CROWNS, CROSSES, AND STARS

CROWNS, CROSSES, AND STARS
MY YOUTH IN PRUSSIA, SURVIVING HITLER, AND A LIFE BEYOND

BY

SIBYLLE SARAH NIEMOELLER

BARONESS VON SELL

Purdue University Press
West Lafayette, Indiana

Copyright 2012 by Purdue University. All rights reserved.
First printing in paperback, 2024.

978-1-61249-912-3 (paperback)

Printed in the United States of America.

Library of Congress Cataloging-in-Publication Data

Niemoeller, Sybil von Sell, 1923-
  Crowns, crosses, and stars : my youth in Prussia, surviving Hitler, and a life beyond / Sibylle Sarah Niemoeller, Baroness von Sell.
    p. cm.
  Includes index.
  ISBN 978-1-55753-618-1 (paper : alk. paper) -- ISBN 978-1-61249-211-7 (ePDF) -- ISBN 978-1-61249-210-0 (ePUB) 1. Niemoeller, Sybil von Sell, 1923- 2. Niemoeller, Sybil von Sell, 1923---Family. 3. Aristocracy (Social class)--Germany--Prussia--Biography. 4. Prussia (Germany)--Biography. 5. Niemoeller, Martin, 1892-1984. 6. Spouses of clergy--Germany--Biography. 7. Germany--History--1933-1945--Biography. 8. World War, 1939-1945--Personal narratives, German. 9. Jewish converts--Biography. 10. Immigrants--United States--Biography. I. Title.
  CT1098.N54A3 2012
  943.086092--dc23
  [B]
                              2011047704

I dedicate this book to my son, Ulrich Marcus Niemoeller, and in memory of those family members who chose the dangerously narrow path of resistance over indifference to evil. Some of them paid the ultimate price for their courage—my father, my mother, my husband Martin Niemoeller, and my cousin Werner von Haeften. Their lives and their memories are my greatest blessing.

Contents

Editor's Note, *Richard Libowitz*	xi

PART ONE: THEY EVEN CLOSED THE CANDY STORE

Prologue	3
Chapter One: September 1914	6
Chapter Two: Augusta	11
Chapter Three: Anna	16
Chapter Four: Father	20
Chapter Five: My Arrival	24
Chapter Six: Berlin	27
Chapter Seven: New Men in My Life	31
Chapter Eight: The New Pastor	35
Chapter Nine: Rabble-Rousers	40
Chapter Ten: The Godfather	43
Chapter Eleven: The Third Reich Begins	48
Chapter Twelve: A Pastor's Growing Doubts	51
Chapter Thirteen: Nazis on Parade	53
Chapter Fourteen: Life in the Third Reich	55
Chapter Fifteen: Royal Sons	60
Chapter Sixteen: School Days	62
Chapter Seventeen: Family Choices and Special Neighbors	65
Chapter Eighteen: Uncle Mirko	70
Chapter Nineteen: Nazi Actions	72
Chapter Twenty: A Meeting with the Führer	75
Chapter Twenty-One: Problems at School and at Home	78
Chapter Twenty-Two: Uncertain Reactions	82
Chapter Twenty-Three: Boarding School	84
Chapter Twenty-Four: My Meeting	89
Chapter Twenty-Five: Pastor Made Prisoner	91
Chapter Twenty-Six: Triumphs of the Führer	94
Chapter Twenty-Seven: Prisoner 569	96
Chapter Twenty-Eight: Growing Up	99

PART TWO: DESTRUCTION UNLIMITED

Chapter Twenty-Nine: Conspirators	111
Chapter Thirty: Out of and Into School	113
Chapter Thirty-One: An Aspiring Actress	116
Chapter Thirty-Two: A Visit Home	119

Chapter Thirty-Three: Good-bye to My Godfather	123
Chapter Thirty-Four: The Incipient Actress	127
Chapter Thirty-Five: The War Comes Closer to Home	130
Chapter Thirty-Six: Shortages	132
Chapter Thirty-Seven: Resistance	134
Chapter Thirty-Eight: Rescue Efforts	136
Chapter Thirty-Nine: Danzig	139
Chapter Forty: The Final Attempt	142
Chapter Forty-One: Revenge	146
Chapter Forty-Two: Aftermath	150
Chapter Forty-Three: More Illegal Activities	152
Chapter Forty-Four: A New Career	155
Chapter Forty-Five: Thoughts of Home	159
Chapter Forty-Six: The Prisoner of Dachau Receives Tragic News	161
Chapter Forty-Seven: The War Closes In	162
Chapter Forty-Eight: Last Visit to Dachau	167
Chapter Forty-Nine: Arabella	169
Chapter Fifty: Freedom	172
Chapter Fifty-One: Continuing the Trek	174
Chapter Fifty-Two: War's End	176
Chapter Fifty-Three: The Russians are Coming	180
Chapter Fifty-Four: With the Americans	184
Chapter Fifty-Five: Joining the British	188
Chapter Fifty-Six: British Intelligence	191
Chapter Fifty-Seven: Return to Berlin	193
Chapter Fifty-Eight: The Confessing Accuser	198
Chapter Fifty-Nine: Surviving in Berlin	201
Chapter Sixty: Help from Many Sources	206
Chapter Sixty-One: A New Job	209
Chapter Sixty-Two: The News of My Father	212
Chapter Sixty-Three: Grandmother	215
Chapter Sixty-Four: Interlude: Journey into the Unknown—July 1986	217
Chapter Sixty-Five: New Sorrows, New Jobs	220
Chapter Sixty-Six: The Airlift	223
Chapter Sixty-Seven: Cold War	225
Chapter Sixty-Eight: Discomfort and New Life	227

PART THREE: THE PROMISED LAND

Chapter Sixty-Nine: A Test Case	235
Chapter Seventy: Living in America	240
Chapter Seventy-One: The New Yorker	243
Chapter Seventy-Two: The Today Show	246
Chapter Seventy-Three: In Love Again	248

Chapter Seventy-Four: Hollywood	251
Chapter Seventy-Five: Tragedies and Other Events in Europe	253
Chapter Seventy-Six: Events in America	256
Chapter Seventy-Seven: Divorce, Despair, Deliverance	258
Chapter Seventy-Eight: Back to Berlin	261
Chapter Seventy-Nine: Life with Martin	264
Chapter Eighty: Under the Rug	267
Chapter Eighty-One: Married Life	270
Chapter Eighty-Two: Martin and the World	273
Chapter Eighty-Three: Life in Germany	276
Chapter Eighty-Four: Rebellion	279
Chapter Eighty-Five: Film and Farewell	281
Chapter Eighty-Six: The Work Is Finished	284
Chapter Eighty-Seven: East Germany	286
Chapter Eighty-Eight: New Beginnings	289
Chapter Eighty-Nine: A New Life	292
Chapter Ninety: Questions of Faith . . . and Answers	294
Chapter Ninety-One: Conversion	298
Epilogue: August 1996	302
Index	305

Editor's Note

More than a decade has passed since I had the good fortune to meet a sharp-eyed, sharp-tongued woman and was regaled by the stories of her distinguished family and the roles she and they played throughout the twentieth century. She spoke of her father, Ulrich Baron von Sell, trained as a diplomat, severely wounded in war, forced by circumstances to turn from the foreign service to a business career, eventually to become the financial adviser and closest friend of Germany's last monarch, Kaiser Wilhelm II, who would, in turn, be godfather to the baron's children. She told of growing up during the Third Reich within a household adamantly opposed to its dictates, in which it was finally decided that passive resistance to Nazism would not suffice and what the price of that decision might be. She also spoke of the courageous pastor, Martin Niemoeller, who became an exemplar to the world by remaining unmoved by the earthly might of Adolf Hitler, and whom she would marry, decades later.

Crowns, Crosses, and Stars is Sarah Niemoeller's story, the saga of a remarkable woman living in tumultuous times; born a German baroness, trained as an actress and an accomplished equestrienne, she was involved with myriad groups resisting both Hitler's dictatorship and his genocidal efforts. Post-war, she assisted British Intelligence during the occupation period and experienced the trials of the Berlin Airlift before coming to America to create a new life for herself and her son. As an American citizen living in New York, she met and befriended many notables within politics, religion, and the arts before her return to Germany to wed Martin Niemoeller, resuming her life in the United States only after his passing ended a loving marriage, after which she began yet another phase in her life as an author, a public speaker, and a member of the Jewish People.

My task has been to weave Sarah's narrative into a relatively straightforward time line while allowing digressions for stories involving some of the hundreds of men and women—nobles and commoners, heroes and villains, the famous, infamous, and the "ordinary"—who have played a part in her life. The task has been a challenge and a delight. My only regret is that space limitations precluded more of those tales from inclusion.

Crowns, Crosses, and Stars is a saga at once fantastic and fascinating. My thanks to Professor Zev Garber, the *Shofar* series editor who originally approached me, to the staff at Purdue University Press, including Charles Watkinson, Rebecca Corbin, and Katherine Purple, for their invaluable help with the manuscript, and, most of all, to Sarah Niemoeller, for the opportunity to bring her story to you.

—Richard Libowitz
Temple University, July 2011

Part One
They Even Closed the Candy Store

Prologue

"There she is!"

A muffled whisper at first, like the rustling of dry leaves, slowly swelled into an outburst of unrestrained joy on the deck of the *Italia* as the weather-beaten veteran of the seas finally neared her destination, the harbor of New York.

"There she is, there she is!" we shouted.

Yes, indeed, there she was, the magnificent Statue of Liberty, the endearing symbol of Freedom in the New World.

Through the April early morning fog, faint outlines of the famous skyline of Manhattan had slowly begun to appear on the horizon. It drew closer and clearer, finally taking shape as the ship, now accompanied by tugboats, slowly navigated along the narrows between Brooklyn and Staten Island.

During the afternoon preceding our arrival, the *Italia*, sailing under the flag of Panama and groaning with old age, had cast anchor on the open sea. A coastal vessel had appeared from which several United States immigration officers emerged to climb aboard our ancient carrier. They would subject the immigrants to one last thorough screening before allowing them to set foot on American soil.

When the ship had begun its two-week journey from Hamburg, at least half of the passengers were emigrants, so-called Displaced Persons, from Eastern countries. At the Canadian port of Halifax, our first stop in the New World, most of them had gone ashore. Their reason for selecting Canada over the United States as a new homeland was a practical one; the Canadian authorities were far more liberal in their admission of foreigners, their vast territory desperately needing laborers in nearly all occupations.

Although I had recuperated from near-constant seasickness, I barely felt up to facing what seemed to be a final grilling by authorities of the nation I had chosen as a permanent home. Was I really and irrevocably going to be admitted, or would they find a reason to reject me and send me back? To my relief, the two immigration officials seemed sufficiently satisfied with my solemn promise neither to assassinate the president nor to prostitute myself in any way. I swore not to become a burden to the nation graciously opening its doors to me, a refugee whose financial means were, at best, limited. There were few promises I would not have made, just so long as they enabled me to regain firm ground under my feet.

Like almost all of my fellow passengers, I traveled with light luggage, the lightest item by far being my wallet, which contained twenty-two dollars as my "starting capital." However, there was one truly valuable treasure that I carried with me, my command of the English language, which would put me far ahead of the vast majority of newcomers to America's shores.

On the evening before our arrival in New York, I had packed my two shabby suitcases and actually managed to sleep fitfully for a few hours until, at the break of dawn, I went to join the crowd already gathered on deck. My heart was pounding. Could this be true? Was I really going to arrive in the land of my dreams, America?

"When all of this is over, promise me that you will go and find your luck under another star, so you and your children can live in freedom."

How could I forget my father's pleading voice in these powerful words, which had haunted me ever since he spoke them during our final conversation, a few days before the ill-fated attempt to assassinate Hitler on July 20, 1944, before my father was taken away to a place from which there would be no return? How relieved he would be to know that his only daughter was about to find not just one new star, but indeed forty-eight of them, every one welcoming her to a brand new world, a brand new life.

Rising from the water, out of the morning mist, on our left side the gigantic lady, the Statue of Liberty, had appeared amid the shouts of "There she is!" So it was not a dream; it was true, I was about to arrive in America, and I saw no reason to hold back the tears that were long overdue.

Next to me stood a young family, obviously from Eastern Europe. The black-bearded father held his small boy firmly by the hand, their skullcaps and long curls over the ears identifying them as pious Jews. The mother, a tight white scarf hiding every strand of her hair, clutched a little girl to her breast. Slowly, almost without noise, we seemed to slide past the statue greeting us in her majestic beauty. The rising sun made her face shine like gold.

The final lines of Emma Lazarus' poem, "The New Colossus," engraved on the statue's base declare:

> Give me your tired, your poor,
> Your huddled masses yearning to breathe free,
> The wretched refuse of your teeming shore.
> Send these, the homeless, tempest-tost to me,
> I lift my lamp beside the golden door!

I, too, was coming as a beggar, tempest tossed, from the very country that for the second time in one century had thrown the world into disaster, the nation of Heine, Goethe, Beethoven, and Bach, my ancestors' fatherland. I had grown up in a family who decided to walk the dangerously narrow path of resistance against evil instead of joining it, determined to light a candle in the darkness instead of cursing it. The price for their courage had been high.

After passing the statue, Ellis Island came into sight, a locale that only a few years earlier would have been my first stop in America. With its multiple buildings, Ellis Island had served as the point of arrival for millions of émigrés hailing from the "old countries," the final purgatory before reaching heaven. Many never managed to pass through the gates to freedom, refused admission because of a slight cough, a faint shadow on the lungs, an eye infection, or perhaps a temporary infirmity not successfully concealed that turned anticipation into despair. A stutter, a single wrong answer—easy enough because almost no immigrants spoke English, and few immigration officials had mastered foreign languages—and the hope for a better life burst like a soap bubble.

Although millions of mostly Eastern European immigrants had been admitted before and after the turn of the century, during World War II only 250,000 refugees were fortunate enough to be accepted into the United States. Among the people from all walks of life who had escaped the Nazi terror were the elite from Germany and Austria, as well as from other countries groaning under the boots of the German invaders. Overwhelmingly, though not exclusively of Jewish descent, these members of the elite were politicians, authors, poets, journalists, artists, actors, movie directors, physicians, and scientists. Some of the grateful newcomers belonging to the latter category presented their host nation with a very special gift, a priceless gift that needed no gift wrapping and not even a suitcase: the atom bomb.

Even before the *Italia* had reached its final docking place in the harbor on Manhattan's West Side, I knew that nothing would ever be able to drag me out of America. The seven years that I allegedly would need to feel at home in New York shrank to less than an hour. This was now my city; my first life was over and a second one, a new and exciting life, was about to begin. Look forward, forward, forward. The past was now behind me. Or was it?

Chapter One
September 1914

Sweltering heat hovered over the German town of Potsdam on this late summer day when a black coach, pulled by four black horses, its curtains tightly drawn, came to a halt on the cobblestones in front of a modest villa with a little garden in front. The somber-looking vehicle, with the silver imperial insignia on the doors, the coachman's hat, and the saddle cloths of the four horses with their silver bridles, was all too well known in this most prominent Prussian garrison town. It was the private coach of her majesty, Empress Auguste Viktoria, spouse of Wilhelm II of Hohenzollern, Emperor of Germany, King of Prussia, the "Kaiser." Helped by a footman, a tall, black-clad, and black-veiled lady emerged from within. Wherever the imperial coach appeared during these days since the outbreak of war, people would stop in the street, turn around, sadly shake their heads, and whisper: Another one! Another one!

The empress, a kind and sensitive soul, had decided that it was her duty to personally inform the families of those officers in the Imperial First Guard, the kaiser's own regiment, that their son, husband, father, or brother had died a hero's death for emperor and fatherland on the battlefield. She was, in fact, a messenger of death.

On this fateful late summer day, Auguste Viktoria walked alone through the small front yard, stepped into the villa, and was received by a curtsying maid. Seconds later, the twenty-three-year-old lady of the house learned that her young and cheerful husband, his majesty's First Lieutenant Baron Ernst von Hohenstein, had fallen, together with his white horse, in the battle at St. Quentin on August 29, 1914.

The widowed baroness, Augusta Bertha Ottilie Helene, born in the Alsatian town of Colmar in 1891, was the fifth of seven children of Konrad and Helene von Brauchitsch, née von Korn-Rudelsdorf. Her father, General Konrad Louis Eduard von Brauchitsch, commander of the Alsatian garrison, which in those days was part of the German Reich, had followed in his illustrious forefathers' footsteps, choosing the traditional military career and, with apparent ease, climbed the ladder all the way to the top.

The general had every reason to be proud of his family, which could authentically be traced back to Charlemagne. An adventurous ancestor from Russia by the name of Velislaus von Brocovice had made his way west. Around the turn of the millennium, the descendants of this noble dynasty were noted as robber knights and eventually became military leaders and statesmen. A considerable number of his relatives, Konrad not among them, still owned vast estates in the east of the German Reich.

My mother was a pretty little girl with cascades of chestnut-colored curls and the family's traditional light-blue eyes. Nobody would pay any attention to her complaints about frequent and nagging headaches, which later developed into migraine attacks that would haunt her for the rest of her life. She should pull herself together, the stern governess told her. Furthermore, in the expert opinion of tiny Frieda Hahn, there was no such thing as lamenting over not being able to do this or that; the stereotypical answer little Augusta Bertha Ottilie Helene received was "Quite simple! Just do it!"

As was customary in aristocratic circles, children grew up in the care of nurses, governesses, and a variety of other more or less qualified servants. Until they were able to sit properly at the dining table, Siegfried, Hertha, Hildegard, Konrad, Augusta, Eberhard, and little Hellmut (who died at age two) took their meals separately and saw their parents only at bedtime. Children, so the general opinion ran, should rarely be seen and never heard.

The general, lord and master of a large family, could have enjoyed many more years of active service, had it not been for a rather bizarre incident that ended his military career brutally, abruptly, and prematurely. During a traditional game hunt, an extremely nearsighted fellow hunter managed to mistake the imposing figure of the commander for that of a deer, firing a generous load of buckshot into his unfortunate victim's head. By some stroke of luck this did not cause life-threatening injuries, yet entailed a disaster of monstrous dimensions. In spite of all efforts, the doctors were unable to remove all of the tiny pellets embedded within his noble scalp; the general discovered to his horror that he was unable to wear the obligatory spike helmet, without which a Prussian officer was as unthinkable as a lady without a corset. After his resignation, at the zenith of his career, he took out his helpless rage on the ones closest to him, his family.

Helene, whose limited intelligence was no match for that of her brilliant husband, totally worn out by too many pregnancies and the social demands made on her as a commander's wife, had to bury her dream of someday moving to a little, vine-covered house. Since the family estates were occupied by his older brothers, Konrad calculated it best if the family moved to Potsdam, the cradle of Prussian militarism. He figured that, with his majesty's elite regiments stationed there, the chances to marry off his three daughters to spouses of noble descent, wealth, and prominent social standing would be better than anywhere else. In those days, a Prussian general's pension was limited; thus the financial consequences of the accident were devastating.

The castle of Rimburg near the Dutch border, in the Brauchitsch family for many generations, had not gone to Konrad. The ancient fortress, the foundation of which was laid during the reign of Charlemagne, offered a hint of what life before the Middles Ages had been like in Germany. With a moat, walls ten feet thick, secret underground passages, dungeons, torture chambers, and an honest-to-goodness family ghost, bravely weathering all attacks over the centuries, it had proved to be impregnable as well as indestructible. Over a millennium, each new owner had not only repaired damages suffered during numerous war activities, but added a new item, like another wing or a tower. Through fortunate circumstances, Konrad's firstborn son, Siegfried, would inherit it, in turn leaving it to his son, my cousin, also named Konrad.

With the two older sons already serving as officers in the military, the three daughters and young Eberhard had no choice but to stay home with their parents until a fairy godmother might appear and change their lives.

The move to Potsdam was followed by two events, one of them delightful and certainly satisfactory, the other one of heartbreaking nature. The oldest daughter, Hertha, became engaged to a young man, a commoner, who made up for this shortcoming with apparent wealth and social standing. This happy event was overshadowed by the tragic death of fourteen-year-old Hildegard, who succumbed to typhoid fever, leaving only Augusta, by far the most beautiful of the three sisters, who had just returned from one year in Miss Friedlander's Finishing School for Girls in Geneva.

Eberhard, the lanky nestling who, for mysterious reasons, had come into the world with black instead of the usual reddish-blonde curls, was still attending secondary school. From whence their youngest son's dark hair and totally non-Germanic looks originated, remained a puzzle to his bewildered family. A nasty rumor reached the general's ears that his very own flesh and blood had even been called *Judebueble*, "little Jew boy," by street children, which caused his father to gnash his teeth, because Jews, according to his irrevocable conviction, had no place in his Teutonic clan, at least not as long as he had any say in it. But there would be Jews soon enough, although he would not live to witness this family disgrace.

On the subject of disgrace, there was a rather earthshaking surprise that "little" Eberhard Hubertus Hellmut Konrad, his six foot five inch frame towering over the entire clan, had in store for his dumbfounded parents. After graduating with high honors from the humanist high school, the brilliant son informed them that he had not the slightest intention of becoming an officer. Instead he planned to enroll in a technical university, his goal being a degree in engineering. This announcement had the effect of a bomb. An engineer? Never, never, never had a member of this renowned family expressed such a vulgar and undignified desire. He might as well aim to be a night watchman; the outrage would be the same.

Augusta and her brother shared the gloom with the disenchanted, constantly lamenting mother, the general's manservant, and Frau Minna Plinke, the squat and resolute cook. Not in the slightest intimidated by her employer's temper outbursts, she insisted on personally fastening the gigantic white napkins around the general's neck at mealtime, and every Saturday she cooked his favorite meal, a dish of lentil soup in which a fried herring had to swim!

Everybody else groaned under the general's foul moods, his face now adorned with a red-and-white sprinkled beard. Because of a lack of physical exercise, an extreme love of food, and large quantities of heavy red wine, Konrad had gained in corpulence, and the belly he carried could no more be described as an embonpoint.[1] Locking himself in his study, he would emerge from it only to eat. What made the atmosphere in the house even more unbearable was his growing habit of not uttering a single word to anyone, sometimes for weeks. Buried in his vast library, he kept himself busy studying the natural sciences through countless volumes of heavy books and journals. He also joined a society that had as its goal the purification of the German language from all the ugly, undesirable, and totally redundant foreign terms, mostly of French origin, that had invaded his cherished mother tongue.

Cleansing the German language was not the society's sole concern. It was believed that the Germanic race was badly in need of purification. Certain theories, recently developed by noted personalities about races in general and the "Jewish race" in particular, seemed well-founded and met with the general's interest, if not wholehearted approval, an approval that was not necessarily shared, but had to be silently tolerated, by his immediate family. The brooding hermit arrived at the conclusion that indeed there *had* to be something about the Jews that made them seem so undesirable, *everybody* said so, and *everybody* could not be wrong. Certainly not the esteemed British author Houston Stewart Chamberlain, Richard Wagner's son-in-law, whose well-founded anti-Semitic theories were shared by the French Comte de Gobineau and the German Protestant "court preacher" Adolf Stöcker. The historian Heinrich von Treitschke, Germany's self-proclaimed philosopher, had publicly declared that "The Jews are our misfortune!"

In other words, the religion for which the Jews had suffered over almost two millennia, their stubborn refusal to accept Jesus as the Messiah whom they had brutally crucified (as Christians were taught), was not of vital interest anymore. What really mattered was the race, this "dangerously alien, evil and inferior race."

Konrad von Brauchitsch would not live long enough to witness his own family's multiple intermarriages with Jewish spouses. He would never know that his youngest son, Eberhard, who had graduated from university with an engineering degree, became not a night watchman, but the manager of the *Junkers Werke*, Germany's largest airplane manufacturer. In New York he married a beautiful, artistic, and black-haired girl named Maria, whose non-Aryan parents had fled the pogroms taking place in their hometown of Odessa. This marriage secured the youngest member of the Brauchitsch clan a place in the "*Semi Gotha.*"

The *Gotha Almanach*, nobility's "Who's Who," listed all members of aristocratic families within and outside of Germany. In my grandfather's unshakable conviction, shared by most of his "caste," anyone whose name was not printed in the *Gotha* did not count. Around the turn of the century, its publishers, the "Kyffhäuser Bund" in Munich, had the brilliant idea to publish a supplementary volume to the original *Almanach*, the so-called *Semi-Gotha*, mercilessly exposing those members of nobility who had contaminated their pure blue and Aryan blood with that of the "foreign Jewish race." This special edition later became a most valuable source of information for the man who had decided to wipe the Jews from the face of the globe.

Eberhard was not even the first member of his family to see his name printed there, my mother having beaten him to it. Her first husband, the young war hero, had a Jewish grandmother who, after her baptism, became a baroness while saving her husband's family from bankruptcy. Although there were instances in which true love motivated a nobleman to marry a Jewish girl, others were the consequence of a financial dilemma on the part of a noble family. Whatever the reason, all such a union required was baptism of the bride, qualifying her as a new member of the family: Sarah became Louise and Rebecca would henceforth be known as Katharina. While unions between Christian men and Jewish women had become acceptable, those between Jewish husbands and Christian girls of noble birth were frowned on in aristocratic, bourgeois, and Jewish circles.[2]

Although the original purpose of the *Semi-Gotha* had been to expose those members of the aristocracy to shame over their ill-begotten alliances, the publication would eventually lead to consequences of a dimension unforeseen by even the most radical anti-Semite, when the overwhelming majority of the German people decided to accept an Austrian ex-corporal with a ridiculous hairdo and a shoe-brush moustache for their sovereign leader. His gratitude for this specific Kyffhäuser edition would be boundless. This book would save him considerable efforts to track down those who had tainted their heritage by allowing their blood to mingle with that of the alien and unclean Jewish race. It provided the Nazis not only with information down to the third and fourth generation, but also with the addresses of all those who would now fall under the Nuremberg "Laws for the Protection of German Blood and Honor."

Like an act of revenge after the demise of Hitler, the pendulum would swing in a most undesirable direction; the standard *"Gotha"* meticulously revealed, in embarrassing detail, the names and positions of those aristocrats who had fallen for Hitler. The Nazi virus had spread to the highest circles, even invading royal dynasties. Members of the Hohenzollern family, the Duke of Coburg and Gotha, grandfather to the present king of Sweden, closely related to Britain's queen, as well as the House of Hesse and Nassau, to mention just a few, had not considered it beneath their dignity to don the brown and black uniforms of the SA and the SS. Beating them all was Duke Josias von Waldeck-Pyrmont, who proudly accepted the appointment as SS Gruppenführer and Inspector General in charge of Hitler's concentration camps. The list of German aristocrats unashamed of selling themselves to "crime incorporated" was a long one.

Chapter Two
Augusta

Back in Potsdam, nineteen-year-old Augusta Ottlie Bertha Helene von Brauchitsch was ready to enter society, an occasion that would include her presentation to the Majesties in Potsdam's Imperial Palace during the Annual Imperial Ball, the most exquisite social event of the 1910-1911 season. The honor of being introduced to the imperial couple was by tradition restricted to daughters of high birth, worthy of meeting and mating with the young officers of the elite regiments.

Wilhelm II of Hohenzollern—seated next to Empress Auguste Viktoria on his imperial throne in the back of the ballroom, dressed in one of his favorite operetta uniforms, and ecstatic in the knowledge of being the cherished idol of his subjects—kept twirling the carefully groomed moustache with his right, ring-adorned hand, letting his watery blue eyes wander over the illustrious crowd. One by one, the young debutantes would approach the throne between their parents, following an announcement by the master of ceremonies, the Imperial Lord Chamberlain, who personally escorted them to the steps of the throne. The Kaiser's left hand, like the right one richly decorated with sparkling diamond rings, was kept carefully hidden behind his back, as he had been taught from early childhood. The withered little hand on a short and useless arm was a defect with which he, Prussia's crown prince, Queen Victoria's favorite grandson, had come into the world.

The parents' delight over their daughter's impending presentation to the Majesties was dampened only by the costs for Augusta's ball gown. Yards and yards of elaborate velvet, choice silk, and delicate lace were needed; expert hands transformed the outrageously expensive material into a masterpiece. This task could not possibly have been entrusted to Philomena, the clubfooted little seamstress who came into the house twice a year to sew, patch, and mend what needed sewing, patching, and mending. The gown, stitched by the town's most fashionable dressmaker, tore what turned out to be a bottomless hole in the family budget. But the finished product was breathtaking; it resembled a fluffy white cloud, fit for a royal princess.

On the evening of the ball, her eyes modestly cast down, a well-rehearsed expression of humility on her face, the debutante seemed to float through the halls of the imperial palace between her parents toward the majesties. Her chestnut curls had been arranged balloon-style on top of her head in the fashion of the time. With apparent ease, she performed the mandatory deep curtsy, practiced a hundred times, and her youthful freshness caused a smile to appear on Auguste Viktoria's kind face. Her imperial spouse, a benign twinkle in his light-blue Hohenzollern eyes, ogled the beauty in front of him with unconcealed approval; Augusta's main concern at that moment was to manage the gown's long train, borrowed from a relative for the occasion.

There was no question after the ball as to who had stolen the show. Even Augusta's mother, who had anxiously watched the proceedings through her pince-nez with other matrons from the so-called "dragon's rock," with a sigh of relief agreed that her daughter was the undisputed queen of the evening. Her dance card filled within seconds, Augusta had the time of her life, waltzing in the arms of her admirers.

Those were glorious days, the best that Prussia had ever experienced in its one hundred and fifty year history. The mere idea of war seemed as far removed as the moon. It was common knowledge that the German nation under its incomparable emperor was the envy of many. What could be more important for Potsdam society than the ball season, compared to which all other events became oblivious? Potsdam, after all, was the undisputed center of the nation, perhaps the world.

Throughout the first winter following the debutante ball, a carefree Augusta managed to twist a vast number of eligible bachelors mercilessly around her little finger. She loved to dance. But, whether a waltz or a polka, twirling around was only permissible in one direction, clockwise, and never, never counterclockwise. The Lord Chamberlain himself, with the eyes of an eagle, watched for possible offenders of this unwritten court rule. It was up to him to decide who would be allowed to dance close to the throne. For that supreme honor, the girl had to put on a winning yet humble smile with zest and spirit while dancing, but clockwise please!

Among the officers in their elegant gala uniforms were some not quite as eligible as others. They included the German imperial princes as well as those from other nations serving in the Prussian elite regiments. After returning to their home countries like Austria, Russia, Greece, or Bulgaria, they would eventually be required to marry mates of equal birth. While it was encouraged and even desirable for a girl to dance with future monarchs, falling in love would, without doubt, entail heartbreak and even full-blown scandal because, in the highest society, there existed an eleventh commandment that was strictly enforced: thou shalt only marry a spouse of equal birth. A future king could only wed a princess and not a countess or a baroness. Any deviation from this rule inevitably led to trouble for all parties involved. The only way to legitimize such an undesirable union was a marriage "to the left hand," a morganatic alliance, barring possible offspring from inheriting the royal title, let alone succession to the throne. An exception to these stern rules was the English royal dynasty, which simply required a princess royal to be Protestant and not divorced. These much more humane conditions, considered outrageously liberal in other monarchies and therefore most undesirable, were frowned upon in pre-World War I Germany. But even in Prussia there had been examples of futile attempts to prevent a royal prince or even a king from following his heart. Friedrich Wilhelm III—a ruling monarch and grandnephew of the childless King Frederick the Great—had, after the death of his beloved wife, the legendary Queen Louise, married the Countess Mathilde von Harrach in a morganatic ceremony.

While recognized and accepted as his lawful wife, the privileges and title of an imperial princess were denied her.

For Augusta, the die was cast when the first ball season ended. Baron Ernst von Hohenstein, a first lieutenant in his majesty's Imperial Guard, who had won her heart and hand, came from old southern German nobility. Few knew that his background was rather exotic; not only did he have a Jewish grandmother, but his maternal great-grandparents included a notorious couple, Lord Nelson and Lady Hamilton. Since the family estate on Lake Constanz, bordering on Switzerland, went to his older brother Hans, Ernst, as was the custom for all younger sons, had been forced into a military career.

Following the wedding one year later, Augusta and her husband moved into a modest villa on a quiet Potsdam street. Money was scarce, and it would not be easy to maintain the lifestyle required for an officer of the Imperial Guard. A carriage, two horses, the officer's batman, and at least one female live-in servant were mandatory; it was unthinkable that the young bride should be required to cook and clean. After all, fellow officers like the future kings of Greece and Bulgaria or the Duke of Coburg and Gotha, a member of the British royal family, were quite likely to drop in unannounced. Was the lady of the house supposed to open the door herself, adorned in a kitchen apron? That situation was unlikely for the simple reason that Augusta did not own such a vulgar garment. One day, the ringing of the bell had gone unnoticed in the salon where the playful young woman had, for fun, fastened a blue ribbon into her husband's hair, when in the open door stood the future king of Greece, who did not quite know what to say.

The honeymoon was over before it had really begun; in 1914 Wilhelm II declared his war, proclaiming that from now on, "he knew no political parties anymore but only Germans." With a never before experienced enthusiasm, all men of eligible age hurried to arms, eager and ready to defend their beloved fatherland and what it stood for, against enemies who begrudged them wealth, glory, Prussian traditions, and most of all, their cherished kaiser, first cousin to Britain's king as well as to the tsar of Russia.

The war against France, the notorious and hereditary foe, was but a few weeks old when Augusta's young husband met his death during the battle of St. Quentin, his snow-white horse having been shot from under him. Disaster, the bereft young woman would soon discover, rarely strikes once or even twice, but as a rule three times; in addition to Augusta's early widowhood, her mother succumbed to heart failure, the shock from which caused her father to suffer a massive stroke, robbing him of speech. From then until his death three years later, he was only able to express himself in gurgling sounds, accompanied by fits of helpless rage. Little Minna Plinke, the faithful cook who refused to leave her master until his death, was the only person able to handle him.

The twenty-three-year-old woman, with no financial means, soon forgot her playfulness. She had no choice but to don the mandatory widow's veil and wrap herself from head to toe in ghastly black garments that, due to a cruel tradition, would be required of her for the next two years. The widow's peak on her head made her look like a starving little chickadee.

She was not alone in her misery as the streets of Potsdam soon filled with more and more black-veiled figures, resembling flocks of huge owls. Seemingly indefatigable despite her grief, Augusta raced between her own house and the home of her horribly afflicted father, paying no attention to the cough that had begun one day and would not go away, until her condition was diagnosed. What ailed her had a name, whispered in horror behind cupped hands: consumption.

Augusta's frantic search for a position that paid enough to keep her household going was over. She had been considered as a lady in waiting at the emperor's court in spite of doubts expressed by the Lord High Steward, who believed that the young baroness, while delightful, would be incapable of conforming to the strict rules of court etiquette. Now, with that ghastly shadow on her lungs, quick help was needed and ultimately offered by her fallen husband's bosom friend. Carl Edward George Albert, Duke of Saxe-Coburg and Gotha, royal prince of Great Britain and Ireland, belonged to the family from which Prince Consort Albert, first cousin and husband of Queen Victoria, had come. The duke and duchess saw to it that the widow was taken to a sanatorium in the Black Forest where, against all expectations, the patient regained her strength.

While still recovering there, correspondence began between the young war widow and a certain baron, a captain in the field, seven years her senior. The letters were exchanged from bed to bed, because the man was slowly recuperating in a field hospital from several operations after receiving a deep wound in his left temple, caused by a shell splinter. No stranger to Augusta, Baron Ulrich von Sell had been among her dance partners at the Annual Imperial Ball. Although she considered him attractive, she had been in awe of the serious expression in his deep-set gray eyes. What she only found out later was that he had gone to war with the explicit wish to die. Disregarding the eleventh commandment, he had allowed himself to fall in love with a young girl of royal descent, whose father, not amused when the young baron asked for his daughter's hand in marriage, yanked her away; eventually she wed a prince. After the end of the war, coinciding with Augusta's discharge from the sanatorium, the first properly chaperoned meeting between the two pen pals ultimately led to their betrothal.

In May of 1919, the modest wedding ceremony took place in Potsdam. Aside from the precarious economic situation, the new bride was, after all, a warrior's widow and Ulrich von Sell had lost his three brothers in battle. The groom's mother had not exactly welcomed this union, regarding her last living son's matrimonial choice as a personal insult. No doubt, the bride's descent and her background was beyond criticism, but nothing would change the deplorable fact that the bride, admittedly through no fault of her own, was a widow, and as such, quite obviously not a virgin. In her stern mind, this made the bride no more desirable than an apple that someone had already nibbled on.

Augusta's new father-in-law, the retired Prussian Major General Baron Wilhelm von Sell, came from a succession of military leaders and statesmen; he had a red bulb-like nose, a drooping moustache, and was called *Mannchen*—"Little Man"—by his stately wife, who towered over him by several inches. *Mannchen*, as became evident soon after the disaster of the German defeat, could not be counted on for the emotional support his heartbroken wife needed in her terrible grief. It seemed as if he had made the decision to ignore a world in which there was no place anymore for the monarch he had sworn allegiance to after a war that had claimed the lives of three of his beautiful sons. Gradually, he lost all contact with his environment, and he ceased to talk. Taken to a nearby sanatorium, he lingered in a twilight zone, a nebulous dreamworld that no one could share. He died six months before I, his first grandchild, was born.

Chapter Three
Anna

The newlyweds moved into an apartment in the Neue Königstrasse in Potsdam. Housing was scarce in those days, and the couple considered themselves fortunate to have a roof over their heads—one they could afford, which was spacious enough to house three people (because without at least one servant, life in their impoverished but noble circles was still unimaginable). The servants just happened to be a little poorer than their masters, a situation accepted as being absolutely normal by both parties. As far as shabbiness was concerned, the new domicile could hardly be surpassed. In the vast lot behind the dismal building, leading all the way down to the Havel River, a coal company maintained its booming but dirty business. Instead of trees and grass, there was a sizeable mountain of black coal heaped in the center of the court, from which angry clouds and sizeable rats emerged as soon as workmen dug their shovels into it.

The rooms—including the kitchen, with its coal burning stove and cold water faucet, the living room, the bedroom, and the servant's quarters—with high ceilings and narrow windows, mercilessly faced north. Central heating and running hot water were unknown in Potsdam, so a rickety boiler in the stark bathroom required a basket full of expensive firewood and pressed coal in order to produce hot water each Saturday night. The arched gateway, leading from the street to the court, was used by the workmen of the coal firm who, on their way in or out, would relieve themselves against the stone walls near the entrance door. This rather nasty habit caused the stringent odor that insulted the noses of all those entering or leaving the house. For the young couple, their new domicile had only one advantage: it was cheap. But it was also dark and damp.

Finding a servant, a maid for all seasons, would have been a difficult if not hopeless venture, had it not been for the resourcefulness of the young baroness with the attractive little dimple on the tip of her nose, an inheritance from her mother. Somehow she had received word of a very capable person in the neighborhood who was looking for a new position. Her employers had decided to retire to their country estate, planning to take their staff with them. Anna, the cook, had rolled her eyes in horror at the very idea and informed her mistress that her days of serfdom were over; she would stay in Potsdam, where she belonged. Since Anna enjoyed the reputation of a veritable jewel, many a Potsdam matron would have given her right arm to engage the woman, but before anyone could lift a finger, the young Baroness von Sell had already persuaded Anna that she and no one else could be entrusted with managing the new household.

Anna Troppa, who at thirty-one was considered an old maid, was of pure Vendish stock. Notorious for their valor, fearlessness, and death-defying ferocity, this Slavic tribe from southern Serbia had, some thirteen hundred years before, invaded the vast wasteland between the Vistula and Elbe Rivers. They occupied an area that would only some five hundred years later be inhabited by Germans; Berlin—much to the chagrin of the Germans and especially the Nazis—had been founded by the Vendes. After centuries of battling, the remaining Vendes, instead of returning to the regions of their origin, eventually settled in the Spreewald, southeast of Berlin, where the Spree River, with its countless tributaries, had created a landscape quite unique in Germany. Waterways were used for connecting the various villages instead of country roads, their vehicles long, narrow boats rather than horse-drawn carts. During the winter months, with the river arms frozen, sleds replaced the boats, and the entire population donned ice skates to get from one place to another.

Converted initially from paganism to Catholicism and later to the faith of Martin Luther—not necessarily by their own free will—the Vendes maintained their traditions over the centuries. Stubbornly resisting assimilation, they lived in enclaves, married exclusively within their own tribe, and clung to the habit of wearing colorful costumes. Even after five hundred years, they obstinately declined to speak the language of their host country, German, despite the fact that Vendish or Sorbic, with a strong resemblance to Serbic, had over the centuries slowly been reduced to a spoken language. By the turn of the century, no more books existed in Vendish, and neither the pastor nor the village schoolteacher was able to write Vendish anymore. But everyone spoke it, in spite of the fact that by the time Anna was born in 1887, all children were required by the state to attend the local elementary schools, where German was mandatory. Aside from learning the basic subjects, they received their religious instructions in the "foreign" German language and were taught to believe in the Protestant-Christian God and the Holy Trinity. Like most of her people, Anna kept a few of the old deities locked in a separate chamber of her heart, considering them a lot more competent in cases of emergency. Ghosts and spirits enabled her to contact the deceased, a fact the pastor did not necessarily have to know.

At some point in the nineteenth century, it had become customary among the poor village population to send their daughters to the city as cooks, maids, and nannies. Also in great demand were wet nurses from the Spreewald; a girl who gave birth to an illegitimate offspring would, after merciless beatings by her father, tearfully leave her little bastard in the care of her family, to put a strange baby to her bosom in Berlin or Potsdam.

Anna had just turned fourteen when her parents began to ponder which of their two daughters, Anna or Marie, her younger sister, should be sent off and which one kept home, when Aunt Maike, Anna's godmother, made the family an offer they felt could not be rejected. The maiden aunt, before reaching the age of sixteen, had given birth to a baby boy out of wedlock and, leaving him with her parents, accepted a position as a wet nurse with a well-to-do Jewish family in Potsdam. Over the years, she had climbed the servants' hierarchy ladder all the way to the top. As chief housekeeper she was facing a carefree old age, had it not been for a ghastly accident; on a beautiful summer day, in the basement kitchen, Aunt Maike had poked her head into the shaft of the apparently stuck food elevator to see what was holding it up, when it came crashing down on her.

Her desolate employers gave her a funeral fit for a queen; following her coffin, which was covered with exquisite wreaths and floral arrangements, marched what seemed to be the entire female Spreewald population, all in their Sunday best. Among the countless mourners was Anna, who adored funerals, and tried very hard never to miss one. Where else could she cry to her heart's content? Where else indeed, except later in those new movie theaters, where silent films showed life as it really was![3]

Back in 1902, Aunt Maike had informed Anna's parents that a practically custom-tailored position awaited their older daughter in Potsdam. The employers, an aristocratic family, had as their only condition that the girl would be strong and healthy. Qualities like honesty, diligence, and loyalty went without mentioning. That was how fourteen-year-old Anna's life took a dramatic turn. On the day of her confirmation, her godmother presented her with her very first pair of real leather shoes. Within a week she left her village with the traditional wicker basket holding her clothes, the colorful garments of her tribe's national costume, which she wore with pride for the rest of her years. Her new life began as a second kitchen helper in the Potsdam residence of Major von Strehlow, a position from which she would soon advance to kitchen helper number one and, after ten years, to first cook.

Everyone appreciated her as a hard worker, praising her ability to make her own decisions. Furthermore, during the course of a dozen years, she successfully taught herself the kind of modestly winning smile that would touch the hearts of the people with which she came in contact. What a nice and well-behaved girl, what excellent manners, everyone thought, which was precisely what she wanted everyone to think.

By the time the war ended in disaster, Anna had reached the age of thirty-one, in those days ranking as an old spinster, which in itself did not particularly bother her, remembering with a shudder her own parents' marriage. Although not pretty by commonly accepted standards, she was certainly impressive in appearance. With her broad face, high cheekbones, flat nose, and low forehead, her ebony black hair parted in the middle, a tightly knotted bun on top of her head, she was a classic physical example of her Slavic people. However, few people suspected that behind her low brow was an alert and cunning mind, which under different circumstances would have enabled her to become anything from a criminal lawyer to a field marshal. Her most striking feature was a pair of strangely light, seemingly century-old eyes from the distant grassland of Asia, resembling those of a wolf, eyes that never missed anything, not even in the dark, or so it appeared. Any speculation that Genghis Khan himself might have been among her ancestors seemed not at all remote. Quick-witted and smart, she possessed a strong will. Her occasional outbursts of rage enjoyed a legendary reputation in Potsdam.

When the beautiful young baroness, with her chestnut-colored hair and the little dimple at the tip of her nose, presented her case, Anna, displaying a particularly demure expression on her broad face, immediately grasped the situation. Admittedly, the wages were low, but here she was dealing with someone who quite obviously had no overwhelming interest in running a household. Consequently, she would not be likely to interfere with the housekeeper's decisions, interference being something Anna thoroughly despised. And, above all, there were no ill-behaved brats! She decided to jump into the new adventure headfirst, her gambling instinct telling her that, while there was little if anything to lose, there was something of great importance to gain—independence.

From the first day, she set out to lull her new mistress into the false belief that she—the *Frau Baronin*, the baroness, and no one else—was in charge. As far as the *Herr Baron* was concerned, he met her wholehearted approval and admiration. Here was a truly noble gentleman! Although serious and distant, he was never unkind, treating her with the utmost courtesy, even going so far as to jump from his chair when he saw her approaching with a heavy tray, just to open the door. With a never before experienced ardor, Anna's heart went out to the poor *Herr Baron*, who had lost his three brothers in the war, barely surviving with the deep shrapnel wound in his temple that caused him so much pain.

Chapter Four
Father

The tragic expression in Ulrich von Sell's deep-set gray eyes was not only the result of the war. In the life of the thirty-five-year-old war veteran, grief and sorrow had begun early. His all too brief childhood ended on the day the sensitive eight-year old, small for his age, was sent to the *Kadettenanstalt* in Berlin-Lichterfelde, one of the renowned military academies reserved for the Prussian elite. His father, General Wilhelm von Sell, with the drooping moustache and slightly pinched, watery blue eyes, resembling a benign seal, had been successful in climbing almost to the top of the military ladder. His paternal grandfather, born only five years after the death of the Great Frederick, Prussia's legendary ruler, had served his monarch as a General of the Infantry and later as Lord Chamberlain and cabinet member at the court of the Duke of Mecklenburg-Schwerin, who eventually rewarded the nobleman for his excellent services with the hereditary title of a baron. The family coat of arms proudly displayed two three-pointed crowns, one in the left upper and the other in the right lower corner, opposite each a staff with a coronet-adorned serpent coiled around it. Above this impressive crest was the baron's crown, with its seven peaks.[4]

At the advanced age of forty, he surprised his friends by falling in love with Hedwig von Rosenstiel from Marienwalde, an estate of vast dimensions in West Prussia. Her father, Wilhelm von Rosenstiel, whose ancestors had, centuries before, come across the Baltic Sea from Sweden, saw himself faced with the awesome task of having to marry off three daughters who, in family circles, were named "the intelligent one," "the kind one," and "the beautiful one." Hedwig was neither overly intelligent nor particularly kind, but her beauty was undisputed, Looming over her cheerful little husband with the bulbous nose that became redder as the years proceeded, she looked down on him with a slightly pitying and patronizing expression in her cool eyes. His proposal had been considered a great honor by her overjoyed parents, because the marriage would provide the eighteen-year-old maiden of Prussian gentry with the enviable title of a baroness. From this rather odd union would spring four handsome boys who, as soon as they had been taught to read and write by private tutors, as was customary in the circles of the elite, were shipped off to a military academy.

The second son, Ulrich Adolf Wilhelm Günther, met with this cruel fate shortly after his eighth birthday. Tearful pleas to spare him fell on deaf ears. After all, how was a Prussian general supposed to finance the education of four sons in accordance with the status his rank and social position demanded? With the military academies tuition-free for the offspring of aristocratic Prussian officers, who could afford to forego this unique chance, this supreme honor?

Law and strict order prevailed within the high walls of the institution behind which the little boys disappeared. Sentiments, feelings of any kind, were considered a luxury and were to be left behind at the clothing depot, where the new cadets received their uniforms. "The foremost lesson you will learn is obedience!"—this sentence was drummed into the cadets' ears several times daily—"Only once you have learned to obey, can you give orders." The whole atmosphere, the spirit of the new surroundings, was characterized by commands on one side and obedience on the other, amounting to brutal contempt for simple human dignity. Discipline, merciless drill, and blind obedience marked a cadet's life from six in the morning until dark, with hardly a minute to relax. From the day of his arrival, Ulrich endured a living hell.

The true meaning of utter helplessness became only too clear to the unhappy child who, despising physical violence, found himself the target of frequent vile and cruel attacks by big bullies. More than once, he would seriously consider suicide as the only way out of his misery. Twice a year, for Christmas and during the summer, the cadets were allowed to travel home. The first half of the vacation was needed to recuperate from the hardships of military life, after which the all too fast approaching date of return to the hated place cast its dark shadows over the remaining weeks. In his mother's opinion, all these alleged hardships would serve to shape a boy into a man. His brothers did not complain, so why did he not pull himself together and get tough, especially in view of the fact that there was no alternative to the military education? Ulrich would never forgive her.

For obvious reasons, Ulrich von Sell showed no desire to choose the military as his career. The idea of eventually joining the general staff as a professional officer, possibly becoming instrumental in the shaping of world history, held no attraction for him, so he decided not to follow in his esteemed ancestors' footsteps. But, since his graduation from the military academy alone would not qualify him for admittance to a university, he reluctantly accepted the advice of his superiors, who were well aware of the young man's outstanding potential, and attended the so-called *Selecta*. In this seminary, carefully chosen cadets received advanced instruction in history, mathematics, languages, and all the fields that would eventually enable them to enter the diplomatic service.

After graduating with exceptional honors, the eighteen-year-old second lieutenant proudly strolled down Berlin's magnificent avenue Unter den Linden. Donning his brand-new uniform for the first time, he resembled a child dressed up as an officer. Two years later, the serious young man left the Prussian War Academy, a place of education favored by Europe's royalty, where he had been carefully and thoroughly prepared for a future in the diplomatic corps. Successfully circumventing the obligatory beginners' posts, he met with a rather unique stroke of well-deserved luck in 1910, when he was handpicked as aide-de-camp by Theobald von Bethmann-Hollweg, Chancellor of the German Reich since 1909. He moved into his new residence in the chancellor's palace on Wilhelmstrasse, and before even realizing it, he found himself in the center of world politics.

Early in 1914, twenty-seven-year-old First Lieutenant Ulrich von Sell accompanied his chief on a last journey to Russia, the purpose being urgent and secret negotiations with the

Kaiser's cousin, Tsar Nicholas II. No special train carried the chancellor and his immediate entourage; a salon car equipped with the bare necessities was hooked to the regularly scheduled train to St. Petersburg. Bethmann-Hollweg despised unnecessary expenditures, favoring one of the most laudable of Prussian virtues: thrift. Thriftiness, advocated by the Prussian kings and particularly by Frederick the Great, to him simply meant the absence of luxury.

The June 28, 1914 assassination in Serbian Sarajevo of the Austrian Archduke Franz Ferdinand, a nephew of Kaiser Franz Joseph and successor to the throne, resulted in Austria-Hungary declaring war against Serbia. After Russia, an ally to Serbia, mobilized her armed forces, the German emperor did not hesitate to declare war against his cousin, Tsar Nicholas II—like himself Queen Victoria's grandson—on the first day of August, and two days later against France. These decisions, in turn, caused England to take sides with her allies Russia and France against the Reich. Proclaiming German mobilization, the kaiser told his jubilant subjects, "As of today, I know no political parties anymore but only Germans!"

On that same morning, Chancellor Theobald von Bethmann-Hollweg, accompanied by his adjutant Ulrich von Sell, went to consult with His Majesty in the Berlin castle. Bethmann-Hollweg's car was stopped by thousands of enthusiastic Berliners, so the adjutant had to step out of the limousine and walk in front of it with outstretched arms to clear the way for his chief. In the afternoon, Ulrich, alone in the backseat of his master's automobile, once more sped toward the kaiser's residence. In a red attaché case he carried a large, sealed envelope containing the Reich's declaration of war against Russia. All that was needed was His Majesty's signature and the date, August 1, 1914. Two days later, Ulrich delivered the declaration of war against France, ready to be signed, to the monarch. Standing next to the desk, he watched the emperor's ring-adorned right hand seal the fate of his people. On the fourth day of August, in his own residence, the German chancellor received Britain's ambassador for a brief conference; passing through the anteroom on his way out, the aide-de-camp could not help noticing that tears were streaming down the shaken envoy's face.

Over the next four years, the flower of European youth was sacrificed on bloody battlefields. The headcount after Germany's unconditional surrender in 1918 showed a total of ten million dead, among them two million German soldiers. According to the general opinion of the defeated Germans, their forces had simply been outnumbered by the enemy. The German Army, invincible in battle, had been "cowardly stabbed in the back" by enemies from within. This legend, the so-called *Dolchstosslegende*, made the rounds until everyone was convinced it was true. The blame clearly rested with traitors from the left: Socialists, Communists, anarchists, and—of course—the Jews. The kaiser, instead of accepting at least a fraction of responsibility for the humiliating defeat, fled his country under the cover of night on November 9, 1918, and was granted asylum in the Netherlands.

While the kaiser had not lost a single one of his six sons, three of Wilhelm and Hedwig von Sell's four sons, who had proudly and bravely fought for the emperor and their nation's glory, were now dead. Miraculously, Ulrich survived a deep shrapnel wound in his left temple. He spent the last months of the war on operating tables in military field hospitals, suffering excruciating pain at the hands of military surgeons under the most primitive circumstances.

After his final discharge, he came home to find his brothers dead, his mother turned to stone with grief, and his own promising diplomatic career over before it had really begun.

Ex-Chancellor von Bethmann-Hollweg had retired to his country estate and was in no position to help his former aide-de-camp. Most of his friends had been killed in battle, and there was no estate for him to retire to, no money to tide him over, nothing! The only indestructible capital the veteran had been able to save was a brilliant mind. His head, which bore a deep scar above the left ear, would never cease to cause him pain. Because he had no alternative, he did what millions were forced to do: he took his place in the long line of the dismally gray army of the unemployed.

It was 1919 and the newlyweds had a hard time making ends meet with their meager savings and a small veterans' pension, from which, among other expenses, Anna's wages were paid. After endless failed efforts to find a decent job, something miraculous happened. Ulrich's field driver during the war, a Jewish corporal named Cassirer, heard about his esteemed chief's desperate situation and offered him a position in his Berlin cable factory. He would never regret acting like a Good Samaritan because the baron, although faced with a completely different line of work, thanked his benefactor by quickly mastering the secrets of a new and alien world: business and finance. To his own surprise, the former staff officer and career diplomat soon detected within himself an outstanding talent for handling money, which would help him advance into a management position with a renowned Berlin banking establishment. Three years later, this newly discovered talent led to a post that would change his life and that of his family, which was about to expand.

Chapter Five
My Arrival

The rat that Anna probably smelled even before my mother was not at all to her liking. A howling brat in the house? Diapers she would have to wash? On the other hand, there was the poor *Herr Baron*, who had lost all his brothers. So, she decided not to quit, but to wait, just like my anxious and excited parents. Finally, there came the night in April when Anna, standing at the foot of the bed, received the baby from the hands of the hurriedly called physician: a girl.

A girl? But everyone had expected a boy!

After overcoming the initial shock, my father's face allegedly lit up when he realized that, after all, a daughter could neither be drafted nor shot. But how in the world would he be able to break this disastrous news to his mother? She, like everyone else, had expected a grandson as heir to the name. Of course, her daughter-in-law was to be blamed; she who had entered this marriage not as a virgin, but an apple someone else had nibbled. A virgin would have regarded it as her duty to give birth to a boy, not an outlandish demand after the loss of her own three sons.

And so, the one true virgin in the house blessed with a child of her own was, without any doubt, a Vendish maiden from the Spreewald, a fact that not even my mother would seriously contest. From the day of my birth, Anna divided visitors into two categories. The first category belonged those few who would, at the mere sight of me, break into exuberant praise about the uniquely exquisite beauty of this bald and spindly creature with huge eyes. The other category, without doubt the vast majority, consisted of my grandmother and all the elderly spinster aunts who did not even make a remote effort to hide their disgust about the new baroness' appearance: skinny arms, big bat-like ears sticking out offensively, and the total absence of hair. The question arose, in case I grew up at all, would there ever be a faint resemblance to a halfway normal human being? Poor, unfortunate parents, they certainly deserved better!

Since the arrival of a girl was not anticipated, no name had been discussed. After a polite but strict reminder by the local authorities (because German law required birth registration to include a name), there were long debates, and finally, my parents managed to come to a satisfactory agreement. I received three names: Sybilla, after the young princess of Coburg and Gotha, the future crown princess of Sweden; Augusta, in honor of my beautiful mother; and Sophia, for my godmother Sophie-Charlotte von Sell, my father's only living spinster cousin.

Around the turn of the century, Sophie-Charlotte had concluded that she would simply not accept the usual fate of a Prussian colonel's unmarried daughter—to become a governess, a librarian, a sister in a Protestant nursing order, or a teacher in a private school for girls of noble descent. She went to Sweden, the country where women even then enjoyed privileges about which their German counterparts could only dream. Mastering the Swedish language, she earned her living as a journalist and writer, publishing several novels in her home country, Germany. One novel in particular had tongues wagging, making the rounds within the immediate family, in the ardent hope of detecting a resemblance between some of the fictional characters and actual family members. But the author, to everyone's dismay, had not considered any of them worth writing about; that was really scandalous!

Sophie-Charlotte, thrilled to be chosen as my godmother, traveled all the way from Sweden to Potsdam to hold me over the baptismal font. Altogether, six godparents had been selected for me. Considering the fact that not a single one was under sixty years of age, their chances of still being alive for my confirmation were extremely slim. To me, it would not make much of a difference because, as far as gifts were concerned, they had decided in unison that they were wasted on a mere girl. The unanimous verdict was to wait until a boy was born. No wonder that, six years later, I picked my own godfather, one who would richly recompense me for their stinginess.

Just when everybody began to breathe a little easier, the worst post-war hardships seemingly overcome, the reichsmark began to crumble and lose value. Germany's economy had groaned under the harsh conditions of the Treaty of Versailles and finally collapsed. Anna, uttering an abundance of Vendish curses, visited the baker, the butcher, and the grocer, carrying a money-laden basket heavy with banknotes in the millions, which swiftly turned into billions and lost value not by the day or the hour, but by the minute, until they outweighed the bare essentials she was able to bring home. This trend continued until October 13, 1923, when a brand new currency, the rentenmark, replaced the worthless valuta, and once more one's banknotes would fit in a regular purse.

While almost everybody had lost something, some had lost everything in the inflation. My parents had owned little, and the little was now gone, as well as Anna's small nest egg. Once more, with the assiduity of bees, the people began to start from scratch. They were too busy to take notice of an occurrence that took place in faraway Munich where, on November 9, 1923, someone had tried to overthrow the government in a putsch, an ill-fated incident that had lasted only a few hours and would soon be forgotten. The newspapers reported several casualties, adding that the main instigator, some obscure Austrian nobody, had been apprehended. Munich was faraway, and the name "Adolf Hitler" did not seem worth remembering.

These events did not concern me in the least, so long as Anna's strong arms held me tight, only releasing me when circumstances made a brief separation absolutely inevitable. It was no surprise, then, that the first sounds I registered were in Vendish and not the German language. Every afternoon, weather permitting, Anna would tuck me into my high-wheeled baby carriage for our daily excursion. Before leaving the house, she underwent a metamorphosis, changing her appearance from that of a mere servant into the magnificent status symbol any aristocratic family could be proud of, a Vendish nanny in all her splendor!

As she stepped out of the house, carefully balancing the carriage with its precious cargo, her wolf's eyes began to scan the immediate neighborhood for potential dangers, lethal enemies lurking to harm her li'l lamb, as well as encounters of a more pleasant nature. There were other Vendish nannies in their colorful garb, pushing their respective charges through the streets and parks of Potsdam, babies that in Anna's expert opinion could not possibly compete with my beauty and intelligence. She almost felt compassion for those ugly creatures, praying that the unfortunate parents would never notice the difference between me and their less than perfect offspring.

It was never long before one of the countless elderly matrons roaming the streets of Potsdam approached us to inquire about my state of health and the progress I was making. Depending on the nature of their comments about me, Anna would either display her faultless teeth in a broad grin, accompanied by a polite curtsy, or she would mumble a few words—three Vendish words to be precise—*"rish me oblish!"* Translated into German, this phrase simply expressed the invitation to kiss her backside.

Chapter Six
BERLIN

I was two and a half years old when the family decided to bid Potsdam farewell and move to the capital. My father now held a position in the management of a Berlin bank, and the future was definitely beginning to look a little brighter.

Our new residence, located on a quiet side street of Berlin-Friedenau, a district preferred by retired officers and government employees, could hardly be described as fashionable. The dismally gray four-story structure, in which we had rented an apartment, was adorned with the kind of stucco work typical of turn-of-the-century architecture. Sparsely clad pseudo-Greek athletes balancing pseudo-Greek pillars on their muscular shoulders alternated with crumbling stone eagles. Inside, the rooms with their high ceilings also displayed an abundance of stucco work. The spacious apartment on the third floor of the walk-up building made the hiring of a second maid mandatory. An added luxury was a central heating system that also provided hot water, making the feeding of individual stoves with pressed coal and wood obsolete. A second staircase in the back was reserved for servants and deliveries.

While my father's study as well as my mother's "salon" faced the street, the huge dining room, connecting the front rooms to those in the back, an arrangement typical for Berlin, as well as kitchen, bathrooms, servant quarters, and bedrooms looked out onto the court, where a scraggly little tree fought for its life. The best thing about this court, which housed the garbage pails and the carpet beating rods, was the weekly appearance of an old organ grinder. He provided entertainment for all of us, and we would throw coins wrapped in paper down to him, which were picked up by a well-mannered, red-capped little monkey.

The building was ruled with an iron hand by the concierge, who had the final say over almost anything that had to do with the house, like deciding who could beat his rugs and when. His assistant was a horrible little Pomeranian with a high-pitched voice, who loved nothing better than to attack the legs of unsuspecting visitors. Madame Concierge, propped up in a booth called the *portierloge*, waited for delinquents who attempted to use the front stairs instead of those in the back, a violation punishable by jail, if she had anything to say (and she said plenty, in much the same tone as the dog, for which she kept knitting little outfits).

There was only one event worth mentioning during our three-year residence in Berlin-Friedenau, but it was one that altered my entire life. A few months after the move, strange things began to happen in the house that nobody bothered to explain to me. For some mysterious reason, the empty bedroom next to mine was rearranged; Anna even dragged my old baby crib down from the attic. Would we have a baby visitor, I demanded to know? My mother had become rather rotund and developed the habit of lying down on the sofa during the day. Instead of playing Beethoven and Brahms on the grand piano in her salon with a slightly hard touch, she now intoned lullabies, which sounded a lot nicer to me. My curiosity, however, was met with Anna's unsatisfactory answer: "Wait hand see, li'l lamb, juss you wait hand see." With all her efforts to speak German correctly, she had never mastered the art of pronouncing an "h" where it belonged, carefully adding it where there was none.

Early one dark morning late in January, my father came into my room. He lifted me from my bed, cradled me in his arms, and after clearing his throat, informed me with tears in his eyes that I now had a brand new little brother. When I inquired about the whereabouts of the stork—who interested me a lot more than any baby—I was told that, unfortunately, the busy bird had to fly off. But, as a consolation prize, he had left me a huge cone-shaped bag filled with candy, so I forgave him his hasty departure.

While I was not too favorably impressed with this toothless, wrinkled addition to the family, everyone else seemed to be in a state of euphoria: my father because of the safe arrival of the long-awaited heir to the name, my mother because her mother-in-law would at last stop harassing her. Anna was happy for my mother, who now had a baby of her own; Anna had decided, in a fit of generosity, to leave the newcomer for her exclusive use. After all, this was fair, because I was Anna's baby, whom she would occasionally share with my father.

Since our move to Berlin had considerably shortened my father's way to and from work, he had more time for me. Father was a very impressive-looking man with a beautifully shaped head. His erect carriage, aristocratic features, and the sad expression in his deep-set gray eyes caused many women to turn around after him. To me, he was the most wonderful man in the world. I would marry him and no one else just as soon as I was old enough. The question about what to do with my mother did not seem a problem for me.

Each evening, I eagerly awaited my father's return, and as soon as he had installed himself in the high-backed armchair by the desk in his study, I climbed on his lap, and he held me tight. My little finger would fit exactly in the strangely frightening dent above his left ear, where he had been shot by the bad, bad enemy. A thin layer of skin had formed over the deep wound, and underneath I felt his blood pulsating, which never ceased to scare me.

As I grew older, I began to ask him questions about the war, which he answered cautiously. What did a trench look like? Were cannons terribly noisy? Why had he not simply run away? Had he shot any of his enemies? Was it very hard to be courageous? Did he ever cry, sometimes, maybe? Why? Because he was afraid? Before each answer he cleared his throat; yes, he had cried on occasion. And in carefully chosen words, he tried to explain what a little girl with my vivid imagination might be able to understand without causing too much confusion and alarm. Somehow, I must have sensed that the war continued to haunt him, that the hell he had been through would never leave him. After a while, his voice usually became low and hoarse, until it appeared that he was just talking to himself and not to me anymore. After all, how could I possibly understand what it had been like, this dark kingdom of death, into which millions of young men, among them his three brothers, my uncles, had vanished? Even though I could not possibly grasp the extent of my father's grief, it was during those moments that, barely sensing his despair, I instinctively knew that I had to show him as clearly as possible how much I loved him.

The memories of the inferno would haunt him for the rest of his days, even invading his dreams. At least once a week, in the middle of the night, he screamed during a nightmare. The bloodcurdling shouts were usually followed by a brief moment of frightening silence, after which my mother's soothing voice was heard, trying to wake him and calm him down. Not until I was a teenager did I realize that fathers in other families did not scream during the night. I had been under the impression that this was normal.

On the wall of my father's bedroom hung a picture that never ceased to make me shudder. It depicted poor Jesus with the crown of thorns, and depending from which side I looked at it, his eyes would either be shut or wide open, and they seemed to follow me wherever I went. At age three, possibly as a direct consequence of my father's nightmares, I began to climb out of my bed at night, evidently fast asleep, and wander through the house. More than once I showed up in the parlor, with guests still present, some of whom were vastly amused by the little ghost with wide open eyes. Others whispered behind cupped hands that this kind of behavior was, at best, rather odd. Maybe I was moonstruck or otherwise deranged, like Aunt Hedwig, my maternal grandfather's sister? Or could it be that the Vendish nanny, the woman with the heavy accent and the light, almost luminous eyes of a wolf, had cast some kind of spell on this helpless little creature with sparse hair and spindly legs? Anna, outraged by such remarks, muttered her favorite three-word invitation, swept me into her apron, and tucked me back into my bed.

My beautiful mother with her natural chestnut curls, trademark of the Brauchitsch family, sometimes casually touched my head and, with a distinctly regretful tone in her voice, whispered what a misfortune it was for me to have inherited my grandmother's "plain" hair. Although I did not understand the meaning of the word "plain" yet, I sensed that it was not complimentary. In later years, she would add that if indeed I should, against all predictions, reach a halfway normal size, I would never, never be as beautiful as she was. I had freckles, a pointed nose, huge eyes, and my deplorably narrow shoulders were definitely sloping! Why did I not have my cousin Gerlinde's broad build? For her it would be a pleasure to buy pretty dresses!

But for me? What a waste!

As a suitable punishment for my imperfect exterior, up to age fourteen I received my entire wardrobe at the cruel hands of the elderly, slightly hunchbacked seamstress Philomena, who came to the house twice a year for a week. She wore her fox-red hair in thin, braided plaits wound around her head, and she had a club foot laced up in a high boot. To top her imperfections she was a Catholic, which was absolutely unforgivable in Anna's judgment, but no wonder because Philomena came from the Polish region of Upper Silesia. Crouched in front of an old-fashioned, hand-and-foot-operated Singer machine, she busily stitched, mended, repaired, and "created" my wardrobe from outgrown clothes donated by more fortunate relatives. Having received *plein pouvoir* by my mother, she was free to use her own disastrous taste. My screams of protest fell on deaf ears; a child wore what was put on her, and many poor girls would give an arm and a leg to own clothes like mine. Unfortunately there were no needy children within reach, so Anna and Hilde pitied me.[5]

Hilde, the newly hired maid, a cheerful little sixteen-year-old with a pug nose and brown curls, came from my granduncle's estate, Marienwalde. Having managed to overcome the first hurdle, namely, ingratiating herself to Anna, she was granted the occasional privilege of reading bedtime stories to me, fairy tales by the Brothers Grimm, among which I favored the bloodthirsty ones. Excited beyond description, I used to sit up in my bed, ears cocked in wild anticipation, ready to learn for the fiftieth time about the fate of evil stepmothers rolling toward their well-deserved end in the icy floods of a torrential river, while encased in a barrel trimmed with sharp nails. It sent pleasurable shudders up and down my spine.

One day, unfortunately, my Aunt Gertrud, a spinster and a social worker, decided that this kind of detrimental literature was sheer poison for a tender soul such as mine. Consequently, Grimms' fairy tales were swept off the shelf, replaced by Hans Christian Andersen's allegedly tender and sensitive stories. Beside myself with helpless rage, for weeks I would refuse to listen to a single one of his tales, until one day there came a wonderful surprise. The story of Big Claus and Little Claus surpassed all brutalities I had ever encountered. Big Claus clobbered his grandmother to death with a hatchet; this warmed the cockles of my heart, and I decided to include the unmarried and therefore childless aunt in my evening prayers, for obviously overlooking certain parts in the Dane's masterworks.

Hilde's sudden departure from the house, caused by her mother's death, entailed a chain of disasters: a succession of new maids. The first two did not meet with Anna's approval, knowing that she was irreplaceable; the words "I am quitting," followed by beginning to pack her belongings, usually worked magic.

The next maid fell prey to a mysterious disease that began with morning sickness and was correctly diagnosed by Anna long before the devastating truth dawned on the dumbfounded girl. When the same misfortune befell the following maid, some of the tenants in the building began to speculate. Might it be possible that the *Herr Baron* . . . ? But no, no, no, it was agreed in unison, not him, out of the question! He was such a gentleman, a verdict that was wholeheartedly shared by Anna. No one outranked her *Herr Baron*, not even Kaiser Wilhelm, who had cowardly fled to the safety of another country.

Chapter Seven
NEW MEN IN MY LIFE

On the day of my baby brother's christening in our home, a flock of black-clad, elderly folk, groaning and gasping for breath, managed to climb all the way up to the third floor. Why, in heaven's name, was there no elevator? Since they were not exactly laden with gifts, all they had to carry was their own weight. Just as in my case three years before, an almost unanimous decision had obviously been reached not to waste good money on such a small child, even though this time it was a boy. Almost unanimous, because there was one exception.

Prominently displayed on the dining room table, for everyone to admire, lay the exquisite gift that the prominent godfather had sent: a huge platter of heavy, solid silver, with an imposing "W" engraved under the imperial crown. The generous donor, however, was absent because he had made the solemn vow to set foot on German soil only if invited to resume his rightful place on the throne.

Wilhelm II of Hohenzollern, in faraway Doorn, after learning the happy news of the little boy's birth, had spontaneously offered himself as a godfather. From my father's days as an adjutant to Chancellor Bethmann-Hollweg, the kaiser had followed the highly gifted young man's career with keen interest, well aware of the tragedy that had struck his family. As an expression of their gratitude, my parents added the new godfather's name as an additional burden to the names already selected for the heir: Friedrich Wilhelm Adolf Konrad Ulrich, so far the last Baron von Sell. Together with his own father's and his new godfather's name, those of his three fallen uncles had come to life again in the tiny baby.

With respectful reverence, champagne-filled glasses were raised in a toast to His Majesty, causing tears to sparkle in Prussian eyes, after which my father stunned his guests with yet another surprise, the glad tidings that the ex-kaiser had offered him the position as administrator of his substantial private capital, his privy purse. He would be entrusted with the welfare of a fortune vaguely estimated at fifty-five million reichsmark.

Wilhelm had promised his subjects prosperity and a glorious victory in the four-year war, which instead had ended with the shameful defeat of Germany and my father's promising career as a diplomat. Instead of facing responsibility, the kaiser had fled his country and people, seeking asylum in the Netherlands. As an act of retaliation, the rulers of the new German Republic stripped the fugitive of all his possessions. However, for reasons never explained, his entire property soon was returned to him, including some 250,000 acres of land in Germany, castles, fortresses, mines, and various real estate of inestimable value.

Thirty-seven freight cars, loaded with precious family-owned property, were sent to Holland, including gold, silver, china, jewels, furniture, paintings, sculptures, Wilhelm's private automobiles, and his vast collection of outrageously extravagant uniforms.

What would remain a mystery forever was where all these treasures were eventually stashed. The new domicile, "Huis Doorn," which held fifteen rooms not including the annexes, was by no means a castle, but it was a comfortable and moderately spacious country mansion surrounded by a romantic moat, embedded in a park with an abundance of trees, flower beds, and meadows. Not exceeding an area of five acres, the estate had been purchased by the new resident from its previous owner for just over one million Dutch guilder.

Assisted by a staff, my father assumed the duties of the ex-monarch's financial advisor and administrator in his new office, Unter den Linden in Berlin, located in the Dutch Palais, a city palace owned by the Hohenzollern family. Frequent trips to see his new chief in the little town of Doorn, not far from Utrecht, would take him away from his family for a week or two each month. There he was assigned his new residence in the "Orangery" opposite the main house.

Although not a monarchist and certainly anything but fond of the Hohenzollern family, my father must have had a soft spot in his heart for the unstable, stubborn, and often unbearable old ex-sovereign, who had taken such a steep fall from almost god-like heights into obscurity. And this vain old ex-potentate, who, by his rash and immature decisions, had been mainly responsible for throwing the world into disaster, loved him back with all his heart, more than his own sons.

When my father suggested to my mother that, for practical reasons, we should move to the penthouse on top of the Dutch Palais on Unter den Linden, he met with furious resistance. The family residence above the office? Where her husband would be available day and night to any demands and whims of the Hohenzollern family? Had he taken leave of his senses? And her children? Should they grow up in a cement desert, learn to roller skate and ride their bicycles in an asphalt jungle? Little as I was, the mere possibility of living in a palace struck me as extremely attractive, because in my mind, it would have qualified me as a veritable princess. [6]

Instead of moving to the Palais, my mother did what she did best. Behind my father's back, she began negotiations with realtors, and when she found what she wanted, she presented her ideas to my father in such a way that he felt that the whole idea of moving to the rural suburb of Dahlem had been his very own idea. For the first three years, we lived in a rented house; in 1933, my parents decided to build a home of their own. The modest yet stately white house, with a red roof and red wooden window shutters, vine and wisteria eventually climbing all over the exterior, was situated on a quiet street lined with red-blooming hawthorn trees. The garden offered a well-kept lawn, an abundance of fruit trees, a stately birch, and a row of tall firs as well as a sandbox for my brother, a swing for me, and a seesaw for both of us.

Unlike the elegant suburb of Grunewald, with its pompous Victorian mansions, well-manicured parks protected by high walls, and thick hedges, the medieval village of Dahlem, settled seven hundred years before, had managed to retain some of its original rural character. The estate, with its manor, at the time of our arrival still a working farm with horses, cattle, pigs, sheep, and fowl, was surrounded by rolling meadows and fields where corn, wheat, rye, and oats were grown—a child's paradise.

Across the street stood the village church of St. Anne's, built with local fieldstones. Over the period of seven hundred years it had bravely defied all attempts to be destroyed by fires, war, and the Reformation, only to be restored to its simple beauty after each disaster. Now Lutheran, it was surrounded by a romantic cemetery with magnificent trees.

The dense forest bordering the village of Dahlem, the Grunewald, had not too long ago been a haven for elk, bears, wild boar, and deer, where shortly before World War I, my father had still been hunting. The capital of Berlin, on the shores of the Spree River, lay embedded in the "Green Forest" of unspoiled swamps, lakes, and clear brooks, like a diamond set in a circle of emeralds.

The question of which elementary school I should attend for the first years of my education was answered by the combined protest of a number of Dahlemers, in unison rejecting the unacceptable idea of sending their elite offspring to something as vulgar as the local public elementary school. They were not about to expose their children to the unhealthy influence of possibly ill-mannered, low-class mates from whom they would learn terrible words and, infinitely worse in Anna's mind, catch fleas, mites, and lice. The problem was solved by hiring a retired teacher and renting a single room to serve as a classroom in an annex of the estate manor.

After several years, St. Gertraude's School for Girls, right around the corner from our house, would accept me for my high school education.

We were just a dozen children for whom going to school on the estate, a working farm, was great fun. Herr Meyer, the teacher, deathly afraid of offending his wards' parents by spanking their children as was still customary in public schools, was sweet and tender. If he felt that corporal punishment was inevitable, he draped the delinquent across his knees and gently applied a thin bamboo cane like the bow of a cello on the respective bottom. It was not pain that counted, it was the shame!

During the breaks we would sneak into the stables, admire the horses, cows, and pigs, sometimes watching certain startling activities we were not supposed to even notice. Despite speculation among us, we decided not to share our newly acquired knowledge with our parents. The chickens fled in panic when we appeared, as we loved to grab them and whirl them around until they lost their sense of balance, fluttering about like drunks.

I was in third grade when my father decided that the time had come to send me to Sunday school. My parents were the kind of Christians who limited their church attendance to services on Christmas, Easter, and other special occasions such as baptisms, weddings, and funerals. Because of his days in the military academies, my father's opinion of organized religion in general and the Protestant clergy in particular was not overly positive; however, he decided to use me as an experimental guinea pig, expressing the hope that the minister was not one of those pietistic twaddling relics he despised; I was the one who would discover that the pastor of St. Anne's was neither particularly old nor did he twaddle.

One Sunday, my father himself escorted me to the church, making sure that I would not find more amusing things to do, which indeed was within the realm of possibility. I was outraged because, instead of the leather pants in which I spent my days, a dress was forced on me, after receiving a badly needed scrub in the bathtub. I was to look like a girl so, adding insult to injury, Anna fastened a white taffeta bow, resembling a propeller, in my hair. My father, taking me firmly by the hand, personally delivered his pouting, freckled firstborn to the spinster in charge of the children at the church entrance. As a greeting, I stuck my tongue out at her behind my father's back, before reluctantly taking my assigned seat in the first pew.

On the altar stood an aged, white-haired clergyman, but next to him was someone else. Pointing to the man by his side, the old minister explained that this was our new pastor, who would succeed him in office, now that he had decided to go into his well-deserved retirement. I pricked my ears and took a good look at the man who bore a distinct resemblance to my father. He was a little younger, his complexion darker, his eyes almost black. I gave him the toothless grin becoming an eight-year-old, received a smile back, and felt my dogged obstinacy melt like butter in the sun.

When he began to speak to us, it was not about the precious little Jesus child at all, but instead he talked of his time as a submarine commander during the war, explaining what it had been like to be in a ship below the surface. Fascinated beyond description, I held my breath, and after the service, I skipped all the way home. This had not been bad at all! However, my parents definitely deserved punishment for ruining my original Sunday plans by forcing me to attend a religious service; I decided to withhold my interesting information from them, at least for a while.

A new pastor? My father inquired. Indeed? What a surprise! A young one? What was his name? His name? With a bored look, I ostensibly shrugged my shoulders. How would I know? Besides, he did not interest me in the least! Not one bit! On one of the following Sundays I learned his name: Martin Niemoeller.

Chapter Eight
The New Pastor

On January 14, 1892, a son was born to Heinrich Niemoeller, who was serving as pastor in Lippstadt, a sleepy little Westfalian town with some thirteen thousand inhabitants. At baptism the little boy received the names Emil Gustav Friedrich Martin, the last one, by which he would be called, in honor of Martin Luther.

The rectory, an ancient Westfalian frame house, was situated in the shade of the six-hundred-year-old Church of the Augustines. Here the Lutheran pastor lived with his wife, Paula, whose ancestors were Huguenots. From her southern French grandmother, Paula inherited her dark black eyes and complexion, characteristics she would pass on to her son Martin, together with a southern French temper, undiluted by the proverbial cautious prudence of his Westfalian father. What both temperaments have in common, however, is an equally proverbial stubbornness.

The second of the Niemoellers' five children, Martin was small for his age, painfully thin, with slightly protruding ears; his most prominent feature was a pair of dark, burning eyes. His outbursts of rage would be as notorious as his willingness to repent, his seemingly inborn sense of fairness and justice—character traits that would accompany him throughout his life. The romantic garden behind the rectory stretched all the way down to the Lippe River, a child's paradise. Here the sheep grazed, and Martin let his most prized possession, a sheet metal boat, glide on a long string into the water, imagining himself as a captain on the high seas. For him, there was not the slightest doubt that someday he would be a real captain on a real ship.

At age seven, he became the undisputed leader of a regular street gang; his most faithful allies were his two sisters who, without question, delivered all their precious discoveries to their older brother. There was a lot of love and tolerance in his family, which was quite remarkable in comparison to the frugal strictness and prudery prevailing in most evangelical pastors' homes. Martin would later state, "We were on a leash, but on a very long one."[7]

After his sixteenth birthday, Martin was sent to England for the summer vacation. He lived with a physician's family, pious people, requiring him to attend church services daily, and twice on Sundays, when even playing the piano was not permissible. He loved London, where he would roam the streets, travel by horse-drawn streetcars, enjoy his favorite dish, which was steak and kidney pie, and take extensive strolls on the banks of the Thames and on the docks. He admired the big ships. Later, as a naval officer, he still maintained that as far as appearance and behavior were concerned, British naval officers served as the one great example to their German colleagues.

Being more certain than ever that his future would be the sea, he set a modest goal for himself: to become Chief of Staff of the Imperial German Navy. The idea of becoming a pastor like his father never even occurred to him. However, there was one particular experience, the memory of which would not leave him for the rest of his life.

One day, the fourteen-year-old accompanied his father on a pastoral visit to a member of his congregation, a seriously ill coal miner. Calling on his parishioners at home was regarded by the pastor as his foremost duty. What better way was there to know his flock, to find out about their problems, wants, and needs, offering his advice, concern, and help? In the coal miner's wretched basement dwelling, located in the poor section of Elberfeld, they found the prematurely aged husband and father of five dying of tuberculosis, a common disease in those days. Letting his eyes wander through the shabby, sparsely furnished quarters, young Martin noticed something that attracted his attention. Hanging on the naked wall was a framed epigram, which read: "What would Jesus say?" The youth had no idea to what extent those four words would determine the course of his life.

After graduating from the Humanistic Gymnasium in Elberfeld with the supreme honors of a *Primus Omnium*, he entered the Imperial German Navy as a cadet, the first step toward his goal of becoming Chief of the German Fleet. Growing up in a traditionally conservative family, he had been taught, in accordance with the generally accepted teaching of the church, that a pious Christian is a good citizen and consequently a good soldier, a dogma that young Martin saw no reason to doubt. One of his comrades at the Northern German Naval Academy in Flensburg-Mürvik was named Karl Dönitz, a thin and humorless youth with a pinched face. He was not popular, but was regarded as conceited and abnormally ambitious by his comrades, who maintained that he cheated in class. He possessed those Prussian virtues that are considered of secondary importance: ambition, perseverance, discipline, and blind obedience. They would, several decades later, enable him to rise to the top of the German Navy, under Adolf Hitler.[8]

The outbreak of World War I found Martin jubilant, sensing that, for the first time in history, the war at sea would play a decisive part. His promotion from second to first officer on several warships led to the rank of commander of a submarine, the U-56, during the last year of the war. His orders included laying sea mines in the Mediterranean not far from Marseille. However, all efforts to torpedo a French vessel near the harbor of Dakar were unsuccessful, and the steamer disappeared. Forty years later, one of the passengers from that vessel wrote to the former submarine captain, then President of the World Council of Churches: "My dear pastor, so it was indeed you being after my life! Thank God you did not succeed because you would have robbed yourself of a sincere friend and a true ally in your efforts toward world peace!"

The writer, who would become a close friend, was Albert Schweitzer. Martin would never cease talking about his years at sea. Memories of exciting, dangerous, and even funny events would follow him for the rest of his long life.

In 1918, the collapse of Imperial Germany shattered the young naval commander's plan of becoming chief of the German Navy. Martin's last official function was the outright refusal of a military order. He declined to carry out a command requiring him to deliver two German submarines to England as part of war reparations. He knew he could get away with this act of disobedience because he could explain that under no circumstances would he ever consider remaining in a much reduced and certainly not very glorious postwar navy. "I fought for four years," he declared before his commanding officer. "I neither wanted nor signed this armistice and, as far as I am concerned, those who did can take the ships to England," he continued. "I will take no part of this action. I refuse!" On March 27, 1919, his career as a naval officer was finally over.

Less than a month later, on April 20, Martin's father conducted the wedding ceremony of his oldest son and Else Bremer, the sister of his unforgotten friend Herrmann Bremer, whose ship had sunk in the Irish Sea. When proposing to Else, her father had asked a very obvious question: "Just what tangible goods did the two young people possess to justify such a step?" He received the answer: "A lot of courage!" Courage was urgently needed, because the twenty-seven-year-old ex-captain did not have the slightest idea what to do with a life that had once seemed so promising and secure.

What would Jesus say?

What indeed would Jesus say? Would he say "yes" to the question that Martin entered in his diary on September 17, 1919, five months after his wedding? "Will I become a theologian?"[9]

"The profession of a pastor, my boy, is the freest in the world," Heinrich Niemoeller told his son.

Jesus says, "Yes!"

With eagerness, Martin began his studies at the University of Münster. A lot of learning was ahead of him, including the *Hebraicum*, the command of Hebrew required of a Protestant pastor for his ordination. To keep his fast growing family from starving, he worked part time as a railroad laborer; by the time he was ordained in 1924, three children had been born, to be followed by three more before 1930, and in 1934, Martin Niemoeller Jr. would come into the world.

For the rest of his life, Martin Niemoeller would reject being called a "theologian." He did not think too highly of systematic theology; it was of no importance to the pastor, for whom the only significant message remained the gospel of Jesus, the man from Nazareth. At age eighty, he still stated, "All my life I have tried to tell my vicars to forget the theology they were taught and instead make the message of Jesus Christ the center of their teachings and their lives."

Following his ordination, the thirty-two-year-old minister's first sermon turned into an unexpected disaster—he stuttered, groped for words, and became hopelessly stuck. The church council regretfully decided that, since the young pastor obviously lacked the talent to deliver sermons, he would be put to better use in the administration. But Martin would not give up. In utter dismay, he turned to his father, pleading with him "to loan him his own pulpit." His father agreed, and this time Martin had no problem preaching his sermon. He would never get stuck again. There was another bit of advice from his father that he would take to heart: "Preach in such a manner, my son, that even the dumbest little confirmand can understand you."

For six long years, however, he found himself confined to working in the Home Mission, in close contact with Pastor von Bodelschwingh, who would later play a decisive role in refusing the Nazi-ordered "euthanasia" in Bethel, an institution for the mentally and physically handicapped. Thoroughly disappointed and discouraged about his life as an office employee, the pastor was ready to resign in 1931, but then a miracle happened. The congregation of Dahlem had an opening for a third minister and offered him the position. This, he felt, might well become the chance of a lifetime. With Else, the housekeeper Dora, six children, and even some goldfish in a jar, he moved to Dahlem, home to an affluent congregation with 13,000 members, contributing almost 800,000 reichsmarks each year in church taxes. His only concern: would this atmosphere of wealth harm his children?

The new pastor made his debut on a beautiful Sunday in June 1931, holding the children's service in the ancient church of St. Anne's, prior to the adults' service, which would follow an hour later. Among the children in the first pew, he spotted a small girl. She was thin; her impudent little face with the pointed nose covered with freckles and her two missing front teeth did not exactly enhance her appearance. Her hair was fuzzy, and she was constantly fidgeting in her seat. She was furious, because she was not there by her own free will. "You will obey my orders," Baron Ulrich von Sell had informed his daughter that morning, just when she attempted to sneak out of the house for a game of field hockey.

My initial encounter with the pastor of St. Anne's had two consequences worth mentioning. The first was that I soon found myself wandering over to the rectory, a spacious red brick mansion adjacent to the cemetery of St. Anne's on Cecilienallee. To my infinite relief, the suspicion that a pastor's children had to be unbearably well behaved proved totally unfounded. The spacious house was brimming with youngsters, three boys and three girls between four and twelve years of age, four of them blond and blue-eyed, and two with black hair, dark complexion, and black eyes. They all seemed to have inherited their father's vivacious temperament and high spirits. To my delight, I found that I blended in rather well, one extra child not making much of a difference. Being used to a somewhat subdued atmosphere prevailing in my own home, I was fascinated by this noisy bunch.

The children's mother, her hair a premature white, had a hard time controlling us, particularly when we chased each other through the house playing hide-and-seek. Once in a while the study door was pushed open and the father, with a thundering voice, promised us a sound thrashing if this hullabaloo did not stop at once. He was, after all, trying to work on his Sunday sermon. This outburst caused instant silence that lasted five minutes at the most, after which hell broke loose again. The first time I had sought quick refuge under a table but was assured that "barking dogs never bite." Nobody recalled the pastor actually carrying out his plans. The only person with real authority was little Dora, the housekeeper, a resolute wisp of a woman with a mop of tousled, carrot red hair, who knew how to put a swift end to the pandemonium by distributing juicy slaps, from which I, the runt of the litter, was by no means exempted.

As a second consequence of my first Sunday school visit, my parents decided to attend church more regularly, ultimately forming a close relationship with Martin and Else Niemoeller. As far as the political inclinations in 1931 were concerned, the pastor expressed a lot more optimism about the future than my father, although the two men agreed that the hard times were by no means over. Dark clouds were threatening on the horizon.

Chapter Nine
Rabble-Rousers

On Pentecost Sunday, I succeeded in persuading my parents to let me accompany them to the grown-up service. I was now old enough and pretty tired of legends and fairy tales about sweet baby Jesus. Besides, on that specific Sunday, the pastor's father, Heinrich Niemoeller from Elberfeld, was expected to officiate. The Niemoeller children had shared a delightful secret with me: their grandfather's false teeth had a tendency to fall out during the sermon. What a wonderful prospect! In wild anticipation, I took my seat in the pew, but to our dismay, the dentures stayed where they belonged. Instead, the congregation was in for a surprise of a different nature. Throughout the second part of the service, loud noises from the street reached the ears of the worshippers. Outside, on Cecilienallee, a crowd of people had gathered to watch a spectacle taking place opposite the church.

A group of men in brown uniforms with shoulder straps and army boots were marching in formation, forward and back, with one of them bellowing orders. Intermittently they shouted marching songs that I had never heard before, one about "brown battalions and millions looking hopefully up to the *Hakenkreuz.*" Like the armbands the men wore on their sleeves, the flag that one of them carried showed the swastika, a black, spider-like emblem on a white circle surrounded by red.

Were they soldiers, I inquired? My father, who looked even more serious than usual, explained to me in a low voice that these brown-clad figures were not soldiers, but members of an extremely dangerous gang, belonging to a political party led by a certain Adolf Hitler, who hoped to become chancellor of a new "Reich." Were it not for the old president, Field Marshal Paul von Hindenburg, the revered war hero, who would not permit this agitator to realize his plans, there would be cause for concern. But what would happen, I kept insisting, if this whatshisname came to power anyway? "Dear child," my father replied, "in that case we can only pray for God's mercy." Glancing up at him, I noticed that his face looked ashen.

Similar performances outside the little church, designed to disturb services, would be repeated on the following Sundays. On one occasion, a man in a brown uniform, waiting until enough bystanders had gathered around him, began a very loud and lengthy speech. Once in a while, he would pause to shoot threatening glances into the crowd. The Germans, he yelled, had to renew themselves as a *Volk*, find their true identity as a people, something that could not be achieved by praying and blubbering pious hymns. He pointed a finger at the church and added that it was most likely filled with reactionaries dead set against Adolf Hitler and his wonderful ideas.

"We will show them," he shouted, shaking his fist, "those renegades, Communists, Bolsheviks, anarchists, Jews, goddamn them! *Juda Verrecke!* Croak, Jews! *Sieg Heil* and forward march!" These developments deeply disturbed my parents, so the atmosphere in our house became gloomier by the day.

St. Nicholas Day was observed in every German house with children on the sixth of December; on that date in 1932, a bombshell went off at home. The Saint's ill-tempered male servant, Knecht Rupprecht (a strictly German invention), usually came to the house to threaten us with a rod. Reciting a well-rehearsed prayer would put him into a gentler mood. My brother and I often wet our pants, after which he would open his voluminous bag onto the living room floor, out of which came candy, gingerbread, marzipan, nuts, and apples. Until the previous year, I had firmly believed in this nasty old man's existence, if for no other reason than he was strangely familiar with amazing details of my wrongdoings throughout the past twelve months. Now, for the first time it dawned on me that underneath the crimson cloak, the hood, the white beard, and the red nose was none other than Uncle Putzi, one of my mother's three brothers, who managed to irritate us with boring jokes.

Boldly expressing my well-founded doubts, he took off his costume, exposing a brown uniform, complete with shoulder strap and knee-high boots, his left shirtsleeve adorned with a swastika band. Noticing the horrified look on my parents' faces, he explained that he was on the way to a meeting of the SA, Adolf Hitler's storm troopers, who had joyfully welcomed him as a full-fledged member. My father commented that by accepting men with noble names in their ranks, this gang of terrorists attempted to raise its status from notoriety to acceptability. He then asked politely whether Uncle Putzi, a former naval officer, had taken leave of his senses by lending his good name to an unspeakably vulgar mob.

Uncle Putzi, the color on his stupid face having changed to that of a freshly boiled crayfish, panted with indignation. Then he took a deep breath. Didn't my father realize that the only man able to restore dignity, law, and order in the beloved fatherland was Adolf Hitler? This God-sent leader whose sole concern was for Germany to resume its rightful, God-given place at the top of all nations? Had he not read the uniquely informative book *Mein Kampf* (*My Struggle*), in which Hitler laid down all his glorious plans for the German people with such wonderful clarity?

Indeed, retorted my father, he had read this concoction of garbage, the product of a warped mind, its author being a demagogue of the worst kind, a frustrated would-be architect suffering from megalomania!

At this point, my uncle was beside himself, the tip of his pointed Aryan nose now white as chalk. Could it have escaped my father's attention, his voice a pitch higher, that very distinguished personalities had not found it beneath themselves to proudly join the SA? Even the kaiser's son, August Wilhelm, performed his duty just like anyone else who believed in the ideals, the high goals of the National Socialist German Workers' Party.

"What ideals," my father inquired, "what goals?"

Well, for instance more *lebensraum*[10] for the German people, this most Aryan race of all, trying to overcome the miserable consequences of the Treaty of Versailles. Hitler would not rest until all those responsible for signing it received their deserved punishment: the Communists, anarchists, and of course, the Jews, those foreign, syphilis-inflicted subhumans, parasites in any decent society. But, he ended, not to fear, the savior is on his way!

"Great," my father quipped. "Now, instead of 'Christ, the savior is here,' you can sing 'Adolf, the savior is here.'"

That did it! Uncle Putzi stamped out of the house.

I profited from this new situation insofar as the broad shoulders and golden curls of Gerlinde, Uncle Putzi's daughter, would not be mentioned anymore as a highly desirable example for me to follow.

Only thirteen months after this ghastly encounter, what Uncle Putzi had wished for so ardently, and what my father had feared with equal passion, became reality; Hitler came to power only weeks after the venerable, wonderful, and equally senile Reichspräsident Paul von Hindenburg had told my father, "Not as long as I have something to say, will this Austrian painter's apprentice become chancellor!"

My father had been in constant contact with the old head of state, not necessarily by his own free will. His master in Holland, still in need of a scapegoat on which to blame his misery, had made Hindenburg the target of his hate, maintaining it had been he who strongly advised the monarch to leave the country after the lost war. Angry letters were exchanged, and it was my father who had to carry the handwritten epistles from Doorn to Berlin and back.

Several years later, Uncle Putzi and Aunt Edda would pay an unwelcome and unannounced visit to our house. Both decorated with the red-rimmed black metal spider on their lapels, they expressed their grave concern over the fact that neither my brother nor I were members of the Hitler Youth. For reinforcement they had brought one of their own Teutonic sons along, in the splendor of his uniform, a glorious specimen of a German boy serving the führer, meant as a shining example for weaklings like us. His scanty pants just barely covered what my brother and I called the *peepeenuller*. Unfortunately, we just happened not to be home to admire him.

Chapter Ten
The Godfather

Having mastered the art of writing, I finally found myself in the position to do what I had planned for years, to inform my father's employer, my little brother's imperial godfather in faraway Holland, about me. So far he had ignored my existence, directing valuable gifts for Christmas and birthdays exclusively to his godson, who on account of his pudgy cheeks was never called by one of his impressive five first names, but "*Dicker*" which, in plain language, meant "Fatso." Determined to rectify this situation, I tore a page from my school writing pad, asked my mother for an envelope, and proceeded to compose a letter to Germany's last monarch, which I dared not entrust to the mail, but boldly handed to my father for personal delivery the next time he went to Doorn.

In 1933, even though my father was still conservative in his political thinking, he was dead set against the Hohenzollern clan's ambitions to regain access to the throne. But deep in his heart, he felt compassion for the lonely old man in his self-chosen exile, who, after his plunge into obscurity, continued to live in a make-believe world in a make-believe court atmosphere. My father felt a strong duty to protect his master not only from the disastrous influences of those in his entourage, headed by an ambitious wife, but also from himself. After the kaiser's devoted wife, the Empress Auguste Viktoria, died in 1921, the old man was so distraught that his friends feared for his life. They arranged a visit to Doorn by the widowed Princess Hermine of Schoenaich-Carolath, née Princess Reuss. Wilhelm fell into their trap; only nineteen months after his wife's demise, he married the princess, twenty-eight years his junior, and insisted she be called "her majesty." Too late, the bridegroom discovered that Hermine was quarrelsome, scheming, and downright malicious. She would leave no stone unturned, including approaching the Nazis, to ascend the throne of Germany.[11]

As I became older, I overheard remarks not meant for my ears, which caused me to wonder if the bond between the two men was really just incidental. Illicit alliances had always been part of life at the courts, certainly not excluding the Hohenzollerns, where the mistresses and their illegitimate offspring received settlements of estates and titles. Not even Wilhelm I, the kaiser's revered grandfather, had exactly been a pillar of virtue. Neither had the kaiser himself. It was among my father's duties to take care of the various financial obligations, including alimony payments to an undisclosed number of out-of-wedlock descendants from as far back as the turn of the eighteenth to the nineteenth century. My maternal grandmother bore a striking resemblance to Queen Victoria, her light-blue eyes a trademark of the Hohenzollerns.

Daily life in Doorn resembled that of a ruling court, of miniature proportions. The kaiser continued to bestow medals of merit to deserving underlings. There were even courtiers and sinister intrigues, fortunately not dangerous enough anymore to cause a world crisis, but instead remained tempests in a teapot. If it had not been for the 1919 law doing away with aristocratic titles, the ex-sovereign would probably have issued new patents of nobility. Unlike in Austria, where even the "von" was stricken from a noble name, the change in Germany had not been so drastic, simply declaring a title as part of one's name. This meant that my father was not to be called Baron Ulrich von Sell anymore, but Ulrich Baron von Sell. It was that simple, and nobody was too offended.

Among His Majesty's favorite hobbies in exile was one that did not exactly meet with the undivided joy of his guests. He had gotten into the habit of felling trees by the hundreds. Their trunks, after being stacked in a corner of the park, were sawed by hand and chopped by axe into logs of firewood. All this was only partially accomplished by the kaiser himself, so his guests were invited to chip in. All male visitors were to report to the shed early in the morning and were put to work regardless of age, profession, or rank, most of them aghast at such a proposition. Nobody was exempt, not even princes, counts, barons, statesmen, physicians, or scientists. The only known exception was my father, who for once in his life had reason to praise the deep scar in his temple, which served as a valid excuse. This strange hobby became an obsession, resulting in the deplorable fact that the stock of trees in the park and nearby forests dwindled to an alarmingly small amount. Why nobody put a stop to this activity remained a mystery. Another puzzle was what the kaiser did with all the leftover wood. After generously supplying everyone near and far with enough firewood for decades, he proceeded to adorn mountains of thick round trunk slices with his signature, donating them to baffled visitors, whether they liked it or not. After having practically shaved his park, the old woodcutter complained bitterly about not being able to take a stroll without being observed, stubbornly refusing to see a logical connection between his own actions and their disastrous effect. But then, logical thinking had never been among his virtues.

When the news made the rounds that Hermann Goering intended to appear as a guest in Doorn for a private dinner party, it was my father who was chosen to let the party crasher know that he had not been invited. This and other, equally unpleasant, encounters laid the cornerstone to a relationship between my father and the deeply insulted Goering that can only be described as disastrous. Needless to say, Goering swore revenge, and he got it a few years later when he decided to simply take over Rominten as well as other possessions by simply disowning the rightful proprietors.

My very first epistle to the kaiser must have vastly amused him. Not wasting unnecessary concern with etiquette, I simply addressed him as *Lieber Kaiser*, "Dear Emperor," and proceeded to inform him about my existence, suggesting in no uncertain words that he accept me, the sister of his *real* godson, as his godchild, too. There were a few spelling mistakes and minor ink spots, but my father respected my wish and handed the letter unopened to the rather surprised imperial recipient in Doorn. This was, to my utter delight, the beginning of a rather lucrative friendship. By return mail, I received an answer from my new self-chosen godfather, handwritten with the purple ink pencil he favored, and signed with the huge flourish-adorned name, Wilhelm. Underneath were two letters, I. R., which my father explained stood for *Imperator Regis* and meant "Ruling Emperor."

When a blue scooter with shining chrome arrived on my birthday, complete with bell and brakes, I knew I had played my cards right, convinced that the *Lieber Kaiser* himself had selected this wonderful gift, maybe even tried it out in the local toy shop. Since I had recently learned the art of knitting, I decided to reciprocate by sending him one of my elaborations, a white pot holder with red rim, a true work of art and of love. He could use it, I figured, to lift pot lids during his inspections of the imperial kitchen.

Before realizing it, he had advanced to the position of a *postillon d'amour* on the highest level. Only once did he have cause to reprimand me. I had asked my imperial pen pal for a signed photograph, which he promptly sent, so in my enthusiastic thank-you note, I informed him that his picture was now on my bedside table.

My father looked me straight in the eyes and explained that "bedside table" was an embarrassing phrase, a no-no, and therefore unmentionable to someone like His Majesty. Why? Because this specific piece of furniture contained a particular object of crockery known as a chamber pot that, while admittedly extremely useful, should, under no circumstances, be associated with an emperor, not even one without a throne. From now on, he added sorrowfully, my mail would have to be subject to his censorship, which, fortunately, did not last beyond the next letter, because the kaiser obviously preferred my rather unique style, ordering that mail from me be handed to him unopened.

To add a little more spice to my letters, I blew some of the events in my life out of proportion. During a trip to the Dolomites, I had the bad luck of breaking one of my skis, an accident that left me unhurt and overjoyed at the same time. I hated skiing, particularly since my little brother was a real champion. I was pretty certain in the assumption that I was not about to get a new pair soon. This incident served as a perfect opportunity to describe what happened in a letter to the *Lieber Kaiser*. In sordid details, I described how, high up on a dangerous glacier, the ski broke under me while speeding down a steep hill. I found myself clinging to a shrub while hanging upside down over a yawning abyss. Pondering whether I should mention fire-spitting dragons threatening in the depths, I decided against it. Remembering all my death-defying Prussian ancestors, I told him that I managed to remain calm, cool, and collected. Eventually, I was rescued and, I added, I did not even cry, because I was a brave soldier, and soldiers do not cry. After reading this hair-raising description, the kaiser turned to my father and exclaimed, "and that brave little soldier did not even cry!"[12]

When a shiny dynamo lamp for my bicycle arrived a few weeks later, I felt I should reciprocate and decided to crochet a tea cozy for him in white and blue wool. I knew he loved tea, and now he would be able to keep it hot.

When, I inquired, could we visit our godfather in his fabulous castle? After all, he must be heartbroken never having met me and his regular godson? The only member of the family the kaiser remembered well from the golden days was my mother, as she floated by his throne as the belle of the ball.

It turned out that there existed a rather formidable and invincible obstacle that kept blocking our way to Doorn, and that obstacle was her majesty, the "Empress" Hermine. Her arch-enemy's family coming for a visit? Over her dead body! She would rather jump out of a window than tolerate such an insult. It was bad enough that my father, against her explicit wishes, was not only still in her husband's employ, but seemingly closer to him than ever. What happened next hit us like a flash of lightning out of the clear blue sky. There seemed to be enough curiosity in Hermine's jealous mind to meet us, provided it was on her own terms, on her turf, and as far removed from her husband as possible.

Returning home from school one day, I found the house in an uproar, Anna in a fit of hysteria; "her majesty" had summoned my mother, my brother, and me to appear at the Dutch Palace on Unter den Linden for tea that same afternoon. This, my mother knew, was a command performance as well as an act of revenge, cleverly devised in my father's absence. In a wild rush, my brother was stuffed into his white sailor suit, while I donned its counterpart for girls, a sailor dress, complete with collar and sailor's knot, a white taffeta bow resembling a propeller fastened on top of my head, after which the three of us jumped into a hastily summoned taxi.

This being my first visit to a real imperial castle, I was beside myself with excitement. The white-haired, white-gloved butler, with his drooping moustache and the air of an archduke, courteously addressed me as "young gracious baroness," which caused my mother to first gag and then inform him that the title was a total waste on a brat like me. I hated her for it. He led us to what he called the imperial chambers. Chambers? Because majesties, unlike us, my mother whispered, did not just live in rooms, they resided in chambers.

Entering through a double door with heavy green velvet drapery, I noticed in semi-darkness a lady clad in a gown of flowing green silk, draped on a sofa with the languor of a huge, probably poisonous snake. Graciously summoning us to come closer, she stretched a limp hand out for my mother to kiss, who then sank to the floor in a deep curtsy, a gesture I knew she hated with a passion. My brother, who, in sharp contrast to me, was always well-behaved, politely bowed his head, while I did my own version of a curtsy by first squatting down and then jumping up into the air, offering my hostess the inquisitive grin of an abundantly freckled and momentarily toothless eight-year-old.

Where was the crown, I kept wondering? "Her Majesty," whose cat's eyes reminded me of little Snow White's evil stepmother, did not offer me an apple, but, with a sweet-sour smile, handed me the biggest box of chocolates I had ever seen. Maybe my father's descriptions of her had been a little exaggerated? Without delay, I began to tear the silk bow and the luxurious wrapping paper open, ignoring my mother's warning glances and, in record time, managed to wolf down half its contents, poisoned or not. My brother received a striped sweater in monstrous colors, hand-knitted by Hermine herself, which reached all the way down to his ankles, making it obvious that he would never grow into it. Eventually, it landed in our dog's basket.

Following these preliminaries, tea and fine cookies were served by the butler, and Hermine's rather monotonous monologue began to make me feel drowsy. After an hour, the three of us were finally dismissed. We had not even reached the street, when I got what was coming to me in the shape of several juicy slaps across the mouth. I bawled all the way home, this time by subway. The endless trip had to be hurriedly interrupted at one point when my chocolate laden stomach turned inside out, and we barely made it from the subway car onto the platform. To maintain that the stationmaster was displeased with the mess I left would be an understatement. And it must have been his choice of down-to-earth words, some of which not even I was familiar with, that caused my mother to react with a rather severe migraine headache.

This was our first and last encounter with the "empress," who wasted no time to utter snide remarks to my father about his precious daughter's conduct. Grasping for adequate words, she tried to describe my uncouth behavior, which, as far as she was concerned, had been beyond description. My father, in turn, informed me about this crushing verdict, but I could not help noticing the twitching around the corners of his mouth. In fact, he could hardly keep a straight face.

Chapter Eleven
The Third Reich Begins

Late in 1932, the riots organized by Hitler's brown-clad storm troopers, called the "garbage brigade" by my parents, became even more blatant and obnoxious. It seemed as if they were already practicing what one of their favorite marching songs threatened:
Heute gehört uns Deutschland und morgen die ganze Welt!
"Today, Germany is ours, tomorrow the entire world!"

On January 30, 1933, a German miracle happened. In spite of Reich President Hindenburg's repeated derogatory statements about the Nazis in general and Hitler in particular, it was he who appointed the man from Braunau to the position of Reich Chancellor. The choice was cheered by the Germans, who saw their dream of a mystical, mythical leader come true at last. A knight in shining armor would deliver them from the evils of a parliamentary democracy, not to mention the threat of Communism. Hitler's shining armor consisted of an ill-fitting yellow-brown uniform with shoulder straps, accentuating his rather narrow, slanting shoulders and wide hips, complete with baggy breeches, clumsy army boots, and a slouch hat with an enormous peak to conceal his allegedly beautiful blue eyes.

Early in January, Hindenburg had summoned my father for an urgent meeting, the purpose being a special favor the president, now in a state of advanced senility, wanted to ask of the kaiser's confidant. Would he take a letter, a personal message to His Majesty in Doorn? The once close relationship between the two men had turned into bitter hostility over the kaiser's constant accusations that it had been Hindenburg who advised him, practically forced him, to leave his country. This unfair and unfounded charge lay as a heavy burden on the old warrior's heart; it had been the emperor himself who, instead of facing the consequences, had deserted his people and fatherland in an act of unprecedented cowardice and was since in dire need of a scapegoat.

On the morning following January, 30, 1933, my father came down to breakfast looking decidedly different; his face seemed naked. As long as I could remember, his upper lip had been graced by a very becoming and well-trimmed little moustache. Now it had disappeared; he had shaved it off. There was no room, he explained curtly, for two moustaches in the world in which he had to live. Taking one look at his drawn face, it dawned on me that, beginning today, life would probably not be the same anymore, and I remembered his answer to my question a few years before: what would happen if the Nazis came to power?

"Then, my dear child, may God have mercy on us."

What was mercy, I wondered?

Meeting with Martin Niemoeller a few nights after the Nazi victory, the pastor still expressed the hope that Hitler, against all predictions, might well become instrumental in bringing about the renewal of the German people, leading them back to their roots as a "*Volk.*" As far as the church was concerned, there was absolutely no reason to worry; Hitler himself had guaranteed its untouchability and independence. Martin would soon have ample reason to change his opinion.

On March 21, 1933, with pomp and glory, the new chancellor was officially presented to the German people by Reich President Hindenburg, the spectacle taking place in Potsdam's ancient Prussian Garrison Church, the *Garnisonkirche*. After all, asking for God's blessings seemed appropriate. "An act of sheer blasphemy," my father remarked.

Surrounded by the Old Guard, representatives of the armed forces, the storm troopers, high officials of both churches, delegations of industry and nobility, an ostensibly demure, well-dressed, and soft-spoken Adolf Hitler, keenly aware of the importance of this day, solemnly promised to be a good führer. At the same hour, only a few miles away, opponents were dragged into Sachsenhausen Concentration Camp: Communists, Socialists, trade unionists. Hitler had wasted no time honoring his threat to get rid of his enemies. "I am," he would declare only one year later, "the Supreme Judge of the German people!" But by that time, Germany had already ceased to exist as a constitutional state. Law and outward order prevailed, but it was the law and order of unabashed terror.

To the majority of Germans, the political as well as the economic situation looked promising, the future rosy. The führer had sworn to wipe out the disgrace of the lost war, and instead of unemployment, there was now work in abundance. Thousands were busy building the autobahn, for which the Nazis would claim full credit; in fact, this project had been started several years before the new regime took over. Armed with shovels, an army of laborers now found work hacking away by hand what could easily have been done by machines. But masses of determined workers shouldering spades were a lot more impressive in the media. This wonderful expressway was constructed for the Germans to travel in their very own Volkswagens, those miraculous little vehicles created by one of Hitler's most ardent admirers, Ferdinand Porsche. The car inventor would do very well for himself from then until the end of the war, employing Jewish concentration camp inmates, systematically worked to death by practically all branches of German industry. The magnificent highways, unique proof of German craftsmanship, knowhow, and willpower, would not be enjoyed by happy Aryan Germans on pleasure trips in their own cars, but only a few years later, would be used by army vehicles carrying troops and ammunition to the fronts in the West and the East in a war that the führer had planned all along, the one that would finally create well-deserved *lebensraum* for his people, ample living space for superhumans to rule and subhumans to serve.

On February 27, a fire devastated the Reichstag Building and was immediately denounced as a Communist plot against the new government. A dim-witted Belgian sailor by the name of Marinus van der Lubbe, a member of the Communist party, allegedly confessed to singlehandedly setting the fire, the nature of which suggested that the deed could not possibly have been committed by just one person, but only with the cooperation of at least a dozen others. More Communist suspects were apprehended, and a trial before the *Reichsgericht*, forerunner of the infamous *Volksgerichtshof*, the People's Court in Leipzig, sentenced van der Lubbe to the guillotine. Rumors kept making the rounds that the crime had, in fact, been concocted by none other than Goering with the sole purpose of blaming and subsequently punishing the Communists.

After this incident, my father called the attention of his friend Martin Niemoeller to the fact that the führer was well on his way to following the warnings directed toward his enemies in *Mein Kampf*.

Chapter Twelve
A Pastor's Growing Doubts

Within the first three months of the new regime, Pastor Niemoeller's initial optimism was shattered, as was his naive faith that the führer would keep his solemn promise not to interfere in church affairs. With the *Reichskonkordat* of July 30, 1933, Pope Pius XI declared total neutrality between the Holy See and Nazi Germany where Adolf Hitler, by birth a member of the Catholic Church, had been successful in winning the support of the majority of bishops. Since the terms of the treaty clearly guaranteed the inviolability of the Catholic Church, they hastened to pledge allegiance to the new government, closely followed by the Protestant clergy, who eagerly declared their loyalty to the regime even before being asked to do so. Hitler was euphoric; his hopes of having churches on his side had been surpassed. Now he had every reason to believe that he had been fully accepted.

For the majority of Germans, the traditional bond between state and church, between throne and altar, had not ended just because there was no throne, no monarch anymore. Their new kaiser's name was Adolf, and he saw every reason to be pleased by the developments. Backed by the churches, he would build a mighty bulwark against Bolshevism, as well as the powerful "International Jewry" still lurking in the background. He officially declared the two Christian churches to be the solid foundation of state and family life. Their rights, he promised, would not be touched. What more could anyone want? Too late, some of those who trusted in the new führer's promises realized their error in judgment.

Soon after the cleverly orchestrated Reichstag fire, Hitler was ready to begin his war against the Jews. The chicanery and harassments against them were soon to be followed by laws barring them from all walks of life in Germany. It would not take long until the phrase "You shall not live among us as Jews" was shortened by two words to "You shall not live among us." Two more words, "among us," would later be omitted.

Pastor Martin Niemoeller finally realized that all his hopes for a better Germany and a better government had been lost. He wasted no time, warning his congregants from the pulpit to "bow to God's will and practice love toward all human beings, Christians, Jews, and Pagans alike." And he gave his young confirmands the option to either "obey the orders of the Nazi party or God's commandments," emphasizing that "we must obey God more than man." These occurrences were swiftly reported to Hitler, who was not amused. He came to the decision that, as far as the Lutherans were concerned, a new and united German Protestant Church was needed, which would practice undivided loyalty and obedience to him and his party. Unlike the Catholics, who were one united body, the forty-five million German Protestants belonged to no less than twenty-eight different branches of the Lutheran and Reformed churches.

The führer determined that the Jewish Old Testament, filled with weird, ridiculous stories and endless lamentations, in their concept totally incompatible with the Teutonic perception of life, would eventually be eliminated. The decision about what to do with the Jewish Jesus seemed, for the time being, fairly easy.

Of course he was *not* a *Jew*; he was the first *Christian*! That is why the Jews had to kill him! "Christ, the savior, will come again," promised the Christian creed. The German people had to be convinced that the true savior had already come, and that his name was Adolf Hitler.

This new church would have no room for Christians of Jewish descent, neither as members of the congregation nor as clergy. In April 1933, a decree was introduced, which was called the "Aryan paragraph." It contained the following passage: "Anyone who is not of Aryan descent may not be appointed as a pastor or official. Pastors and officials of Aryan descent who marry non-Aryans are to be dismissed."

The order would not only be ignored, but publicly denounced as unacceptable by the pastor of Dahlem. "A Jew who confesses Christ as his Lord is certainly my brother," he simply declared, "and I will not deny him membership in the congregation of a Christian Church."

German Protestants now found themselves divided by a deep rift. On one side were the Nazi-oriented "German Christians," eagerly abiding by the new laws, and on the other side were their brand-new counterpart, the "Confessing Church." This new branch of the Protestant Church, preceded by the formation of the "Council of Brethren" and the subsequent "Pastors' Emergency League," had been established by the penitent Pastor Niemoeller. Any Christian who decided to join the "Confessing Church," as a minister or a member, pledged obedience to Jesus Christ over the Nazi regime. Hitler's answer to this unexpected defiance was the nomination of Ludwig Müller, a clergyman in the rank of an Evangelical bishop, to the position of "Reich Bishop," head of the German Christian Church. This obscure little man would soon be nicknamed "Ludwig the Desperate."[13]

The rejection of the "Aryan paragraph" resulted in mass arrests of pastors, whose names Martin now read aloud from the pulpit each Sunday. The führer himself slapped Martin with an official suspension from office, an act that the pastor ignored. Financially supported by his congregation, he continued to preach, teach confirmation classes, and officiate at baptisms, weddings, and funerals. Each Sunday he denounced the Nazi evil from his pulpit, branding the so-called "positive Christendom," propagated by the Nazis, as antithetic to the teachings of Jesus.

Soon, the little church of St. Anne's could not hold the masses of the faithful anymore, so services in the nearby and more spacious Church of Jesus Christ were added. Some Sundays Martin had to preach two or even three sermons. Those who came from the city by subway heard the stationmaster call out at the Thielplatz station in Dahlem: "Anyone for Pastor Niemoeller get out here!"

However, Martin was beginning to find out what it was like to have Hitler for an enemy, for the führer had decided that the rebellious clergyman needed to learn a lesson, one he would not easily forget.

◦ Chapter Thirteen ◦
Nazis on Parade

The charade of Potsdam had sent my father into a fit of rage. He learned that not only had the kaiser's fourth son, August Wilhelm, attended the spectacle in his brown storm trooper outfit, but also his older brother, "Crown Prince" Wilhelm, nicknamed "Little Willy," saluted the new chancellor while wearing a black World War I uniform.

In the late spring of 1933, a big parade was scheduled in honor of the chancellor. My father decided to take our family to his own office in the Dutch Palace on Unter den Linden, where we would able to watch the spectacle without getting cold feet. He wanted us there so that we would never forget. We took a taxi for the lengthy ride into the city, and upon entering my father's office suite, we met with a crowd of friends and employees. The old white-haired and white-gloved butler carried around a tray with tea. When he came to me, he filled a dainty little cup, reverently bowed his head, and again addressed me as "most gracious baroness." Fortunately, this time my mother was not around to set him straight, so I thanked him with a gracious smile.

It was a cold evening and the sun had gone down, leaving the city in twilight. Excited beyond description, I climbed onto the sill of the wide-open window. In front of the building were masses of people in a state of euphoria, waving little swastika flags. A storm trooper with a fat shaved neck above his brown uniform collar offered me one, but I caught my mother's threatening look just in time. The flag itself had been designed by Hitler; the hooked cross, resembling a large spider, would become the most cherished and feared symbol of Nazi Germany, standing for ultimate victory of the Aryan race.

Thousands of Berliners lined the streets, eagerly awaiting the motorcade, the open car carrying its precious cargo, Hindenburg and Hitler. Endless formations of soldiers marched swiftly by our window, members of the *Reichswehr*, the post-war German Army. The presidential convertible was followed by police squads, platoons of brown-clad storm troopers, Hitler Youth formations, and—in black outfits with shoulder straps, skull symbols on their lapels, sleeves, and caps—Hitler's very own guard, the newly formed *Schutzstaffel*. In runic style their insignia displayed two letters: SS.

Total darkness had fallen over the city, illuminated only by the flickering light of hundreds of torches, enhancing the macabre atmosphere of the scene. No demonstration of Nazi power, no ceremony would ever be imaginable without torches, so most of the party events took place at night. In my father's opinion, the führer had reason for shunning the light of day, the darkness having the distinct advantage of concealing the revolting ugliness of the Nazi representatives of the new Aryan master race, like Hitler, Röhm, Ley, and Himmler.

Fire as the source of light and life was interpreted as a mythical Teutonic symbol; its purifying powers would eventually light the darkness in the extermination camps, with flames shooting up from the smokestacks over the crematoria of Auschwitz, Treblinka, Sobibor, Majdanek, and all the other places where human bodies were burned. On May 10 that same year, flames were to consume the books of unwanted authors, such as Heinrich Heine, Thomas Mann, Heinrich Mann, Kurt Tucholsky, Émile Zola, Marcel Proust, Upton Sinclair, André Gide, and H. G. Wells. On that day, an allegedly spontaneous torchlight parade led by students had halted on the Opernplatz in Berlin, opposite Humboldt University, not even a stone's throw away from the kaiser's palace. A hysterically screaming mob watched as thousands of books, piled high not by hooligans out of control, but by faculty, students, and burghers alike, were reduced to ashes. Similar actions followed in almost every German town that same year. In the words of Josef Goebbels, "these sacred flames marked the end of an old era and the coming of a new one, in which there is no room for Anarchists and Bolsheviks and Jews!" It had been Heinrich Heine who once made the ominous prophecy that where they burn books, they will eventually burn people.

In my father's office, still crouching on the windowsill, I finally heard the long-awaited, exultant cry, "They are here! Here they come!" I almost fell out of the window. Indeed, the president's car slid slowly by, not even twenty feet away from me. Policemen wearing shakos with tightly fastened chin straps stood on the running boards to guard the two men. In the back of the car, next to the seated president, stood the new chancellor, who every once in a while lifted his right arm in the Nazi salute. There he was, in all his glory, the man about whom my father had remarked that if he had used his former legal family name of "Schicklgruber," the whole disaster could have been avoided.

"*Heil, Heil, Heil!*" the crowd shouted.

I saw no reason not to join in, shrieking at the top of my voice. This was fun! After a while it occurred to me that nobody in the room was joining in. I felt my father's hand on my shoulder, and as I turned to him, I noticed that his face was chalk white. He stood motionless, and it seemed that the smoke of the torches had caused his eyes to tear.

~ Chapter Fourteen ~
LIFE IN THE THIRD REICH

Due to the new political situation, which demanded increased caution, our social life became more restricted. Unfortunately, this did not affect the regular invasions of family members seeking a cheap vacation in our spacious, vine-clad white house with the red window shutters and beautiful garden. Several times during the year, my grandmother appeared, to stay with us for a few weeks. Accompanied by her slavish servant Martha, like a gray shadow behind her, she always seemed eager to display the utmost humility of a pious Christian. My father maintained that she was downright bigoted. Occupying the main guest room on the second floor, she maltreated my mother's grand piano for endless hours during the day, making abundant use of the pedals. Only my father's arrival abruptly stopped her. She never tired of lecturing me about the duties of a Prussian girl of Christian noble birth. After all, the granddaughter of two and great-granddaughter of three Prussian generals, related to royalty with at least fourteen noble ancestors in her pedigree, was expected not ever to speak unless being spoken to, nor to oppose orders, humble obedience being the foremost virtue of any female. I was not to pick my nose, make faces, cry, complain, lie, or bite my fingernails to the quick, as was my unfortunate habit at the time. Instead, I should display humility, piety, and fear of God. Later, I would be sure to wear my plain hair in a simple, knotted bun, my entire appearance of such supreme modesty that a man of aristocratic standing, preferably one with a large estate, would be honored and happy to ask for my hand in marriage!

Marriage? Living in a castle in some godforsaken area held no special attraction for me! So, she asked, what would I like to do instead? A librarian, maybe, or perhaps a governess or a nurse in some noble order? My reply focused her sharply: I was actually thinking about becoming a demimonde! Not having the faintest notion of this word's true meaning, I had lately overheard my mother using it in connection with an imperial Prussian princess in the habit of cheating on her husband. The announcement left my prudish grandmother speechless, which had been my purpose.

My father instilled in his children the importance of behaving in such a way that could serve as an example to those around us and particularly the ones beneath us. "Noblesse oblige" meant that high birth was not only a privilege, but a duty, an obligation to others, mainly the ones dependent on us, at our mercy, those helpless and too weak to fend for themselves. After all, for hundreds of years, our ruling "caste" had determined the fate of so many others entrusted to us.

The outstanding social events in our house during the winter were the formal dinner parties, requiring weeks of meticulous planning and preparation. Since Anna would barely permit the maids, let alone a second cook in *her* kitchen, the planning of the daily menus was left up to her. Anna prepared meals in the true tradition of Prussian frugality, the consumption of food considered a somewhat obscene function, performed exclusively in order not to starve. Anything beyond that was considered gluttony and a luxury in which the French, who seemed obsessed with this vulgar habit, might indulge. Eating, particularly in my mother's opinion, was something so banal that not even a thought was to be wasted on it. Vegetables were mercilessly cooked to death and drowned in a white sauce. Fish, usually cod, was boiled until it fell apart. I was almost a teenager when I discovered that there were more than two kinds of fish in the world; aside from cod, the only other kind served at home was the traditional carp eaten on New Year's Eve. Anna preferred the fish's eyes as a special delicacy, crushing them with a sickening sound between her teeth. The most disgusting dish, served with minute regularity, was a hash consisting of leftovers, the looks of which made me wonder if it was to be eaten or if it had already been eaten. Only my father's presence at the table improved the quality of the food. He ate with lightning speed, a habit from his military school days where anything not eaten quickly was stolen from one's plate by hungry comrades.

No matter what, my mother demanded that we had to clear our plates. Sometimes, she made me sit for hours, after which I usually threw up. Why was I so ungrateful? Why did I not remember those poor children in the world, or the starving soldiers in their trenches, who would gladly give their right arm for delicious food like mine? No great comfort to me, especially in view of the fact that starving children and hungry soldiers in trenches were extremely hard to find in my immediate neighborhood. To my mother, the quality of what was served was not half as important as the fact that the maid, in her black outfit with the white apron and the pretty white headdress, was standing by the door throughout the entire meal. That custom had to be dropped after January 30, 1933, because the presence of a maid, no matter how reliable she seemed, reduced the table conversation to general and unsuspicious topics. The price for telling even a comparatively mild joke about the regime—let alone a word of criticism—could mean years in a concentration camp. Or worse.

There were a few pleasant exceptions, which all too rarely broke the monotony of the dismal menus. Yeast dumplings, for instance, snow-white, fluffy, and featherlight, served with a dish of stewed prunes, which, like crisp brown potato pancakes with applesauce, not only surpassed all culinary delights known to me, but, according to Anna, improved in taste when served cold the next day. On several occasions, I dragged school friends home to partake in our midday meal, in the vain hope that yeast dumplings or potato pancakes would be served. Each one of the victims came only once, after which the news of the disaster made the rounds at school, temporarily turning my social status into that of a leprous outcast.

The formal banquets in our home were scheduled to take place several times throughout the season as means of reciprocation to all those who had been hosts during the past year. For a fleeting moment, Prussian frugality became an alien term. Some of the ingredients needed for such an occasion arrived via railroad express from the various family estates.

Depending on the time of year, the train delivered venison, hares, wild ducks, woodcocks, partridges, as well as our favorite birds, the pheasants with their colorful feathers.

A few days before the big event, my father would spend several evenings at his desk, laboring over a regular battle plan: the seating order at the dinner table. It was no easy task to determine who was to be seated next to whom and who must, for reasons known only to him, definitely *not* sit next to whom. An expert on protocol at the highest level, he juggled all the given possibilities until fairly certain of having at least ruled out the gravest mistakes. Of course, there would always be one guest who felt insulted. Pleasing everyone was just not possible. The selection of the proper wines from his exquisite collection in the hermetically locked wine cellar was more than a task—it was a ceremony that he never left to anyone else.

Much as Anna revered my father, her opinion of men in general was devastatingly low, with one other possible exception, as she grudgingly admitted. His name was Karl, one of Crown Prince Willy's very own butlers. Graciously lent to us by his master for the various dinner parties, he was the only member of the male gender that she tolerated in close proximity; as soon as he appeared on the scene, she spread her tail feathers like a peacock. Bearing a distinct resemblance to a tall, grave bird in his black tailcoat and white gloves, Karl took instant command of the situation with inimitable dignity. Under his expert supervision, the festive table was extended by several boards to seat twenty-four people. The sparkling crystal competed in shimmering luster with the family silver on the exquisite snow-white damask tablecloth, decorated with the two five-armed silver candelabras, gifts from His Majesty. With superb proficiency and the air of a grand duke, Karl would later direct the serving of the meal, one course after the next.

An hour before the arrival of the guests, my father subjected his study, the parlor, my mother's salon, the hall, and particularly the dining room to one last, thorough inspection. The delicate white china with golden-green rims, also a present by the kaiser from his private porcelain manufacturer, gleamed. The mandatory four glasses stood in front of each plate: green glasses for the white wine; goblets of various sizes for red wine and port; and the tall, slender vessels for champagne. Armed with a tape, Karl had carefully measured the distance between each setting, making sure there was exactly the same space for everyone. As a final touch, my father lit the oriental candles distributed throughout the downstairs rooms, which sent a uniquely pleasant fragrance drifting all the way to the upstairs where my brother and I were confined throughout the evening. This measure had become necessary ever since the two of us had hidden under the table, waiting for all the illustrious guests to be seated. Sparing the ladies, we concentrated on the gentlemen's shoes, tying the laces together in such a way that getting up later led to disaster. Some were less amused than others.

We knew that Karl, in whose eyes we were not just ordinary brats, but the little baron and baroness, would secretly sneak up at regular intervals, carrying covered plates with tasty little morsels. Especially appreciated was the ice cream, hand-produced by Anna, who had cranked the handle of an old-fashioned ice machine in the laundry room for hours.

Precisely at seven o'clock the doorbell rang, announcing the arrival of the first guests. At least one of these major social events was reserved for titled members of our very own and special class, into which one had to be born, most of us being blessed with the fourteen noble ancestors necessary to count as authentic true blues, *Uradel*.[14] Those belonging to a slightly lower class had received their noble titles through a decree by the emperor for special services rendered, like our neighbor "von Tirpitz," son of the kaiser's famous admiral. The other, and certainly more amusing, gatherings included dignitaries of bourgeois descent, diplomats, foreign correspondents, and the like.

Restricted exclusively to parties reserved for aristocratic guests, the first toast would be drunk to His Majesty in faraway Doorn, complete with three "hurrahs," followed by a moment of respectful and emotion-laden silence, during which handkerchiefs usually went into action. As the Nazi era continued, some of the names had to be dropped from the guest list for several sad but valid reasons; their bearers had either left the country, disappeared in a concentration camp, or were simply not politically reliable enough anymore.

Anna, being more caste-conscious than anyone else in the house, had her favorites in each category, but the one guest that nobody else could match in her eyes was the French Ambassador André François-Poncet, whose own receptions in the beautiful French Embassy, frequently followed by exquisite house concerts, enjoyed a legendary reputation. Opening the door for him was Anna's privilege, which she was not about to share with anyone. As soon as the big black limousine with the tricolor flag pulled up in front of the house, she would drop everything, hastily don her best white apron, push Karl and the maids aside, and race to the door to politely curtsy for François-Poncet, who never failed to give her the kind of ingratiating smile that made her feel like a real lady.

The second visitor on her list of favorites was the American correspondent for the Associated Press, Louis P. Lochner, who delighted her with little jokes in accentless German, his mother being of German-aristocratic descent. Edoardo Senatra, the Berlin correspondent for the Italian *Messagiero*, was also among the more interesting guests. An extremely good-looking man with a dark complexion, he was usually full of very entertaining stories. Because of his exotic features, he was frequently mistaken as a Jew, which led to all sorts of complications between the Nazi authorities and the Fascist Italian Embassy. He usually arrived in the company of Otto and Edith Stargardt. Even though we were not related, we called them "uncle" and "aunt." Aunt Edith was the daughter of the legendary Louise Wolff, in musical circles known as "Queen Louise." She was indeed the queen of music worldwide, her deceased husband having founded a music agency before the turn of the century, which she operated with unique proficiency. Ranging from Brahms to Yehudi Menuhin, nearly any musician—composer, conductor, violinist, pianist, or opera star—had at one point in his or her life been involved with Louise's agency. This remarkable lady escaped the grip of the Nazis by dying just before her agency was closed, her publishing house Bote & Bock taken over by "Aryans." Uncle Otto, a renowned judge, and Aunt Edith, later deported, were lucky enough to survive three years in Theresienstadt.

Berlin's lord mayor at the time, Dr. Heinrich Sahm, was a close friend who graciously permitted us to call him "Uncle Sahm." Being a giant in size, we eagerly (but in vain) used to wait for him to bump his head when entering the house. He had a kind, somewhat crumpled, prune-like face and never forgot to delight us with sweet little surprises. Time permitting, he would even let us climb into his limousine, advising the chauffeur to drive us around for a little while. Bursting with pride, we crouched on the leather upholstered backseats, pressing our noses against the windows in the ardent hope of being spotted by schoolmates in this hour of glory, which would raise our status to unbelievable heights. One year, Uncle Sahm presented my father with a birthday gift as unique as it was dangerous: a roll of ordinary toilet paper, which he had, sheet by sheet, adorned with hand-scribbled political jokes, a job that must have kept him busy for months. Bearing in mind that each one of the jokes represented several years in prison, the value was inestimable. Unfortunately, there were not too many people with whom my father was able to share this priceless collection, which ultimately went the way of all toilet paper rolls.[15]

Among the visitors who were titled members of our own class was a family friend, Kurt von Schleicher, who had held once the same office that Adolf Hitler took over on January 30, 1933, the position of Reich Chancellor. Seventeen months later, on June 30, 1934, Uncle Kurt and his wife were killed in their home by gunfire, victims of Hitler's SA, who in a surprise attack shot the couple in cold blood during what would go into history as the "Night of the Long Knives."

After dinner, the ladies joined my mother in her salon for liqueur and mocha, while the men, enjoying cognac, kirsch, and exquisite cigars, gathered in the host's study. After the last guest had left at eleven o'clock sharp, my father usually turned to Anna to thank her and ask her expert opinion about the illustrious visitors.

Chapter Fifteen
Royal Sons

Several times a year, a sleek sports car would roar down our quiet street, coming to a screeching halt in front of the house. "Little Willy" would emerge from the car, without a chauffeur and usually unannounced, an event that caused my mother extreme anxiety. His Imperial Highness—casual, lanky, and totally carefree—loved surprises. He always turned up without his wife, a habit having something to do with Crown Princess Cäcilie being a very, very "poor lady." For a while I wondered if her husband did not give her enough allowance, until it dawned on me that this poverty had nothing to do with a lack of finances.

The crown prince, who never failed to ingratiate himself to us by extracting English drops from the deep pockets of his elegant English trench coat, addressed my father with the familiar "*du*." He loved teasing my father for working so hard. His Highness used to inquire why he did not play tennis instead. Such tactless remarks, coming from someone who had never performed a day's work in his life, rightfully infuriated my father, who, through hard labor and financial expertise, had been able to considerably increase the Hohenzollern fortune.

Moreover, the prince seemed to forget that, during those first crucial months after the kaiser's abdication, it had been Ulrich von Sell whom his father had called for help, begging him to spend many nights at Cecilienhof Castle in Potsdam to protect the imperial family from Communist assassins. Adding insult to injury, Little Willy had nicknamed him *General Leichenbitter*, "General Undertaker," referring to my father's special weakness for funerals. The nickname stuck. My father's obsession with burials may have had something to do with the sad fact that the bodies of two of his fallen brothers had no graves. Or could it have been some dark foreboding that he himself would not have one either?

One of the imperial princes who never honored us with his presence was August Wilhelm, the fourth son of the kaiser and a constant source of irritation and anger for the old man in Doorn. He had decided to ignore his father's stern warnings, usually conveyed to him by my unfortunate father, and paraded around the country in one of his brown uniforms, never missing a Nazi rally. It was no secret that his wife, Alexandra Viktoria, the former Princess of Schleswig-Holstein-Sonderburg, was a bit lax in her view of the sanctity of marriage, which ultimately led to the couple's divorce. My mother had nicknamed her "the lollipop"—on which men had sucked.

My father had no illusions about the Hohenzollerns' attitude toward the new regime in general and that of "her majesty" in particular. In pursuit of the burning desire to see her husband, with her at his side, on the throne again, she would do anything that brought her closer to her goal. If flattering Adolf Hitler and his gang was part of the game, she would gladly play it. Emperor by Hitler's grace? My father shuddered. All he could do was try and prevent the worst, like barring August Wilhelm from appearing in Doorn for his father's birthday in a storm trooper's swastika-adorned outfit.

Several times during the year, the kaiser's fifth son, Oskar, came for tea. His wife Ina Marie had been born Countess Bassewitz, so their marriage was considered a morganatic one by the Hohenzollern statutes. While the outraged imperial father did not quite cut the family ties, he had barred the prince from a possible, although most unlikely, succession to the throne. "Oskars," as they were referred to by my parents, detested the Nazis. My brother and I always looked forward to their visit because they never failed to bring us Swiss chocolate. Their appearance in the house was topped only by that of one other guest, the uncontested favorite among all imperial visitors, whose eagerly awaited arrival once a year was anticipated with almost the same eagerness as Christmas Eve, even in Anna's expert opinion.

The Princess Irene was the widow of the kaiser's younger brother, Heinrich, who had died the same year we had moved to Dahlem. The princess came from the House of Hessen and bei Rhein, her sister Alexandra having married Nicholas, Russia's last tsar.[16] The first time the princess announced her forthcoming visit, my father decided that I—dressed in a brand-new white frock with puffed sleeves, the sash tied into a bow on my little behind, with white knee stockings, and black patent leather buttoned shoes—should present her imperial highness with a huge bouquet of pink roses. My mother, remembering with a shudder my curtsy performed for Hermine, taught me how to do a proper court curtsy.

When the day came and I finally stood in the door of my mother's salon, holding a bouquet bigger than myself, I slowly approached the guest of honor sitting on the crimson sofa. Even though she wasn't wearing a crown, with her beautiful white hair, partially covered by a widow's peak, and her elegant black robe with a white lace collar, she looked like a queen. With an amused smile, she summoned me to come closer. Just as I proceeded to sink deep down in my long-practiced curtsy, I stumbled and practically fell into the princess' lap. She simply picked me up, bouquet and all, lifted me on to her lap, and gave me a big genuine kiss. I was beside myself.

She possessed a keen sense of humor because once, just before her appearance in our house for dinner, our schnauzer Rumpel (last name Stilzken) had been able to steal and wolf down an entire veal roast from the kitchen table. When my mother confessed the disaster to her, the princess laughed till she cried. One of her two sons, Prince Waldemar, an ardent anti-Nazi, was also a welcome visitor in our house. Before his first visit, my father took my brother and me aside and informed us that Waldemar was a hemophiliac.

In wild anticipation of a gruesome spectacle, we inquired if he would spurt blood all over the place, and we were a little disappointed when told he would do no such thing. My father then proceeded to enlighten us about the incurable hereditary disease that, like an evil curse, haunted the European dynasties, passed on from apparently healthy and unsuspecting mothers to their sons. Since the royal families were all related, they were more or less all afflicted.

Chapter Sixteen
School Days

Like vermin, the Nazi big shots had infested Dahlem's stateliest residences, after the rightful Jewish owners were chased out. Behind high walls, embedded in luscious parks with swimming pools, these "prolet-Aryans," a term invented by my father, were guarded by SA or SS with dogs from attacks by Communists or, worse, Jews.

St. Gertraude's School for Girls, which I had been attending since the spring of 1932, had been invaded by Nazis. In my class was Bettina von Ribbentrop, daughter of the future Nazi ambassador to England. She was a head taller than I, and once I had to climb on a bench in order to slap her across her sheep-like face. Fortunately, she did not report this insult at home, but for days I waited for the Gestapo to come for me. There were two sisters, offspring of the notorious *Reichsfrauenfuehrerin* [17] Gertrud Scholz-Klink, miniature editions of their mother, including their hair in plaits draped around their heads in a Teutonic fashion. Mechtild Rust, older daughter of the Minister of Education Bernhard Rust, received a well-deserved failing mark, but her teacher, Dr. Schroeder, was to bear the consequences. He did not land in a concentration camp, but he was transferred to a godforsaken village in the East. Gudrun Himmler, by a stroke of luck, was in a lower grade. Except for Inge Lutze, her father the SA Chief Viktor Lutze, all Nazi brats arrived at school in their fathers' luxury limousines, swastika flag and all, snubbing their chauffeurs, who submissively opened the car doors for the snot noses. At age sixteen, Inge would die in the same car accident that killed her father; we all mourned her loss.

By the summer of 1933, certain changes at St. Gertraude's began to become quite noticeable. Not overnight, but little by little, three different categories of teachers had begun to emerge. The first category consisted of staunch anti-Nazis, the second one ardently in favor of Hitler, while the third group, initially opposed to the regime, eventually fell for it, either through mounting pressure or by a true change of heart. These turncoats, eager to make up for their initial errors, were dangerous. Our homeroom teacher, an elderly, yellow-faced spinster with matching yellow bags under her eyes, thin gray hair knotted in a tight bun, had become a turncoat in favor of the Nazis. One morning, her voice trembling with emotion, she informed us that she had placed her dear departed mother's framed picture on top of the radio when the führer spoke, so she could partake in the new euphoria.

Hitler's heroic portrait soon graced the walls of every single German classroom. Instead of the traditional "good morning," a teacher would be required to lift his or her right arm in the new Hitler salute when entering a classroom. By the manner in which this "wing flapping," as we called it, was performed, we were soon able to determine whether it came from the heart or not.

At a tender age, when a young girl's mind should have been occupied with dolls, games, fun parties, and mischief, I received my first instructions in "conspirative behavior." Being a fast learner, it did not take me long to differentiate clearly between what I heard at home and what was taught at school, and to act accordingly. Soon I was able to sense and recognize imminent danger and learned how to cope with this strange kind of schizophrenia, regarding it as a game, a very perilous game, eventually enabling me to walk the dangerously narrow path over an abyss without falling down.

One day, late in 1933, we were handed questionnaires in class, accompanied by the order to have them filled out and signed by our parents. They contained questions about the student's "Aryan" descent. I turned to my bench neighbor, Ditte, a lively and cheerful little girl with an audacious face and wiry brown pigtails, to inquire what "Aryan" meant. Was that a religion, maybe? But she did not know either. My concerned parents told me that this term had nothing to do with religion but with "race."

What the school wanted to find out was which students were Jewish. Jewish? All I knew about the Jews was what I had been taught at Sunday school, namely that they did not believe in Jesus. Were they heathens? My father tried to explain to me that Hitler hated the Jews, all Jews, including those who had converted to Christianity. But this hate could not possibly include children like Susi Epstein, Ellen Levy, Lore Ginsberg, Ellen Lachmann, Lore Rachwalski, Eleanor Sadowski, Susi Sinsheimer, and Anita Frank. Or could it?

In class, Susi Epstein showed me her questionnaire, which stated that she was of pure Jewish descent; like my own, Ditte's read that she was a "pure Aryan." This was a mild overstatement, as I was soon to find out, after a Nazi teacher, not amused by one of Ditte's fresh answers, told her that it was not wise for an obviously non-Aryan pupil to display impertinent manners. In a fit of rage, Ditte ran home, demanding instant retaliation. That was the day her parents took Ditte and her two older sisters aside to tell them that their mother, although a baptized Christian—and with her husband a faithful member of Martin Niemoeller's Confessing Church—came from a Jewish family. Living as unostentatiously as possible was not only imperative—it could mean the difference between life and death.

Proud and privileged to share this well-kept family secret, I had come to a major decision: what I needed was a second home. I loved my parents, but the atmosphere of constant gloom persisting in our house over the worsening political situation and the harassments in Doorn began to leave its mark on me. So I fell into the habit of wandering over to Ditte's house after school more and more frequently. I enjoyed the laughter at the table, where I was soon accepted as one of the family, calling Ditte's parents "Mummy" and "Pappy." The quality of the food served in the beautiful house was infinitely superior to ours, with Ditte's little Alsatian-born mother carefully supervising the preparation of the meals.

After the incident at school, I sometimes heard my own parents ponder a possible move to another country. These discussions, however, usually ended before they really began. First of all, where would they go? Furthermore, the idea of leaving their fatherland to a bunch of hoodlums without a fight was considered cowardly, unacceptable, and not in line with Prussian virtues. They wondered how long they would be able to keep me out of the Hitler Youth, the *Bund Deutscher Maedel*. The invitation to join was slowly giving way to pressure, the kind that my brother was spared for another couple of years. What both my mother and father were soon to realize was that putting up passive resistance, going into "inner emigration," was not enough. Nothing was achieved just by avoiding saying "*Heil Hitler.*" After the führer had established himself as a dictator, an organized coup d'état was now more or less out of the question. So one had to resort to other means of active resistance, not ruling out Hitler's assassination.

Assassination, I asked? My father explained that this was just another word for murder. In my dreams, or rather nightmares that followed this explanation, I saw my father attack Hitler with a bloody hatchet.

Chapter Seventeen
Family Choices and Special Neighbors

It was around this time that my parents reached three important decisions. The first was to bring a governess into the house. More than my brother, who was well-behaved and polite by nature, I had definitely outgrown Anna's authority. Growing up like wildflowers, roaming the streets after school, was leading to trouble. The time had come to hire a governess from either England or France. What we needed was closer supervision, and furthermore, my father wanted his children to become fluent in at least two languages besides their native one.

The first lady was an elderly professional governess from Switzerland. Small, with short, slightly bowed legs, slanted eyes, and excellent references, she had been the companion of a little princess, and she obviously expected us to be as angelic as her former charge. With her hopes soon shattered, she quit after six weeks. I suspected that the real reason for her early departure was Anna's "cuisine," which she found not fit for human consumption. My mother was sorry to see her go because, with her in the house, she had been able to speak French again.

Next came a succession of young English ladies. First was Betty, then Joy, and finally Nell, all of whom hailed from London, were fun-loving, and were almost as mischievous as their charges. I would never have anticipated that knowledge of English would one day literally save my life. Nell so loved being a part of our family that she stayed with us until the outbreak of the war.

My parents' second decision was that we should learn to ride. A superb horseman, my father expected both his children to follow in his footsteps, or rather, hoofsteps. While my brother by far preferred skiing, I soon became the expert hoped for by my father. A nearby stable with beautiful, privately owned horses seemed ideal. The instructor was a fierce-looking man, a former sergeant major in the cavalry, who insisted I climb back on the horse each time it threw me into the dirt. Placing cigarette paper between the saddle and my knees, he would throw a fit if I ever lost it. The knees and the saddle were to be inseparable. Even in tears after breaking my collarbone, I was expected to get back into the saddle. If I balked, my father used a long whip to bring me back to my senses. "Wipe the saddle with your ass!" he kept telling me, and I did not disappoint him.

The third decision had something to do with our summer vacations. So far, my mother, my brother, and I had spent at least four weeks a year with relatives on one of the vast family estates in Pomerania or West Prussia. One summer, we had been invited to Hohenfinow, the estate of my father's former chief, Reich Chancellor von Bethmann-Hollweg. Staying with aunts and uncles meant cheap recreation, at the same time furthering the stabilization of family ties. In Marienwalde, on the estate of my paternal grandmother's family, our favorite vacation spot, developments of a rather unpleasant nature forced my parents to change their vacation routine. At the ripe age of seventy-five, my uncle had succumbed to the brown temptation, getting into furious arguments with my father. The solution was henceforth to travel somewhere else for the summer. It was the old *Reichspräsident* von Hindenburg who suggested a particularly romantic spot in the Bavarian Alps. This undertaking turned out to be a complete flop. To his utter dismay, my father found that someone else had beaten us to the beauty of Berchtesgaden, which included the majesty of the white-capped Alps, clear streams, and luscious green meadows. He came to the conclusion that we were not to share the formerly pure, now contaminated, mountain air with the resident of the nearby "Berghof" on the Obersalzberg, Adolf Hitler.

The following year we traveled to the picturesque village of Kreuth, south of Munich, three miles north of the famous spa with the same name, where emperors and kings from all over Europe had come for centuries to restore their health. Kreuth became a true hit. For the rest of our lives, we were to regard it as our home away from home. On a hill, opposite the white village church with its slender steeple, not far from the blue mountain lake, the Tegernsee, stood the four-hundred-year-old farmhouse where we occupied several modest rooms. To our delight, there was no bathroom and no running water in the entire place; a steady flow of fresh mountain water continually filled the hollow tree trunk in front of the house.

By far the most unsanitary installation was the "toilet." It consisted of a stall on the second floor, providing a wooden seat with one opening for an adult and a smaller opening for a child's rear end over a gaping, dark, and smelly hole. Finding the place, even in the dark, was easy—all one had to do was follow the fragrance. Why my parents, used to the luxury of several bathrooms in our Dahlem house, put up with this medieval inconvenience remained an enigma. They probably considered being exposed to most primitive conditions as educational for us.

Following an ancient tradition, the farmhouse and the stable were under one roof, which meant that entire squadrons of very hungry flies could travel from the stable to our rooms without a detour. Anna was horrified, because she frequently got her hair caught by one of the honey-colored, sticky, corkscrew-like fly strips hanging from the ceilings, with their wriggling victims stuck to them. Much to her dismay, she had to prepare our meals in the farmer's kitchen, whose family used to eat from one pot placed in the center of the table. This was already progress, because a century ago, the table just had a cavity in its middle into which the food was dumped. But above all else, Anna hated the fact that everyone around her was Catholic. Catholic? There was no excuse for it in her eyes.

In sharp contrast to Anna, I was fascinated by every aspect of Catholicism: the Sunday masses, the priest's chanting, the kneeling, the endless, monotonous prayers, the rosaries, the smell of burning incense. I made it a habit to accompany Kati, the farmer's daughter, to the church each evening, where I watched her ring the bells that hung high up on the steeple and had to be operated by ropes. After first feeling the weird sensation of being pulled into the air by invisible forces, I soon mastered the art of bell ringing, so that eventually

Kati let me do the job all by myself. In front of the mirror, I practiced crossing myself and soon noticed a benevolent smile on the face of poor Jesus on the cross, probably in happy anticipation of seeing me convert to Catholicism.

My favorite place was the stable, where I loved to position myself behind a cow, until she deposited a large, greenish-brown, warm blotch into which I jumped full force with bare feet. Marie, the farmer's wife, not only taught me the art of milking a cow, but she allowed me to be present when a calf was born. My mother never entered the stable, so she had no idea of the events that took place there. Sometimes I was even invited to participate in pulling a calf out of the mother with a rope. After its appearance, the calf remained connected to the cow by something resembling a ghastly, slippery telephone cable. Finally, a disgusting-looking pudding popped out, and that was the end of it. Now with full knowledge of the birth process, I kept wondering how the calf had gotten into the mother in the first place. But even after watching a certain mysterious spectacle, I still was unable to put two and two together.

The stable housed the village bull named Germanius, a huge and ferocious animal with a ring through its nose. Disobeying my mother's stern warnings never to get close to this monster, I soon made friends with him and found that the safest hiding place was right under him, particularly when punishment threatened on the horizon. Nobody even dared to get near me. Germanius seemed to enjoy a fabulous reputation, because farmers from near and far kept dragging their cows up the hill to pay him a social visit. As soon as my mother spotted the four-legged visitors turn the corner, she called her children inside to discuss with them matters of the utmost importance that could not possibly wait. It dawned on us that we were being deprived of something highly interesting and educational, so we decided to hide in the barn as soon as we saw the procession making its way toward the stable. The cow was led into a fenced outside area while Hansl, the farmhand, dragged out the bull, who obviously knew exactly what he was supposed to do. The poor cow, with the snorting bull jumping her full force, almost went to her knees. I could not believe my eyes, remembering the pigs on the Dahlem farm. But they were swine and were supposed to behave like swine. This, we concluded, was true cruelty to animals and should probably be reported to the humane society. But Hansl, whom we consulted, just gave us a sheepish grin when we mentioned the outrage. He did not even offer a satisfactory explanation as to why the roosters chased hens and then did what Germanius had done. He probably didn't know himself.

It was in Kreuth that I first realized the consequences of the Nazis takeover among the population. Like an axe, the issue not only managed to split the village into two opposing camps, but even caused rifts within families. While our farmer's family was violently opposed to Hitler, some of the neighbors displayed the party emblems on their clothes. Thanks to the cunning old priest, no cases of denunciation occurred. He kept threatening his flock from the pulpit that whoever performed an underhanded act, like reporting his neighbor to the police or to the party authorities, should consider himself excommunicated immediately. And excommunication meant going straight to the devil. Everybody knew that! And everybody shuddered! The old rascal even went so far as to ask if anyone could imagine the führer, a baptized Catholic, being excommunicated. Before the congregation was able to grasp the logic, the sermon was over.

All through the glorious summers, we swam in the nearby lake, took lengthy bicycle tours, picked wild strawberries, and waded through the stream in an effort to catch trout by hand, fearing nothing but the day when we would have to leave our paradise. My father, like my brother and myself clad in lederhosen, would climb the nearby mountains. While my brother joined him as an ardent climber, wild horses could not drag me up a mole hill.

During our summers in Kreuth, the one event surpassing all others was the annual visit to Bad Kreuth, the famous international spa, only a few miles south of the village. There, at a safe distance from the spa buildings, in a simple Bavarian-style house, lived the man once destined to become the king of Bavaria, Prince Albrecht von Bayern from the house of Wittelsbach, heir to the throne. The Bavarian monarchy had shared the fate of so many other European dynasties at the end of World War I, ceasing to exist.

Albrecht was born in 1905, the eldest son of Crown Prince Rupprecht and his wife, the Duchess Marie Gabriele, who had died when Albrecht was a little boy. Her death was followed by several others within the family, so the five-year-old, once asked by a relative how things were at home, laconically retorted, "All they ever do at home is die!" Albrecht, related to the better part of European royalty, preferred the simple life over a residence in a glamorous castle. One of the reasons for seeking solitude may well have been that his Hungarian-born wife Marita, the former Countess Draskovich von Trakostjan, a lovely, soft-spoken woman with the face of a gothic Madonna, had not been formally recognized by the Wittelsbach family as an "equal." That fact would have barred her husband from a throne already denied his father. Only years later would the family permit the princess' status to be changed from a mere "serene" to "royal" highness.

Crown Prince Rupprecht, the son of King Ludwig III and Marie Theresa, Archduchess of Austria-Este, Princess of Hungary and Bohemia, had also chosen a life of seclusion in one of his castles on Lake Starnberg. There, he quietly raised his children from a second marriage, not far from Schlossberg, where his unfortunate forty-four-year-old uncle, King Ludwig II of Bavaria, had drowned himself in the lake, taking his physician with him. It was there that I, some twenty years later, would be invited to visit with the royal couple. While my father never took us along on his visits to the aging crown prince in Leutstetten, our entire family was heartily welcomed by his son, Prince Albrecht, his wife, and children in Bad Kreuth. The absolute highlight of our vacations were the meals with the royal couple, their twin daughters, Marie-Gabrielle and Marie-Charlotte, called Pussi and Lotti, who bore a striking resemblance to their Habsburg ancestors, and their little brother, Franz Josef, called Franzl. Max Emanuel, the last son, in those days a baby, would, half a century later, take over the responsibilities of the House of Wittelsbach as Duke of Bavaria.

Prince Albrecht, an extremely handsome man in his early thirties, with brown curly hair and brown eyes, wore a well-groomed moustache, one that my father did not seem to mind in the least. Preferring lederhosen over formal clothes, he sought his friends among the natives, who, although treating him like one of their own, never forgot that aside from being their buddy, always good for playing funny pranks on people, he was their undisputed "king." Everybody in the village addressed him as "royal highness" but with the familiar "*du.*"

There were no governesses or private instructors for the royal children, who, like all others, made their way to the village of Kreuth, barefoot in the summer and on skiis in the winter. The only difference between them and the others pupils in the one-room school was probably that they were spared the rod. They were taught the basics of reading, writing, and arithmetic by the esteemed village until the point when their parents decided to leave the country and seek refuge from the hated Nazis in Hungary. Unlike the Hohenzollerns, the Wittelsbach family was united in their steadfast refusal to give in to any of the Nazis' attempts to win them over. No scum, Rupprecht decided, would ever cross his threshold. Hitler, in turn, did not forget the constant insults, and he later took his revenge by incarcerating Rupprecht's entire family.

Unfortunately, Hungary was not quite far enough, because Hitler's influence would eventually stretch through half of Europe. The entire family, including little Max Emanuel, was picked up by Hitler's henchmen and dragged through several concentration camps, including Dachau and Flossenbürg where, huddled in barracks, freezing and starving, with corpses piled up outside, they shared the hardships of all the other prisoners. Only by a miracle were they spared the fate of their cousin Mafalda. This second daughter of Italy's King Vittorio Emanuele had become the victim of Hitler's rage against her father for siding with the Allies toward the end of the war. Married to the German Prince Philip of Hessen, an SA Obergruppenführer, Mafalda died in the Ravensbrück Concentration Camp. Rupprecht himself managed to survive, hidden by a family friend in Rome.

◦ Chapter Eighteen ◦
Uncle Mirko

In 1934, a new term invaded my vocabulary and my life: concentration camp. I learned its true meaning in connection with Uncle Mirko. Not actually related to us by blood, the Russian-born nobleman and industrial magnate, a giant in stature, was among my father's closest and most trusted friends. He owned a sizeable estate in Mecklenburg, acquired for his wife, Olga, who preferred breeding horses over appearing in Berlin society at her husband's side. Uncle Mirko kept a city apartment, which he occupied during the week, not necessarily always alone, as I gathered from certain whispered remarks at home.

He had the delightful habit of carrying chocolate by the pound into our house, so his visits were regular feasts for us children. He also delighted in showering my parents with all sorts of expensive gifts. Just to make sure there would be enough to drink, he brought supplies of vodka and champagne with him every time he made an appearance, of which he consumed veritable streams without ever showing outward signs of intoxication. His imposing size, accompanied by a deep bass voice, never ceased to cause my mother great anxiety as soon as she saw him, laden with packages, step out of the taxi. She knew only too well that he loved to persuade my father (who, due to his head injury, could not tolerate alcohol beyond a moderate amount of wine with dinner) to consume that one little glass too many, which resulted in vile headaches.

One day, Uncle Mirko's wife came to our house in a frenzy. She had hurried to Berlin after being informed of her husband's arrest by the Gestapo. Ordered to bring a change of underwear for him to the notorious Alexanderplatz Prison, Olga had in turn received a bag filled with her husband's blood-stained clothes. Horrified, she asked my father for advice, but he could do little to comfort her. A few weeks later, Olga was notified that the prisoner had been transferred from Berlin to the Sachsenhausen Concentration Camp north of Berlin, for "re-education." Since the Gestapo did not need a warrant for arrest, nor an explanation, the charges were not disclosed, and she resigned herself to the possibility of never seeing him again. However, after several months, he came back as suddenly as he had disappeared, seemingly unharmed and in the same boisterous spirits as before.

After having been apprehended and slapped with the charge of illicit currency dealings for the huge industrial concern he represented, the Gestapo had first dragged him to prison and ultimately to Sachsenhausen. At some point, he obviously made his tormentors an offer that they did not dare refuse. He simply suggested his release in exchange for the solemn promise not to reveal the names of high-ranking Nazi officials involved in illicit financial transactions, which would cause a terrible scandal. Since, according to him, his incriminating information, to be revealed after his death, had been deposited in a safe place, his would-be henchmen could not get rid of him fast enough. They practically kicked him out, although not without stern warnings never to disclose to anyone what he had experienced. This order sent Uncle Mirko into fits of hollow laughter, knowing that, under the circumstances, there was not a thing anyone could do to him. But from then on, just to be on the safe side, he carried a loaded gun and, drinking just as much if not more than before, proceeded to enlighten everybody about the gruesome details concerning the "re-educational practices" in Sachsenhausen.

The event of Uncle Mirko's arrest caused me to develop nightmares about my father. What would I do if "they" came for him? This mortal fear never left me. Adolf Hitler had entered my personal life, and it seemed he had come to stay. Shortly after this incident, my parents went to the opera, a rare event because my father was usually too tired for a trip back into the city after a day's hard work. However, they returned home long before the opera was over, and I learned what had occurred. In their seats they were kept waiting for almost fifteen minutes, after which something happened for which they had not been prepared. Accompanied by his brown entourage, Adolf Hitler appeared in the "imperial box," now the "Führer's Box," next to theirs. Everyone stood up, and "*Heil*" shouts shook the house. My mother, having been told about the alleged magnetism of Hitler's eyes, in a whim of curiosity turned her head, and for a few seconds her eyes met those of the führer. Instantaneously, she was overcome by an attack of violent nausea and a splitting headache, so my father had to lead her out to comfort her until she was able to be taken home. It took her a few days to recover from what she called an encounter with Satan personified.

Chapter Nineteen
Nazi Actions

On June 30, 1934, a bomb exploded. Hitler decided to put a bloody end to what was reported to him as an attempt on his life by his own SA. The instigator, the führer's long-standing comrade Ernst Röhm, an extremely repulsive-looking individual and a homosexual, was among the SA members who fell victim to the executions that the führer himself had ordered. During the massacre that followed, the "Night of the Long Knives," the Nazis rid themselves of as many known or suspected adversaries as possible. The count of those murdered, at random and in cold blood, was in the hundreds. Among the dead was Kurt von Schleicher, the former *Reichschancellor*, along with his wife, riddled by bullets in their Berlin suburban home. The previous week, the Schleichers had been our dinner guests.

Late at night, a truck with armed SA had stopped in front of our house. They left after trampling through the rooms in search of "the baron." It later became evident that my father, having left the same morning for Doorn, had missed the bloodbath by a few hours. In the afternoon following his return a few days later, while seated at his desk in the study, the telephone suddenly rang, and he motioned for me to take the call. Identifying myself by name as I had been taught, I heard a shrill voice, demanding to talk to "the *Herr Baron*," who put the phone to his ear after just giving his name. I watched his face turn gray and, after half a minute, without uttering a single word, he put the receiver down.

"That," he said, "was Goering!"

The fat man had called to warn my father that the next time he might not be so fortunate to escape his fate.

Hermann Goering, as my father was well aware, had held a special grudge since the day my father had admonished him for showing up without an invitation at a Hohenzollern family gathering. The humiliated party dignitary, at the time President of the German Reichstag, had not taken this blow kindly. In revenge, Goering made it a habit to show up unannounced at the various Hohenzollern country properties in Germany, particularly the East Prussian estate of Rominten, which happened to be my father's favorite hunting grounds. Some ten years later, after the imperial family had fallen out of grace, Goering, now *Reichsmarschall*, took possession of Rominten, eventually stripping it of precious paintings, carpets, furniture, and other valuables. He transferred the loot to Karinhall, his pompous home near Berlin, named after his deceased Swedish first wife, the Baroness Karin von Fock-Kantzow.

Of all the Nazi leaders, it was Hermann Goering for whom my father felt the coldest contempt. Here was a man from a decent family, a German Air Force officer decorated for bravery with the Pour le Mérite in World War I, who should have known better than to team up with gangsters. Moreover, he had elevated himself to the position of a self-styled god, one who would determine who was Aryan and who was not. The voice I had heard on the telephone would continue to haunt me.

A little more than one month later, on August 2, 1934, Paul von Hindenburg died at age eighty-six. The last obstacle preventing a still somewhat restrained dictatorship from turning into open terror had been removed. Since no plan for a successor to replace the president had been made, his death meant that the führer was now the sole and undisputed ruler over Germany. He wasted no time in proclaiming that, beginning now, he alone represented the law. Soldiers swore allegiance to Adolf Hitler. Germany had ceased to be a constitutional state.

We were in Kreuth when the news broke about Hindenburg's death. My poor father, who had just begun to recuperate after a week's vacation, hastily threw a few things into a suitcase and rushed off to Doorn, sensing that, with Hindenburg gone, "her majesty" would now go berserk in her efforts at persuading Hitler to let her husband resume his place on the throne. His worst expectations were by far surpassed. While my father, as usual, succeeded in talking some sense into the old man, he knew from bitter experience that his sound advice would fly out the window as soon as he turned his back.

Fate had more blows in store for us that year. My mother's youngest brother, Eberhard, the one who rejected an officer's career, had made it all the way to the top in the management of Junkers Airplane Works. From his marriage to the beautiful, black-curled, and totally non-Aryan Maria had sprung two little boys, Matthias and Hans-Conrad, our favorite cousins. The family had rented a house on the lake, the Tegernsee, not far from Kreuth, for the summer. One day, Aunt Maria bruised her knee in the garden, and the neglected little wound became infected, ultimately developing into a severe case of blood poisoning. Rushed to the local hospital too late, she died only minutes before her leg was to be amputated. She left behind sons too small to grasp the horrible truth and a completely distraught husband, who would follow her to the grave not long after.

The little orphans, according to the newly introduced Nuremberg Race Laws, were now defined as "*Mischlinge ersten Grades*," first-degree half-castes. Without the protection of their Aryan father, the boys were not only extremely endangered, but possibly doomed. The urgent question arose: what to do with them? An emergency family conference was called, during which Uncle Putzi had the nerve to state that his brother's marriage had already been enough of a disgrace for the illustrious family, contaminating pure Aryan blood. The sons, age five and three, now presented a possibly grave danger to the rest of the clan, something that—as far as his own reputation as a member of the party and the SA was concerned— could by no means be taken lightly. Any connection with his nephews would definitely put his hopes of getting a post with the *Reichsrundfunk*, the Berlin radio station, in jeopardy. The children were, and there was no other expression, "*Judenstämmlinge*," Jewish offshoots. The rest of the family agreed that steps had indeed to be taken, not to protect the family, but to protect the orphans. My father came up with the only acceptable solution: the boys would be sent to Switzerland, to be educated at the famous "Ecole d'Humanité," where their mother's only sister, herself a refugee, was a faculty member.

In the fall of that miserable year, Uncle Otto came storming into our house one Sunday morning, urgently demanding my father's expert advice. They had awakened to find a Star of David smeared on the front door, together with the word *Judenschweine* (Jewish pigs)! Uncle Otto announced that he was on his way to the police precinct to report this outrageous event, and had it not been for my father's stern warnings, he would have gone through with it.

Not long before this incident, the notoriously vile Nazi paper *Der Stürmer* had printed on its front page a photo of an elderly Jew running the gauntlet with a grinning mob watching. A painted sign around his neck read: "I will never complain to the police again."

But they were not really Jews, Uncle Otto protested, they were baptized Christians, faithful members of Martin Niemoeller's Confessing Church! Had he not received the Iron Cross for bravery in World War I? Could the church or their pastor not help them? Surely, under his protective wings, nothing bad could happen to them?

Since the assault was not repeated, the Stargardts felt encouraged in their hopes to remain exempt from molestation. Like countless other German Jews, they permitted themselves to be lulled into a treacherous sense of safety from which they would be torn a few years later, when Hitler proceeded from step one—"You shall not live as Jews among us"—begun a mere two months after his installation as chancellor, to "You shall not live among us." The third and last step—"You shall not live!"—would, for technical reasons, have to wait a little while longer. Misjudged and underestimated not only by the old garde, but by the entire civilized world, the dictator's secret of success was that he planned actions incomprehensible for the normal human brain. While many of his future victims still lived under the illusion that they really had nothing to fear, the well-oiled Nazi machinery began functioning with meticulous precision before anybody realized what was happening.

Even in the face of open terror, there were those Germans who naively maintained that the Reich's many wonderful and positive developments certainly outweighed the negative ones. Wasn't a mistake here and there within the realm of normalcy? After all, nobody was perfect, and certainly not a government. Most likely, the führer did not even have knowledge of these singular incidences. Growing pains, that was all it was!

Growing pains? Growing into what, my parents wondered? These abuses were not the inevitable and admittedly deplorable by-products of an otherwise honorable regime, but crimes against human dignity and human lives. Not only did Hitler know about the crimes, but they had sprung from his brain. "By ridding the world of the Jews," he had written in *Mein Kampf*, "I am doing the Almighty's work."

Chapter Twenty
A Meeting with the Führer

For Martin Niemoeller, the year 1934 had begun with a rather interesting encounter on January 26, one that would eventually seal his fate.

"Is Hitler really a great man?"

In anxious anticipation, Else Niemoeller searched her husband's face. For many hours she had been waiting for his return, not certain she would ever see him again.

"No," he replied dryly, "he is a great coward!"

And with those words, he stamped into the house.

Earlier that day, a telephone call had informed Martin that the führer wished to see him at once. Upon arrival in the old *Reichskanzlei* in the center of Berlin, black-clad SS men directed him to a vestibule, where he soon found himself in the company of more than three dozen members of the Protestant clergy as well as party functionaries. While he pondered the purpose of this rather unexpected situation, Hermann Goering made a sudden entrance, rudely brushing by the pastor without a word. He was wearing an unobtrusive civilian suit rather than one of the fantasy uniforms that he would favor in his later years.

Finally, the door opened, and the visitors were ushered into the inner sanctum, Hitler's study, where the führer was seated at his desk, its size well-befitting his megalomania. He demonstrated his sentiments by not rising for his "guests." Presiding Reich Bishop Ludwig Müller, of the German Christian movement, a meek little man, stood motionless behind his lord and master, as if he was trying to hide.

Positioned in a half circle in front of the enormous desk, the visitors waited for Hitler to make the first move. He finally rose, and Minister of the Interior Wilhelm Frick introduced everyone present by name. At the moment Martin's name was mentioned, Goering began attacking the pastor by shouting that a telephone conversation between Martin and his secretary had been overheard by the Gestapo that very morning, revealing that he was contemplating evil actions against the Reich and the führer's life. This outburst startled the pastor who, for some time, had suspected that his phone might be bugged. He remembered only one conversation that morning with his secretary, during which she had told him the latest joke: that President Hindenburg was called to Hitler's deathbed, with Pastor Niemoeller present to administer extreme unction! The nature of the talk, Goering maintained, clearly disclosed that it was held in a secret code. In his mind, there could not be any doubt that Martin was receiving support by foreign powers, their goal being to eliminate Hitler.

This seemed to be the cue for Hitler to go into one of his famous tantrums. Flailing his arms, foaming at the mouth, and yelling at the top of his voice, he screamed insults and threats at his visitors as if they were ill-behaved children. In his rage, he singled out Martin, rambling on in an endless monologue, until he finally ran out of breath. The moment had come for the pastor to speak out. His only deep concern, he said, was the fate and future of the German people, which caused Hitler to give him a dirty look. "You leave the German people to me," he screamed back, "and limit yourself to see that they go to heaven."

As far as Hitler was concerned, the meeting was over. Having regained his composure, he proceeded to stalk from one man to the next, stretching out his hand to bid everyone good-bye. Standing in front of Martin, the pastor continued holding Hitler's hand with a firm grip and decided that he must speak out one last time. "*Herr Reichskanzler,*" he said in a strong voice, "the responsibility for our people has been entrusted to me by God, and neither you nor anyone else in the world has the authority to take it from me." The führer, speechless due to the boldness of this remark, abruptly withdrew his hand, turned around brusquely, and left the room without another word. On his way out, Martin turned to Goering with a question about the charge of outside support of the Pastors' Emergency League.

"I have proof," was the fat man's brief answer.

That same evening, eight Gestapo men invaded the pastor's home to ransack it for incriminating evidence. A few days later, a bomb exploded in the rectory hall, fortunately not injuring the pastor, his wife, or any of their six children.

Martin had no more illusions; he knew that his days of freedom were numbered. How long would it take Hitler—before the meeting a halfway calculable adversary, now an open and omnipotent enemy—to apprehend, arrest, incarcerate, and execute him? He was now more certain than ever that Hitler blamed him for the failure to create a United German Protestant Church, an institution whose full support he desperately needed until such time when he could replace it with the National Socialist ideology. Could it be that an arrest of the pastor, whose picture appeared with frequency on the front pages of British, French, and American newspapers, might provoke anger in those countries with which he still intended to remain on friendly terms, at least for the time being?

What had struck the führer as particularly insulting during their encounter was that the former U-boat commander had left him, a lowly ex-corporal, with the devastating feeling of having been called to order by a superior officer. Ever since the day of their meeting, Hitler threw a fit whenever the pastor's name was mentioned. He was not very gracious about taking orders, let alone insults.

Martin, with a shudder never experienced before, realized that on January 25, 1934, he had been eye to eye with ultimate evil, an evil he would keep fighting to the best of his abilities. Ignoring his permanent suspension from office, signed by Ludwig Müller, he continued to speak out even more ardently against evil, aware of the presence of the special visitors Hitler sent to his services, who reported every one of his words to their master, Heinrich Himmler. Since there was no such thing as an unobtrusive Gestapo official, the men in their long black leather coats were immediately spotted from the pulpit by the pastor, who courteously welcomed them: "I notice that our brethren of the Gestapo have no hymnals, so would the ushers be kind enough to supply them with some?"

The "brethren" were not amused, but they stayed because they had to.

On November 10, 1934, Reich Minister for Propaganda Joseph Goebbels entered these remarks in his diary: "The attitude of the church is giving us a severe headache. Pastor Niemoeller preaches in Dahlem. Should we blast him or prohibit him from speaking? We shall do neither!"

Nine months later, on a beautiful Sunday morning in August, while the church bells of St. Anne's rang, a seventh child was born to Martin and Else Niemoeller. The little boy received the name Martin Friedrich Eberhard after the three Dahlem pastors: Martin Niemoeller, Friedrich Müller, and Eberhard Röhricht. Six weeks before his second birthday, his father was taken from him.

Chapter Twenty-One
Problems at School and at Home

At regular intervals, I came home from school with news of a frightening nature. A course called "national-political instruction" was now taught on Saturdays by Dr. Kadner, a stocky brute, who had lately been parading around the school in his yellow-brown SA uniform, complete with black boots, shoulder straps, and swastika. As far as my attendance in his classes was concerned, Dr. Kadner had reason for suspicion. Almost every other Saturday I was, according to a written excuse from my mother, stricken with some life-threatening illness, from which I miraculously recovered by Monday. I was small for my age and allegedly prone to all sorts of diseases. Weak, sickly, rebellious, and—on top of that—not a member of the Hitler Youth, the teacher asked himself? A renegade, a typical product of the notoriously decadent class, the aristocracy, a pernicious caste that, Dr. Kadner was certain, the führer would eventually want to deal with in his own way. Even though, he had to admit, there were a number of highborn people, including dukes, counts, and barons, who had proudly joined the party, the SA, and even the SS.

Although the mere appearance of Dr. Kadner gave me the creeps, I had discovered a wonderful secret weapon. He had undoubtedly examined the note verifying my Aryan heritage, on which my mother had stated her maiden name in all its glory. "Von Brauchitsch? Very interesting," he remarked one day. "Do you know there is a famous general by this name?" I took the chance to enlighten him about all my illustrious ancestors. "No, no, no," he replied, "I mean the one, who is not only the "führer's" esteemed military advisor, but the bearer of the Golden Party emblem, the three-star general?"

At that moment, I taught myself a first lesson in the art of name-dropping! "Oh, you mean my favorite Uncle Walther," I remarked nonchalantly, causing his lower jaw to drop in awe. No need for him to know that this particular uncle was not my mother's brother, but one of her numerous cousins, and for obvious reasons persona non grata in our house. My father tolerated no connections whatsoever between us and the man who lived only three blocks away.

Not too much later, lightning of a particularly frightening nature struck close to home. A family living on our street decided to send their son, who at age fifteen had suddenly developed a severe case of epilepsy, to a reputable medical institution in western Germany, realizing they could not handle his terrible attacks at home. Believing that he was getting the best of care and treatment that might improve his condition, they instead received a letter that the boy had, unfortunately, succumbed to a fatal kind of pneumonia. The inconceivable news contained the information that he had been cremated, the urn with the ashes being on the way to the family. The letter ended with "*Heil* Hitler" and some doctor's signature.

In 1935, the term "euthanasia"—Greek for helping the incurably ill to die in dignity—had taken a different, deadly meaning in the language of the Nazis. By the time the mass murders were publicly denounced from the pulpit by the "Westfalian Lion," the Catholic Archbishop von Galen, long after Pastor Niemoeller's incarceration, well over 70,000 of those classified as "unfit to live" had already died. Handicapped human beings, ranging from epileptics and people with Down syndrome to the physically crippled, from clearly recoverable to definitely incurable, were killed in cold blood, adults and children alike, in hospitals and mental institutions, some of them church-affiliated. Their murderers were doctors, nurses, deacons, and deaconesses who would, after the war, resume their positions as if nothing had happened. After the archbishop's protest in 1940, the murders stopped, but were resumed later. Galen remained unharmed, because Hitler knew better than to touch such a high-ranking official of the Catholic Church, the institution he himself had never officially left.

Alarmed by horrifying rumors, people tried in vain to bring their loved ones home from hospitals and mental institutions, particularly the children whom they had entrusted to recommended medical facilities. In those days, pneumonia turned out to be a very popular cause of death. Two years after our neighbors lost their son, a second case shook the neighborhood, also involving a teenager.

In 1935, an order was issued that on all Nazi commemoration days, swastika flags were to be displayed by all Germans, excluding Jews, who were no longer considered German citizens. Among the days to be observed was the führer's birthday on April 20; November 9, honoring the memory of those "martyrs" fallen in the ill-fated *Hitlerputsch* in 1923; and May 1, Labor Day, a Socialist holiday since the middle of the nineteenth century. On these occasions we were herded like sheep into the school auditorium. There we had to endure endless speeches praising Hitler and his ideology. The ceremony inevitably ended with the singing of not one, but two German national anthems. First, "*Deutschland, Deutschland über alles*" and then the "*Horst Wessel*" anthem, named after the Nazi idol who was allegedly murdered by reactionary forces. My father informed me that the worshipped hero had in reality been a pimp, a term I did not quite understand at the time. Singing one rather lengthy stanza of each anthem would have been punishment enough, but to hold our right arms outstretched in the Hitler salute during the entire procedure was sheer torture. Being caught in the sinful act of resting one's arm on the shoulder of the person in front called for severe punitive measures. Green with envy, I thought of all the nations completely satisfied with one anthem instead of two. Unfortunately, it was Dr. Kadner who spotted me with my arm for a split second on a neighbor's shoulder, and I received a stern admonition for disgracing our führer, who had dedicated his entire life to the future of Germany. My uncle, the three-star general, would be beside himself with disgust!

The flagstaff in front of our house had been dismantled the day after the Nazi takeover. This, however, was not a sufficient excuse; there were windows from which a flag could hang. But our windows remained empty, the reason being that we did not own a flag. Belligerently checking the housefronts, the newly appointed *Blockwart*, so called because he was responsible for one block, rang our doorbell. A *Blockwart*, ranking at the bottom of the Nazi hierarchy and seemingly insignificant in status, was still an important functionary. Chosen for political reliability, he usually qualified as an efficient neighborhood snitch for the Gestapo. Among his duties was to report anything he found suspicious (for instance, the absence of the Nazi flag).

Bestowing ranks on his followers had been one of Hitler's most ingenious accomplishments among a people traditionally obsessed with the importance of titles, uniforms, decorations, and emblems. These honors reassured the bearers of their own importance and significance as a small yet vital cog in a gigantic, well-functioning machine, a machine of death and destruction.

"Where is your flag, *Volksgenossin*?"[18] Adolf Kroepel, in civilian life a janitor, inquired in a threatening tone. "The flag?" my mother, her Hohenzollern-blue eyes displaying total innocence, responded. She herself had fastened it to an upstairs window that very morning. Most likely, the nasty, nasty wind had blown it down. "In this case," the disgruntled party official observed, "it would be on the ground, wouldn't it?" This sacred symbol somewhere in the mud? Yet it was not to be detected anywhere, so my mother voiced her speculation that someone must have stolen it. After all, did he not know there were so many bad people in the world?

"Well," he barked, "you'd better get a new one. And fast!"

My mother went out and bought a flag the size of a man's handkerchief. She adorned the white rim around the swastika with the pencil-scribbled message: "*Nur für kurze Zeit*," "for a short time only." On the next flag day, she attached it loosely to the upstairs toilet window, making sure that it would soon fall into the front yard. This time a boy in his Hitler Youth uniform with alarmingly short pants rang our bell.

For a short time only? For how much longer? My mother, in despair over her unfulfilled expectations, began to consult clairvoyants. Like the practice of psychiatry and psychology now branded as Jewish black magic, the art of foretelling the future was punishable by law. But my mother had her secret sources of information, one day returning triumphantly from a consultation with a fortune teller with the delightful news that Hitler would be gone by the time "the cherries bloomed." Unfortunately, the lady had failed to inform her of the exact year. After the cherries in our backyard had bloomed, ripened, were canned, and eaten, without Hitler paying the slightest attention to the prophecy, my mother turned to another source of knowledge, who assured her that the Nazi nightmare would definitely be over by the time "the leaves fall." The trees dropped their leaves, which were swept away without the remotest sign of a political change. Another spring came, and once more the cherries bloomed, forcing my mother to repeat her predictions. A third Cassandra voiced the rather startling forecast that the Russians would come to Berlin. She could see them climbing over her garden fence. Unfortunately, the old lady was careless enough to share this interesting bit of information with a client who took it straight to the Gestapo. Without wasting precious time on a proper court procedure, the seventy-year-old woman was sentenced to a gruesome death on the guillotine in Berlin's Plötzensee Prison, the macabre sideline being that there had not just been one witness to the prediction, but two.

The second witness was a tiny, grass green, and very tame parakeet who, when the Gestapo tried to catch him, kept screeching at the top of his shrill little voice: "The Russians are coming, the Russians are coming!"

Chapter Twenty-Two
Uncertain Reactions

Despite the brutality with which the Nazis proceeded to tighten the screws on the Jews, few of them were able to interpret the handwriting on the wall. This, in Uncle's Otto's unshakeable opinion, would pass, and he steadfastly kept rejecting the urgent pleas by Aunt Edith's son from a former marriage to join him in the United States. Leave their beautiful house for no reason at all? The Nazis would not dare to touch him, the highly decorated World War I veteran. Leaving now would look like they had something to hide. When he finally realized he was fighting a losing battle, it was too late.

While the 1936 Olympic Games in Berlin offered Hitler the opportunity to present the new Reich to the world in all its glory, the idea of having so many foreigners on his turf caused him uneasiness. Loathing the unbearable thought of non-white and non-Aryan competitors possibly winning silver or even gold medals, he was thrilled when the entire French team, marching by his box, saw fit to raise their hands in the Hitler salute.

During the games, a handwritten memorandum was delivered to Hitler, signed by five clergymen, among them the pastor of Dahlem, which read:

> If blood, nationhood, race, and honor are declared the most important German values, the Protestant Christian will have to resist in obedience to the first commandment. When Aryanism is glorified, forcing him into hate of the Jews, Christian brotherhood must stand in his way.

The führer decided he could not afford the risk of a scandal during this magnificent event, for which the city had been carefully prepared. All anti-Jewish signs were temporarily removed in order to lull the visitors into the belief that Germany was now a truly free, healthy, and happy nation. But when the last foreign guest had gone, the terror returned. Hitler took swift action, throwing seven hundred pastors of the Confessing Church into concentration camps. Surprisingly, Martin Niemoeller was not among them.

At my school, regular class expeditions to the Olympic stadium had taken place, from which Ditte and I, with the exception of the Jewish and half-Jewish girls now the only students not in the Hitler Youth, were barred. Our parents had decided to ignore the entire event, my father maintaining that he knew without going that one ox would outrun the other.

The führer had refused to shake hands with Jesse Owens, the triumphant African American athlete.

"No wonder," a classmate remarked, "negroes are animals!"

After this national spectacle, the atmosphere at home became more depressing every day. While not yet so noticeable for my little brother, for me, a young girl with hopes for a bright future, it was hard to endure. "What explanation will we give those who come after us," father asked, "for not having even raised a finger in the face of naked terror."

Chapter Twenty-Three
Boarding School

My mother had long toyed with the idea of sending me away to boarding school. She came up with a suitable place, a private institute in Eberswalde, a bleak little town north of Berlin, where mainly daughters of aristocratic descent were accepted. In my mother's mind, several birds could be killed with one stone. Not only would I be forced into the circles where I belonged, but I would also be removed from the company of Ditte.

The two of us had become known in Dahlem as the "diabolical duo." During the periods between governesses, who could have prevented the worst, we specialized in playing pranks on neighbors that amused few, if any, least of all the local police. We boldly stole flowers from other people's gardens, bound them into beautiful bouquets, and sold them, sometimes even back to their rightful owners. Using my little brother's air gun, we became experts in busting windows. After school, disregarding our homework, we would roam the streets on foot, by bicycle or on stilts, in search of trouble. As a consequence, our identical report cards showed an alarming number of failing marks.

What had become clear was that our parents seemed unable to cope with such misbehavior. Some of our pranks were reported by my father to the kaiser, but he only laughed. That was easy for him, my father complained. He did not have to live with me.

Ditte's parents were extremely eager to see all this nonsense come to an end, because they now lived in mortal fear that Ditte's mother's Jewish identity would be detected. It was still a family secret, and she had masterfully erased and forged some of the names and dates in her family tree, which now revealed that she had only one Jewish grandparent. Married to an "Aryan" husband, the danger of her deportation was drastically reduced. Still, they lived as unobtrusively as possible, avoiding public attention.

In boarding school, the company of girls from my own "caste" would not only improve my behavior, but cause present catastrophic marks on my report card to go up. My grandmother was jubilant. Finally!

Aside from dreading to leave Dahlem, my parents, my brother, Anna, Ditte, her family, and my freedom behind, one fact caused me grave concern: I would not be able to take the mandatory two years of confirmation instruction, taught by my idol, Pastor Niemoeller. By now, I had developed a full-fledged crush on the pastor. Watching him in the pulpit, dark and handsome, I secretly began to picture myself by his side as the love of his life. Oblivious to the fact that he was a married man with seven children, who never gave me more than an occasional fleeting smile, I found myself drifting into a dream world. The very thought of touching his hand would cause my heart to pound, my face to turn the color of a boiled lobster. Aside from my father, he was the most attractive man I had ever seen. I had reached the heroic decision that, should the Gestapo ever attempt to arrest him in church, I would throw myself between him and his persecutors, relishing the thought of becoming a martyr for his sake.

During my last winter at home, Ditte and I had been permitted to join a very exclusive dance circle, where the offspring of carefully chosen families were taught the foxtrot, the tango, the slow and the fast waltz, the forbidden "swing," and the "Lambeth Walk." For the first time, we became aware of boys as the other gender, having received stern but enigmatic instructions at home about behavior in the company of fifteen-year-old "males." Despite my crush on the pastor, which was, to me, almost holy, I had now gotten into the habit of falling in and out of love almost every week, usually with boys who had no use for me, a year younger than the rest of the girls, and unlike Ditte, not having even begun to "develop." The pink ball gown that my father had picked out for me to wear at the final party somehow did not fit around the chest. Asking Leonore, a rather well-developed Jewish girl in the dancing circle, for her expert advice, she suggested I put cotton into my bra. My what?

After Easter vacation in 1937, I was shipped off to serve my two-year sentence in exile, my clothes as well as linens and towels having been marked with my name by Philomena. On the day of my deportation, Anna, who dissolved in tears, cursed my callous mother, using all the Vendish profanity in her command. How was she to live without her "li'l lamb"? How could the *Herr Baron* stand by and tolerate such an act of cruelty? I wondered how my "godfather" in Doorn would take the shattering news. Maybe, with some luck, I could escape and somehow make my way to Holland. I had visions of him standing there with open arms, into which I would throw myself: "Oh, you poor, poor child," he would exclaim. However, I sobered when I pictured "her majesty" throwing a fit, demanding my swift removal.

How was I to survive, I asked myself upon deliverance to my new surroundings? Misled by my expectations that the institution was located in a spacious mansion, surrounded by a luscious park, I was in for my first shock. The school consisted of several buildings on an ugly small-town street, surpassing one another in shabbiness. The institute was run by three homely spinsters with pinched faces and short cropped hair, called "Chief One," "Chief Two," and "Chief Three." They were assisted by several equally old-maidish instructors who, while being academically acceptable, lacked even rudimentary qualifications essential in dealing with thirty young girls on the threshold of womanhood.

Chief One and Chief Two, both in their early fifties, resembled two rocks that had rolled down a high mountain until they looked practically alike. While Chief One had no nickname, Chief Two was called the "Hen," even though she resembled a dachshund with her short legs. Chief Three was the "Magpie." Having had a British mother, she taught excellent English, exclusively wearing black and white clothes. The only color on her person was a constantly dripping red nose. All other teachers were underlings, ranking so far below the ruling trio that they were not honored with nicknames, not even the housemother, a chinless and listless creature, who tried in vain to endear herself to the three chiefs by constantly snitching on her charges.

Sharing a spartan bedroom in one of the tenement-like buildings with two girls, one of them a princess, I soon got a taste of the strictly enforced Prussian virtues: obedience, discipline, precision, and punctuality. And frugality! Each floor was equipped with a single bathroom, its wood-burning stove providing hot water for the traditional Saturday night bath. The sparse bedroom furniture consisted of a bed for each girl, a dresser with three drawers and a porcelain washbowl on top, and a jug filled with cold water for the daily hygiene. Since we were not supposed to ever see each other nude, nakedness being considered not only indecent, but downright sinful, we each had a screen that surrounded this private area. The only source of light was provided by a dim, twenty-five-watt bulb dangling from the ceiling. The sheets on the narrow, rickety bedsteads with their thin, well-worn mattresses were changed once a month, the single towel once a week.

If the food at home had been nothing to brag about, at the school it was barbaric. Weak tea was served in the mornings, accompanied by slices of dark bread with either margarine or jam, but never both. Meat was provided once a week: smelly fish on Fridays. Unsightly vegetables swam in a white sauce in which, according to older inmates, fat maggots had been sighted more than once. Twice a week, a chocolate or vanilla pudding from some cheap mix was served for dessert; at least it was sweet.

Before breakfast we were chased around the block in two-by-two formation by teachers, one in front and one in the back, sometimes followed by compassionate glances from passersby. Upon our return, we were subjected to a brief prayer service in the main building. The daily hymn, announced the evening prior, had to be memorized by everybody overnight, because Chief One had the habit of picking a girl at random to recite it from beginning to end. Stumbling or stuttering, a sure sign of being a bad Christian, resulted in a lengthy and severe lecture that usually ended with mention of Martin Luther and Frederick the Great as shining examples, after whom we should strive to model our lives. Before being permitted to take our places at the breakfast table, we had to file by the three head spinsters, kissing their hands while sinking into a deep curtsy. In the afternoons, with our homework done, we were again taken for a brisk walk either into the nearby woods or through the rather dismal town.

The worst by far was that I, used to roaming freely after the departure of the last governess, now found myself under constant supervision. Even the toilet was not a safe retreat; a teacher was sure to hammer at the door in case a session took too long. More than four sheets of toilet paper was considered wasteful, and therefore unchristian.

The languages spoken during the meals alternated between German, English, and French on a weekly basis. Experiencing my first English week, I became immediately aware that my fluent command of it visibly upset Chief One. Her greatest joy was to find fault with at least one of the pupils, for either making mistakes, being too fat, too thin, too picky, or too greedy. She would not rest until her unfortunate victim finally broke into tears.

Among the three most deadly sins was not being of pure Prussian noble descent, a misfortune that had befallen two or three among us. The second unacceptable inadequacy was being Catholic. And the third sin, illness of any kind, from a cold to an upset stomach or worse, was also unforgivable. Being sick was not advisable for the simple reason that a bedridden student, neglected or ignored, had to rely on the kindness of her friends for survival. Those few unfortunates among us who wore eyeglasses had it coming to them every single day! Could we, pray, imagine Martin Luther or Frederick the Great with eyeglasses? Well then, why such folly? At our age? Ridiculous!

Whoever refused to clear her plate at the table, after receiving ample instruction about the poor hungry soldiers in the trenches, was made to sit until the food had been consumed or the victim threw up, whichever came first. By far the most sordid dish that appeared on the table was "hash," a concoction of leftover meat. For gourmet food, we should go to France, the French being obsessed with such obscene luxury. No wonder, I thought, that was probably why they won the war! But I knew better than to say it aloud.

The most feared punishment for any misdemeanor was to be stricken from the list of lucky ones permitted to travel home once a month for a weekend. Prussian daughters, it was hammered into us, girls of "our caste," obeyed blindly; they did not care about food, clothes, or mammon in general! I did my best to follow the rules, but there soon came one occasion when I would refuse to obey an order and lived to talk about it.

On the first Sunday after my arrival, we were marched, in the usual formation of two-by-two, into the old brick church for the obligatory service, guarded by a teacher in front and another in the back. Once, a long time before, a pupil had broken out of the line, and before anyone was able to stop her, she had run to a passing beer wagon pulled by two huge horses, mounting one of them. The perturbed animal, bolting under the unexpected burden, could only be brought under control after a few blocks. The coachman almost suffered a stroke, and the outraged headmistress promised the culprit a foreseeable and richly deserved end in the gutter. (In spite of her sinister prophecy, the defiant pupil of royal descent, instead of ending in the gutter, made it to the throne of a European monarchy.)

No sooner had the old minister, with his carefully groomed white beard resembling a pompous goat, opened his mouth to twaddle a lengthy sermon, than I smelled a rat! No doubt, the man was a "German Christian." A German Christian to prepare me for my confirmation? Over my dead body! That same afternoon, collecting all my wits, I marched into the lion's den, the office of Chief One, the headmistress. Seated at her desk, she put down her black cigar, piercing me with icy blue eyes, one peering through a monocle. I declared my determination not to grace the church and its German Christian pastor with my presence ever again.

Speechless at first, after letting her eyes wander to the ceiling and then out the window, she asked me if I, a meek little sausage, considered myself an expert on Christianity. German Christian or not, the word of God still was the word of God! I calmly explained that my parents were members of the Confessing Church, Martin Niemoeller being our pastor and friend. For a moment, she was silent. Indeed, she said after a while, in a decidedly milder tone of voice. Indeed! After taking several puffs from the cigar, blowing blue smoke rings into my face, she came up with a surprising answer. In that case, she would inquire about another church with an appropriate pastor who taught confirmation classes. The condition would be that I not tell the others, but keep our conversation a matter of strictest confidence. For a fleeting moment, I felt the bond of a secret alliance between us. Neither she nor any of the other teachers were Nazis—otherwise my parents would not have sent me there—but unless some discretion was practiced, the authorities were in a position to close the school in spite of its excellent academic reputation.

A few Sundays later, without a word of explanation, not just I alone, but four of us were sent across town to attend church services held by Pastor Reichmuth, a brave and upright member of the Confessing Church. When I told him about my connections with Pastor Niemoeller, he almost fainted. His round face and benign expression reminded me of a full moon, and I decided to fall in love with him, even though his trousers were decidedly too short and his eyeglasses in the wire frame looked a little ridiculous.

∽ Chapter Twenty-Four ∽
My Meeting

One afternoon, a few weeks after my arrival, four of us girls set out to march into town on our way to the bookstore, accompanied by our chaperon, the chinless housemother. Passing an apartment building, we observed a big black limousine parked at the curb with an SA man at the wheel. While we were still wondering what a car that size was doing in the area, the front door of a nearby house opened and out stepped four men in civilian clothes, surrounding a fifth man wearing a trench coat, his head covered with a soft, wide-brimmed hat, not unlike the one my father wore on his hunting trips. Suddenly, our housemother froze. She was the first one to recognize the man in the middle by his moustache. It took me but a split second to realize that I was at arm's length from Adolf Hitler.

Before anyone had a chance to scream *"Heil,"* the führer, in an obvious fit of joviality, decided to shake hands with us dumbfounded girls, who seemed glued to the sidewalk. When he came to me, a pinched smile on his face, offering his hand in a somewhat limp handshake, I looked him straight in his allegedly mesmerizing blue eyes. What I expected was the same reaction my mother had experienced once at the Berlin opera. Would I be sick as well? To my own amazement, I felt absolutely nothing! Lightning did not strike, the earth did not open up, and I did not hear bells ring. I was simply not able to reconcile this rather common-looking man, not much taller than myself, with the hoarsely screaming, wildly gesturing villain I knew from newsreels.

There was neither exhilaration nor devastation; I did not even feel an urge to throw up. What would stay with me was the memory of his shoe-brush-like moustache just a foot away from my face and the fishy touch of his fingers. After he and his entourage had sped off in the limousine, my classmate Lucy began to weep hysterically, informing us that she would never, never, never again wash the hand that *he* had touched. When she sank to the ground to kiss the sacred spot upon which Hitler's holy foot had trod, the housemother caught her just in time.

Just when I had come to the conclusion that we had been fooled by a Hitler impersonator, the local papers proudly reported that the führer had indeed honored the town of Eberswalde with his presence, paying a private visit to the mother of a deceased comrade. So much for the closest encounter I would ever have with the man I had been taught to loathe and fear for as long as I could remember.

I continued to regard my enrollment in the school as a personal insult. Never would I forgive my mother for sending me away (and probably not my father either, for tolerating it). There was only one fringe benefit: I found out to my delight that the problem of my nonexistent membership in the Hitler Youth, the "League of German Girls," had somehow solved itself. Under the false assumption that I was a registered member in Berlin, nobody even asked that I "rejoin" in Eberswalde. For the first few weeks, I had been obsessed with the urge to escape, if necessary running away to Timbuktu, but each plan had to be dismissed because my limited funds would not take me farther than the next street corner. While one of my roommates managed to cry through several nights in a row, I decided that cursing out loud served as a better outlet for my anger, using my rich vocabulary in German, English, French, and Vendish. Saying "*rish me oblish*" in the presence of the second headmistress once caused her to ask what it meant. It is Vendish, I explained, for "noblesse oblige."

As a last resort, I wrote a lengthy letter to Doorn, expressing my feelings. All outgoing as well as incoming mail was subject to inspection, so I got into the habit of secretly depositing my private letters in a public mailbox behind the teacher's back while on our way to church on Sundays. A few weeks had passed when an envelope with the imposing, unbroken imperial seal on the back of the luxurious envelope was handed to me by the dumbfounded Chief One; she had not dared to open it. Nonchalantly, I read it, and then showed it to her. It had the desired effect insofar as she must have reached the conclusion that if the kaiser liked me well enough to send me handwritten letters, maybe I was not so bad after all.

The days that separated me from freedom crept by all too slowly. Six glorious weeks of summer vacation! Home at last on July 1, while Anna was busy packing our bags for Kreuth, including tennis rackets and fishing equipment, disaster struck. I had run over to greet the Niemoellers, in the secret hope of catching a glimpse of my adored hero, and when no one answered the doorbell, I had climbed inside through an open cellar window in the back of the rectory. Strangely enough, the place was empty. Before I was able to sneak upstairs, however, their housekeeper Dora caught me and whispered that the pastor had just been arrested by the Gestapo, and I should go home—fast!

A few hours later, Else Niemoeller, dissolved in tears, appeared at our house. After her departure, my father informed us that, under the circumstances, he could not possibly accompany us on our trip to Kreuth. He would stay in Berlin to offer the Niemoeller family all possible assistance.

Chapter Twenty-Five
Pastor Made Prisoner

The pastor of Dahlem had continued to preach his inflammatory sermons to larger and larger crowds. During the last days of June 1937, he traveled to hold services in Bielefeld, Wiesbaden, and in the historic *Paulskirche* in Frankfurt where, in 1848, the National Assembly had taken place. In a state of exhaustion, he arrived home on July 1 to find four Gestapo officials waiting to arrest him. This time, they hinted, he should not count on an early release. He was permitted to pack a few necessary items before being taken to the Berlin Police Headquarters on Alexanderplatz. There he was subjected to a brief interrogation, after which the heavy door of a stark prison cell in the notorious Moabit Prison closed on him. Although not overly alarmed by his arrest, the sixth one so far, he had a notion that this time his confinement might very well last longer, perhaps even a lot longer. Only nine days prior, as if moved by a dark foreboding, he had urged his Dahlem congregation "not to give in to evil, but instead obey God more than man!"

The prisoner, stretched out on the hard wooden planks in his cell, slept soundly during that first night, his nervous anxiety having given way to an overwhelming feeling of relief. "The responsibility has been taken from me," he later confided to his wife in a letter. "Lord Christ himself is now steering the ship." What he experienced was a boundless trust in God.

On the day following his arrest, the Gestapo paid another visit to the rectory. For one entire day, they rummaged through the house for proof of illicit activities. They not only took personal documents and the pastor's private diaries, but also, from the wall safe, stole the sum of thirty thousand marks, property of the Pastors' Emergency League. In the meantime, Hitler and Goebbels were in a state of euphoria, for once in total agreement that, for too long, Dahlem had been allowed to become a festering sore, "an abscess on the body of the German people," as Goebbels publicly denounced it, for which there was only one person to blame: Martin Niemoeller. On July 2, 1937, Goebbels was finally able to enter gloating remarks in his diary: "Pastor Niemoeller arrested at last! A brief notice in the press. And now sentence him until he is blue in the face. (He must never be free again!)"[19]

His opinion was wholeheartedly shared by the führer.

The final straw had been a letter typed by Martin and addressed to the Minister of Justice Franz Gürtner, which bore the date of June 17, 1937. In the letter, the pastor complained in no uncertain words about the mass arrests of innocent citizens and clergy who were members of the Confessing Church. One passage in the letter was particularly infuriating; the writer had the impudence to quote Hitler himself from *Mein Kampf*: "When freedom is violated, the best ones meet in prison."

He added that, "Since Christians are obviously treated as outlaws, the time has come to call injustice INJUSTICE, truth TRUTH, a lie a LIE, as well as violence and terror VIOLENCE AND TERROR."

The pastor concluded his letter with the words: "I had to write this, so coming generations will not be able to blame me for having kept silent in the face of injustice."

Hitler decided that he would not tolerate any more audacity from this dangerous agitator, figuring that by simply removing the shepherd from his flock, the leaderless Confessing Church would soon break apart. His prognosis, unfortunately, would not prove to be altogether erroneous.

What the führer had not taken into account was an unexpected wave of protest by numerous international leaders, a tremendous echo in response to his action throughout the world, a world he believed he had enchanted after the glory of the Olympic Games. Only a few days after the pastor's arrest, Hitler's Deputy Rudolf Hess received a sharply formulated note from George Bell, the Anglican Bishop of Chichester, England. A declaration of protest was read from the pulpits of numerous churches in Germany: "Martin Niemoeller's arrest touches all Protestant Christians, whose hearts are filled with deep concern for our people." If Hitler had ever planned to quietly dispose of his foe in one of his concentration camps like any other victim, he now changed his mind; he wanted everybody to realize what a villain the pastor was, in a trial with a verdict that would shake the opposition!

In the meantime, the prisoner with the number 1325 was waiting in his cell. He had permission to write and receive letters. Soon his tight domicile became too small for the loads of mail that arrived from all corners of the free world. Each letter was carefully examined and censored by dismayed Gestapo officials occupying an adjacent cell. Before long, the situation was getting out of hand, and the captive was only allowed eight letters or postcards per day.

He was permitted to consult with his defense lawyers and granted a visit from his wife, who was shocked by her husband's appearance. He was pale, his faced bloated from the revolting prison food. She succeeded in securing extra rations for him. Moreover, with his eyesight failing, he received his first eyeglasses. From then on, Else would see her husband once every ten days for half an hour, closely monitored by guards. Each time she brought a different child along. With the exception of Martin Jr., who was too young, the children fully grasped the seriousness of the situation. The prison chaplain's initial question to his colleague in office, "Brother, why are you in prison?" was answered with the well-deserved quip, "Brother, why are you *not* in prison?"

Eight months, the time needed for trial preparation, passed quickly. The pastor was treated like any other criminal, his days subjected to a rigid routine. After scrubbing his cell floor on his knees, he was allowed to write, read, and to study the Bible. The only living creature he spotted from his small cell window was a falcon, circling high in the air. He decided that this beautiful bird enjoying freedom must be a good omen. His deepest concern, other than for his family, was the state of the Confessing Church. Alarming and depressing news reached him about internal controversies, petty quarrels, and general pessimism, which seemed to overtake his Dahlem congregation. As William Shirer would write decades later,

"While the resistance of the Niemoeller church was not completely broken, it was certainly bent!" That was precisely what Hitler had been counting on.

The trial began on February 7, 1938, before a *Sondergericht*, a Special Court, set up in Moabit, from which the press and public were barred. The numerous charges against the defendant, covering fourteen pages, were read, and the testimony by forty-two witnesses was heard. My father was among the most important witnesses. During the twenty-three days of intense court hearings, one charge after another had to be dropped, including that of high treason, leaving practically only the accusation of disobedience by violating the "pulpit clause," illicit activities such as speaking from the pulpit after the suspension pronounced by the führer.

On March 2, 1938, a verdict was reached, sentencing the pastor to a seven-month confinement in a *festung*, a "fortress," rather than a regular prison, plus a fine of two thousand marks. Since the defendant had already spent almost eight months in prison, he was free! Or was he?

In the courtroom, Else Niemoeller was the first to congratulate her husband, together with the Chaplain of the Swedish Embassy Pastor Forell. A radiant Martin Niemoeller exclaimed, "This is better than an acquittal!" For the moment, the dark prediction of Hans Bernd Gisevius, a close friend and an extremely well-informed official in the Ministry of the Interior, that "Martin Niemoeller will *never* be free," was forgotten. At home, seven children anxiously awaited the return of their father, the house was filled with flowers and the suitcases packed for a badly needed vacation on the Baltic Sea; however, they waited in vain. Pastor Niemoeller, on his way home from the court building, disappeared, and it seemed as if the earth had opened up and swallowed him.

Chapter Twenty-Six
Triumphs of the Führer

Ten days after ridding himself of his foe Martin Niemoeller, an ecstatic führer proclaimed his native Austria part of the *Grossdeutsches Reich*. The country of his birth had "come home" to the Reich! Not quite under its own power, but with the helping hand of the Nazis, who, ruthlessly squashing whatever opposition might have existed and overturning the weak democratic government, now met with a rejoicing people. The date of the Nazi invasion of Austria coincided with an event that Hitler felt was clearly in his favor. After the death of Pope Pius XI, the former Papal Nuncio, Eugenio Pacelli, was chosen to succeed him as Pius XII. Having spent many years in Germany, the new head of the Catholic Church had been largely responsible for the formulation of the infamous *Reichskonkordat* in 1933 under his predecessor, reaching a very satisfactory arrangement between the Holy See and the Nazi government.

His sixth sense told Hitler that from that moment forward, he would encounter even fewer difficulties with Rome than before. A nominal member of the Catholic faith, like Goebbels and Himmler as well as twenty-two million Germans, including twenty-five percent of the SS, he was more certain than ever that the Vatican would formally guarantee continuation of the neutrality policy manifested under Pius XI.

My father, who arrived in Doorn shortly after Austria's *Anschluss*, found "her majesty" away on one of her frequent pleasure trips. The kaiser was ecstatic over the latest political developments. Gloating over England's helpless fury, he stooped low enough to even express admiration for Hitler's latest coup. More than ever before, he was now certain that what the expanded fatherland most urgently needed was an emperor! If the British and French were to invade Germany, so he fantasized, a German Army without an emperor would be helpless and totally ineffective.

After dinner, with no one else present, my father succeeded in convincing the kaiser that the chances to resume his throne were now indeed worse than ever before. The old man, close to tears, sank into a state of depression. The following day, he suffered an attack of angina, which the attending physician believed was serious enough to summon Hermine back to the patient's bedside. The patient, in turn, made it very clear that he did not wish to see her.

On his next trip to Holland, the Gestapo searched and interrogated my father at the border in the most humiliating manner. His appearance in the Berlin court as a major witness on behalf of Pastor Niemoeller had increased his notoriety on the Nazis' blacklist. Shortly after the trial, the Gestapo paid an extended visit to our house. I was home from boarding school for this memorable occasion. In long black leather coats, the foursome barged in, and one of them did precisely what we had been warned about: he marched straight through the hall into the dining room and turned on the radio. My parents, who relied on BBC London as the only source of authentic information, had instructed us always—*always*—to turn the knob back to a German station. Listening to foreign news, at this point cause for arrest, would later cost an offender his life.

To his visible disappointment, the Gestapo officer found only *Deutschlandfunk* blasting the usual Nazi propaganda. After hours of thoroughly searching the house from cellar to attic without a warrant, never disclosing what they were looking for, they gloatingly discovered the Niemoeller court files, which were promptly confiscated.

The gang leader asked my father if he was a supporter of a traitor, the number one "enemy of the State." My father answered that Martin was a friend. The informal interrogation continued, with the leader asking if my father had any travel plans, if both of his children were in the Hitler Youth, and if he himself was a member of the party. My father responded in the negative to all of these questions. The leader responded that while he was not under arrest quite yet, my father would surely be found when the time came.

Chapter Twenty-Seven
Prisoner 569

The news of Martin Niemoeller's disappearance traveled quickly beyond the borders of Germany, making headlines in the Free World's media outlets. However, it took four agonizing weeks of waiting before Else received the first note from her husband, a crumpled piece of paper, with whole passages made illegible by the black ink of the censors.

At least he was alive!

Jubilant over the outcome of the trial, the pastor had returned to his cell on March 2, 1938, to gather his belongings. All he wanted was to go home—to his wife, his children, and his congregation. But the limousine, with plainclothes Gestapo officials riding along and following in separate cars, did not take him to Dahlem. Speeding northeast instead of southwest, it soon reached the site of the Sachsenhausen Concentration Camp, which, at that date, held 30,000 inmates. Each inmate passed through a gate adorned with the wrought-iron words *"Arbeit macht frei!"* ("Work will make you free!").

Niemoeller was swiftly registered and mug shots were taken: front view, right side, left side. He was stripped of all personal possessions including his Bible, hymnal, golden watch, and wedding band. After this humiliating procedure, he was led to a long, low building, the bunker, down some stairs into a cell, one of several in a row, all with iron doors. His dungeon was seven steps long and four steps wide, the furniture consisting of a cot with a straw mattress, a shelf with a jug of water on it, a footstool, and a bucket in the corner. High up on one wall, serving as a window, was a hatch.

The next morning, in the splendor of his sleek black uniform, a visibly disturbed high-ranking SS officer named Baranowski, commandant of Sachsenhausen, entered the cell.

"Pastor Niemoeller," he said in a fairly civil tone, "you are here as the führer's personal prisoner. Since I have not come across a similar case, nor have I been advised how you are to be treated, I have to ask you if you have any complaints or wishes."

The totally unexpected outcome of the trial by the Special Court had caused Hitler to throw a temper tantrum that beat all records. It revealed to him that, even at that late date, there were still judges in Germany who, boldly defying his authority, based their verdicts on the law and nothing but the law. Beside himself with rage, he summoned his entire cabinet, only to have Minister of Justice Franz Gürtner inform him that there were absolutely no legal grounds on which the pastor could be held.

"In that case," the führer bellowed, "the man shall be my personal prisoner."

In response to the question of whether he had any complaints, Martin, now prisoner number 569, demanded the return of his Bible, hymnal, wedding ring, and watch. "We do not permit dangerous books like the Bible," was the angry reply. But, to his great surprise, it was handed back to him within minutes. Two weeks later he received his ring, watch, and hymnal. The pastor was totally unaware of the fact that the commandant, not having received any instructions concerning the treatment of this prominent inmate, felt extremely uneasy. His position was a uniquely precarious one; if he treated his ward too well, it might cost him his job; if he mistreated him, perhaps his life. The prisoner was obviously the führer's treasured private possession, so Baranowski decided to play it safe by simply leaving him to rot in solitary confinement, like a potato in a cellar.

For three years, Martin would be kept in his dark, half-underground cell. The hatch high on the wall provided the only source of air, and by climbing on the stool, he was able to catch a glimpse of daylight. Through the narrow opening, he could hear but never see his fellow inmates being marched to and from work. Soon he made it a habit, while standing on the stool, to quote passages from the Bible to them, in a clear and loud voice. His only companions were the SS guards who threatened to beat him to a pulp if he did not stop his forbidden activities. The pastor was unafraid, even though he had no way of knowing that those threats were empty; the führer would decide his fate. He now wore prison garb: striped pants and a crude greenish-blue jacket, with a red triangle identifying him as a political prisoner. Within six months, the number on his uniform was changed to 10506.

Four weeks went by before Else was finally informed about her husband's whereabouts. After two more months, a Gestapo car took him from Sachsenhausen to Berlin Police Headquarters, where he was allowed to meet with his wife for the first time, and from then on at irregular intervals.

In Sachsenhausen, the news of the famous pastor's arrival spread through the camp like a brushfire. The inmates were blissful! Surely now, the Free World could not remain silent any longer, and they all would soon be released, a fervent hope that would never materialize.

Although the German media tried to hush up the whole affair, the international news reported on the pastor's fate. German ships in New York harbor were picketed, the signs warning not to travel by German boats as long as Pastor Niemoeller was in a concentration camp. While petitions from many countries were ignored by the Nazis, money donations and gifts from total strangers poured into the Niemoeller household for support of the fatherless family, often accompanied by heartwarming notes. Farmers sent bread, butter, honey, and eggs.

Although never physically abused, Martin, used to the company of his wife and seven children, craved human companionship; more than any other hardship, he suffered the excruciating pains of his solitary existence. Since nobody in the camp was permitted to catch a glimpse of him, his daily walks, accompanied by armed guards, took place in darkness, after the others had been locked up. He was intentionally led by poles that lined the paths between the blocks, on which inmates were routinely strung up for punishment; some were dead, some still alive. Trips to the commandant's office were undertaken in a covered wheelbarrow or even a hearse. The lonely man came close to giving up more than once; he suffered from deep depression and, due to the constant darkness, his eyesight was getting worse. He reached the conclusion that he was forgotten, forsaken by the world, and, most certainly, by his church. Could he go on? Is that what God expected of him? He did not know the answer.

What would Jesus say?

The only one in a position to answer his question was Adolf Hitler, who habitually flew into a wild rage whenever the pastor's name was mentioned. With the unexpected abundance of protests pouring in from all over the world, it had begun to dawn on the führer that what he held in his hands was a priceless jewel, a pawn of inestimable value, that he might one day use to his own advantage. There was no hurry; after all, he could still have him killed whenever he liked—tonight, next week, or in ten years.

A story made the rounds, according to which Hitler consulted an astrologer, asking the question how long he, the führer, was going to live. The alleged answer: "Mein Führer, you are going to live one day longer than Pastor Niemoeller."

Chapter Twenty-Eight
Growing Up

Following my fifteenth birthday, my mother gave in to my nagging and took me to a beauty parlor where I received my first permanent wave. Monsieur Jean (his real name was Herr Krause, chief coiffeur in the Hotel Bristol) had taken a regretful look at my mousy hair, plain as my grandmother's, and hastened to assure my mother that the attempted procedure, while not capable of performing miracles, could only improve my—here he cleared his throat—rather plain appearance, unaware that reflected in the looking glass I noticed his eyes wandering to the ceiling in helpless despair. After endless hours of sadistic, medieval torture, I was finally permitted to look at the finished product in the mirror. To my delight, staring back at me was a woman of the world, a femme fatale! Even Monsieur Jean was in awe of this unexpected transfiguration. On her next visit, my grandmother almost fainted: artificially curled hair? A girl of *our* caste? She truly was going to be a "demimonde"! The next surprise on my way to the gutter would probably be lipstick, or worse!

A notorious late bloomer, I had finally developed female curves, making the purchase of my first brassiere and a girdle mandatory. The days when I had been as flat as a flounder, fingernails bitten to the quick, were now definitely a thing of the past. With an air of nonchalance, I paraded through the bedrooms at school, leaving my gown open so anyone could admire my latest acquisitions.

An incident that had occurred during Easter vacation must have had something to do with finally growing up. One day, after complaining of severe abdominal pains, I was rushed to the hospital, where the red-faced surgeon with huge hands was already busy sharpening his knives. Appendicitis, of course! What else? No need for lengthy examinations. Four weeks after the removal of the little scoundrel, to my horror, I found myself writhing once more with the same kind of pain. Could it be that I had two appendixes? But this time, there was blood where it was not supposed to be. Obviously, I was closer to death than anybody had told me. Sharing my fears with Ditte, she confided in me that she, too, was experiencing this unpleasant event each month. It dawned on my mother that it had not been the appendix causing me such discomfort after all. I was handed a blue cardboard box wrapped in unobtrusive brown paper, containing items called sanitary napkins, and informed that this "ailment," unfortunately, would befall me once a month for the next forty years—the sad lot of nearly every female in the world!

But why? I asked in despair. Because, my mother replied, God, in his infinite wisdom, had "arranged it that way." In her mind, it was another error in His divine judgment, the reason behind the mistakes being that the Almighty was not married. That same summer, my reluctant mother took the opportunity to enlighten me about the facts of life, facts that by that time I had already made it my business to find out from classmates. In Kreuth, passing a meadow with cattle, she pointed at one animal, or rather at a certain part on its body, explaining that men were also endowed with what I saw dangling there. Then she began to stutter about certain activities that took place between married people, after which a baby would be on its way. I need not worry, she ended; the good news was that this would not take place but once in a long while. The bad news? It was a wife's duty to go along with her husband's wishes.

The greatest miracle following my transformation would be another enjoyable experience: falling in love with someone other than Pastor Niemoeller. I had already been kissed while on a skiing vacation in the Dolomites. The kisser had not been a clumsy, fumbling boy, but the ski instructor himself. He had grabbed me in the dark outside the hotel, and his kisses, to my utter surprise, did not bear the remotest resemblance to those of my father. Unfortunately, the next morning, just when I was sure that he would ask my parents for my hand in marriage, I found that he had already departed, which probably had something to do with his wife and three children. Faster than expected, I recuperated from this disappointment when, at long last, true love came my way.

Among the Prussian geese at the institute were two exotic birds—two sisters from China. Their father, a Chinese general and advisor to General Chiang Kai-shek, had, after the Japanese invasion of his homeland, whisked his two daughters to Germany and placed them in the well-recommended boarding school where they would be safe. Aside from being safe, they almost died from homesickness in the rough climate of this alien and hostile country. For the duration of the Christmas vacation, their father had rented a villa in Dahlem just around the corner from us, so he and his daughters could be together during the holidays. Overjoyed, I had accepted an invitation for afternoon tea at their house.

While seated at the table laden with Far Eastern specialties, in glorious anticipation of wonderful things to come, the door opened and in walked the man of my dreams. Introduced as a cousin, I learned that the slender young Chinese man in a German officer's uniform was one of the foreigners attending the War Academy in Munich, where he would receive the necessary instructions for the liberation of his country, which was planned by his father.

His father?

Throughout the vacation, the four of us went ice-skating and visited movie theaters. I also worked myself into a frenzy, a state of mind not minimized by the fact that the target of my infatuation did not seem to pay any particular attention to me, while I, in my fantasy, had already worked out a future together. Before drifting off to sleep at night, I imagined how my beloved, his hand firmly holding mine, would bravely step before his family, announcing his irrevocable decision either to be permitted to wed this fair young maiden or commit hara-kiri. (At the time, I did not know that hara-kiri was not a Chinese, but a Japanese specialty.) Eventually, the mighty father, reduced to tears, would give in and bless our union! Totally unaware of my passion, my unsuspecting future bridegroom returned to his military academy, and I never saw him again; in faraway China, General Chiang Kai-shek would never know what he had missed.

Back at school, my expanding figure required several visits to the local seamstress, who did her best to let out my dresses in the respective places. It was in the fall of 1938, that I, now permitted to go to town by myself, was passing what had been pointed out to me as a "temple," the place of worship for Jews. Curiously, I peeked through the open iron gate and caught a glimpse of a gray little man with a round black cap on his head, busily sweeping the yard in front of the sanctuary. For a moment our eyes met before he abruptly closed the gate. I felt overcome by a sudden urge to tell him how much I hated the Nazis. The memory of not having done so, meaningless as it might have been, would later fill me with guilt.

On a dark November evening—during an inconsequential school anniversary celebration—the janitor's wife stormed into the hall, yelling at the top of her voice, "Fire, fire, the town is on fire." Looking out of the window, we saw the red sky. Chief One decided to take a walk down the hill to find out what was taking place. A handful of us were allowed to accompany her, while most of the others preferred to stay with the dry cake and sickeningly sweet punch.

Approaching the same street I had walked only a few days before on my way to the seamstress, we found ourselves in the midst of howling masses, and then, finally, I saw it: the synagogue was ablaze. To my surprise, fire trucks positioned on each side of the synagogue directed their hoses not to the source of the fire, but to the neighboring houses.

"Why do they not save the synagogue?" I whispered to a man with a slouch hat standing next to me. "Because," he murmured through clenched teeth in a flat Berlin twang, "first they set fire to it, and now they are afraid their own houses might burn down." The horrified look on my face prompted him to add, "Don't you understand? Those assholes are after the Jews."

"*Deutschland erwache—Juda verrecke!* (Germany awake—Judah kick the bucket!)" chanted the chorus of the people who jammed the entrance to the synagogue. In the front yard, boys dressed in Hitler Youth uniforms deposited on the ground some objects that they had hauled out of the temple resembling torn, smoldering parchment rolls. In a wild frenzy, they trampled on them and shouted, "*Gott sei dank, nun ist's vorbei mit der Juden tyrannei!* (Thank God, the tyranny of the Jews is finally over!)"

A moment later, SA men in brown uniforms pushed a few people out of the building adjacent to the synagogue, dragging them to a waiting open truck. Behind them stumbled the little caretaker I had seen a few days before. Was this the moment that my father had referred to when, trying to answer my question about what would happen if Hitler came to power, he had replied: "Then, my dear child, may God have mercy on us!" My eyes met those of the headmistress, whose white face seemed to have turned to stone. Without exchanging a single word, we slowly walked back to school, on our way encountering chaos, including broken windows of Jewish shops, now looted by the bloodthirsty mob of German burghers. Jewish shop owners were chased through the streets by screaming crowds. Drawing near the school, we heard the well-known German folk song being sung by those who had stayed behind: "*Kein schöner Land in dieser Zeit als hier das unsere weit und breit.* (There is no country more beautiful than ours, near or far.)"

Indeed?

I sent a detailed written report to my parents that ended with the words, "Jewish shops were looted and people behaved like wild beasts!" My mother kept it through the war. Later, the BBC informed us that the terrifying incident I witnessed had by no means been a singular one. Throughout Germany, during *Kristallnacht*, the "Night of Broken Glass" as the Berliners would call it, a total of 119 synagogues and 171 houses had been set on fire, and another 76 Jewish houses of worship and 815 shops were completely destroyed. The death of 36 Jews was reported, plus an equal number of seriously injured. An estimated 20,000 Jews were arrested and dragged to concentration camps.

The November 9 pogrom and its consequences would also touch my life personally, causing a beautiful relationship to come to an abrupt end. While on a skiing trip in the northern Italian Dolomites with my mother and brother during spring vacation in 1937, we had met a lady from Berlin. Staying at the same hotel, I soon became very fond of Irma Lange and her twenty-year-old-son, Hanns. This incidental acquaintance turned into a friendship, and after returning to school, I soon received an invitation to visit the Lange family at their estate on the Spree River at Rahnsdorf, outside Berlin.

Walter Lange was one of Berlin's most prominent furriers. Theater and movie stars, and lately the wives of Nazi officials, had their stoles, coats, and jackets created in his elegant store on Luetzowplatz. By far the most prominent among the illustrious clientele was none other than Hermann Goering, which meant that, at regular intervals, Walter Lange would drive to Karinhall, his car laden with exquisite ermine, sable, and chinchilla furs for the *Reichsmarschall* and his wife.

Situated in the Schorfheide outside of Berlin, the pompous estate left nothing to be desired as far as luxury was concerned. Being in the habit of simply taking what he liked, the place later overflowed with great artifacts stolen from museums and private homes throughout the Nazi-occupied territories. The obese man's favorite hobby was tinkering with a fabulous electric train system that occupied a huge upstairs room. Whenever he felt in a particularly gracious mood, he would invite honored guests to join him in the fun. Walter Lange was one of those lucky people.

In wild anticipation, I had counted the days until Christmas vacation and another weekend in Rahnsdorf. The house, a regular little mansion, was located amidst a park on the romantic Spree River. There were sheep, dogs, cats, and, best of all, several beautiful horses, so I could ride with Hanns, for whom I had developed the inevitable crush of a teenager. Soon after the occurrences of November 9, I received a letter from Irma Lange. She told me that, for my own sake, we should not plan another visit to Rahnsdorf.

I almost fainted. Had I done something to annoy her? Devastated, I continued reading and learned that she felt it was only fair to tell me that she was Jewish. She would certainly understand if I broke off my friendship with her, a friendship that could well pose a real danger for me. Whatever I decided, she would understand and still love me like a daughter. Needless to say, I went to Rahnsdorf over Christmas vacation. When I left, Irma Lange withheld the news from me that my holiday visit would be the last one. Hailing from Vienna, her siblings had already fled to England; she hoped that, as the wife of an "Aryan" husband, the Nazis would allow her to do the same.

When Walter Lange drove once more to Karinhall in December 1938, he courageously and boldly asked the man, who had boasted that he alone decided who was Aryan and who was not, for permission to send his wife and son to England. By that point, the Nazis had closed the German borders from the inside, preventing Jews from emigration. Goering, feeling supremely god-like that day, granted the wish. Soon after, Irma and Hanns made it safely to England, though their eventual destination was Australia. I felt relieved and sad at the same time, and of course I could not know that I would never see Irma Lange again.[20]

During my next visit home, I found my father not only visibly shaken by developments in general, but specifically by those that had occurred in Doorn. The kaiser, assembling his sons around him, labeled the atrocities on November 9 a "crime," calling the culprits "gangsters." He strictly prohibited his son August Wilhelm from continuing to associate with the Nazis. As a result, "Auwi" threatened his father with reporting these defeatist remarks to Goering. Crown Prince "Little Willy," in despair, pleaded with his father until the old man moderated his order.

My father was shocked, not so much by the sons' behavior, which he had expected, but by the old man's fickleness. The fact that Jews had been among the kaiser's close friends, even while he was a ruling monarch, did not keep him from making the most outrageous anti-Semitic remarks.

Returning to school after Christmas vacation, I had no inkling that it would be for the last time. On January 27, the kaiser had celebrated his eightieth birthday in Doorn, surrounded by his entire family. The guest of honor was the Dutch Crown Princess Juliana. At the last moment, my father had been able to avoid a major upheaval by preventing Wilhelm's only daughter, Viktoria Luise of Hannover-Braunschweig, whose husband and sons were members of the SS, from wearing a diamond pin in the shape of a swastika on her festive gown. Physically barring her entrance, he told her that with this kind of adornment, she would first have to step over his dead body.

Four weeks after Hitler's invasion of Czechoslovakia on March 15, I packed my belongings. For one last time, I entered the lion's den, the office of Chief One, to bid my farewell. A letter from the headmistress had reached my parents, suggesting that another school might be more suitable for me. While allegedly far from expelling me, the faculty had determined that all efforts to turn me into an obedient member of the school community had netted no positive results. The main cause, in spite of a high degree of intelligence, was my stubborn refusal to conform to set rules. What a wonderful compliment; I was in seventh heaven! "Conforming" was a hostile word in my vocabulary.

Chief One, seated behind her desk, a monocle covering one eye, a pinched smile on her thin lips, and a black cigar resting on an ashtray, reminded me that I should never forget to follow the shining examples of Frederick the Great and Martin Luther. Patronizingly, she inquired what I intended to do with my life. Possessed by Satan, I nonchalantly informed her that my future would be the stage. The stage? Not as an actress, she hoped? I nodded, trying hard to keep a straight face. Indeed, I would become an actress and a dancer and a movie star. Watching her turning a little green around the nose, I added the crowning suggestion that I might even join a circus.

Her eyes searched the ceiling in a vain attempt to find a suitable answer. "Your poor, poor parents," she was finally able to gasp.

I was dismissed.

Without looking back, I climbed into the cab and left the hated institution, realizing that what they had tried to teach me in vain were two things: first of all, that only the elite, our "caste," counted in this world, and furthermore, that subordination and blind obedience were the keys that opened the doors to a respected existence. I was determined to give Martin Luther and Frederick the Great a fair chance to disappear from my life just as fast as possible!

My confirmation in the Church of Jesus Christ in Dahlem was planned for Palm Sunday. Ardent hopes that Pastor Niemoeller would be the one to guide me in my transition from a mere child to a full-fledged member of the Confessing Church had remained an illusion. Instead, his courageous young substitute, Pastor Helmut Gollwitzer, officiated at this memorable occasion. In a pitch-black confirmation dress, the hymnal tightly pressed to my now well-developed bosom, I probably resembled a hundred-year-old scarecrow. With an ostensibly demure expression on my face, together with thirty other confirmands, I walked to the altar. I had arrived at the conclusion that the only way by which I could possibly help Pastor Niemoeller to survive was if I became very, very pious and prayed a lot. For this memorable event, I had selected a passage from the New Testament attributed to St. Matthew: "For what is a man profited, if he shall gain the whole world, and lose his own soul?"

At home, a big party was given in my honor. With few living godparents, most of the guests were friends. Among the many gifts was one from the kaiser, a gold pin with little diamonds in the shape of a half moon. Irma Lange had sent a precious turquoise armband.

My parents gave me a golden ring with a blue stone, engraved with our coat of arms. It had been in the possession of my family for a long time; the last one to wear it was the grandfather who had died six months before my birth. Altered for me, I would never take it off, I swore. However, I did remove it once, but that is another story. I also received a beautiful antique mahogany desk with five drawers and four slender legs that would, no doubt, entice me to do my homework. Homework? Who needed homework? I already envisioned myself sitting there, graciously signing photos for my ardent fans.

Soon after, I informed my parents of my professional intentions. My plan, unheard of in the family so far, so distressed my father that he had to share it with his majesty only a few days later, provoking a rather unforeseen reaction. The kaiser broke into a fit of Homeric laughter, put his intact right arm around my father's shoulder, and spoke the memorable words, "So the courageous little monkey wants to be an actress! My dear, dear friend, this, of all people, should happen to you!" He could barely compose himself. The highly amused kaiser had referred to me as "the little monkey" ever since I had called a visiting young officer, who revealed himself as a Nazi, a monkey.

A welcome consequence of the old man's reaction was that my parents gave me permission to try out for the entrance exam at Berlin's most noted acting academy. I had every reason to be rather pleased with the "godfather" of my own choice, who, at least this time, had not let me down.

After returning home, my parents made the serious mistake of permitting me to go back to my old school, where Ditte was now a grade above me. To my undivided horror, my home room teacher was Dr. Bach, a sly Nazi turncoat. Inquiring about my nonexistent membership in the Hitler Youth, a verbal exchange between us led to a very nasty letter written by him to my father, ending with the remark that girls like me had no place in his school or in any other decent German school. My poor parents were in a predicament; they really did not know what to do with me. With no other school in the country permitted to accept me, my graduation would not just be in jeopardy, it was out of the question. Worse, there was now the acute danger that I might be taken away and placed in a Nazi reform school. After the summer vacation, some kind of solution would have to be found.

The summer of 1939 was unusually hot. It seemed that never before had the garden produced such an abundance of flowers, their sweet, heavy fragrance almost unbearable. In the early morning of August 26, my mother's birthday, I watched my parents walking side by side through the garden. There was something greatly disturbing in the way they walked and talked; my father looking as if he carried a load too heavy for him, his face gray and distorted with grief and pain. He had just received the notification that, in case of war, he, now fifty-five years of age, would be drafted to active duty into Hitler's *Wehrmacht*.

There had been incidents at the Polish border, probably staged by the Nazis. On September 1, the führer's hoarse voice came over the radio, announcing that German troops were now striking back. With a shudder, I remembered Hitler's cold, limp handshake.

"Are we going to have a war?" I inquired.

"Yes," my shocked mother replied, "another war!"

I demanded to know what this would mean for our lives. After all, wars, as everybody knew, took place on battlefields and certainly not in the streets of Dahlem. My mother told me that there probably would be a blackout, and all the young men will be inducted into the armed forces. Clothing and food would become scarce, with new ration cards each month or even each week for everything. Even matches, I asked? Surely not candy?

Tearing my bicycle out of the garage, I raced to the store opposite the Dahlem Dorf subway station, where I came to a screeching halt. I noticed a sign on the door, scribbled with pencil on a piece of cardboard: closed for the duration of the war!

For the duration of the war? Did this mean until the war was over? What if it lasted more than just a few days or weeks? Or even months? I just could not believe it; the unthinkable had happened. They even closed the candy store!

Part One Notes

1. Excessive stoutness.
2. The unique situation in which one of Konrad von Brauchitsch's very own granddaughters converted to the Jewish faith without compulsion by outward circumstances would, later in the century, cause considerable upheaval within her birth family. In unison, the decision was reached to throw the black sheep overboard. Breaking with traditional family rules and principles had, over the centuries, led to rather dramatic acts of official expulsion from the clan. In this particular case, the culprit was quietly dropped like a hot potato, an act the happy convert found extremely easy to live with.
3. The horrific account of Aunt Maike's fatal collision with the food elevator would later become one of my favorite bedtime stories, particularly since Anna had a talent of adorning this tragic event with new and atrocious little details as the years went on. Until Grimm's fairy tales entered my life, it remained the undisputed preferred story in our repertoire and became a part of the secret world that Anna and I shared, from which even my beloved father was excluded.
4. Unfortunately, the Duke of Mecklenburg-Schwerin forgot to present his faithful servant with something a little more tangible than the title, like a handsome country estate, as was quite customary in those days. This omission would affect the lives of his two sons, Friedrich and Wilhelm, who were left with no choice but to pursue military careers. While Friedrich made it to colonel, Wilhelm reached the rank of a major general.
5. As revenge, for which I received many thrashings, I took sadistic delight in creeping underneath Philomena's chair with a wicker bottom, sticking needles into her behind, a wretched act that made her shriek out loud.
6. How close I came to that dream I did not learn until much later in my life when it was revealed to me that one of the kaiser's sons, childless himself, had been dead set on adopting me. Unfortunately, I had not been for sale.
7. A rather remarkable incident occurred when, at the age of fourteen, Martin decided to drop his habit of thumb sucking and take up smoking cigars while doing his homework in the seclusion of his attic room. One day, his unsuspecting father stood in the door and found his son wrapped in a cloud of blue smoke. "My boy, you are smoking?" he exclaimed. "Well, well, I guess from now on we shall order our cigars together!" The leash was long indeed.
8. Dönitz would admire the führer and what he stood for. The führer, in turn, would reward his eager subservience by ultimately naming him as his successor in office at the end of April 1945. He would receive a well-deserved sentence of twenty-five years in Berlin's Spandau Prison as a convicted Nazi criminal, charged with carrying out orders, to which he added his own, which had unnecessarily sacrificed the lives of thousands of young German sailors.
9. After leaving the Navy, the young man had decided to become a farmer. Working as a hired hand in Westfalia brought him back to the soil, back to his "motherland." Only after realizing that he had no money to buy his own farm did he resign, writing in his diary, "shall I become a pastor?"

10. Living space.

11. Insanely jealous of anyone close to the old man's heart, my father soon became her main target. During a brawl, she demanded that Ulrich von Sell be dismissed; with his healthy right fist, the ex-monarch pounded the table and thundered, "He stays!" Of course, she would stay, too. From that day on, my father did not even dare accompany her for a walk through the park, for fear that she should jump in the moat and accuse him of pushing her in.

12. For a while, he would refer to me as "the little soldier," until something happened a few years later that caused him to forever call me "the little monkey."

13. While the pastors of the Confessing Church bravely defended the rights of their members who were Jews by Nazi definition, few concerned themselves with the fate of those Jews who still practiced the "Mosaic" faith. When Niemoeller, like the vast majority of his forefathers raised in the anti-Semitic Lutheran tradition, finally came to realize the detrimental consequences of this exclusion of the "Jewish" Jews, it would be too late.

14. Nobility dating back at least to the sixteenth century.

15. My father's favorite joke was about Hitler purchasing a carpet in a store. The salesman asking him, "Should we wrap it, or do you wish to eat it here?" Allegedly, when seized by one of his fits, the führer not only foamed at the mouth, but fell to the floor, biting into the carpet. What I would have given to see such a fit!

16. The tsar had been murdered with his entire family, including the little Tsarevich Alexander, a victim of the "royal disease," hemophilia.

17. National German Women's League leader.

18. A Nazi term for "fellow German."

19. *Nur aber ver knacken, dass die Schwarte knacht!*

20. It would take sixty-one years until Hanns, still living in England, was able to trace my whereabouts after the German version of my autobiography was published by Ullstein. His mother died just a year before we were able to reconnect.

Part Two
DESTRUCTION UNLIMITED

Hell is naked before Him, and destruction hath no covering.

—Job 26:6

Chapter Twenty-Nine

Conspirators

"Murder," she said, without lowering her voice, "they are contemplating murder!" Returning home one evening in the late summer of 1941, I was about to cross the hall into the garden, when my mother held me back. "Do not disturb them now," she warned. Through the open terrace door, I saw two men seated on the bench in the back of the yard, engaged in what seemed like a serious discussion.

The sun had already begun to set but I was able to identify one man as my father, the other as Colonel Achim Oster, a family friend. Both were in shirtsleeves, riding breeches, and high, shiny black boots, indicating they had returned from a ride through the Grunewald, the vast forest surrounding Berlin. While unable to understand the actual words, their gestures indicated the extremely urgent nature of the debate.

Since his brief and not very glorious guest appearance in the *Wehrmacht* had come to a sudden but not unexpected end, my father was once more a civilian. Unqualified for active duty due to his World War I head injury, he had been drafted to serve in a military mail censoring center in Berlin, with Admiral Wilhelm Canaris as his immediate superior. There, he used his position to provide employment for those among his friends considered politically unreliable or racially unfit by the Nazis. Furthermore, he had made it a habit to destroy mail that would have otherwise been detrimental for the writer or the recipient. Most of these letters had been secretly handed to him by a woman named Maria von Maltzan. It was not until after the fall of the Third Reich that her anti-Nazi activities were revealed. The Countess Maria von Maltzan, by profession a veterinarian, was a daredevil. In her ground floor apartment, she had hidden her Jewish lover, Hans Hirschel. Not only did he survive, but with him literally hundreds of Jews for whom she provided hiding places.

After someone snitched on my father, he was reported to the Gestapo. That someone later turned out to have been a teacher from my old school. Only the intercession of Canaris saved my father from a court-martial or worse. Hastily discharged from the *Wehrmacht*, with tremendous relief, he took off the hated uniform he had regarded as a personal insult and returned to civilian life.[1]

I remembered one specific evening before his dishonorable discharge, when I found him in the study, his revolver before him on the desk; he had been informed of his pending transfer to Paris. Noticing the horrified expression on my face, he explained that, rather than being forced to parade around the Nazi-occupied city wearing a German uniform, he would take his own life. The only reason for not going through with his plan was his family. What would become of us? So he tucked the little gun, an Ortgies 6.35, back in the desk drawer.

Discussions about a possible coup d'état that would end the life of the dictator had, for some time, been a normal conversation topic at home. Since our household staff had recently been reduced to Anna, talking without fear of being overheard and reported made us feel a lot safer. At some point, my parents had come to the decision that little could be accomplished by not saying "*Heil* Hitler" or refusing to join the party. The situation called for action, and if action included murder, so be it. The head of the snake had to be crushed.

Since June 26, 1941, the plan to kill Hitler seemed to have entered a new, more acute phase. On that day, I witnessed my father break into tears of helpless rage after the radio blared the triumphant news that the Germans had invaded the Soviet Union. Stalin, the führer's esteemed accomplice and ally in the satanic pact formed in September 1939, had—overnight—been turned into a despicable villain. Only twice before had I seen tears in my father's eyes: in 1934, when my Aunt Maria died of blood poisoning, and when Nazi bombs destroyed his beloved Rotterdam.

Several attempts on the führer's life, instigated by the same group of conspirators, had failed due to unforeseen circumstances, and time was running short. Each new day meant more destruction, more victims. But where, when, and under what circumstances would a coup have even a remote chance of succeeding? Who was there, not only willing to do the deed, but, at the same time, in a position to get close enough to the intended target? There was not merely the question of finding enough courageous, death-defying men ready to put their lives on the line; Hitler's death alone would not be the answer. What about Goering, Goebbels, and Himmler? How would the German people react? Would the armed forces be willing to accept a totally new situation? A new government?

Clandestine cells had formed all through the Reich, small enough to remain inconspicuous; would it be possible to unite them in a joint venture before being detected? In his search for dependable candidates, my father had even paid a visit to our neighbor, my uncle, Field Marshal Walther von Brauchitsch, forcibly retired by Hitler as Chief of Staff of the German Armed Forces. He could have saved himself the time and energy. With his second wife a raving Nazi, Uncle Walther declared he could not participate in such an underhanded action. My father considered himself fortunate not to be reported to the Gestapo.

The old military guard having long ago reached a state of total lethargy, declined their support. After Hitler had achieved supreme power, some among them came to the decision that, while secretly despising the führer, it might not be advantageous to stand in the way of his anti-Bolshevist crusade. Others maintained that an act of violence against Hitler was inconsistent with their alleged Christian faith, indicating that they were still bound by their oath of allegiance. All of these circumstances limited the number of people willing to risk their lives by participating in a plot at a point when highly organized resistance had been dismissed as out of the question for many years. With precious time slipping by, the circle of those carefully screened men permitted in the führer's immediate vicinity had dwindled to a handful, so that the chance of an actual assassination became more and more unlikely.

Chapter Thirty
Out of and Into School

After my high school education had come to an untimely end, just weeks before the war, my parents realized the necessity of removing me from the acute danger zone, fearing that Dr. Bach, the Nazi teacher and Gestapo informant responsible for my dismissal, might not be satisfied with my mere disappearance. One fact was clear: no other high school in the entire country would admit me as a student, let alone allow me to graduate.

My parents' concern about my status as a school dropout was surpassed only by my infinite relief. Since I was under eighteen, the mandatory age for admission to acting school, my father demanded that I learn an honest, respectable profession first, one of true and lasting value, like that of a secretary or a librarian. Even if I were not to be forced to earn my living, it would prepare me for my future as the spouse of a noble estate owner, the normal destiny for the granddaughter of two, and great-granddaughter of three Prussian generals. However, if at age eighteen, against all expectations, I still insisted on my foolish ambitions, he would solemnly promise to give his permission to take the state exams, where experts would hopefully confirm a total lack of talent, once and for all!

In order to get me out of danger, I was shipped off to Uncle Mirko's estate, not too far from Berlin, which he had purchased to keep his wife happy. The estate, which included fine horses, was vast and splendid. The castle-like manor, which had more rooms than I had ever seen under one roof, was surrounded by a moat and a beautifully landscaped park. There was only one issue that prevented me from reaching the state of happy oblivion: Uncle Mirko's wife, Olga. She disliked me the instant I arrived. Her disapproval changed to open resentment when she discovered that I was aware of something she tried to keep secret: Olga had a lover!

For this knowledge I deserved punishment, so I was given little, if any, opportunity to enjoy the countryside, to learn about farming and gardening, or to ride one of her superb horses. Instead, she decided that I should work, starting literally at the bottom, the cellar, where I was to appear at six o'clock each morning to peel mountains of potatoes under the cold eyes of "Mamsell," the chief cook, a rather unfortunate-looking spinster. The potatoes were not for our consumption, but for the Polish prisoners of war who worked as field hands, replacing the German men now bravely defending their fatherland in Poland.

Some of the POWs were usually delegated to help with the peeling, I liked their company; they were rough and tough but we had a good time singing and laughing as soon as the old battle-ax left the room. Soon my hands began to look a mess. Rubber gloves were out of the question A real *deutsche Frau* proudly displayed her cracked, red hands.

My only consolation was the weekends, when Uncle Mirko came from Berlin to spend two days with us. Two days during which the tall, young officer, stationed at the nearby Luftwaffe airfield, had to temporarily return to his quarters at the barracks. In her husband's presence, Olga knew better than to order me around; she treated me almost like a human being. Unfortunately, I made the fatal mistake of writing home about staying up until the wee hours of the morning, drinking champagne with the carefree guests that my uncle usually brought along. In true Russian tradition, the nights ended at daybreak with the glasses being smashed against the fireplace. Nobody ever told me to go to bed, so I didn't. After I had written the first detailed letter home, my stay at the estate came to a rather abrupt end; my mother came to pick me up herself. The conversation between her and Olga was held at a volume that did not require eavesdropping.

Within a month, I was sent to an agricultural school for girls in the little town of Miesbach in Bavaria, where I would have the guaranteed supervision needed for a seventeen-year-old. The best thing about the new location was that Kreuth was close by; I was permitted to go there each free weekend. One month after my arrival in Miesbach, an event took place that I was never to forget. Up until that point, I had been successful in withholding the fact that I was not in the Hitler Youth. My standard explanation had been that, while naturally a member in faraway Berlin, why on earth bother to transfer for a mere six months? After the war, I would often be lauded for my "courage" and even "heroism" by refusing to join this organization. But it was not so much courage, let alone heroism that kept me out. I simply loathed being one in a crowd; I hated the physical closeness of so many girls, the constant smell of sweat, marching in formation, and the loud singing. In short, it simply was a tendency to swim against the stream, which carried through my entire life—mostly for better and rarely for worse.

Unlike in many schools all over Germany, where delinquent girls were harassed and threatened beyond description, I do not remember unbearable pressure by the school authorities or my classmates, at least during the first years of the Nazi regime. As far as pressure from home was concerned—to hold out and not let myself be coerced into something I loathed—there was none either. On the contrary, my father told me that, in case I could not stand it anymore, I should join. He would understand. But I did not. I relished being regarded as an outcast; it was fun, and I truly enjoyed being rebellious.

One morning in the late fall of 1940, we were informed that our führer would be welcoming *Il Duce*, Benito Mussolini, at the Munich main railroad station, some forty-five minutes by train from Miesbach. Of course, we would all immediately don our Hitler Youth uniforms and hasten to the Bavarian capital so we could be part of the joyously cheering crowd. For me there was one snag: I had no uniform. Steadfastly maintaining that the package from home had not arrived yet, I lamented its possible loss in the mail. Luckily, one of my roommates took ill, and while she sobbed into her pillow with anger, I put on her uniform: a black skirt and white blouse, adorned with all sorts of obscene Nazi insignia and numerous swastikas. I was sure God would forgive me, but this spectacle, I swore, was not to take place without me!

Upon our arrival at the Munich station, not yet touched by bombs, an immense crowd awaited us, hooting and chanting in chorus, waving little paper swastika flags in wild anticipation. Just as the train from Rome was about to pull into the station, I managed to slip away from my companions and succeeded in wriggling my way into a front row, behind the police line, only a few feet from the red carpet. Soon, a triumphant cry from the crowd told of the glorious news: the train had arrived and the honored guest was greeted by his host, Adolf Hitler, whom Mussolini had allegedly called "a horrible sexual degenerate, resembling a plumber holding a chamber pot." Some of the people around me broke into tears. Seconds later, the two celebrities appeared, surrounded by the *Leibstandarte*, the führer's own SS guard, tailed by German and Italian functionaries in their black and yellow-brown uniforms.

Whatever one's opinion of Mussolini might have been, he was, without the slightest doubt, a *real* man—a male animal! His face was a deep tan, and dressed in the white uniform he might well have passed for one of those intrepid stage bandits from a Viennese operetta. Rolling his eyeballs and flashing a mouthful of pearly white teeth, he paid little, if any, attention to Hitler's deplorable figure at his side, who was desperately trying to keep up with the short-legged guest's fast pace. For a few seconds both were close enough for me to almost touch them.

Here he was again, the same man whose limp, fishy hand I had touched a few years ago, according to himself the greatest strategist of all time, who had built his power on two principles: chaos and violence. A petit bourgeois, he felt at ease only among his chauffeurs and secretaries, listening to the same platitudes as well as to his own monologues day in and day out. He was known for his habit of watching two German movies each evening and sleeping until noon the next day, and for publicly boasting about not having to learn anything anymore because, "already as a young man in Vienna, he knew everything." Vienna—where he had spent many months in an asylum for homeless men, unable to find a decent place to live for lack of funds and an acceptable position for lack of qualifications.

His left hand clutched his belt buckle tightly; every few seconds his right hand flew up in the German jackknife salute, and was then bent back at the elbow. His eyes were hidden under the enormous peak of a uniform cap, his face a pasty greenish color. The ill-fitting brown garb underscored the shortcomings of his rather unfortunate proportions, featuring narrow shoulders and wide hips.

All of a sudden, unlike in Eberswalde, I felt an irresistible impulse to throw up, remembering the latest rumors that his discarded underpants, probably knitted cotton long johns, were secretly sold by his staff, cut into little pieces, for which lovesick female admirers paid astronomical prices before ultimately kissing them to shreds. A buxom matron in a Bavarian dirndl outfit broke through the police line, threw herself to the ground, and kissed the spot her führer's revered foot had just touched. For the rest of my life I would remember the ecstatic expression on her face when SS-men led her away.

Somehow the months at school passed, and, after finding myself back in Berlin in the spring of 1941, I had to get used to the restrictions the war imposed on all of us—the relentlessly enforced blackout, increasing air raids, and a noticeable shortage of food, coal, and other vital supplies. However, I was young, we were all in the same boat, the house was still intact, and what else but my future career could possibly be of any real interest to me?

Chapter Thirty-One
An Aspiring Actress

The entrance exam for future actors and actresses was scheduled to be held on the stage of the Berlin State Theater, and I had but a month to prepare myself. It was Ditte's mother, the only grown-up who wholeheartedly approved of my plans, who rehearsed with me the parts that I would recite in the audition: Schiller's Maid of Orleans, Shakespeare's Juliet, and, unfortunately, Gretchen from Goethe's *Faust*. On the given day, half dead with stage fright, I entered the theater, an imposing structure in the center of Berlin. I was one among thirty candidates. After being called by name, I climbed the steps leading to the stage. The glaring footlights prevented me from being able to identify any audience members—famous people, teachers, directors, actresses, and actors—who would determine my fate. Somehow, I managed to get halfway through the Maid's monologue, when I was interrupted. Did I have anything else? Dismayed, I began Gretchen's famous prayer, piously kneeling down on the hard stage floor. After the first few lines, I became aware of a terrifying noise coming from the auditorium. It sounded like sobbing; had I really been able to touch someone's heart?

But once more I was cut off by the same male voice. The house lights went on, and the stage lights were turned off. What I noticed bordered on naked disaster; among the two dozen people, some of whom I now recognized, was one actor who hid behind a gigantic white handkerchief, his belly shaking like a huge pudding. To my horror, he was having an uncontrollable laughing fit! I almost sank to the floor in embarrassment. Another famous character actor, Walter Franck, whom I particularly admired, managed to climb on stage. He, too, had obviously been vastly amused by so much tragedy. After clearing his throat and drying his eyes, he was finally able to say, "Well, well, little lady, no doubt you have talent, you even have a lot of talent! But for God's sake, no prayers, no tragedies, please! The Maid? Holy smoke! And Gretchen? Ridiculous! You are a born comedienne!"

Comedienne? I felt limp, already having pictured myself as another Eleanora Duse. "Go home," he added, aware of the devastated look on my face. He gently put his arm around my shoulders in a fatherly gesture and continued, "You will hear from us," as he stepped back down into the auditorium.

"Next one, please."

Somehow I reached home and snuck up the stairs to the safety of my room. What I felt was an overwhelming desire to drop dead. The question was how? There was no poison available, no cup of hemlock, no handy dagger. Jumping out of the window would land me on a soft flowerbed. I could think of no way by which to dramatically and radically end my miserable life as a total failure. So I just sat on a chair, brooding until nightfall. The ringing of the bell announced my father's return from the office. How would I face him? How was I to deal with his relief, if not gloating, over my lack of talent? The telephone rang. Ten minutes later I heard my father coming up the stairs, as usual taking two steps at a time, appearing in my doorway. Before I had a chance to blurt out the disgusting details of my misfortune, he said, "I just received a phone call from Walter Franck; he wants you as his private student."

More surprising than this unbelievable bit of news was something in my father's voice: pride! He was proud of me!

Franck accepted only one private student every two years. Being among the handful of star actors at the Berlin State Theater, he could barely afford the hours as a teacher at the Academy. There were rumors that his steadfast refusal to accept parts in Nazi films, plus his constant absence from the magnificent parties that Goebbels threw at his home, had put him on the propaganda minister's blacklist. Goebbels had taken over the movie industry, singlehandedly deciding not only what kind of films were made, but also who was and who was not to appear in them. Pretty young starlets soon found out there was only one way to stardom, through the limping little Don Juan's bed, much to the chagrin of his wife, Magda Goebbels.

Unlike the film industry, the Berlin State Theater was the undisputed domain of Hermann Goering, who did not particularly care for Goebbels' obsession with female movie stars. Just to annoy Goebbels, Goering permitted himself the luxury of even tolerating actors and actresses with Jewish spouses to remain under "his" roof. Goebbels fumed over the fact that the führer had made it perfectly clear that Goering, his accomplice in the 1923 Beer Hall Putsch and destined successor in office, was untouchable. Goering enjoyed flexing his muscles to demonstrate his power to the man he despised. Consequently, under the safe wings of their obese protector, at least a dozen non-Aryan spouses were exempt from persecution, deportation, or worse. Unlike their benefactor, most of them would survive the reign of the Third Reich.

My training for the stage had one fringe benefit that was not to be underestimated; like all actresses and dancers, thanks to a decree by Goebbels himself, I was now exempt from the dreaded *Arbeitsdienst*, the "Labor Service," a mandatory duty of six month of hard physical work in the hated Nazi uniform on farms and fields. Additionally, my non-membership in the Hitler Youth was old news. Goebbels had decided that culture came before anything else, especially where young future stars with their beautiful bodies, pretty hands, and dainty feet were concerned, which would be ruined by hard labor.

My new teacher had come to the decision that I should not attend the actual State Academy, but receive my training from him and a few competent mentors he had picked out for me. My lessons with him took place in the study of his private residence, and in time I lost my feeling of awe toward the man who, over the span of two years, opened the doors to a completely new world for me.

Coming from a Prussian home, where politics had prevailed as the only discussion topic, I had barely heard of August Strindberg, was totally ignorant of the existence of Kurt Tucholsky, Frank Wedekind, Franz Kafka, Bertolt Brecht, Kurt Weill, and all the other authors whose books had been burned. Now I learned about the actors, directors, composers, singers, and writers who had been stricken from the curriculum in public schools. Franck told me about Elisabeth Bergner, his colleague and close friend, now safely in England, of Fritz Kortner in California, and about Marlene Dietrich, the goddess, the world star, who had steadfastly turned down all offers by Hitler, promising her a triumphant return to Germany. But Hitler's world was not her world, and his Germany was not her home anymore.[2]

My various activities kept me busy. Each day I spent many hours at the barres of Tatjana Gsovsky's famous ballet school, studying classical ballet and modern dance. Margret Langen, considered the number one voice teacher in Germany, taught me to speak and to sing. She also let me in on the secret of correct breathing. God alone knew how I had managed to breathe all the years prior. She squeezed my stomach like a rubber cushion.

After Hitler declared war against the Soviet Union on June 26, 1941, the news reached us that Pastor Niemoeller had been transferred from Sachsenhausen Concentration Camp to Dachau.

Chapter Thirty-Two
A Visit Home

On March 17, 1941, a bitter cold night, Adolf Hitler's personal prisoner was awakened by his guards. He thought there could only be one reason: they were going to drag him to the gallows; executions often took place during the night. To his surprise, he was handed his own clothes, led outside his block to a waiting black limousine, and told to climb in with three Gestapo officials. One of the officials said, "Pastor Niemoeller, we have orders by the führer to take you to Elberfeld for a visit with your father, who has just suffered a stroke." The prisoner could not believe his ears.

In Elberfeld, three hundred and fifty miles away, he found the entire block of his parents' residence surrounded by heavily armed police. No one was allowed to step outside the houses; Germany's most dangerous criminal was expected to arrive in their midst.

Martin found the patient in bed. He was fully conscious and even managed a lopsided smile to greet his son.

"Who brought you here?" Heinrich Niemoeller whispered.

"The Gestapo, father," Martin replied.

Then Heinrich turned to his wife and said, "Paula, give each man a cigar!" Noticing the grim expression on her face, he added, "But not a black one!" The black cigars were his pride and joy; they were expensive, usually gifts, reserved for Sundays only and would, even now, certainly not be wasted on Nazis.

While Martin sat by his father's bedside, a Gestapo official, seated behind a screen, took notes of their conversation. Martin took the old man's hand, and Heinrich said, "Do not ever forget, son, that a lot of people all over the world, even the Eskimos, are praying for you. You must not lose hope!" He continued, quoting Scripture, "Behold, I die: but God shall be with you, and bring you again into the land of your fathers."

His son, after three years of solitary confinement, could not grasp that he was being remembered by anybody. He had no idea that even Mahatma Gandhi was heard to say: "I do not believe that the sufferings of Pastor Niemoeller and others have been in vain. They have preserved their self-respect intact. They have proved that their faith was equal to any suffering." He had no way of knowing that his last twenty-eight Dahlem sermons, living testimony of his courageous resistance against evil, were smuggled to Switzerland and ultimately published. None other than Thomas Mann, the famous German author and Nobel Prize recipient, himself a refugee, wrote the moving foreword.[3]

On December 23, 1940, Martin's portrait appeared on the cover of *Time Magazine*. Depicted to his right was the Christian cross, and to his left was the pastor's emaciated body under the whip of an SA man. The cover was captioned: "Martyr of 1940. In Germany only the cross has not bowed to the swastika." But while the cross, meaning the church, might not yet have collapsed, it was now severely bent.[4]

Since it was late in the day when the limousine left Elberfeld in the direction of Sachsenhausen, the decision was reached to stay in some little town overnight. The prisoner was taken to the local police prison. The cell was filthy and the bed crawling with vermin, so the worn-out man preferred to pass the night sitting up on a hard wooden chair. The former naval officer, trained to rest wherever and whenever he had a chance, slept soundly.

In July 1941, Martin was once again ordered to gather his belongings, and in the company of three other inmates who were Catholic priests, he was taken in an open car all the way to Bavaria, the final destination being Dachau Concentration Camp. Upon arrival, he was locked up in the special cell block for political prisoners.

His new domicile did have a window, but it was small, grated, and the only view it offered was the gallows. And the gallows were used every single day. The prisoner suspected that there was a purpose behind it; witnessing the executions was supposed to break his spirit. But Martin was now far from broken; the new pattern of life seemed to have given him a boost. He was allowed to read books, and he resumed his studies of Roman Catholicism, which he had begun earlier in his imprisonment. Greatly bothered by the indifference of his own church, which seemed to have forsaken him, he began to immerse himself in the Catholic breviary that someone had slipped into his cell in Sachsenhausen. With growing fascination, he found himself closer and closer to conversion. Soon it seemed more than just a rumor making the rounds in Protestant circles; Pastor Niemoeller would embrace the Roman Catholic faith.

While he himself did not suspect that the breviary was put into his hands with the full intent of getting him to convert, the three priests in his block sensed foul play. They even wondered if they themselves might have been purposely placed close to the Protestant clergyman in the hope that their influence might speed up a conversion. What an ultimate triumph it would be to inform the Confessing Church that their revered leader was nothing but a turncoat! But Hitler hoped in vain. The priests made it clear to the pastor that a step of such magnitude must, under no circumstances, be taken under pressure, but would have to be postponed until he was a free man. Michael Hoeck, closest to Niemoeller, even quoted Frederick the Great: "If I should happen to be taken prisoner, any orders I give must be disobeyed." Much to the relief of family and friends, this settled the problem once and for all; Martin Niemoeller would never convert.

Several times over the previous years, the pastor had rejected the chance to be free in exchange for a solemn oath to never again interfere with the führer's orders. For the rest of his days, he claimed that it was Hitler who ultimately saved his life. He knew that, in spite of any promise, once outside, he would have resumed his resistance. The transfer to Dachau had a positive consequence; the prisoner, in spite of all the hardships, now seemed to recuperate from his depression and gain back his mental and spiritual balance.

As far as the activities outside his window were concerned, he noticed that the "hanging crews" changed with every execution. Some of the SS guards volunteered for this gruesome job only because of the generous extra ration of Schnapps, a reward that accompanied each hanging. It was supposed to dull the senses and raise the henchmen's spirit. The view of the gallows, the constant cracking of gunfire at night, and the screaming of the tortured and the dying would haunt Martin for the rest of his days. "I knew that at any time it pleased Hitler, it could be I being strung up there," he later said. "And I was afraid that those who murdered me, an innocent man, would provoke God's wrath and ultimately die in disbelief."[5]

Over the subsequent period of four years, whenever permitted, the three Catholic priests and the Protestant pastor studied the Bible together, with no further mention of conversion. Five times they worked their way through the entire Holy Scripture. During those precious hours, it seemed that the walls of their cell vanished and the bars disappeared.

Pope Pius XII, deaf to the suffering of the Jews and equally unwilling to get involved with the fate of the other imprisoned Catholic clergy in the concentration camps, sent a monthly package of food to the three priests in the political block, from which the Protestant pastor received his share. While Polish Catholic bishops were murdered in the camps, Pius was deeply grateful to the führer for not imprisoning or killing an equally high-ranking German Catholic dignitary, which may explain that the mass murderer Hitler, who would never officially leave the Roman church, was not excommunicated by the Vatican, neither during his evil life nor after his death.

The ordinary captive priests received no packages; they were tortured, starved, and died on the gallows just like all the other victims.

The prisoners in the political block were living in a ghetto within a ghetto, a prison within a prison. Their only contacts, other than with each other, were the special SS guards. The block was equally taboo for ordinary SS or other prisoners, let alone visitors. Once in a great while, a death candidate was allowed a few minutes with either one of the priests or the pastor, before being led to his execution. Among them were political offenders, Communists, deserters, and homosexuals.

At irregular intervals, the inmates of the political block were taken outside to walk in a walled-in yard behind their cell block. At one of these occasions, Niemoeller met Richard "Dick" Stevens. The British colonel, like himself, had years of solitary confinement behind him, at times chained to the wall. With his friend and colleague, Captain S. Payne Best, he had been kidnapped by the Gestapo from Dutch soil during the so-called "Venlo Incident" on November 9, 1939, accused of participating in a "conspiracy against the führer" and charged without a trial as the true brains behind Georg Elser's ill-fated attempt on Hitler's life in the Munich Bürgerbräukeller.[6] The former German U-boat commander and the British colonel soon formed a friendship that would far outlast their years in captivity.[7]

Dick Stevens enjoyed a number of special privileges, indicating Hitler's intention to use him as a possible pawn someday. In his cell, considerable bigger than the others, he was permitted English books, which he shared with Niemoeller, enabling him to vastly improve his knowledge of the English language. Through mysterious connections, Stevens somehow gained possession of a little radio, which was eventually rigged by an inmate electrician for reception of the BBC, information from which he passed on to his fellow prisoners.

On January 14, 1942, Dachau prisoner number 26679, now in captivity for four and a half years, celebrated his fiftieth birthday. Dick Stevens had a surprise for him; according to the BBC, a special service was held in London in honor of the incarcerated hero. Taking place in St. Martin-in-the-Fields, the ceremony was conducted by the Archbishop of Canterbury William Temple, with the Bishop of Chichester George Bell delivering the "birthday" sermon. This news left Niemoeller deeply moved: "To think that I was remembered in faraway Trafalgar Square and learned about it in the solitary confinement of my cell in Dachau!" The event in London infuriated Hitler and Goebbels.

Outside of the ghetto within a ghetto, Dachau was still a concentration camp of the worst kind. Daily, desperate prisoners threw themselves onto the electrified wire fence; one of them was a Soviet POW, Lieutenant Joseph Stalin, son of the Soviet dictator. The electric current, unfortunately, did not kill him. He writhed in agony on the ground, until a guard finished him off with a well-aimed shot. However, neither screams nor gunshots seemed to reach the ears of those citizens living their comfortable lives in the medieval and peaceful little town of Dachau, a stone throw from the concentration camp. Or did they?

Chapter Thirty-Three
GOOD-BYE TO MY GODFATHER

On June 4, 1941, after more than twenty years in exile, Germany's last emperor joined his illustrious ancestors. Wilhelm II of the House of Hohenzollern, who could trace his lineage back almost a thousand years to Burchardus de Zolorin, succumbed to cardiac failure, following several minor heart seizures over the previous months. He was eighty-one.

The Nazi authorities granted my father a visa, enabling him to arrange the funeral. Ever since the German invasion of Holland, it had become increasingly difficult for my father to report to his employer in Doorn and straighten out the confused old man about world events, well aware that, as soon as he turned his back, the kaiser fell prey not just to the evil influence of his second wife, but to all those who flattered his inflated ego by agreeing with whatever he said or did.

He had even seen fit to celebrate the rape of France by the Nazis with a telegram addressed to Hitler, praising this "tremendous victory of our wonderful troops." The führer, in a patronizing mood, had been gracious enough to honor this undignified message with a cool reply. My father sadly realized that in all the years prior to the old man's demise, he had not once expressed the slightest remorse about possible mistakes he might have made while still in power. There had been no insight, no self-incrimination, no regret, no catharsis. Instead, he never tired of eagerly blaming his own failures on various scapegoats.

After the ex-monarch's refusal to accept an offer of asylum by the British royal family, following the Nazi occupation of the Netherlands, Hitler placed House Doorn under "special protection." The German *Wehrmacht*, later replaced by the SS, were in charge of safeguarding the imperial clan. Nobody was permitted to enter or leave the compound without special passes. Wilhelm found himself living in a gilded cage, one he did not even wish to leave anymore after a particularly hurtful incident.

On a cold winter afternoon, he had taken a walk in the park, where he met with a young German soldier standing guard. The old man jovially greeted the boy who, with baby blue eyes, stared at the elderly man. Not only had the youngster failed to recognize him, but in the brief conversation that followed, he displayed total ignorance about the Hohenzollerns, the monarchy in general, and the kaiser in particular. The bitter realization that he was forgotten broke Wilhelm's heart. From that day on, his health took a turn for the worse. Recurring fainting spells eventually confined him to his bed, and on June 4, after seventeen hours of agony, his tormented heart finally stood still.

Following Wilhelm's death, my father arrived in Doorn and immediately went upstairs where the old man lay in state. At the door he almost fainted. The deceased, a peaceful expression on his face, lay on his deathbed in one of his flashy uniforms covered with decorations, the ring-adorned hands folded on his chest on which a bouquet of white roses from the garden had been placed. Seated on a chair by the bed was his "distraught" widow, Hermine, busily scribbling obituary notices, spreading the cards and the envelopes on the dead man's body for the ink to dry. From the windowsill, the radio blared triumphant German Army communiqués at full volume. Seized with speechless rage, my father first turned the radio off and then removed the cards from the bed. Hermine was too dumbfounded to break into her usual shrieks of hysteria.

Hitler considered it beneath his dignity to attend the imperial funeral in person, ordering his deputy, the *Reichskommissar* for the Netherlands, Arthur Seyss-Inquart, to pay the respects in his stead. So my father, as chief of protocol, would have the dubious pleasure of welcoming the gangster with his brown entourage during this historic act, which marked the end of an era.

Wilhelm's last will and testament had determined that the little chapel next to the main entrance gate should serve as a temporary resting place for his body, which was later to be transferred to a small mausoleum yet to be built according to his own plans in the park. A burial in Germany was never even discussed, the ex-kaiser furiously refusing to honor the German people with his presence. After all, they had denied him the throne that was his by God's (not the people's) grace. It never entered his mind that it was he who had forsaken his people after the lost war.

On a gorgeous summer day, with all the flowers in the park in full bloom and birds singing, the somber funeral procession wound its way from the manor to the chapel. The four corners of the black cloth covering the casket were held by four of his faithful, with my father walking next to the cortege. He owed this last honor to the man whom he had constantly tried to protect from his most potent enemy—himself. Wilhelm, up to the end, had remained the conceited, stubborn, moody, and totally incorrigible "old child" that my father had often criticized and even cursed, yet had never ceased to love with the kind of devotion that could only be explained by the mysterious and never disclosed bond of blood. Behind the casket walked the black-veiled widow, the crown prince, crown princess, and other members of the immediate family.

Trailing at the distance my father had set for them, stomped the Nazi gangsters and representatives of the German Armed Forces.

For the last time, honor guards presented arms while a military band intoned the kaiser's favorite hymn. Since he had not wanted a eulogy, passages from the Bible were read by the "court preacher" Pastor Döhring from Berlin, who emptied a golden chalice filled with German soil over the casket, a moment that brought tears to almost everybody's eyes. The brief ceremony ended with another hymn and after that the "Yorckscher Marsch," the military marching tune favored by Germany's unfortunate ruler, who had begun to fade into history.

My father returned to Berlin, his suitcases filled with his own effects and clothing items that had belonged to the last emperor; among them Wilhelm's gray British Field Marshal uniform and a pair of almost unused shiny brown riding boots. With clothes now strictly rationed, a tailor transformed the uniform into a suit for me, successfully solving the problem of the left short sleeve, and a clever shoemaker shortened the riding boots to my size. My father kept for himself the coat that the kaiser had worn on their walks together.

Many years after my father's life had ended in tragedy, I decided to visit Doorn. After all, it was the place where he had spent so much time and energy in wasted efforts to fight off real and imaginary intrigues, to talk sense into the stubborn old fool he loved. He had been, as the kaiser's biographer Reinhold Schneider formulated it, "his master's most faithful, yet his most critical, servant." Immediately after the war, the Dutch government, in a swift and smart move, confiscated the mansion and declared it a museum open to the public. This clever motion, although not quite legal in view of the fact that it had been bought and paid for by the ex-kaiser, prevented the Hohenzollern family from stripping it. Everything remained in its place for tourists to admire.

Having traveled by train from Berlin to Amsterdam and on to Utrecht, I spent the night in a shabby hotel. Too late I realized the true nature of the establishment when certain unmistakable noises reached my ears through the paper-thin walls. My only companion was a very hungry flea. The next morning, after a short bus ride, I found myself in the sleepy, immaculately clean little town of Doorn, headed straight for the "Schloss."

Entertaining the remote hope of still finding someone who had known my father, I revealed my identity at the gate. To my surprise, the lady selling tickets nodded eagerly. "Yes, yes, gracious baroness," she said, "there is someone, let me get him." I felt my knees giving way from under me. After a few minutes she appeared again, dragging a little old man behind her. Coming closer, he took a good look at me and immediately broke into sobs: "The baron's daughter, oh, I can see the resemblance! I was the *Herr Baron*'s personal valet. Such a fine, good gentleman, always he shook hands with me and opened the door when he saw me carrying a heavy tray." Tears rolled down his wrinkled face. Yes, that was my father!

Bowing deep, overcome with emotion, he seized my hand to kiss it and insisted on taking me around the premises himself, showing me everything, including places off-limits for tourists. I followed him to the mansion and across the moat bridge where my father and Wilhelm had fed the ducks from a little basket carried by the kaiser's valet, the one who later hastened to join the German *Waffen*-SS. Walking through the rooms, with each step I felt my father's presence more painfully than ever before. He was everywhere. My guide took me through the downstairs rooms; he did not have to explain, because it all seemed familiar, as if I had just left. There was the dining room with its large round table, where the frugal meals were served. Those unfortunates seated at a distance from the emperor often hoped in vain of being able to clear their plates before the kaiser put down his knife and fork, the signal for everybody to stop eating.

Upstairs in the kaiser's bedroom, I noticed the narrow bedstead where Germany's last monarch had taken his final breath, the dressing table with all the family photographs in silver frames, and his most personal and intimate utensils, including the silver hairbrush and comb, as if the kaiser had just put them down. Seeing these paraphernalia was almost more than I could take.

Leaving the main building, I was taken to the "Orangerie," my father's quarters, his home away from home. There was the glass entrance door, the one the sobbing old man had frequently knocked on in the middle of the night, seeking comfort with his confidant after having escaped his wife's never ending hysterical outbreaks. Back at the gate, I embraced my companion, a last link to my father. I did not cry; tears would have to wait. I did not even allow myself a look back, knowing I would never return.

Chapter Thirty-Four
The Incipient Actress

In Berlin, under the superb mentorship of Walter Franck, I continued my studies, which filled my days to the brim. In the evenings, I would usually watch a performance from the wings in the Staatstheater and return by subway late at night. In case of a night air raid, carried out exclusively by the British Royal Air Force, I sought shelter in an underground station. My strongly developed sixth sense, inherited from my mother, told me that I had nothing to fear from the bombs. That sense would never betray me, even when, late in the war, air raids became more frequent and deadly. Often I would find myself in the cellar of an unknown house, when something told me to leave. Ignoring the angry orders of the air raid wardens, I would run across the street into another building, later to find the place I had left in ruins.

My busy schedule magically transported me from the bleak realities of the war into a world of make-believe, giving me the opportunity to escape the depressing atmosphere at home. Every morning, on the way to the subway, I put myself through the kind of transformation I considered of vital importance for a future stage and movie star. Since, in our Prussian home, the use of make-up, lipstick, nail polish, skirts above the knee, and high heels were frowned upon, I saw myself forced to resort to certain devious activities.

I had paid little, if any, attention to the constant tongue-clucking of my bigoted grandmother about my appearance, but even my adored but hopelessly old-fashioned father had made it clear that only women of a certain, unmentionable profession resorted to making themselves up. No daughter of his would ever sink low enough to run around painted like such a creature. Each morning, on my way either to lessons with Walter Franck, my voice teacher, or the ballet studio, I snuck into a telephone booth, no longer in working order, located next to the Dahlem subway station, which I used as a makeshift dressing room. There, making sure nobody was watching, I underwent a fast but rather thorough metamorphosis. After spreading my tools on the telephone directory, I applied lipstick and powder and, with the help of black or green mascara, turned my eyelashes into fly legs, pulled up my skirt to knee length, changed into high-heeled pumps, and finally marched out of the booth as the demimonde I once had intended to become. On my way back home, the procedure would have to be reversed.

My parents' interest in my education was, to say the least, limited. I was never asked for details. My father's only comment on my ballet training consisted of dry remarks about the shape of my legs, which began to resemble champagne bottles.

My little brother had been shipped off to boarding school. Since he was fortunate enough to be a male and, furthermore, the sole heir to an illustrious name, an institution like the one in Eberswalde, where I had suffered for two whole years, would not be good enough. He was sent to the elite Salem School, the first coeducational facility on German soil, located in a beautiful ancient castle on Lake Konstanz, where European royalty sent their children. Its founder Kurt Hahn, a Jew, had been able to escape to the safety of Britain, where he immediately opened another school much in the same style as Salem, not only preferred by the British royal family, but by other European nobles. My parents hoped that by taking this step, their fifteen-year-old-son would be spared membership in the Hitler Youth, mandatory since 1939.

Ditte had left Berlin to take up her studies in Heidelberg. She had managed the impossible! By boldly presenting false information concerning her Aryan background, after a few days of anxious waiting, she received the news that she had been accepted as a regular student at one of the world's most renowned universities. I had visited her during summer vacation, and upon my return home, Anna gave me one look to let me know that she knew, and she did not like what she knew!

"Lamb," she said, "what have you been doing?" Not expecting an answer, at least not a truthful one, she began to lament the fact that Pastor Niemoeller was not available to teach me about morals. My grandmother, inquiring about my unchaperoned vacation, asked the inevitable question if there had been students of "our caste." No need for her to know about one particular student, who had shown me that making love did not necessarily have to be limited to kisses. As far as his noble descent was concerned, the nephew of the Shah of Iran would easily outrank most German aristocrats.

In the fall of 1941, an order was issued, by which Jews in Germany and in the Nazi-occupied territories had to wear a visible sign of their status as outcasts on their clothing: called a "*Judenstern*," it was a yellow Star of David with "Jew" printed in letters resembling the Hebrew script in the center. With this mark worn openly and not hidden under shawls and scarves, Jews were easy targets, and any man, woman, or child caught without it faced harsh consequences. In addition to this measure, everyone had either "Israel" or "Sarah" added to the name on their identification cards, depending upon gender. Not long after these new rules went into effect, our doorbell rang; outside the gate stood Anita Frank. Of the Jewish girls in my class, she was the one who had been closest to me. However, after returning from boarding school, she seemed to have vanished from her Dahlem residence without a trace. All my efforts to find her had been unsuccessful.

We were both happy to see one another, and she told me that her widowed mother had gone to Switzerland to marry a Swiss citizen, her goal being that she would be allowed to import Anita and Anita's little brother, Reinhard. Although Switzerland steadfastly refused to admit the children, she hoped that, in time, the necessary visa could be obtained. After her mother's departure, Anita found herself alone with little Reinhard, to whom she would now have to be father and mother. Totally abandoned, they went to live in various residences in the city of Berlin until the day when even the Jewish schools were closed. Eventually Anita found a position as a nurse in training in the Jewish Hospital, located in the north of the city, where thirteen-year-old Reinhard found work as an electrician's apprentice.

Two years after her disappearance from my life, Anita decided to take a chance and visit me. She had even boldly removed the *Judenstern* from her jacket, because traveling by public transportation was among the many restrictions imposed on the Jews. With her brown curls, she could easily pass for a farm girl from Pomerania. Unfortunately, there was not much we could do for her. She refused even the remotest suggestion to go underground and become a "U-boat," a practice that had just begun, maintaining that young Reinhard looked far too Jewish for anyone to risk his life by hiding him. A friend of their mother had urged Anita to come and live under an assumed identity on her estate, but she had declined to extend the offer to Anita's brother.

Although Reinhard urged his sister to try and cross over the mountains into Switzerland with him, she would not hear of it, maintaining in her boundless optimism that they were better off trying to survive in Berlin. With or without a valid visa, they now would not gain permission to leave Germany. Many years later, I would learn that Anita Frank had died of typhoid in Bergen-Belsen just days before the liberation. The Nazis, formerly eager to get rid of Jews, had closed the borders. The Jews found themselves in a deadly trap.[8]

Chapter Thirty-Five
The War Comes Closer to Home

Before 1941 ended, our friends Otto and Edith Stargardt were evicted from their spacious home on Schorlemerallee in Dahlem. They were issued a new domicile on the second floor of a so-called "*Judenhaus*" ("Jew house") right around the corner from us, owned by an elderly couple living in a "privileged marriage," meaning that the husband was Jewish and the wife was Aryan. Uncle Otto and Aunt Edith were permitted to take some furniture as well as other personal belongings. The fact that they both had been inducted as forced laborers at the Siemenswerke, in the north of Berlin, led them to believe that they were exempt from deportation. Each day at dawn, the old couple, wearing their yellow stars, set off on foot for the two-hour walk to work, returning home late at night. Grateful still to live among friends, all of whom contributed to their livelihood, they bore their hard lot with dignity and amazing stamina.

For years Otto had rejected the urgent invitations from his wife's son to join him in America. They were even in possession of a visa, which was now void, since the United States had entered the war against Nazi Germany. The former high-ranking judge, a decorated veteran, had steadfastly ignored the impending consequences, maintaining that, since they had not done anything wrong, nothing bad would happen to them. So far, unlike the overwhelming majority of German Jews, they had miraculously been spared abuse and maltreatment. In Otto's opinion, even Hitler had to respect those German Jews who had proven their patriotism and courage in World War I, when Jewish officers and soldiers had fought alongside their Christian comrades. At a time when Jews had just begun to disappear rather than be carted to an unknown destination, Otto deemed all suggestions to go into hiding as undignified. He seemed almost relieved when, in the spring of 1942, the inevitable happened. The Gestapo barged into the *Judenhaus* and announced that Otto Israel and Edith Sarah Stargardt were to report to the Grunewald railroad station the following morning for deportation. The sooner we go, Otto imagined, the sooner we will be back home again. His logic was breathtaking.[9]

The Stargardts were ordered to pack a suitcase with the bare necessities and move downstairs to spend the night with the other inhabitants of the house. The doors to their rooms were then sealed, and all their belongings were confiscated, to be picked up the next day. Confiscated? Meaning that all those beautiful things that they had been able to save from their house would fall into the filthy hands of those savages? My mother perked up her ears, which meant that this would most likely not happen as long as she had her way.

With my father out of town and Uncle Otto considered useless in illegal undertakings, the two women worked out a hair-raising scheme. My cunning mother, in her infinite resourcefulness and with the help of a ladder, determined that the balcony door was not sealed; it was not even locked. All they had to do was wait until nightfall in order to carry out a sinister plot, which required fervent prayers that no air raid or nosy neighbor might bring the devious action they planned—and possibly their lives—to an untimely end. The new moon was on their side, and soon the blackout, usually cursed but in this case highly praised, wrapped the residential streets of Dahlem in pitch-black darkness.

The little wagon, in which my brother and I had spent happy childhood hours, was the designated moving van, the only possible means by which as much furniture as possible could be carted to our house. Once a mere toy, it had lately advanced to the status of a multipurpose vehicle, suitable for carting wood and coal rations as well as horse manure for the garden in the summer, pine cones for heating the stove in the winter, and transporting suitcases to the bus stop or debris to the garbage dump.

Using utmost caution, flashlight in hand, my mother was the one to climb bravely up the ladder and enter the Stargardts' apartment through the unlocked balcony door. Aunt Edith, not fit for such acrobatic ventures, was sure the Gestapo official had not yet bothered to take inventory, so they might as well settle for the most valuable pieces. Aunt Edith chose a little antique Gobelin sofa with matching chairs, a gold-painted wooden rocking chair, an elegant bedroom dresser, several carpets, and silverware. Countless photos, family pictures, and precious documents had been taken to our house months before, which were safely stashed between books in the library.

It took half the night, hours of dragging, lugging, pushing, and lifting, but the bold action went undetected and undisturbed. Even the British bomber pilots seemed to sense the necessity to stay away from Berlin for just this one night. Before the break of dawn, the last item had been safely stacked in our house, where all of it would survive the bombs and even the battle of Berlin, to be returned one day to their rightful and overjoyed owners.

After the risky venture was accomplished, two totally exhausted women sank down on the steps to our house, seized by a hysterical laughing fit over the dimensions of their bizarre situation. Only now did they fully realize the dangers that they had just escaped. What if only one neighbor had watched and snitched? What if the sirens had forced them off the street? They laughed so hard that they cried, holding each other, and by their unrestrained shrieking, they rid themselves of the unbearable nervous tension of hours past.

That same day, the little wagon was used to transport the baggage to the Grunewald station where my mother, now fully realizing the horrible reality, waved a tearful goodbye to her friends. Uncle Otto and Aunt Edith were sent to Terezin, the ghetto reserved for prominent Jews, where they were liberated by the Soviet Army one day before their deportation to Auschwitz.[10]

Chapter Thirty-Six
Shortages

Within the Reich, shortages of all consumer goods were now more noticeable. This did not mean that anybody went hungry, because whatever was needed on the home front was blatantly robbed from the occupied territories, which were ultimately bled dry. Unrationed and in ample supply were the air attacks. "I will change my name to Mayer," the fat *Reichsmarschall* Goering had announced, "if only one single enemy plane drops one single bomb on German soil." However, soon there was no place in Germany out of reach for the British Royal Air Force, later fortified by the American bomber fleet, and hardly a day passed without the sirens announcing another visit.

"We shall erase their cities," Hitler had proclaimed, his threats immediately followed by attacks. While the heavy damage reported from London and Coventry and the high loss of life during the "blitz" were declared justifiable means of war, the air raids over Germany were branded as acts of terror.

Our house was not equipped with even a makeshift shelter, which meant that we spent the raids in what used to be a recreation room in the basement. No sound escaped us, and we soon became experts in identifying the various types of bombs by the noise they made on their way down. Some roared, thundered, and rumbled, while others swished, rustled, and whistled. Allegedly, you never heard the bomb that would turn you to ashes in the rubble of your home. My mother, completely fearless, rejected all suggestions to seek refuge in the public shelter a few blocks away, convinced that in order to save her house, she had to stay in or very close to it. While an air mine would have killed us on the spot, an incendiary bomb could at least be heard and subsequently extinguished before the house burned down.

The closest bunker was a private one, under the mansion of my Uncle Walther von Brauchitsch, former Chief of Staff of the German Armed Forces. He had been fired by Hitler after furious disagreements over the campaign against Russia. In family circles a story was making the rounds, according to which the führer, seized by one of his tantrums, had allegedly thrown a telephone at the field marshal. Uncle Walter was able to avoid being hit by ducking just in time, a practice not altogether alien to him anymore. Another version claimed that the cord had not been long enough to reach the intended target.

For reasons unknown, the demoted old soldier, bearer of the party emblem in gold (an indication of high honor within the party), was still permitted to reside with his Nazi wife in the luxurious "Aryanized" villa, a generous wedding gift bestowed to him by Hitler. My father had a fit at the mere suggestion that his life might be saved thanks to the graciousness of the man who had teamed up with gangsters. Rather than survive in the company of the lady the man married, referred by him only as the "*parteigenossin* Schmidt" (the "party member Schmidt," her maiden name), he would certainly prefer being hit by an honest bomb.

We all remained at home during the nightly attacks from above, my father and I terrified, while my unshakeable mother kept repeating that nothing was going to happen to us as long as we stayed in the house, her intuition never having betrayed her yet. Unlike its owner, the house would indeed survive the air attacks, the Gestapo, the battle of Berlin, the Soviet invasion, and even confiscation by the American forces. Occasionally, the roof was blown off; more often, the window panes were shattered and had to be replaced with sheets of plywood or cardboard. Who cared as long as we were alive?

The one member of the household who was the most frightened as soon as the siren began to howl was Anna. With lightning speed, she donned three of her heavy skirts, one on top of the other and, barely able to move, somehow squeezed herself into the Stargardt's gold-painted rocking chair in the improvised shelter, awaiting the end. With a German Army steel helmet on her head, she bore a striking resemblance to a huge and very angry gorilla. Rolling her eyes in despair, her teeth (or rather, her dentures) audibly chattering, in loud prayer she summoned the help of all the Vendish deities at her disposal.

One night, after months of constant bombings, at the sound of the all-clear signal, she flung the helmet into a corner and, seized by uncontrolled rage, screamed at the top of her voice that she could not take it anymore. And why should she? After all, did she not own a little house in the Spreewald? With a garden full of fruit trees? The apples and pears needed picking, and she knew she could not count on "Itler" to do it for her. Was she crazy to endure this ordeal? 'Hadolf 'Itler, as far as she was concerned, could kiss her backside! Or, in plain Vendish, "*rish me oblish!*" The following morning, gathering the bare necessities, she left us after almost twenty-five years. Back home in her little garden with its heavy-laden fruit trees, she shook her fist and wasted her entire precious vocabulary, cursing the American planes above, whose totally unmoved pilots did not show the remotest interest in her or in the rural area below.

Anna's departure had a devastating effect on everybody, particularly my mother, who had never before entered her or anyone else's kitchen of her own free will. Since she did not know or care to learn about housekeeping and cooking, our home, large enough to keep three servants busy, soon began to show definite signs of neglect. But at this point, when nearly every night brought more destruction, it really did not matter.

Chapter Thirty-Seven
Resistance

In spite of all difficulties, I had managed a trip to Heidelberg to visit my friend Ditte, still a student at the university. So far, nobody had reported her to the Gestapo as "half-Jewish." She had moved into a tiny, shabbily furnished apartment, a typical student hangout, with an extremely inquisitive landlady. This home in the center of town would become the scene of rather unique and strictly unlawful activities.

Around that time, students Hans and Sophie Scholl, highly motivated by their Christian faith, initiated the resistance group called the "White Rose" in Munich. Attempting to shake up the dormant conscience of the Germans to the outrageous crimes committed in their name, they dropped thousands of leaflets within the university compound, which read:

Who among us has any conception of the dimension of shame that befalls us and our children when, one day, the veil falls from our eyes and crimes that surpass any human imagination will come into the light of day?

Reported to the Gestapo by the university caretaker, Hans and Sophie were caught, together with their friends, tried, sentenced to death, and executed by the guillotine. Illegal actions also took place in Ditte's Heidelberg apartment, easily qualifying her for a violent end. With the expert help of medical students, young German soldiers on leave from the front volunteered to have an arm or a leg broken, so they would not have to return to combat. In order to achieve that goal, they were ready to undergo rather brutal procedures, for which Ditte's place seemed ideal. Since no anesthesia was available, the victims were usually knocked out by a bottle of cheap, black market booze before the more or less skillful future surgeons went to work on them.

After making sure that Frau Nattermann, her nosy landlady, had left the house, Ditte turned the radio up to an outrageous volume, blaring Nazi marching songs alternating with Viennese waltzes, in order to drown out screams of pain. Passersby would look up to the windows and shake their heads, lamenting why thoughtless young people, particularly in such serious times, had to be so noisy.

With the sinister deed accomplished, the soldiers were, after nightfall, dragged to the nearest police station or hospital, where they claimed to have been hit by a car or had met with another unfortunate accident, abruptly ending or at least postponing their career as cannon fodder for the beloved führer. By far the worst part, Ditte admitted with a shudder, was the crunching sound of a bone being smashed, which she could hear in spite of the loud music. Little did I know that only a short time later, I myself would be part of an organization dealing with the rescue of illegals.

When, after the Japanese attack on Pearl Harbor on December 7, 1941, the United States had entered the war, my father began to express hope that this development might well destroy the still-threatening danger of a German victory. The "Voice of America," broadcast from London, gave us new courage.

On June 4, 1942, the *Grossdeutscher Rundfunk* reported the murder of Himmler's Deputy, Reinhard Heydrich, in Prague. But our jubilation soon stuck in our throats when the news broke that, in retaliation, the Nazis had erased the village of Lidice, west of Prague, executing all males over fifteen years of age. What none among us knew at the time was that a few months before, on January 20, a conference had taken place in a stately mansion in Berlin-Wannsee, with fourteen high-ranking Nazis in attendance. Presiding over the gathering was *Reichsführer*-SS Heinrich Himmler, whom Hitler jokingly called his "black Ignatius of Loyola." After lunch, the group relaxed by the fireplace over a few glasses of cognac, coffee, and good cigars. They expressed their satisfaction over finally having reached the decision of how and where to annihilate eleven million European Jews in the "Final Solution." A few days later, an overjoyed Hitler was handed the minutes of the meeting. At last, he would see the dream of his life come true! On January 30, 1939, he had clearly stated that "if World Jewry was once more to start a war, this would not mean the end of the German people, but the annihilation of the Jewish race not only in Germany, but in Europe."

Now, with the occupied areas in the East, the problem of killing a high number of Jews away from the fatherland was about to be solved. While there was an ample number of concentration camps within the Reich; it was now time to build centers with the sole purpose of murdering as many Jews as possible in the shortest span of time and at the lowest cost. These killing centers would include Auschwitz-Birkenau, Treblinka, Majdanek, and Sobibor.

Chapter Thirty-Eight
Rescue Efforts

After two years of intense studying, I passed my state stage exams with flying colors and was in the market for my first contract with a theater. Berlin being out of the question for beginners, I had to get used to the idea of leaving Berlin, my parents, and my friends. And Walter Franck. Over the months with him, our student-teacher relationship had slowly developed into a friendship, and eventually into more. At first I was terribly flattered by the attention of this famous man, so much older than myself. I was grateful that he, rather than someone my own age, was to be my first great love. Ultimately, we would go our separate ways, but the deep bond connecting us ended only with his death twenty years later.

There had never been a serious romantic relationship for me involving my dance partners, for the simple reason that "boys" neither interested nor attracted me. Having been a "father's daughter," obsessed with my love for him, I was looking for someone resembling him in looks, elegance, intelligence, and maturity. Walter Franck took great care in teaching me the primary things he believed every woman should know.

The realization that at my young age I had been able to attract a man of his caliber came as a profound shock to me. Throughout my childhood and adolescence, I had been told that, with straight and mousy hair, sloping shoulders, and freckles, I would most certainly never become a beauty like my mother. In other words, aside from being the black sheep of the family, I was also the ugly duckling. Being only five feet, five and a half inches tall, I was also considered the dwarf among a family of red-haired, blue-eyed German giants. But now, to my own surprise, not unlike in Andersen's fairy tale, it seemed that the ugly duckling was about to turn into something else.

The man I loved was gentle, respectful, and observant; I was never to forget all he taught me during my most impressionable years. Whenever, in my future life, I would fall flat on my face, it was usually because I had temporarily chosen to forget the values he had instilled in me. Early in our relationship, he decided it was safe enough to let me in on the otherwise well-kept secret that he was the initiator of a small resistance group, dedicated to the care of Jews who had decided to go into hiding. This activity not only required courage, but skill, cunning, and resourcefulness. Four other Dahlem families, including my own, joined in this important underground railroad.

With a few exceptions, we never knew where the nameless Jews came from. They stayed for a few hours or even days; we took in whoever was sent to us by reliable friends, praying that he or she was not a stool pigeon. One name that kept coming up was that of a certain countess who had worked briefly for my father, instantly identifying her as a persona who could be trusted. Little did I know that Maria von Maltzan, who saved hundreds of Jews, would become my close acquaintance and ally, our friendship continuing until the day of her death in November 1997.

The Countess Maria von Maltzan was by descent the offspring of the highest ranks of nobility; she provided hiding places for hundreds of Jews, including her lover. With the help of the Swedish church in Berlin, she organized her rescue actions, which involved hiding Jews among the furniture returning Swedish nationals sent in freight cars to Stockholm. She was not always lucky, however. At one point, the Gestapo arrested her, and for a week she did not know if she would survive the torture. Another time, during a nighttime rescue action, a bullet grazed her temple, giving her headaches for the rest of her life, part of which she spent with Hans, whom she married after the war.[11]

The greatest danger for Jews on the run were the so-called "Jew-catchers" lurking in the streets, some of whom were Jewish themselves, like the "Blonde Ghost," the notorious and beautiful Stella Goldschlag. One day, Maria found the Gestapo snitch searching her apartment after neighbors had reported "illegal activities." Stella would survive, after delivering close to a thousand Jews into the clutches of the Gestapo, thus saving her parents and herself from deportation.

We know for sure that only one "U-boat" survived. Frau Thiele, alias "Wittenberg," posed as a seamstress off and on in our house and was hidden in the house of Ditte's parents. Frau Thiele's husband and son had already vanished in the East. Eventually, she reached England, and nobody heard from her anymore.

When the Gestapo began to pay us unannounced visits, our family temporarily ended our participation in this intricate system. At that point I found another place, a regular resistance center located in the immediate neighborhood, where illegals, Jewish or not, were hidden and passed on. Located right in the "eye" of the storm, they found asylum. I will describe the details in a later chapter.

Since a city the size of Berlin provided considerably more anonymity than a small town or a village, helped by the destruction through air raids, the number of Jews surviving underground was comparatively high, at first estimated between fifteen hundred and three thousand. Considering that behind each rescuer was a household of at least two or three people, plus an unknown number of helpers—grocers, doctors, and pastors—informed about the action, it is safe to arrive at a total of approximately five to six thousand conspirators, all risking their lives. Among the rescuers were a number of those who had joyfully joined in Hitler's anti-Semitic tirades; however, when it counted, when a next door neighbor was about to be deported, they opened their doors. My maiden aunt, the Baroness Maimi von Mirbach in Potsdam, saved her former piano teacher by actually hiding her in her own apartment for two whole years. The State of Israel would posthumously declare her a "Righteous Gentile." I visited the tree planted in her honor on the Avenue of the Righteous in Jerusalem.

During the years between 1941 and 1943, Walter Franck, still a prominent stage actor, but ousted by Goebbels as a movie star, introduced me to a period in history that was withheld from most of my generation, the "Roaring Twenties," when Berlin, for a brief moment, had been the center of culture in Europe. For a small circle of chosen guests, he arranged evenings at his home, during which he attempted to introduce us to all those artists whose names were not mentioned anymore: Thomas and Heinrich Mann, Kurt Tucholsky, Bert Brecht, and Kurt Weill as well as all the actors who had fled Germany. In a self-crippling act, Nazi Germany had gotten rid of the best among them, either because they were Jewish or, for political reasons, felt they could not stay. On one such occasion, he performed the entire "Threepenny Opera" for us, singing and accompanying himself on the piano.

A highly educated man, he cherished reading Ovid to me, maintaining that the old Roman's conception of love still stood. "At least," Ovid had written, "convince yourself into believing you are in love when in reality you are only motivated by desire. Only when you are convinced you love sincerely, are you permitted to give in to your desire." Even if passionate love later turns out to have been nothing but an illusion, I would never be left with a feeling of having wasted myself.

My first contract as a theater novice had to be signed by my father since I was still a "minor" in the eyes of the law. Unfortunately, the well-reputed State Theater where I began my career was in faraway Danzig, where Hitler's war had begun in 1939. There, being Nazi was a way of life, even among the actors. But, like everywhere else, even among that heap of brown garbage, I found some friends, and we formed an impenetrable club of five kindred spirits.

In April of 1943, while still in Berlin, the news reached us from Radio London that an armed rebellion had taken place in the Warsaw Ghetto. Only after the end of the war would we learn the details. In an area meant to house fifty thousand, half a million Jews had been crammed, hermetically sealed off from the Warsaw population. Over a period of many months, weapons had been "organized," and on the eve of Passover, the heroic, hopeless battle of the Jews against their Nazi tormentors began. The realization that Jews had actually put up armed resistance came as a shattering, as well as embarrassing, surprise to the Nazis. Just how many Nazis lost their lives in the violent uprising was never revealed. At least, not by the Germans, who played down the uprising as a minor "incident."

Chapter Thirty-Nine

Danzig

Danzig was intact, Danzig was historic, Danzig was beautiful. And I hated it at first sight.

"In order to find out about an actress' psyche, I have to see her bedroom," said the General Manager of the Danzig State Theater, which did not amuse me. His watery, bloodshot eyes, with white eyelashes that reminding me of a fat walrus, were already undressing me. With a chin in triple layers, the colors of his face resembled those of a rainbow: red, pink, and purple. This overripe Romeo with the sagging features of his sixty-some years, plus the swastika emblem in his lapel, was not exactly the answer to any maiden's prayers, let alone mine. I decided that I did not even need Ovid's advice; this walrus would definitely not gain entrance to my bedroom or my psyche, not to mention anything else. Once he had grasped the cruel reality, he paid me back by withholding from me all those wonderful parts that I was supposed to play. The worst was that, in spite of being assigned only bit parts, he refused to let me out of the two-year contract.

My first hunch had been right; the whole atmosphere in Danzig, including that of the theater, turned out to be very alien. I felt like I was walking around in a brown fog. Never before had I come into close contact with so many Nazis. I shared my dressing room with a couple of old hags, one of whom kept Hitler's photo on her table; he was going to be a living witness to her glory onstage. After World War I, Danzig had been assigned the truly enviable status of a "Free City." But the Danzigers did not wish to be free; they demanded their slice of the brown cake, of everything the führer offered his fortunate German nation, including this wonderful war, rationed food, and later almost total destruction by bombs.

They got what they desired and what they deserved.

After complaining to my agent about my precarious situation, he informed me that the aged Don Juan had been transferred to his present position from a larger German theater for very embarrassing reasons. He had tried to molest a young actress, which not only got him into difficulties with the girl's outraged father, but also with the authorities. All I had to do was make him an offer he was in no position to reject; if nothing else worked, I should just threaten to snitch on him for attempting to seduce a minor. It worked like a charm. Forcing my entry into the inner sanctum, after receiving a few verbal kicks below the belt, I ignited my rocket. As a result, he swiftly—if ungraciously—released me from my contract, and I returned to Berlin in December 1943.[12]

Back in Berlin, I found the city well on its way to being reduced to a gigantic heap of rubble. My heart bled at the sight of the city I loved more than any other place in the world, now doomed to destruction. Yet deep down I knew that it was wrong to pray for its preservation; each destroyed building would bring us an inch closer to victory over the Nazis. Hitler had been correct in his 1933 prediction that, within ten years, Germany would not be recognized anymore. The Germans, elated over the Nazi bombings of Rotterdam and Coventry, accepted the death of thousands of civilians as a justifiable act of defense. But when, to everyone's shock, the tables turned and German cities were suddenly the target of furious Allied retaliation, and "Anglo-Americans" were branded as inhuman terrorists. The vast majority of Germans chose not to realize a painful but close connection between cause and effect.

Soon after my return home, a little dachshund by the name of Schatzi came into my possession. She possessed a mysteriously wonderful gift; almost exactly fifteen minutes before the sound of the air raid siren, Schatzi began to howl, which gave me precious extra minutes to wake the rest of the family, get my things together, and go down to the cellar before the danger began. As the raids became more frequent and more violent, we decided to seek protection with a neighbor who had built himself a little makeshift concrete shelter, close enough to permit us to run across the street in case our house caught fire.

Although most of the bomb damage so far had occurred in the center of Berlin, Dahlem now suffered its share, inflicted by British air mines. The mines not only destroyed the target they landed on, but their concussion flattened the area around them, although spring, with trees and flowers in innocent bloom, managed to somehow camouflage the worst disaster areas in the neighborhood. Our house, groaning on its foundation, was still standing as my mother had promised, and the best news by far was that the Allies had succeeded in landing on the shores of Normandy and in Italy; it might only be weeks until we were liberated. But, to our dismay, the Allied troops, who met with furious resistance by the Nazis, advanced all too slowly.

Our main concern at that time was to concentrate on getting rid of Hitler. Over the past several years, one assassination attempt after the other by members of the group to which my father belonged either had to be postponed for some reason or simply failed. The bomb placed between two bottles of cognac on board Hitler's plane, carefully set to explode thirty minutes after takeoff, had not exploded. The man who had prepared it, Axel von dem Bussche, a veteran who had lost one leg, also was on board the plane and ready to die in the blast that did not happen.

At a Berlin museum, a high-ranking officer, distantly related to us, had armed himself with explosives, ready to kill Hitler and himself in a deadly embrace, when the führer, by now a full-fledged paranoid drug addict, arrived at a different time and at a different gate. It took my "uncle" some time to dismantle himself. As early as 1939, a plan to assassinate Hitler in Berlin never came to pass because, at the last moment, Hitler went to Munich instead of meeting with Neville Chamberlain.

Civilians continued to die in the bomb raids, soldiers were killed like flies on the various fronts, and in the extermination camps, according to the BBC, every little wheel of the well-oiled death machinery worked with Germanic precision from the moment the Jews were rounded up in their homes to the time when they were gassed. Their belongings, their gold teeth, their shorn hair, and finally their ashes were recycled, to the profit of those who murdered them. With each precious day, thousands of lives were lost. Unlike in the Nazi-occupied countries, where the resistance had the majority of compatriots on its side, within Germany anyone opposing the regime was regarded as an outlaw, a traitor.

Finding myself unemployed, I realized that, unless I was lucky enough to get a new position quickly, I was vulnerable either to be drafted into the "Flak," the anti-aircraft women's corps, or worse, for work in a munitions factory. During these weeks of waiting, my father kept telling me that resistance was possible on every level; if drafted into a factory, I could see to it that every part I worked on was defective. That, he emphasized, was my part in the resistance.

When the municipal theater of Essen offered me a two-year contract, I was overjoyed. Not so my parents because Essen, in the industrial Ruhr region, was a favorite target for air raids. The date set for my departure from Berlin was August 1, when rehearsals for "The Taming of the Shrew" were to begin.

My mother missed her neighbor and close friend, Else Niemoeller, who had recently moved to Leoni on Lake Starnberg in Bavaria, taking Dora, her housekeeper and confidante, and three of her children with her. From Leoni, the monthly visits to Dachau were considerably less strenuous, even though the increased attacks on Munich sometimes made traveling hazardous. Three of Niemoeller's four sons had been inducted into the army, fighting for the man who, seven years before, robbed them of their father. Just before leaving Dahlem for good, Dora had summoned my mother to her mistress, who was feeling very low. In tears, Else made her friend promise that, in case her husband survived Dachau, and she, Else, died in the meantime, and if also my father somehow did not live to see the end of the war, my mother should marry the pastor.

Chapter Forty
The Final Attempt

The humiliating defeat at Stalingrad in January 1943, ending with the surrender of what remained of the once proud German 6th Army by Field Marshals von Paulus and von Seydlitz, sent Hitler into a rage of hitherto unknown dimensions over such "cowardice." This catastrophe, in which 146,000 German soldiers had been killed, 90,000 captured, and the fate of another 14,000 an unsolved mystery, had stifled the loud-mouthed predictions of a quick victory in the East. While Nazi army boots still trampled through half of Europe and North Africa, the chance of actually realizing Hitler's dream of *lebensraum* dwindled by the hour. Moscow was beleaguered but never taken. The population of Leningrad had, with almost superhuman bravery and perseverance, resisted the furious German siege of their devastated city for nearly three years. The price for their valor was almost one million lives—victims of artillery fire, bombs, exposure to the cold, and starvation.

Since the autumn of 1943, under the protective shield of the blackout, the frequency of clandestine nightly meetings in my father's study had increased. Among the participants were Achim Oster, now holding the rank of general; Ulrich von Hassell, Germany's Ambassador to Rome during the early thirties; our neighbor Admiral Wilhelm Canaris; my cousin Hans-Bernd von Haeften, a diplomat; and his younger brother, thirty-two-year-old first lieutenant Werner von Haeften, a lawyer by profession and faithful member of the Confessing Church.

In 1939, Oster had written in his diary that he regarded it his personal duty to "free the world from a monster." Canaris had been dismissed by Hitler as Chief of German Counter Espionage in February of 1944, charged with being politically unreliable.[13] Werner, unusually serious for his age, was recuperating in a field hospital from a serious war injury, after which he would resume his duties as adjutant to General Staff Colonel Claus Count Schenk Graf von Stauffenberg. Late in April 1944, I saw Werner for the last time. Being well enough to return to Stauffenberg's side, he came to say good-bye, and at the door he kissed me. During the past months, he and I had paid little attention to the fact that we were related and had fallen in love. Some strange notion now told me I would not see this strikingly handsome young man with his almost overwhelming charm again.[14]

With rehearsals for "The Taming of the Shrew" scheduled to begin in Essen on August 1, my time at home was running out, so on Sunday, July 16, I decided to take a break from the constant and brutal air raids and visit my cousin Ilse von Schwerin in Pomerania, where she singlehandedly managed a sizeable estate, trying to bring up her four young children after her husband's plane had been shot down over the English Channel.

On the morning of Thursday, July 20, Ilse had sent me to a nearby village with a horse and cart, both groaning with old age, to collect wood. The sun was just beginning to set after a glorious summer day when I returned. From a distance, I spotted Ilse on the front steps of the mansion signaling to me; evidently she had some news that could not wait. Handing over the horse and cart to a stable hand, I ran to her. Hardly able to contain herself, she whispered, "Hitler is dead! They did it!"

They? Who? My father? Werner? Oh, my God!

Yes, she said, it was really true. A bomb had killed the bastard and a whole bunch of Nazis at the führer's Wolf's Lair headquarters in East Prussia.

I knew I had to return to Berlin as soon as possible, but there was no bus or train until the next morning. Around one o'clock that same night, something terrible happened. The husky roar of an all too familiar voice was heard on the radio, causing our blood to freeze. It was, without any doubt, the voice of Adolf Hitler, a little shaky, a lot hoarser. But it was definitely not the voice of a dead man.

A clique of deranged, vile, and despicable officers, most of them of noble descent, he screamed, had tried to kill him. But again, providence had been with him, and all involved in the evil plot would be dealt with at once—no mercy for traitors. They had not only attempted the most despicable crime of regicide, but seriously jeopardized the final German victory over world Bolshevism.

Somehow I managed to reach Berlin safely and found my mother alone in the house, outwardly cool and collected as always. My father had left on July 19 to hide out with Field Marshal August von Mackensen, the ninety-five-year-old hero of World War I, who had participated as an officer in the Franco-Prussian War of 1870-1871. This trip to Mackensen's country estate had been planned when the date for "Operation Valkyrie," the code name for the plot, was postponed from July 15 to July 20. My father was scheduled to return for the conferences that would determine the post he was to assume in a new government.

On the evening before my departure to Pomerania, my father and I had taken a walk around the block. In front of St. Anne's Church, he had suddenly turned to me: "The coup is imminent," he said. "It will take place, and in all probability, it will fail. In my opinion, we do not deserve a break, after all the horrible crimes committed with the full support of the German people. But at least we will be on record for having tried; it will make a difference for those who come after us."

Never before had I so clearly realized the full extent of his contempt for all those who had allowed Hitler to use them for his evil purposes against the tradition of their heritage. "Whatever happens," he continued, "I want you to leave Germany as soon as possible, find a future for you and your children under a different star." Looking into his sad, deep-set eyes, I understood that whatever the future would bring, he knew that he would not be part of it. "They are coming for me," he had screamed in his frequent nightmares that had haunted my early years. Returning home that evening with him, I was struck by the realization that my childhood was over; my father had spoken to me like one adult to another.

On the morning of July 21, Radio London revealed the full extent of the disastrous failure of "Operation Valkyrie," although it did not yet disclose details. Somehow, we learned that my cousin Werner had been one of the key plotters. He had carried the attaché case for his chief, containing two lethal British-made devices, because Stauffenberg had lost one arm and part of the other in battle. The extra bomb was to be used in case the first one did not work, both being equipped with a chemical delayed-action fuse.

The two men had flown to East Prussia from Berlin where Stauffenberg, due to a recent promotion within the general staff, was admitted to Hitler's inner circle in order to participate in an important staff conference. To his dismay, he learned that the meeting, originally scheduled to take place in an underground bunker had, due to the intense July heat and by the führer's own orders, been moved to a wooden structure above ground. This change completely upset the carefully premeditated action because, as Stauffenberg realized instantly, the pressure resulting from the blast would release through the windows. All he could do was place the bomb, unnoticed by the twenty-four participants, under the heavy oak table as close as possible to Hitler's chair, with Field Marshal Keitel seated next to him. Stauffenberg had arranged to be called out for an alleged telephone call by his adjutant Werner minutes before the bomb was to go off.

After Stauffenberg left to take the "call," the two men hastened from the scene as quickly as they could without creating suspicion. Exactly at 12:42 came the detonation, which was so tremendous that the two men had every reason to believe that not a soul had survived. Hurrying to the airport and from there back to Berlin, they arrived in the capital, assuming that Hitler was dead. "Operation Valkyrie" would now go into full action. Instead, at Army headquarters in Berlin Bendlerstrasse, they met with the devastating news that, although the bomb had killed four and wounded several others, Hitler was alive. In spite of the open windows having considerably weakened the power of the explosion, the extent of the blast made the survival of twenty people seem like a miracle. The bomb had caused Hitler to suffer burns, his face was blackened by smoke, his pants torn to shreds. It also burst his eardrums and left one arm partially paralyzed. Only three hours later, the führer, once more saved by the often quoted providence, was able to show the horror scene to Benito Mussolini, who had arrived at the Wolf's Lair at four o'clock that afternoon. Il Duce could not stop marveling about the führer's miraculous salvation.

After long hours of total chaos in the Army headquarters compound in Berlin, it was clear that the Nazis were the winners and that the assassins were the losers. Before the break of day, thirty-seven-year-old Stauffenberg (who was heard to whisper in total despair, "they have all forsaken me"), his faithful adjutant Werner von Haeften, General Friedrich Olbricht, and Lieutenant Colonel Mertz von Quirnheim were executed by a firing squad in the courtyard.[15] Cremated at once, the ashes of their bullet-riddled bodies were strewn over sewage land. Field Marshal Keitel, recalling how Stauffenberg had excused himself just before the explosion, was the first to voice his suspicion to the führer, who, in turn, gave the orders for the execution.

As it turned out, the four men shot by firing squad during the night had been extremely fortunate as Hitler's wrath knew no limits. According to William Shirer, Hitler was "seized by titanic fury." He now gloated over his chance, once and for all, to get even with the caste he despised almost as much as the Jews—the aristocracy! This hated German "elite," with the exception of those with no qualms about joining his gang, had let him feel over the years that he, the proletarian and school dropout, the lowly corporal, the parvenu, would never be socially acceptable in their illustrious circles. Now those who had rejected him as a friend would find out what it was like to have him for an enemy.

Chapter Forty-One
Revenge

At six o'clock in the morning on July 22, our doorbell rang. Four Gestapo officials had been delegated by Ernst Kaltenbrunner, after Himmler second in command of the SS and the Gestapo, to search the house and arrest my father. At the sound of the bell, I had raced to the radio to make sure it was tuned to a German station, and, indeed, the first thing the leader of the gang did was to switch it on. Much to his disappointment, what he heard was *Deutschlandfunk* blaring more details about the evil deed.

In my father's study, my mother explained the absence of her husband. Before she could prevent it, one of the Gestapo officials picked up something from the desk. It was a piece of paper with a telephone number scribbled on it. Aha! A telephone number? Whose telephone number? My mother's cool Prussian blue eyes met with those of the intruder as she told him she really had no idea. The suspicious man dialed it over and over again, then put the receiver down; he could not get a connection. Whatever prompted him to allow my mother to grab the note from him under the pretense that the problem was probably with the downstairs phone and she would try upstairs, would forever remain an enigma. Coming down the stairs again, she seemed a shade paler when she handed him the paper back with the information that she, too, had not been able to get through. After the uninvited guests had left the house, she confided in me what she had done while upstairs; in an attempt to change the number, she had erased two digits and replaced them with different ones. She did not know that the real number in question was that of the designated chancellor in the post-Hitler regime, Karl Goerdeler.

Goerdeler, the former Lord Mayor of Leipzig, had managed to escape arrest and, in spite of his imposing height of six feet, five inches, had made it as far as East Prussia, where a safe hiding place was waiting for him. Not far from his destination, fate caught up with him in a small restaurant while he was eating some soup. Helene Schwärzel, a mousy creature, who identified him instantly from a photo in the local newspaper as a wanted criminal with a huge reward on his head, wasted no time calling the authorities. Sharing the fate of his fellow conspirators, Goerdeler was hanged by the neck. Hitler was not a man of empty words. He kept his promise to sweep the traitors from the face of the Earth.[16]

After eight hours of intense search, during which the Gestapo tore our house apart without finding any substantially incriminating evidence and no Jews, they settled on the veranda, facing the backyard. There they waited for hours for a certain someone to show up and ring the doorbell. But the bell did not ring for the simple reason that I had posted myself at the kitchen window, signaling everyone who came to turn away fast. When the gangsters finally left, they took me along. During the endless ride to Gestapo headquarters in Berlin's Französische Strasse, crammed in the black limousine with the men, I took the precaution of letting my life pass before my inner eye, just in case I did not return home again.

On the fourth floor of the dismal but still miraculously undamaged building, I was delivered to an obviously high-ranking official in civilian clothes. Kommissar Wipper motioned me into his office. Over the years, my father had carefully instructed me on how to behave during a possible Gestapo interrogation. The first rule was never to volunteer any information beyond a yes or a no. "When they get friendly," he had hammered into me, "it is time to watch out." And he also told me to never fall into a well-known Gestapo trap—admitting to something that had allegedly been confessed by another member of the family.

Wipper, his spongy, clean-shaven poker face not betraying any emotion, was civilized. Sitting across the desk from me, he first lamented the lack of qualified personnel in his department, complaining about the extra workload as a deplorable consequence of the latest events. "If it were not for the alertness of the population," he added, looking out of the window, "we would have to hire at least another 50,000 people." I was inclined to agree with him.

During the course of the following two-hour interrogation, I found that he did not seem to be interested in my father, but only in Werner von Haeften, whose death so far had not been mentioned by the media. I had to be extra cautious to refer to my cousin in the present tense. How well did I know him? What was my interest in him? Realizing that, in his opinion, I was probably an accomplice, I boldly told Wipper that Werner and I had been lovers, which solely accounted for his frequent visits to our house. He seemed satisfied with this information. There was no law against a love affair between cousins, was there?

That night I was permitted to return home, but in the morning, they were waiting in front of the house to take me downtown for yet another "friendly" conversation; someone else at Gestapo headquarters wished to talk to me. I was led to Wipper's office, where he and a higher ranking SS officer were waiting. After a few seconds, Wipper tactfully excused himself, closing the door behind him.

When I left the Französische Strasse headquarters, this time after a horrible six hours of questioning with lights blinding me, my head was spinning and what I spat onto the pavement was blood. My left eardrum had been ruptured under the violent blows an SS officer had dealt me with the back of his hand, his SS runic ring leaving a distinct and bloody mark on my left cheek. The hearing in my left ear would remain impaired for the rest of my life. Dominating the physical pain was an overwhelming feeling of red-hot rage screaming for revenge. Not so long as I lived would I forget my tormentor's crude face, his huge butcher hands, and the sickening smell of sweat. I swore to myself never to rest until I found him again, if it meant searching the four corners of the globe.

By next morning, the left side of my face was swollen out of proportion, the ring mark had turned a deep purple, and my aching ear required medical attention. After I came back from the doctor, I found my father had returned home.

"The swine," he muttered in helpless rage when he saw me.

But at least I had survived so far, and I was grateful that the target of brutality had been me and not my mother.

On the following day, they came for my father. No more house search, no questions; they just ordered him to pack a few belongings, and from the window I watched a nightmare coming true, one that I realized had been haunting me all my life. Walking tall between two black-clad Gestapo officials, he did not look back. For weeks, my mother and I had no clue where he had been taken.[17] We were all alone in the house now, since my brother had been inducted into the military and was undergoing basic training with his classmates in some small garrison town not too far from Berlin.[18]

Hitler wasted no time; the group of conspirators considered the main culprits were hanged naked by piano wires suspended on meat hooks at the Plötzensee Prison in Berlin. The first executions took place in front of movie cameras, so Hitler, detesting violence and blood in his physical presence, could enjoy watching his foes slowly squirm to their deaths from the safety and comfort of his living room. Filming this spectacle, however, had to be abandoned for the simple reason that too many of the camera crew kept fainting at the sight of the medieval, sadistic procedure.[19] In quick succession, right after they had been sentenced, the doomed men were either garroted by wires, hanged on ropes, or decapitated by the guillotine. In no case, according to Hitler's orders, would precious bullets be wasted on scum.

A special High People's Court had been hastily set up, with Roland Freisler as the presiding judge, a raving Nazi who tried to intimidate his victims by screaming and hurling insults at them. With belts and suspenders removed, the defendants stood before him, attempting to hold up their trousers, a gesture Freisler hoped would humiliate them and make them look ridiculous. To his dismay, not a single one of the doomed men lost his dignified composure. This was not easy, because most of those facing the court had already undergone terrible torture to force confessions, including having pins driven under their fingernails. By the time the nightmare was over, almost five thousand lives were taken in the wake of the attempt to free the world of the Nazi menace. With the newly introduced practice of *Sippenhaft*, "kin liability," the wives of the assassins were thrown into prisons and concentration camps. Their children, including babies, were torn from their mothers, issued new names, and turned over for adoption to deserving SS families. Among the incarcerated women was my seventy-five-year-old aunt Agnes von Haeften, née von Brauchitsch, and her daughter Elisabeth, mother and sister respectively of Werner, who had been lucky enough to meet with a quick death by bullets, while his brother Hans-Bernd was dragged before Judge Freisler and sentenced to death by hanging. The executions continued for many months, almost until the day when horrified Allied soldiers marched into the camps.[20]

After the defeat of Nazi Germany, voices were heard condemning or ridiculing the conspirators whose lack of know-how caused the blunder. Criticism expressed by those who, for many reasons had chosen their own safety over risking their lives, has to be rejected. The fact that "Operation Valkyrie" was organized and carried out in an amateurish, awkward, and even haphazard manner, with far too many outsiders having knowledge of the impending event, must not be held against the men who dared to attempt the impossible against all odds. They were not professional murderers.[21]

While not all of those involved in the attempt had taken a stand against the regime from the beginning—some had jumped from Hitler's profitable ship only when it was sinking—the core consisted of upright and courageous men from all walks of life: Protestants and Catholics, Socialists and monarchists, liberals and conservatives. Among the officers involved, eighteen had emerged from the elite Regiment Number 9 in Potsdam, rich in the best of Prussian traditions, including Stauffenberg, Treskow, Schulenburg, and Hammerstein. Some had taken the oath of allegiance without too many qualms and fought Bolshevism under the delusion of defending their fatherland and the Christian world until, like young Stauffenberg, they were exposed to atrocities that had nothing to do with defense activities. Following the initial shock, their rage was of a deadly nature when they finally realized that their oath of obedience would have to be replaced by the duty to resist. With this decision, they broke with another, less desirable Prussian tradition: *Kadavergehorsam*—blind obedience. Rejected and branded as traitors, they were determined to risk their own lives and make a statement in the face of inhumanity and indifference. July 20 would take its place in history as the last day of Prussian glory.

It was Allen Dulles who later formulated the opinion: "In retrospect it is easy to criticize German resistance for their delays and failures, but it remains remarkable that, in view of the total failure of the church, in its darkest hour, Christian forces were mobilized and political outsiders were forced to make decisions under unbelievably difficult circumstances."[22]

Chapter Forty-Two
Aftermath

A month after my father's disappearance, Wipper summoned me to his office, an invitation I felt I was in no position to decline. As if nothing had happened, he told me that my father was being held at Lehrterstrasse Prison in the heart of Berlin. He regretted to inform me that, not having confessed and consequently with the date of his trial not yet determined, my father was being kept in strict isolation, and we could not write to him or see him. However, we would receive permission to bring him a package with provisions once a month. Examining the carefully groomed fingernails of his fat white hands and letting his fishy eyes wander from the ceiling to the courtyard, he added in a plaintive tone that he sincerely hoped my father would come to his senses and admit his complicity, the sooner the better, and certainly for his own good! For his own good? I shuddered, imagining just what they might do to him to force such a confession.

Feeling a sudden urge to wring the man's neck, I realized that, in order to free my father, I would be capable of committing cold-blooded murder, starting with this soft-spoken, well-fed, well-mannered, slimy monster across the desk from me, who had once tactfully left the room before the SS brute beat me up. This time, I did not return home with a black and blue face, but with something unique as well as valuable.

During our polite "conversation," or rather his monologue, Wipper had been called away to take a telephone call in the adjacent office. His absence gave me the chance to swiftly steal some of the official stationary neatly piled on his desk, all with the letterhead *Reichsführer-SS—Geheime Staatspolizei*, adorned with a couple of imposing red and green stamps. I stuffed several sheets into my purse, in the correct assumption that I would be not be frisked on my way out. Very soon I was able to put my loot to good use.

Two weeks later, my mother and I received permission to bring a package of provisions to Lehrterstrasse Prison. We took a woolen sweater, some underwear, and a blanket, as well as bread and other perishable goods that we had been able to purchase on the flourishing black market, where the price of a pound of butter was set at three hundred and a pound of coffee at five hundred *reichsmarks*. By far the most precious item was hot coffee in a thermos bottle. We somehow made our way through the mountain of rubble that had once been the city of Berlin in the record time of three hours. Once inside the gate of the dismally forbidding building, we received a stern warning by an SS guard not to dare use the "Hitler salute," of which we, kin of traitors, were considered unworthy. Since we had always avoided the ridiculous wing beating, as my mother called it, this news did not exactly crush us. A young man in the gray uniform of the *Waffen*-SS led us through endless dimly lit hallways and told us to wait our turn on one of the benches. Soon we realized we were not alone. We recognized several of the women, waiting to deliver their precious goods, although none of us dared to betray a glance of recognition.

The air in the corridors was stifling, heavy with the pungent smell of a cheap disinfectant, of fear, of blood, and of naked horror. Black-clad SS men dragged prisoners by, returning them to their cells after an interrogation, some of the victims literally hanging between their tormentors. These spectacles were obviously staged with the purpose of scaring us, who knew all too well about practices in the torture chambers of Gestapo headquarters and elsewhere. At the end of the dark corridor was a cubicle with a small window, from which a uniformed SS man called out a name, whereupon a woman took her bag to him for inspection. At his sight, my mother whispered, "Just look at him, a regular Satan!"

When it was our turn, we approached the window, in which the dark-haired official with the emblems of an *Unterscharführer* (Junior Squad Leader), a sharp nose, piercing eyes, and a pinched mouth examined the contents of our package. We had been told by others that dropping thermos bottles "by mistake" was a favored practice of some of the more sadistic guards, a major disaster because at this stage of the war those valuable receptacles could not be replaced. The Satan handled everything with care, but he seemed to give me more than normal attention. Just when I was ready to leave the window, he motioned me back with his finger.

Oh Lord, what now? Had he found something to object to after all? Summoning me close, with his eyes cast down, he began to mutter something I was not able to grasp at first. Slowly I understood that he was requesting some extra bread or other rations. What was this? A trap? Did the man expect a bribe, or worse? Sensing my uneasiness, he said, without moving his lips, "You understand, I have prisoners here who have no relatives." It sounded like a plea. When he added in a whisper, "I will see to it that your father gets the stuff," I knew that what I had just experienced was real. It was a miracle, a touch of humanity that stood in sharp contrast to those inhuman surroundings. No doubt, this man with the looks of a devil wanted to help, which was later confirmed by others. I learned that at some point of his career, *Unterscharführer* Knuth must have realized that he had made a terrible mistake and had decided to do his utmost under these very difficult circumstances to rectify his deadly error. As time progressed, he became a regular guardian angel for "his" prisoners and their families. On Christmas Day, the fiancée of Theo Haubach, a personal friend and a leading Social Democrat who was to have been named to a cabinet post in the post-Hitler government, came to see him for the last time before his execution in Plötzensee on January 23, 1945. After delivering her goods at the window, Knuth motioned her to wait. After everyone else had left, he led her into his own private office, where Haubach was waiting. After lighting a little Christmas tree, he left the lovers alone for a while so they could say their farewells. All went well until someone got wind of his illicit activities; *Unterscharführer* Knuth did not live to see the end of the war.

Chapter Forty-Three
More Illegal Activities

My mother decided to visit her son, now a private in the *Wehrmacht*, stationed in the small garrison town of Neuruppin. At this point of the war, civilians were not permitted to ride trains without special permits, certifying that their trip was of the utmost importance to the welfare of the German Reich. I told her not to worry, assuring her that I could arrange for a permit to be issued in her name. After I used my stolen Gestapo stationary with one red and one green stamp, which stated "*Reichssicherheitshauptamt*" as well as "*Reichsführer-SS Heinrich Himmler*," to type a neatly forged travel order, I had no difficulty purchasing the ticket. Since I did not want to take a chance of having my mother refuse to leave under these circumstances, I handed her the ticket and the invaluable document through the window just as the train began to move.

After her return, she told me that a train official and a military police officer with the rank of major had stomped into her compartment, taken one look at her papers, and stood in respectful attention.

"Augusta von Sell travels on official business by orders of the *Geheime Staatspolizei*," I had written. Although admitting that she came close to fainting, she managed to give them a stern look with her Prussian blue eyes.

One morning, there was a crumpled piece of paper in our mailbox, covered with my father's handwriting. How it had gotten there remains a mystery. The contents were heartbreaking; he informed us that his deportation to a concentration camp seemed imminent; most of his cell neighbors had already been dragged off. "At least," he ended, "my transfer will save you the ordeal of the trips to the prison."

He wrote that his bleak cell, with a little grated hole for a window too high up for a view, had no radiator, a disaster now that the temperatures had dropped. By far the worst were the nightly air raids; the political prisoners were not permitted to seek safety in the shelter. As soon as the siren sounded, the ceiling lights in their cells, usually burning night and day for added discomfort, were turned off. This brought an immediate invasion of a regular army of bedbugs.

Collecting all my wits, I asked to speak to Wipper in the Französischestrasse Gestapo headquarters. After voicing my complaints, he gave me a hurt look. Shaking his head, he informed me in an indignant tone that, while the circumstances were admittedly regrettable, it was not he who was to blame, but my father himself; as soon as he admitted his guilt he would be moved to another, bug-free cell. There were no plans to transfer him to a "camp for reeducation"; he would stay in prison until after his trial. In the meantime, the alleged bugs, these nasty little fellows, had the beneficial side effect of miraculously speeding up confessions. At this remark he smiled benevolently. I swore that some day I would get even with him.

My contract with the municipal theater of Essen did not last two months; most of the days and nights were spent in local air raid shelters. On the first of September, Hitler, the greatest strategist of all times, ordered all theaters closed. I was rather sad because Essen, in spite of all the bombings, was a pleasant place. The chief director, after recognizing me as a kindred spirit, confided that his brother had been executed, as a consequence of July 20.

While male actors were swiftly sent to the Eastern front as cannon fodder, the women faced induction into the "Flak" or munitions factories. The premiere of Shakespeare's "The Taming of the Shrew" was postponed until after the victory. I was profoundly sad to leave the ruins as well as the ensemble of the Essen theater, having enjoyed, in sharp contrast to Danzig, the total absence of Nazis. It was no secret that even during the prewar years, Hitler knew better than to appear in the Ruhr region, particularly in the notoriously "red" city of Essen.

On the train back to Berlin, Schatzi and I shared the compartment with a rather interesting man in his thirties. He was healthy looking yet not in uniform, which at this point of the war was not only rare, but outright suspicious, so I assumed that he had to be a member of the Gestapo. However, rolling down an embankment side by side, away from the railroad tracks somewhere near Hannover, thanks to a British air attack, I gathered from the nature of his curses that surely I must have been mistaken. After the train was able to resume its journey, my intuition told me that he could be trusted. But who was this heavyset man with the broad Westfalian farmer's face under neatly parted blond hair and slightly slanted, small blue eyes?

At the Berlin Zoo station, the only one not completely destroyed by bombs, he had a car parked. A car? Admittedly, the shabby, three-wheeled vehicle was not a Rolls Royce, but it ran on regular, honest-to-goodness gasoline, which, this late in the war, was as valuable as gold. Delivering me home, he immediately won my mother's heart when he dug deep into the belly of the vehicle for treasures neither of us had seen in a long time: coffee, soap, sugar, chocolate, and cigarettes. Was he a black market dealer? Or worse?

The following day, I received answers to some of my questions. After picking me up in his state carriage, Hans stopped in front of a rather sizeable mansion on nearby Heydenstrasse. Built in a rather ghastly, pseudo-rural Bavarian style, the villa resembled the "Berghof," Hitler's mountain retreat above Berchtesgaden. I was not far off in my observation, because this was the residence of Hitler's pet film star and moviemaker, Leni Riefenstahl.[23] So far, her mansion, having been spared by bombs, was always ready to welcome its mistress, who knew better than to stick her neck out by exposing herself to air attacks, when she had other splendid residences at her disposal.

We entered a little house adjacent to the main building, where Hans introduced me to the "caretakers," Paul and Inge, an ordinary-looking middle-aged couple. They had gotten this enviable position by producing masterfully forged identification papers to their Nazi employer. With Hans' help, the couple operated a superbly functioning resistance center, offering temporary shelter and false papers to deserters from the German *Wehrmacht*, political illegals, and those Jews who had gone underground. Accessible only through a carpet-covered trap door in the vestibule floor, the cellar rooms not only served as hideouts, but were filled with food and other unattainable goods, including a printing press and enough weapons to start a small war. Since Paul and Inge, posing as a married couple, were on the best of terms with their landlady, the house on Heydenstrasse was taboo for the Gestapo; no one would dare search the home of the führer's protégé, which, at this point, was most likely the safest place for illegal activities in all of Germany.

I was received with open arms and soon felt at home with my new friends and the various fugitives who kept popping up from out of nowhere day and night. I knew better than to ask questions; too much knowledge was dangerous for everybody. The Gestapo had their own methods to extract information. With a shudder, I recalled a recent incident when a good friend, Kurt von Plettenberg, had jumped out of a window to his death while being led to another torture session, during which the Gestapo hoped he would spill names. Once, sitting in the kitchen of the caretakers' house, celebrating one of Germany's latest defeats, the doorbell rang. Peeking outside, Paul recognized the visitor and was not amused. He whispered to us that this staff officer, with red piping on his uniform trousers, was no one to be feared; he was too stupid!

Within seconds, food and dishes were shoved out of sight and the illegals—two soldiers and one Jewish lady—had disappeared through the trap door in the cellar. With an inviting gesture, Paul ushered the visitor inside, assuring him that everything was in the best of order. He introduced me as his cousin who had just lost everything through the bombs thrown by these air pirates who would, now that the V2 had begun to operate, pay for their crimes. After allowing himself a cognac, the major hastened back to the waiting army vehicle and sped off to join his squadron at the front, now not even a hundred miles away.

That, Paul explained, was Leni's latest husband, Major Jakob. His facial expression had reminded me of a certain ox in Kreuth. What, I demanded to know, would he do if the visitor insisted on going into the cellar? Very simply, Paul replied, I would have to shoot him.[24]

For reasons he did not care to share with me, Hans habitually wore the white coat of a doctor or pharmacist. All I knew was that he was tremendously wealthy and that he operated some kind of factory in the East. There, much in the style of Oskar Schindler, he employed Jewish workers. What became clear was that his bravery as well as his unlimited funds put him in a position where he was able to bribe anyone. Once, explaining the tingling noise in his trouser pockets, he emptied the contents on the kitchen table: hundreds of diamonds! Some fell to the floor, and he was not even too eager to bend down and pick them up.

My maternal grandfather, General Konrad von Brauchitsch

His Majesty and my godfather, Kaiser Wilhelm II

My father, Ulrich Baron von Sell

The Kaiser and the Baron, strolling at Doorn

With my mother, Augusta Baroness von Sell, née von Brauchitsch

Mother, my brother, Friedrich, and me

With my father at Krueth, our vacation home

My beloved Anna Troppa

Anna and me, her "l'il lamb"

Our house in Berlin Dahlem, which survived both the war and its aftermath

The young actress, ca. 1943

With my cousin, Werner von Haeften, not long before he was killed in the attempted assassination of Hitler

My theater mentor Walter Franck

On Arabella, the regal she-devil

Princess Caroline-Mathilde of Denmark, one of my dearest friends

With Countess Maria von Maltzan—clearly a pair of troublemakers

Pastor Martin Niemoeller

Martin, with confirmands, shortly before his arrest

The happy family—my son, Marcus, Martin, and me

Ready for an evening on the town

Martin (left) with his friend and fellow pacifist Linus Pauling (center)

Martin's grave

My mother in the 1960s, still beautiful

In Jerusalem, by the Western Wall

With Elie Wiesel, who said I must tell my story

The author today

Dahlem, den 10.4.34.

Lieber Kaiser!

Ich danke Dir vielmals für das schöne Bild, dass du mir zu meinem Geburtstage geschenkt hast. Ich habe mich schrecklich darüber gefreut. Ich werde es übermorgen gleich mit nach Eberswalde nehmen. Ich komme nähmlich zu Frl. von Rumpfeldt in Pension für zwei Jahre. Hoffentlich wird es eine recht schöne Zeit dort werden. Vorläufig habe ich noch schrecklich viel zu packen. Wir haben jetzt eine herrliche Zeit hinter uns. Mein Bruder und ich waren doch mit Mutti in den Dolomiten. Wir sind tüchtig Ski gelaufen, und haben alle drei unsere Skier kaputt gebrochen. Nur schade, dass wir im ganzen nur zwei volle Sonnentage gehabt haben. Es sind dort schrecklich viele Leute von Lawinen verschüttet worden.

Nun hoffe ich, dass es Dir weiter recht gut geht und verbleibe mit herzlichen Grüssen
Deine Silla von Sell

One of my letters to "Lieber Kaiser"

Haus Doorn, den 18.XII.1937.

Liebe Sybille !

Für Deinen Adventsgruss danke ich Dir sehr.
Ich freue mich, dass Du gern in Eberswalde
bei Fräulein v.Stumpfeld bist, habe ich doch
schon viel Gutes von dort gehört. Meine Tochter Henriette war auch sehr gern dort.
Und nun wünsche ich Dir fröhliche Weihnacht
und ein gutes neues Jahr!

A letter from His Majesty to his "little monkey"

Chapter Forty-Four
A New Career

Now unemployed, I found myself confronted with the appalling alternatives of either waiting to be drafted into the Flak or being sent to a factory. I did not have to wait long, because the mail brought the notification to report at once to a certain Flak station in Berlin. Only a miracle could save me, and one promptly occurred. I read an ad in the paper that a cavalry academy southeast of Berlin was in desperate need of female horse trainers, capable of replacing men who were being sent into battle as the Soviet Army fast approached the capital. Compulsory induction for this specific position was not possible because the cavalry could only use volunteers competent enough to break a three-year old "remount" from scratch.

The trip to the little town where the cavalry unit was stationed took half a day. To my great surprise and infinite relief, in spite of being thrown several times during the entrance exam, the commander praised my style. I found myself hired as one among the academy's thirty females in uniform, holding the rank of a second lieutenant. Throughout the entire "Reich," there were not more than two hundred female horse trainers doing a man's job.

The stocky female Flak official, with the face of an evil-tempered bulldog, reacted angrily when I reported to her that, unfortunately, I would not be in a position to join her lovely outfit. Having already referred to me as "the offspring of an enemy of the people," she had relished the thought of personally drilling a renegade like me. Not only did the cavalry rank above the Flak, but I personally outranked her, as far as the military hierarchy was concerned.

On the first day of October 1944, I had to report for duty at the academy in Beeskow, where I was issued a uniform and taken to my quarters. I had no first name anymore because only last names were used. Having to deal with horses, I realized that I could not keep the promise I had given my father, to practice as much sabotage as possible, if and when I was forced to work toward German victory. Now I found myself in a situation where this policy could not be applied because horses were not just "material," but living creatures.

The bleak and totally unattractive little town of Beeskow consisted of one long dismal street paved with cobblestones. At the far end, hidden behind high walls and ostensibly impenetrable, lay the compound of the District Military Riding Academy, with its red brick barracks, sheds, and stables situated around the mandatory drill square. A one-story barrack served as lodgings for thirty females occupying three stark wards, each equipped with bunk beds and lockers. An additional highlight was the absence of indoor toilets. The tiled shower room was new but completely empty: no showerheads, no wash basins, not even water. Appliances, we were assured, would be installed just as soon as the war was won, an event that at this point did not seem all too imminent. In the meantime, a single latrine with the obligatory heart carved into the wooden door, conveniently located outside the building, served the needs of the thirty equestriennes; reaching it over unsteady planks during the dark, icy winter nights was an acrobatic masterpiece. Instead of showers, ten of us shared one enamel receptacle the size of a salad bowl, which made the rounds once in the morning and again at night. Since my bunk mate suffered from blooming furuncles on her rear end, washing was more than just slightly hazardous.

The ward to which I had been assigned was equipped with narrow bunk beds, lighted by a naked twenty-five-watt bulb, which dangled from the ceiling over an iron stove that stubbornly resisted all efforts to heat the premises by expelling angry clouds of dense smoke. The straw bags that took the place of mattresses were shaken into shape before being halfway comfortable. Each of us had a narrow locker for our uniforms, personal belongings, and daily food rations.

Our uniforms of bluish-gray cloth consisted of riding breeches, coats with the insignia of the school, and soft slouch hats as well as shirts, sweaters, and a sword belt with the obligatory "God With Us" on the buckle. To my surprise, I received a handsome, new pair of black, soft leather boots with the mandatory spurs, considered part of the uniform. The first batch of girls had been issued men's worn-out army boots, an insult against which they had protested. Well aware of the fact that while they all could be forced to ride, no one in the world could compel them to ride well, they went on strike. As a consequence, an army boot maker was commissioned with the task of making boots to measure practically overnight, at a time when "leather" was not even in the common vocabulary anymore.

Threatening a strike in order to get better food rations also proved to be an extremely effective weapon. We received one square meal a day in the officers' mess, while bread, margarine, some horrid cheese, and equally suspicious-tasting jam were dished out each evening to serve as supper as well as breakfast the next morning. Fake coffee was the only beverage.

My grandmother would have had ample reason for jubilation; seven of the ten girls sharing my ward were members of "our caste," baronesses and countesses, a fact for which there was a simple explanation: coming from large estates, they all owned horses and knew how to handle a remount. All in all, we were a fairly happy crowd. Some of us had already met in boarding school. Outside of the barracks, we got used to being stared at. Enlisted men gave us a snappy salute, petty officers did so with a little less enthusiasm, and officers kept rubbing their eyes before doing anything. One thing was clear—in case of a confrontation with the Americans or the British, not even to mention the Soviets, we would probably be shot at first sight as female werewolves.

The academy's commanding officer, a dapper, elderly gentleman, held the rank of a full colonel. Much to his chagrin, he had only lately been reactivated and dragged from his country estate to assume a post in the cavalry. Colonel Behnke turned out to be just as nice and gentle as his middle-aged deputy, Major Woelle, the squadron chief, who was our direct superior officer. His white hair was neatly parted in the middle, and the color of his face was that of a boiled lobster. The idea of having young women in his squadron, instead of seasoned men, filled his soul with horror, imagining what our unexpected presence might do to disturb the established order of a man's world. But, before our corpulent chief saw reason to worry about the uproar we would cause, he decided the best solution was to treat us as children—kind but strict! We, in turn, reciprocated with naughty pranks.

To show off his authority over us, one nice morning he decided to "inspect" our quarters. Having gotten wind of this intrusion into our privacy, we decided to teach him a lesson, one he would not forget. We knew that an inspection included the lockers, so we took a lot of time and trouble to tastefully decorate them, displaying bras and sanitary napkins, which dangled outside the locker doors. With a martial expression on his red face, Woelle stamped into our quarters, followed by his orderly, who not only stuttered, but was as wall-eyed as a flounder, enabling him to look into opposite corners at the same time. Once in the room, Woelle would have blushed, had it not been for the already existing redness of his face. However, I am certain that he would have loved to either faint on the spot or be swallowed by a hole in the well-swept floor. Gasping for air, he turned around and left, followed by his open-mouthed orderly. This was too bad, because he would never know what kind of surprise was waiting for him in the other room; one of the girls had draped herself, in all her beauty, stark naked on her bed.[25]

During the first few weeks of service, there were days when my bottom was so tender I could hardly sit; eventually, after trying to teach basic manners to seven horses a day at one hour each, I reached a stage where I did not even feel it anymore. Training a "raw" horse from scratch, who took the very idea of bearing a saddle—or worse, a snaffle in his mouth—as a personal insult, was not only exhausting, it was hazardous. Hardly a week passed without at least one of us meeting with a more or less serious accident by either being thrown or kicked, or both. However, our achievements, from six in the morning until late in the afternoon, caused even hardboiled soldiers to stop smirking.

Cleaning the stables and grooming the horses was also part our job, in which we were assisted by Soviet prisoners of war, two of whom were under my direct command, Fyodor and Pavlik. They belonged to a group of some twenty captives who, in their tattered uniforms, were marched from a nearby POW camp to the compound under heavy guard at the crack of dawn. While Fyodor did not dignify me with as much as a glance, Pavlik and I hit it off from the start. He took the broom out of my hand and said, "*Du nix arbeiten, you nix raboti, Pavlik raboti.*" ("You don't work. You don't sweep. Pavlik sweep.") And that, to use Humphrey Bogart's famous words, was the beginning of a beautiful friendship. The seventeen-year-old kid, from a village not too far from Moscow, had been captured by the Germans the year before. With his whitish-blond straw-like bristles and constantly inflamed eyelids, he resembled a badly made up circus clown. Since Pavlik sounded forbidding to me, I called him Pawlee.

Compared to the horrors most Soviet prisoners had to endure, our outfit was sheer paradise. Living conditions in their POW camp were appalling, but they soon found out that, once inside our compound, they were safe. What they dreaded were the Sundays, where all they could do was lie on the cold, bare cement covered with a handful of straw, waiting for Monday morning to come around. It was warm in the stables, there was plenty of soft hay and straw, the work was light, and we shared our generous bread rations with them, looking the other way when one of them took a snooze. More important was that, during my time at the academy, I never witnessed one single incident in which a prisoner was mishandled. One of the reasons was that this kind of conduct would not have been tolerated by the commander. Furthermore, it seemed that people who dealt with sensitive creatures like horses were opposed to violence; therefore, beatings were unthinkable. Pavlik, obsessed with an urge to please me, had somehow managed to get hold of a small Russian-German dictionary, literally in shreds, teaching himself enough to delight me with a new word almost daily. Once when he had done a sloppy job rubbing down my favorite horse after heavy exercise, I yelled at him that if it happened again, I would beat him up until he resembled *puppenlappen* ("rag dolls"). *Puppenlappen*, he inquired? That word had no place in his limited vocabulary; "Pawlee nix know what means!" He kept repeating *Puppenlappen* over and over, until it became his favorite word. Once I had explained it in detail, he laughed until he cried at the very idea of me making *puppenlappen* of him. Wiping his snotty nose on his shiny sleeve, he kept muttering "Pawlee *puppenlappen*," "Pawlee *puppenlappen*." He could not get over it.

One morning, he came up with a rather touching surprise for me. From across the drill square I saw him lurking at the stable door, and I greeted him with my usual "good morning bristle head." Making sure nobody was watching, he stuck a half-crushed purple aster, which had seen better days, up my nose. Where he had stolen it, God only knew. Accompanying his thoughtful gift, he stood at attention and said in halting but flawless German: "My dear lady, I love and adore you." He must have practiced that sentence all night, and I almost cried.

Once he knew I could be trusted, he let me in on a deep dark secret, namely that he believed in God. *Nobody* was ever supposed to find out, especially not Kommissar, a fellow prisoner, who would beat him or worse. He made the universally understood gesture with his finger of having his throat cut. Kommissar, a sinister-looking creature, was feared by all the POWs. On the day when Kommissar, not quite without my interference, was transferred to another camp, Pavlik was in seventh heaven; he actually had tears in his red-rimmed baby blue eyes.

Berlin and Beeskow were now separated by light years, or so it seemed. The war was as "total" as the Germans had wished, the Eastern front moving closer by the minute. The retreat of the beaten German Army was still declared by the media as a smart strategic maneuver to lure the enemy into a deadly trap.

Chapter Forty-Five
Thoughts of Home

The thought of my mother being alone and my father still waiting for his trial in his cell drove me almost out of my mind. So I decided to have a confidential talk with the commander. After listening to my story, he let me in on the secret that his family, too, had been hit by the Nazis, his brother-in-law executed. While in no position to officially grant me leave for personal reasons, he saw no reason why I should not be sent to Berlin on a very delicate and secret mission as his special courier. I left his office with a stern warning that one of the officers, a captain by the name of Winkler, was a Gestapo stool pigeon. I was able to return his favor with my news, namely that one of the girls in my dormitory had all the earmarks of a Gestapo snitch. Inadvertently, I had overheard a conversation between her and the officer in question, dealing with a new girl who had joined us directly from Nazi prison.

Barbara, confused and depressed, still suffering from torture, had been engaged to one of the plotters who was ultimately sentenced to death by Roland Freisler. She had been dragged before his court, and her own father, a Nazi general, had asked Freisler to impose the most severe penalty on his renegade daughter. Allegedly, even Freisler was somewhat irritated by her father's request. Miraculously, she was set free and somehow joined our outfit. We soon discovered we were kindred spirits. However, because her was health ruined, she did not survive for very long, while her father, receiving a general's pension, outlived her by decades. No one bothered to bring him to justice.

During the first week, a very special event was scheduled, one that I quickly decided would have to be celebrated in my absence—the oath of allegiance to Adolf Hitler, which took place in a ceremony on the drill square. Not that this forced oath would have meant anything to me, but I still decided to avoid it. Using the old trick of rubbing the thermometer to the necessary temperature of thirty-nine degrees Celsius, I reported sick, as a matter of fact, fatally ill. Suspecting something fishy, the medic informed Woelle, who came into our dormitory to judge for himself whether I was going to live or die.

On tiptoes, he cautiously approached my cot. Was it bad? Did I feel terrible? Should he summon the doctor? After putting his fat white hand on my cool forehead, he did not even bat an eye, but wished me a speedy recovery. As he was leaving, he turned around in the door to inform me that, unfortunately, this uniquely wonderful ceremony could not be repeated for my sake. Wasn't that too bad?

One weekend, I was issued a twenty-four-hour pass, identifying me as the commander's special courier sent to Berlin on some confidential mission. At the academy's front gate the guard suspiciously examined the document from all sides, saluted, and I was on my way to Berlin. I had called my mother on the telephone, which miraculously still functioned, to learn that she had received permission to bring a package to my father. In Dahlem, turning the last corner, I breathed a deep sigh of relief; the house was still there after the previous night's particularly nasty air raid, the roof missing some tiles and a lot of broken windows.

That same afternoon, entering the Lehrterstrasse Prison in the cavalry uniform, my mother by my side, the SS guards gave me odd looks. *Unterscharführer* Knuth suppressed a grin, and with a gruff loud voice, he criticized several of our items, then whispered, "Your father is all right."

Returning to the barracks, I made one of the worst discoveries of my entire life; my wallet was missing. While I had stuck my special "courier" pass into an inside pocket of my uniform jacket, I vaguely remembered putting some of my possessions on the luggage rack. In the wallet were at least half a dozen of the stolen sheets with the *Reichsführer-SS* letterhead. If found by the wrong people, it would mean the end not only of me, but probably the entire family. Over the next few days, I moved around in a kind of black, sticky fog, unable to eat, sleep, or share my horrible fears with anybody. I even consulted with my little Ortgies friend about a terminal solution if worst came to worst. Two days later, the time bomb exploded.

After lunch I was summoned to the commander's office. Instead of the expected black-clad Gestapo henchmen with ankle-length leather coats, two dumpy girls in Hitler Youth uniforms were waiting for me, in the background the visibly nervous colonel. They gave a snappy salute and reported, not without pride, that after finding the wallet on the train, they searched it, discovered my identity, and consequently, my whereabouts. "Wasn't that wonderful?" they both asked me with a heartwarming smile. Wonderful was hardly the expression! I was ready to have them beatified and canonized for saving me from the guillotine. Only on my way out, it dawned on me that they must have believed me to be a Gestapo agent. But, almost skipping all the way back to our barracks, I decided that this was something with which I would have to live.

By the time Christmas rolled around, my father was still in his bug-ridden cell. We had been issued another pass and were able to take him a few gifts. On Christmas Eve, the British bombers decided to take a well-deserved rest; they made up for it the following day.

Chapter Forty-Six
The Prisoner of Dachau Receives Tragic News

The prisoner in Dachau spent his eighth Christmas in captivity, never knowing what the next hour might bring for him. He had no idea that he was, in all likelihood, Adolf Hitler's most precious hostage, to be used as a pawn at the right time to the führer's advantage.

Just as the year 1944 came to an end, Niemoeller was struck by a blow, compared to which all his previous suffering seemed almost negligible. A gruff SS guard informed him almost casually, "By the way, your daughter died." For twenty-four hours, the prisoner was left guessing as to which of his three daughters the man was referring, but a dark foreboding told him that it was Jutta, his youngest and favorite child, the apple of his eye. Of the seven children, she was the one who was helped into the world by her father, no doctor or midwife having been available. Beautiful in appearance, with her father's dark complexion and the eyes of a doe, she was mature far beyond her years. Although cheerful by nature, there were indications that she had sensed her early death.

Indeed, it was sixteen-year-old Jutta who, despite all medical efforts, succumbed to diphtheria. Her last request, to visit her father, had been turned down by the Gestapo. The devastated father's petition to attend her funeral was rejected.

Only weeks after this tragedy, his oldest son, Jochen, the only one to follow in his father's footsteps as a pastor, came home for a brief furlough from the front. Before returning, he handed his sister Hertha a sealed envelope with the instruction to give it to his mother in case he did not come back. His premonition did not betray him; he was killed in action in Pomerania. Else took Jochen's letter to her husband in Dachau; he was on the brink of a total breakdown. He rebelled against God. Why could not he have died instead of his son, for whom he would have joyfully laid down his own life? But once more Jochen, even after his death at age twenty-two, was able to console his father, who had often jokingly referred to him as "the pastor's pastor": "Be cheerful in hope," Jochen ended his last brief note, "patient in tribulation, and keep on praying."

Chapter Forty-Seven
The War Closes In

The people of Berlin groaned under the brutal assaults from above, which turned the once proud capital into a not so proud mountain of debris. The British Royal Air Force, with vast supplies of air mines on board, kept attacking at night. Only after such a device had hit its target did one hear the terrible swishing noise it made on the way down. To assure perfect aim, the pilots now dropped luminous devices, appropriately named "Christmas trees" by the Berliners, in order to illuminate the scene before unloading their precious cargo.

The American raids took place in broad daylight and were exclusively directed at industrial centers. We learned to almost enjoy watching them from the garden, flying at high altitude above the house in majestic formation, ignoring the furious attacks by the German flak battalions. Rarely, it happened that a plane was hit and, after going into a spin, ultimately plunged to the ground in a fiery ball. If the pilot made it to safety by parachute, he was faced with the possibility of being lynched by an outraged mob before the authorities arrived.

With the Soviets rapidly approaching from the east and, at a somewhat faster pace, the Western Allied ground forces from the west, we nursed the hope of being liberated by the British or the Americans. Now voices were heard from those who had so far loudly praised every German victory in Russia, labeling the Russians as *untermenschen*, subhumans. Something must have changed their minds, because they assured everyone that, even if the impossible became fact and the Red Army reached Berlin, we had little, if anything, to fear. They would march into the city in an orderly formation, probably with military bands playing those wonderfully rich and moving Russian folk songs, eager to set a shining example for the whole world to watch! Basically, they maintained, Russians were good-natured children, dim-witted but eager to pick up the German culture. Others expressed the weird theory that intentionally luring the enemy deep into the heart of Germany was probably the führer's most ingenious strategic move. The Red soldiers, in awe of so much German civilization, would simply be too embarrassed to display anything but their best behavior. While certainly no match in discipline to the orderly Germans, the Soviets could simply not afford to behave in anything but an exemplary manner.

Orderly Germans? Like the German intruders? The *Einsatzgruppen*? The SS? The torturers and the henchmen in the concentration camps who did not hesitate to string up their own compatriots by piano wires on meat hooks? After the hell endured by the Russian people at the hands of the invaders, the SS and the *Wehrmacht* alike, thousands of towns and villages erased from the face of the Earth, the violent deaths of millions deeply imprinted in their memory, they would be eager to demonstrate exemplary behavior to their tormentors? We just could not believe our ears.

Back at the academy, during one night in early January, we were awakened by the rumbling, ground-shaking noise of distant thunder. A thunderstorm in the middle of winter? Since there were no accompanying flashes of lightning, we soon grasped that what we heard was the unmistakable sound of ground battle fire, probably Russian field artillery. The following morning, Pavlik whispered into my ear that, according to the unfailing POW grapevine, "Russian brothers come soon. Du nix Angst. You nix fear, Pawlee protect," he reassured me. During the following weeks, a pathetic and never-ending procession of vehicles began to clatter down the main street, ranging from makeshift hand-pulled carts, covered wagons, and elegant coaches pulled by dead-tired and emaciated horses, among them exquisite thoroughbreds. Some of the vehicles had been turned into regular little huts, equipped with roofs and smoking chimneys on top, dogs running underneath. They were packed with mountains of household goods, bedsteads, and bedding.

The fugitives from East and West Prussia, from Pomerania and Silesia, on the frozen roads for weeks, had left everything behind in fear of being caught by the Soviet Army. Bundled up against the cold, some of the old men's beards had turned to icicles. They told stories too horrible to be believed, of farmhouses set ablaze by the Mongols and Tatars, mass rapes of eighty-year-old women as well as five-year-old girls, while the farmers were nailed to the barn doors. All we could do for those desperate people was supply them with bread, hot soup, and ersatz coffee.

Only for the horses' sake did they agree to take a brief rest in the compound, crammed into stables, barns, and halls for as long as it took their animals to recuperate; then off they went again, westward, westward, as if chased by furies. We had to deal with casualties, mainly small children and old people, who had dropped dead from sheer exhaustion, their cold corpses dragged along by their relatives for miles to the next village, in the hope of a decent burial. Beginning as a trickle, the stream of wagons soon swelled to hundreds, then to thousands, and we stopped counting.

It was after one particularly exhausting and bitter cold night that a terrible stabbing pain in my chest made breathing almost impossible. The medical officer diagnosed double pleurisy and ordered me into the infirmary at once. Colonel Behnke came to my bedside and told me that, since the academy was going to be evacuated, the entire unit would be moved west to a place near Potsdam. Feeling that I should not be left behind, he strongly advised me to go home to Berlin on official sick leave at once, if I felt at all up to it. Gathering my few belongings, with a fever of forty degrees Celsius, I left Beeskow that same day. Pavlik broke into pitiful sobs at the news, like a child wiping his red-rimmed eyes and his eternally runny nose on his ragged, all-purpose sleeve. Never, never, never would he see me again, he howled in despair like some abandoned animal, with Fyodor silently looking on.

While recuperating in Dahlem, the familiar roar of the attacking airplanes and the falling bombs turning the sky over the dying city a bright red during the nights was now reinforced by a constant grumbling of artillery fire that came closer every day, until it eventually drowned out all other sounds. In February, Frau Thiele came once more into our house. She had survived so far, thanks to the help of the brave, resistant families in our neighborhood. Now she was confident that she would make it all the way to safety. Since the aftermath of July 20, 1944, we had not dared to accommodate any more Jews in our house for fear of unannounced visits by the Gestapo. At this stage, however, Gestapo members were too busy going underground themselves, naked survival being the utmost priority.[26]

The air raids caused the rain and snow to seep through the damaged roof down to the second and first floor. The dark foreboding of a major battle made us realize that the end was near; as the Berliners put it, an end with horror was still better than horror without end. Business at Leni Riefenstahl's house was still going on as usual. The magnificent resistance center remained intact and undetected. There cannot be any doubt that the mistress of the house never had the faintest notion of what occurred under her own roof. Neither did she find out that I relished sleeping in her comfortable bed through a few nights. We were all sworn to silence about the secret rescue activities that went on at her residence, fearing that, after the war, it would provide the lady of the house with a welcome and badly needed alibi as a fierce anti-Nazi.

With my father still languishing in the Lehrterstrasse Prison, which would ultimately be leveled during the actual battle of Berlin, my mother did something that she dared not share with me beforehand. During the last days of March, she decided to approach Ernst Kaltenbrunner, Heydrich's successor, to plead with him for her husband's life. Upon her return home, although seemingly composed, she suffered a long overdue nervous breakdown, realizing she had confronted ultimate evil, face to face. After recovering sufficiently to report about her encounter with Satan personified, she stated that, as far as she was concerned, he had not even listened to her plea to release her "totally innocent" husband, who, after all, was a highly decorated World War I veteran, a man who had lost his three brothers in battle.

To her own surprise, she had somehow gained entrance to the devil's inner sanctum, where she found the hideous-looking, almost seven foot tall man with his ghastly scarred face seated behind his huge desk and wearing his black uniform. Obviously he saw no reason to rise from his chair for the wife of an enemy of the state, a damned Junker. Standing before him, she presented her case, after which she was swiftly dismissed. She left convinced that nothing she said had made the slightest difference to this sadistic brute, who was known to travel to extermination camps to join in the killing or just watch executions for his personal enjoyment.

One month later, on the morning of Friday, April 13, three days after my birthday, the phone, miraculously still in working order, rang in the hall. Taking the receiver, I could not believe my ears. On the other end was my father, his voice a hoarse whisper. He was free; would I come and get him? No, not at the prison, but rather at the Lehrterstrasse S-Bahn station. I do not remember how I made it there, walking, running, and stumbling the long way into the heart of the city, sometimes using the S-Bahn, which was still erratically running. It seemed to me that angels carried me on their wings.

Anxiously scanning the mobbed, badly damaged Lehrterstrasse station platform across from the prison, I could not detect anyone even remotely resembling my father. When I finally saw him leaning against a pillar, giving me a faint wave with his hand, my heart almost stood still. With his shaven head and gray beard stubble, he resembled a vagrant. I would not have recognized him in clothes that were almost rags after nine months of captivity, a string-tied bundle with his belongings at his feet. His face was bloated out of proportion, a typical symptom of hunger edema, after having existed on a diet of watery soup, interrupted once monthly by our small food packages. We fell into each other's arms, oblivious to the world around us; I had him back and he was free, as free as anyone could be under the harrowing circumstances.

Then my eyes fell on a figure standing next to him in the gray uniform of the *Waffen-SS*, the field branch of the regular SS. Obviously one of those just drafted and not older than fifteen, he resembled a child crammed into a grownup's uniform. To the youngster, seeing a father and daughter reunited was obviously more than he could take. Tears were streaming down his baby face; he could hardly contain himself. My father explained to me that the boy had helped him carry his things from the cell to the station. As he turned around to leave, his shoulders shaking with violent sobs, I knew that he, too, would probably like to see his own father again.

Somehow we made it home, walking, taking an unexpected tattered bus, and riding a few stops on the underground. All the way we just held on to one another, unable to speak. I do not remember having stopped crying for more than a few seconds. At home, taking a good look at him, he seemed even worse than at first glance. His swollen face was a hectic red, his arms and legs covered with countless red spots showing the traces of bed bugs. Lacking fuel for the central heating system in our house, my mother and I managed to gather enough wood and some coal to build a fire under the old boiler in the laundry room, ultimately dragging buckets of hot water up to the bathroom for his first bath in nine months. Black market soap and a soft towel were long-forgotten luxury items.

After twenty-four hours he began to talk. With a feverish glow in his burning, sunken eyes, he spoke incessantly for hours and hours. It had been terrible! Early that morning, an SS guard had come into his cell, brusquely ordering the prisoner to gather his belongings. This was the moment my father had been dreading—his deportation to a concentration camp. Just before he stepped into the courtyard, ready to board the Black Maria,[27] after habitually sticking his hands out to be handcuffed, the guard told him that he was free.

Free? Why? How? We would never know! He was even handed official discharge papers, granted permission to make a phone call, and two hours later I was there. Upon his request to say good-bye to *Unterscharführer* Knuth, he received the answer that the *Unterscharführer* was not "available anymore." The news that he had been executed for behavior not befitting an SS official would reach us only years after the war.

In terrible monologues, which did not require a reaction or an answer, the words seemed to fall out of him, quite obviously the only way to rid himself of an unbearable burden. When it came to describing the physical and mental torture, his voice became a hoarse whisper, and he had to stop several times before being able to continue. After endless nocturnal interrogations with the light almost blinding him, there was always the same ritual. Back at his cell door, the handcuffs were taken off, followed by a kick of the guard's boot in his back that sent him flying into a corner, accompanied be the threat that *tomorrow* severe measures would be taken to make him spill the truth. He had nightmares about being tortured to the point where he would do what was expected of him before being delivered to the hands of

Roland Freisler: spill the names of anyone involved in the conspiracy. Through the prison grapevine he had been informed that his friend Hans von Plettenberg had jumped out of a window to his death on his way between the cell and the interrogation room. Had it not been for the support and the encouragement of *Unterscharführer* Knuth, my father said, he would probably not have made it through the nine months of hell.

It took a week, most of which we spent on mattresses in the cellar, until he was mentally and physically able to take a brief walk around the block with me. Cooped up in the tiny, cold cell for so long, enduring agonizing sciatic pains without medication, he had literally forgotten how to use his legs. Frequently, he would take my hand and turn around as if expecting to be picked up again. Walking by destroyed houses toward St. Anne's Church, we saw a young soldier in uniform hanging by a rope from a lamppost. The wind caused his stiff body to swing back and forth. Around his neck hung a crude cardboard sign that read, "I was a coward and not worthy of fighting for führer and fatherland." That was my father's welcome back to his beloved Dahlem.

We had reached the spot where a year before he had made me promise to leave Germany after the war; once again he grabbed me by the shoulders, repeating his request. I should promise to go and find a "new star" for myself and my children. Something in his eyes and his voice told me in no uncertain terms that even now, after his miraculous liberation, he did not include himself in my future. "They are coming for me, help, they are coming for me," he had screamed in his nightmares throughout my childhood. Yes, "they" had come for him! But now he was back, back for good! Or was he?

With the air raids having come to an end, the noise of the planes above was now replaced by the roar of heavy artillery, the infernal hooting of bazookas, and the wailing of so-called "Stalinorgans," huge firing devices mounted on wide gun-carriages, their multiple barrels reminiscent of organ pipes. Not bothering to change into bedclothes anymore, we fell asleep from sheer exhaustion whenever possible. There was still water, sometimes even electricity, and we had enough basic food to last us for a while.

Chapter Forty-Eight
Last Visit to Dachau

On April 21, 1945, a Saturday, Else Niemoeller traveled from Leoni on Lake Sternberg to the Dachau Concentration Camp for the last time. It was the day after Hitler's fifty-sixth birthday, which he spent in the Reich Chancellery bunker in the beleaguered capital of Berlin, surrounded by some of his most faithful accomplices and the woman who would become Eva Hitler for the last few hours in her life. While Soviet troops encircled Berlin, preparing to penetrate the heart of the city, the Americans were approaching Munich from the south. On April 7, Martin wrote in his diary that, for the first time, the roar of cannons could be heard.

The chaotic atmosphere prevailing in the entire camp did not escape Else; everyone seemed busy packing, the offices having already been stripped of furniture and appliances. The time allotted with her husband was brief. She found him more depressed and nervous than ever. Rumors had reached him through the camp grapevine that a number of prominent political prisoners from other concentration camps all over the "Reich" had been brought to Dachau to be deported with him.

Among the new arrivals, hermetically sealed off from the other inmates who would soon be driven from the camp like cattle, were the former Austrian Chancellor Kurt von Schuschnigg with his wife and little daughter, former French Minister-President Léon Blum, the Italian General Sante Garibaldi, Commander in Chief of the Greek Forces Alexander Papagos, the two British spies Best and Stevens, and the Prime Minister of Hungary Miklós Kalláy. In addition, the German generals von Falkenhausen, Halder, and Thomas, as well as a number of surviving members of the Stauffenberg family, including Colonel von Bonin, who refused obedience to the führer, and Hjalmar Schacht, Hitler's former finance minister until he fell out of grace.

"They want to deport us. I don't want to be deported," Martin continually repeated, though he had hardly a say in the decision, should it come to pass.

As the situation grew more precarious, the pastor, his nerves at the breaking point after eight years of captivity and the loss of two children, lost his composure. The prospect that he and other high-ranking inmates would indeed be taken south as Hitler's most valuable hostages sent Martin into a fit of rage. The Catholic priests, in despair over not being able to calm him down, summoned Colonel Dick Stevens in the hope that the British officer would talk sense into their raging fellow prisoner. Martin threatened to kill anyone who would force him to leave his cell against his will. Dick finally succeeded in convincing him that, in order to be liberated by the Americans, they had to leave the camp, which was still crawling with SS. With her heart heavier than ever, Else Niemoeller left Dachau. When, if ever, would she see her husband again?

⇜ Chapter Forty-Nine ⇝
Arabella

With Dresden practically bombed out of existence on February 13 and 14, the last major target of the Allied air attacks had been Potsdam, the cradle of Prussian military glory where, in 1933, the established Christian church once permitted Adolf Hitler to disgrace the tradition-rich old sanctuary, the *Garnisonkirche*, with his presence. The heart of the ancient town was in ruins, including the Garrison Church, with its belfry in shattered pieces strewn on the street below. Had my grandmother survived?

Monday, April 23 marked my grandmother's eighty-fifth birthday, and aware of my father's anxiety over his mother's fate, I decided to ride my bicycle the fifteen miles to Potsdam to see if she had made it through the air raids, figuring I could be home again by nightfall. Just in case something unexpected should keep me from returning that day, I took a rucksack with the bare necessities. My parents, although reluctant to give their permission for this expedition, had learned to trust my sixth sense that, like my mother's, bordered on clairvoyance.

Donning the mandatory steel helmet to protect me from bullets and shell splinters, I hugged my father for one last time. He made me promise "to be careful." Before turning the corner at the end of our street, I looked back and saw him wave his hand from the front garden gate. For the rest of my life, I would remember this last gesture. With my shiny black little friend Ortgies safely tucked in a holster on my belt, I began my journey into the unknown with an amazing degree of confidence. Berlin was burning—so what?

The torn-up streets of the western suburbs, with their hastily erected barricades, offered a picture of devastation. Soldiers and civilians alike, cardboard signs around their necks, were hanging from trees and lanterns, while piles of grotesquely shaped black objects were stacked on the sidewalks, the carbonized remains of bodies pulled from bombed houses, shrunken to the size of pressed sticks of charcoal through the intense heat. Buildings were ablaze everywhere, frantic survivors hauling their belongings from one cellar to another, dead horses lying where they had fallen, with hungry people already lining up for a welcome meal, greedily watching men with knives cut the still warm bodies into portions.

There were a few German military vehicles and soldiers in sight but not a single Russian yet. Amidst the deafening, honking noise of the Stalinorgans, and in spite of constant artillery bombardment, I reached the main road leading to Wannsee and, ultimately, Potsdam, thanking God that my bicycle enabled me to squeeze past the masses of refugees on foot, dragging carts and wagons, in a panicky effort to escape westward, always westward!

I found my grandmother in her apartment, alive and well. The only gift I had for her on her birthday was the news that her last son had survived the Nazi prison. On my way out, she unfastened a golden chain from her neck that held a beautiful golden medallion adorned with countless little diamonds, which I had craved ever since I could remember. In it she had kept locks of hair from her three dead sons. She encouraged me to hurry home.

It was still early afternoon, so I decided to return via Krampnitz, located a few miles north of Potsdam, where my cavalry unit was now stationed. This rash decision probably saved my life. Before reaching the Krampnitz academy, I was almost thrown off my bike by a series of massive detonations nearby. In front of the compound, lined up in an orderly formation of vehicles and horses, was my unit's five officers, the non-commissioned officers and soldiers, Russian POWs, and lots of horses. Colonel Behnke informed me that the bridges connecting Potsdam and Berlin had just been blown up. Since I could not return to Dahlem, I had to go with them, and he would not take "no" for an answer. We would have to take our chances trying to reach the American lines, now reportedly west of the Elbe River, a hundred miles away.

Since all the other girls had been sent westward weeks ago, I would be the only female in the convoy. He added that, since I was able to ride like a man, even able to roll a cigarette with one hand while in the saddle, I could probably shoot like one, too, if necessary. He ordered me to take the lead at the front between him and the "good" captain, followed by the major and the veterinarian, while the "bad" captain, the Gestapo snitch, was placed at the convoy's far end—at a safe distance. Only a few weeks earlier he had reported two of the girls to the Gestapo for making defeatist remarks. Reassured by little Ortgies' presence, I could not wait to get my hands on him.

To my horror, I was the one designated to mount the commander's private horse, Arabella, the snow-white Trakehner mare who tolerated but a chosen few on her aristocratic back. Being among those chosen people, she greeted me with an ingratiating snarl of her yellow teeth. Arabella was a so-called "killer horse," a somewhat deranged animal with very odd behavior patterns that could never be normalized. Since horses were unable to talk, it was impossible to determine the cause of such an unfortunate development, the presumption being that some traumatic experience in her early years lay at the root of the problem. Literally on her way to the horse butcher, she had been rescued by the commander, who purchased the four-year-old mare for his private use. He had not been able to resist the wicked beauty of this moody, unpredictable, and totally asocial witch with her long, dark gray mane, the deep blue eyes of a diva, who was fully aware that a well-aimed kick from her dainty little hooves could kill a man. The colonel had found to his dismay that he, her savior, was not among the chosen few she permitted in the saddle. So whenever he felt bold enough to mount her anyway, one of us was delegated to chase her through the ring on a lead for at least half an hour, to sufficiently tire her out.

Her resourceful tricks included either plopping to the ground together with the rider or pumping herself full of air while the saddle belt was fastened, only to let the air out later, causing the saddle to slide to her belly. I could not remember one single time that she had not tried to bite me on the back when I tried to bridle her. Another one of her favorite games was to gallop close to a tree in the woods at top speed, in the diabolical hope of tearing the rider's leg off, While she had learned to fear and therefore obey me, I was now determined to teach her to love me. After all, we were going to be a team, one relying on the other.

The riderless horses not pulling carriages would have to be led by the reins, so each Russian prisoner was assigned to walk between two horses. This meant that our traveling pace was determined by their speed, unless we wanted to risk losing a man and/or two animals. Arabella gave me a poisonous look, indicating that she was not overly amused, but, as if she sensed the urgency of the situation, she graciously tolerated me in the saddle.

Night was already falling when our convoy moved through the front gate of the academy. Directly behind us, at a respectful distance from Arabella's hind hooves, each leading two horses, were Fyodor and Pavlik ("Pawlee"). At the unexpected sight of me, his red-rimmed eyes brimmed with tears of joy, which were wiped on his snot-shiny tattered sleeve. Oh, he was so happy, and he would take such good care of me—no reason to worry! *"Du nix Angst"*; I should not be afraid. In Pawlee's imposing presence, who would be afraid?

The decision was to ride by night, when the roads were not quite so crowded by the masses of refugees. During the second night, somewhere on a cobblestoned road between two deserted villages, I must have fallen asleep on the horse from sheer exhaustion, only to wake up on the hard and cold ground, the steel helmet having prevented my skull from bursting like a coconut. Above me, I spotted three pairs of eyes—the slightly triumphant look of Arabella's and the horrified expressions of Pawlee and Fyodor. Was I hurt? *Alles kaput*? *Nix kaput*? After knocking the dirt off me, the two heaved me back into the saddle again. *Karasho? Karasho!*

Another reason for riding at night was to avoid being hit by low flying planes, whose pilots delighted in firing from their cockpits toward anything that moved. The casualties had to be left by the roadside in the ditches. On our long journey into the unknown, I must have taken identity papers from at least two dozen corpses, which I later sent to the Red Cross. But not even the darkness provided enough safety, especially with Arabella shining like silver in the dark, so more than once we just barely managed to dash into some underbrush before the pilots took aim.

"You goddam fucking idiots," I felt like screaming. "Not me, please, not me!"

It must have been then that I discovered my curses were in English, and I decided to henceforth think and speak in that language.

Faraway in the distance was our guiding star, most likely a powerful American spotlight, searching the heavens. This bright pillar, reaching all the way up to the sky, moved slowly back and forth, obviously with no other purpose but to show us the way to freedom, to salvation. The star of Bethlehem could not have been any brighter.

Chapter Fifty
Freedom

In the early morning hours of Wednesday, April 25, two open trucks left Dachau Concentration Camp. The first one held the group of prominent prisoners; the second held their wives and children. Martin's premonition had not betrayed him; they were taken out with the purpose of being eventually used as hostages. Accompanying SS guards, armed to the teeth, were ready to carry out orders, any orders. The two big vehicles made their way through the pitiful masses in their striped rags, thirty-five thousand survivors driven on foot from the camp by the SS. Not a sound was heard except for the muted murmur of the prisoners. Some of them, recognizing the cargo on the passing trucks, lifted their hands in a last weak salute, a gesture that brought tears to the pastor's eyes. This long procession of emaciated inmates dragging themselves forward would, of course, not be noticed by the German population who, during the previous twelve years, had mastered the fine art of selective sight.

Colonel Stevens had managed to bring his little radio along, from which they learned that, while General Patton was about to take Frankfurt, the US 7th Army was approaching Munich. They found out later that, in his Berlin bunker, Hitler had given the order to "liquidate" all the prisoners en route south, foremost the hated pastor. Under no circumstances were any of the special prisoners to fall into the hands of the enemy.[28]

After leaving the ruins of Munich, the trucks sped toward the town of Rosenheim, ultimately reaching the autobahn. An island in the Inn River, a deserted former labor camp, filthy and vermin-infested, provided a first place of rest. After two days and nights, they continued south; at Innsbruck, three tight-mouthed, sinister-looking SS guards and one SS officer from Buchenwald, with the rank of *Obersturmbannführer*, were taken aboard: the death squad. The convoy was now heading in the direction of the Italian border. After hours of waiting at the Brenner Pass, they eventually stopped at Villabassa in southern Tyrol, several times barely escaping attacks by low flying Allied planes.

Under the eyes of the SS, the prisoners were finally able to rest on some straw in the town hall while the guards drank themselves into a stupor. Captain Best was able to swipe a note from the *Obersturmbannführer*'s briefcase, the execution order from Berlin; however, before it could be carried out, a German Army unit marched into the village and sent the baffled SS guards fleeing.

Soon, all 136 prisoners were liberated for a second time by the US 7th Army, who made it through deep snow to the Hotel Pragser Wildsee, where the captives had been locked up for the previous two days. The Americans provided food, drink, and clean clothes for their charges. The miracle of their actual liberation was due to a bold act of disobedience by a young US lieutenant named Alfred de Jonge. He decided not to follow the command he received to bomb the Hotel Pragser Wildsee, sensing that the place was filled with Hitler's prominent prisoners, among them Pastor Niemoeller. Instead, he ordered his platoon to move forward and take the hotel. Not a single shot was fired, and within minutes, twelve nightmarish years came to an end.

There was one US Army device that impressed Martin as particularly ingenious; icy water was pumped from the lake, heated by sending it through the radiators of a military truck, which ultimately came out hot through makeshift showerheads in a tent. Armed with soap, fresh towels, and brand new clothes from US Army supplies, the freed prisoners, happily discarding their tattered, striped convict garb, felt as though they had passed through a fountain of youth. This was the first bath and the first clean clothes for Martin and his fellow hostages in what seemed like an eternity.

During the next few days, they all lived under the illusion of being in heaven, after which a convoy of twenty-eight vehicles lined up to take them to Verona and from there by military aircraft to Naples, where the British commander had prepared a festive welcoming ceremony. A special surprise awaited the pastor; a former confirmand who had been able to escape Nazi Germany greeted him in the uniform of an American officer. Martin, who was most in demand by the media, visited Marshal Alexander for lunch. Now wearing a khaki shirt, with his pipe in one corner of his mouth, he presented himself to the numerous photographers. His command of English was admired, and he was pumped for every single detail of information. But even a broad smile could not disguise the deep lines in his emaciated face.

After five weeks his patience ran out. Eight years had gone by, and all he wanted now was to go home to his family. The Americans flew him to Wiesbaden but, instead of releasing him, he was detained for more questioning. At that point he lost his temper, threatening to go on a hunger strike. In vain, the American captain tried to tempt his angry charge by reading him the daily menus. Finally, the pastor was issued a US Army vehicle that would take him to Leoni on Lake Starnberg. On the way, it happened that they were stopped by American Military Police, checking the suspicious-looking pass permitting a German national to be outside after the otherwise strictly enforced curfew. After one glance, the flabbergasted sergeant asked, "You don't want to make me believe you are *the* famous Pastor Niemoeller?"

"I cannot deny it," was the answer, whereupon the sergeant quipped, "You know what I want to do with you? I want to kiss you!"

In the early morning of June 24, 1945, Else Niemoeller woke up to the sound of a familiar voice outside her window. Even in his strange-looking clothes, including a slouch hat, she immediately recognized her husband, alive and well. His greatest anguish, the death of his two favorite children; his sublime triumph, the fact that against all odds he had survived his tormentor, Adolf Hitler.

Chapter Fifty-One
Continuing the Trek

Every completed mile brought us a little closer to our goal, the American or British lines, promised by the light in the far distance. Would we ever reach it? Managing about ten miles in twenty-four hours, with the horses and the Russian POWs setting the pace, we made slow but steady progress. In between we rested, sleeping for a few hours in some underbrush, in stables, barns, empty farmhouses, and deserted mansions. We sank down on bare wooden or concrete floors, piles of straw, and magnificent, oversized beds, still warm from those who had decided to leave in a hurry.

Since we all had to eat, I stole potatoes and cabbage from cellars, canned meat from pantry shelves, enough wine to make everyone happy, and caught and cooked chickens after they had been decapitated by Fyodor and Pawlik with the proficiency of executioners. One of the wagons in our convoy was filled to the brim with bread and booze, the key having been entrusted to me. They could not have picked a better person, because I dished out both to whoever asked. Enough schnapps, we found, was very helpful in lulling us into a nice, warm feeling of false security.

The only thought that made me sick was that my parents had no idea of my whereabouts. After five days and nights, something occurred in the little town of Neustadt on the Dosse River that almost brought our journey to an abrupt and possibly tragic end. With night setting in, we were just about to resume our weary journey, with the vet and me at the head of the convoy. The others were still some distance away when, suddenly, a motorcycle came to a screeching halt right under our noses, causing Arabella to perform a perfect yet unexpected levade.[29] The man on the bike with a sidecar did not even bother to turn the engine off; what he had to say would not take long. I recognized the SS emblems on the license number as well as on his helmet, identifying him as one of the feared "Field Police" hunting for deserters; even at this stage of the game, I almost panicked. After determining that we were not in the possession of official marching orders, he told us in no uncertain terms to immediately turn back east to Berlin to help defend the city as was our duty. His machine gun hung casually across his back, an oversight he would have no time to regret, since both the vet and I were armed.

Memories of young soldiers dangling from lampposts because they did not want to go on fighting for Adolf Hitler flashed through my mind. Not me, I decided, not me, not at this point or ever will I return to hell.

Precisely at that moment, with a low flying fighter plane roaring above us, for a split second my eyes met with those of the vet next to me. The infernal noise of the plane engine, plus the rattling of the motorbike drowned out the two gun shots. One of the bullets carried special greetings from my friend Ortgies, the other one carried best wishes from the vet's handgun.

Shortly after this incident, our column started moving, passing the SS man, now slumped over the sidecar of his vehicle that had rolled halfway into a ditch with the motor still running, another unfortunate war casualty, most likely hit from the cockpit of the plane! The vet and I had committed the perfect crime unnoticed, probably saving not only our own lives, but our entire unit.

After the seventh night, while passing through a deserted village, an old man approached us, whispering that, according to a special radio bulletin, Adolf Hitler was dead. The führer had fallen in the battle of Berlin, which he had helped defend like a hero, fighting to his last breath for his fatherland, for his people,

"Not for me," I wanted to shout! "Not for me!"

But warned by my instinct, I decided to postpone long-overdue screams of ecstasy until this delightful report, the best one in twelve years, was confirmed. I had survived this far, so now I could surely wait just a little longer.

Chapter Fifty-Two
War's End

The battle of Berlin would officially end three days later. It dawned on me that I must have left only hours before the iron clamp closed around the city and its three million inhabitants. Steadily and forcefully, the gigantic Russian tanks, with thousands of miles behind them, made it forward, mercilessly attacked by furious but futile German attempts to hold back the enemy. The tanks' monstrous size, preventing swift and effective movements, made them easy targets for the German anti-tank weapon, the "*Panzerfaust*," small enough to be operated by the children now drafted into the *Wehrmacht*. The Red Army did not enter Berlin in an orderly formation; they had to conquer it street by street, house by house. While dead Russian soldiers would be buried at once by the roadside, Germans were left lying where they fell. Of the 135,000 German soldiers still stationed in the Berlin garrison, 70,000 survivors were captured and marched East; only a handful would eventually return. A last minute offer by the *Wehrmacht* to negotiate peace vastly amused the Russians. Wasn't it a little late for negotiations?

When the battle was finally over, Stalin offered his heroic soldiers the battered Nazi capital as a free-for-all on a silver platter, a well-deserved reward for years of unspeakable suffering. Now the Germans, men, women, and children, the very old and the very young, the guilty and the innocent, Nazis and anti-Nazis alike, got a taste of what it meant to be invaded by an army that, through dogged determination, under inhuman conditions, and after four long years, had triumphed over the devastators of Russia, forcing the enemies to their knees on their own turf. The red flag displaying a hammer and sickle now flew from the Brandenburg Gate.

It was just before dawn; I had fallen asleep on the floor of a farmhouse when a knock at the window awakened me. Oh God, what now? Had *they* gotten wind of our evil deed after all? Then I heard Pawlee's voice: "Open, *pasholsk*, open!"

"Thank you, Lord!" I said aloud.

Pawlee's red-rimmed eyes peeked in from the outside, his nose flattened on the glass. What the hell did he want? When I opened the window, he put a finger to his lips and whispered! "Gitler kaput, war kaput, SS kaput, krkrkrk, boomboom, bangbang, *karasho*!" Grinning from one ear to the other, not without admiration, he threw a significant glance at little Ortgies on the table. So the rascal knew what had happened by the Dosse River after all! With Fyodor like a shadow behind him, Pawlee began to mumble in a mixture of German and Russian until I finally grasped that "Russian brothers" were close, and he and Fyodor would like to join them. No longer prisoners, but instead soldiers again in the Red Army. I had to suppress a fit of hysterical laughter at the utter absurdity of the situation; two Soviet POWs about to be liberated asking a female German, with the rank of an officer, for permission to escape. I just could not believe it!

"Go," I told them. "Go, run fast, don't turn back, and be very, very careful. Hurry up, scram, what are you waiting for?" But Pawlee wasn't through with me yet. They were both hungry, he signaled, and his longing look went to the large loaf of black army bread next to the Ortgies on the table. Through the window, I handed him the entire loaf, not without stern instructions to share it with Fyodor, because otherwise I would—"da, da, da," Pavlik ended my unfinished sentence. "You make *puppenlappen*, rag doll, of Pawlee." He took the words right out of my mouth! Both gave me a smacking kiss on the cheeks and—*spassiva, dasvidaniya*—I watched them disappear into the fog, suddenly horrified at the thought of never seeing them again. I almost cried, but I decided it would have to wait; there was no time for tears now.[30]

At roll call on the last morning of our journey, the Nazi captain noticed the disappearance of two Soviet subhumans. Foaming with rage, he promised to personally massacre them. But in order to do that he would have to catch them first!

The sun was just about to rise in the east when, moving slowly across the marketplace of the deserted village, we noticed white sheets hanging from windows that, I was certain, over a period of twelve years had been graced by swastika flags. Nobody was in sight; the entire population was invisible, probably hiding in the woods or the cellars of their houses. It was so quiet that we could have heard a pin drop. Before we had time to wonder about the deadly stillness, we heard a thunderous noise. Was it the *Wehrmacht*? The Red Army? Around the corner and heading straight toward us came a huge vehicle, the biggest tank I had ever seen, with a white star painted on it. Behind it was an army car—a jeep, as I later learned—from which two figures in khaki battle fatigues emerged. With machine guns, they motioned us to bring our convoy to a halt. This was not the Red Army!

It did not take me long to determine that we were in the process of being captured by the United States Armed Forces. Could this really be true? Had we actually made it to the American lines, without losing one man or one horse on our tiresome road from Berlin? The two soldiers, who turned out to be officers, informed us that we were now their prisoners. Two young men captured a convoy of forty enemies and as many horses, eighteen Russian POWs, and me. I would learn that we were dealing with none other than the renowned US 82nd Airborne, their legendary reputation and the name of their equally legendary commander Major General James Gavin having been frequently mentioned by the BBC since the invasion of Normandy.

Everything happened with lightning speed. Several more tanks with white stars came rattling across a wheat field in order to provide cover for our captors. Jumping from one tank came another officer, shouting, "You fucking Krauts! The war is over, and you have lost." The words were followed by the order for everyone to throw his rifle or pistol on the ground in the center of the village square. Since I was the only one able to understand the cordial invitation, I translated it for all to hear and obey. The men, visibly relieved by the uncomplicated manner in which the war had ended for them, filed by to rid themselves of their weapons. "That goes for you, too," I screamed at the Nazi captain, who pretended not to understand, and I could not resist adding a message that I had wanted to deliver ever since I met him: "You filthy Gestapo rat fink." Turning to one of the American officers, I informed him that while, to my knowledge, there was not one rotten egg among all of the men, this captain presented a most disgraceful exception. The young man inquired politely if the Gestapo office should be shot; this could easily be arranged. I told him that just handcuffing and separating him from the rest would suffice for now. This lowdown stool pigeon should definitely have to suffer the consequences later.

Although everyone had surrendered his weapon, I just could not bear to part with little Ortgies quite yet. It had, in all likelihood, been instrumental in saving a lot of lives, among them my own. Since nobody seemed to pay attention to me, I boldly hid my friend under my jacket. Fully anticipating to be included in the group of POWs now marching into captivity, I was surprised that nobody showed any specific interest in me, or in Arabella, who tried with all her might to follow the others. Since I wore a civilian coat over parts of my former uniform, nobody identified me as a member of the military.

Where was I supposed to go, I asked? "Why don't you go home, girly?" one of my liberators suggested naïvely. Home? To Berlin? With the Red Army just around the corner from us? "Well," he said, "why don't you come with us, consider yourself confiscated. We do need an interpreter." On the spot, he appointed me the official interpreter; as a first lieutenant and platoon leader he was entitled to make such earthshaking decisions. By the way, was I British? How come I spoke English with this funny British accent? "No," I replied, "I am a fucking Kraut."

"A damned fucking Kraut for an interpreter?" another officer interrupted in what I noticed to be an unmistakable Viennese accent. In all likelihood he had not left his native country of his own free will, and I was probably a raving Nazi, a spy, a werewolf! Thoroughly disgusted, he shook his fist in my face. From a respectful distance, watching this whole scene unfold before their eyes, the Russian POWs stood looking helpless and bewildered. Who was in charge now? What would become of them? Where would they be sent? One of them by the name of Igor, whom I had called "Goliath" due to his impressive size, cap in hand, slowly walked toward the Austrian-American officer. Goliath had never smiled, and I had always felt uneasy in his presence, now recalling with horror that I had yelled at him once for not rubbing a horse down properly. Pointing at me, "Goliath" began to talk to the unfriendly American, who seemed to understand Russian. Or was it Russian? No, it was not Russian, it was not English, and it was not German. When they suddenly fell into each other's arms, it dawned on me that the strange yet somehow familiar sounding language they were conversing in was Yiddish. One Jew had recognized another.

I saw the American nodding and Goliath turned around, slowly coming toward me. Well, I thought, after making it this far, just because this brute wants to take revenge on at least one German, this is where my life is going to end. Looking down at me from his imposing height, he grabbed me around the waist, lifting me in the air with outstretched arms like a paper doll, then pressed me to his bosom and gave me a wet kiss, one for each cheek. "Nix forget Goliath, you hear?"

"You are a lucky little lady," the Viennese officer managed to say with a crooked grin, "you have just been canonized! So if you still want to be our interpreter, it is OK by me. We can surely use you!"

What did surprise me was the uncalled for haste with which the Americans motioned the captured convoy on: *schnell, schnell,* fast, fast, get moving! Their captives were prisoners of war, what was the hurry, I wondered?

After bidding a last farewell to all the men in my former unit, they went in one direction, and a reluctant Arabella and I went in the other. Following the jeep to the next village, we finally stopped in front of a seemingly deserted, rather pretentious-looking mansion, located on a little river, a tributary of the Elbe. In the hall, the first thing I noticed was a faded rectangular spot over the fireplace, leaving no need to guess whose portrait had hung there until very recently. This place had been the residence of the *Ortsbauernführer*, I learned, the home of the leading Nazi of the district. To my delight, I found a pantry filled with fresh and canned food and a stable for Arabella, with straw, hay, and oats galore. The kitchen stove was still warm and used dishes were in the sink, indicating that the owners had seen fit to leave in a hurry.

I was told to rest until the next morning when I would be picked up. After accommodating Arabella, I fell into one of the beds. The idea of being able to sleep lying down in a proper bed was almost too good to be true. My last thought was that this had been, by far, the greatest day in my entire life! In my dreams, I heard a tank rattling by under my window, and then another one and another one. What a wonderful noise!

◈ Chapter Fifty-Three ◈
The Russians are Coming

The next morning I awakened to an uncanny silence, and it took me a few moments to fully recall the events of the previous day. I went downstairs and, peeking outside, immediately noticed the total absence of American soldiers, tanks, or jeeps. In the stable, Arabella gave me one of her benign looks. I ran back upstairs and looked out the window. Something was definitely very, very wrong, but what? Then I saw it!

Slowly winding its way toward the village from the distant woods came a procession that resembled a tape worm, a seemingly unending stream of trucks, motorcycles, and rickety carts pulled by little shaggy horses, accompanied by soldiers in mud-colored uniforms. There could not be any doubt; this was the Red Army! Horror-struck, I realized that the war was not over by far, and if I did not act fast, I was going to be "liberated" a second time. I grabbed my few belongings, threw the knapsack over my shoulder, and raced into the garden where I hurriedly buried the golden medallion with diamonds on the golden chain that my grandmother had given me, my ring with the coat of arms, and the diamond pin from the kaiser in shallow sand under a bush; they would not catch me, and they would not have my jewels.

In a panic, I headed for the stable to retrieve Arabella, but I was too late. The head of the convoy was just about to reach the first houses, so I raced across a narrow bridge over a river behind the mansion, letting myself plop down into the reeds on the other side. Just in the nick of time, because I spotted the first Soviet soldier with his Kalashnikov, a machine gun, across his chest stomping into the front yard, and I heard his coarse, guttural roar: "*Matka—Frau!*"

Arabella, I thought, what are they going to do with my horse?

Pressing myself against the ground as flat as a flounder, I did not dare to move a muscle. Would Red soldiers make it across the bridge and find me? And then what? The presence of my friend Ortgies hidden in the inside pocket of my jacket was somewhat reassuring; if worst came to worst, I would definitely turn to him for help, whatever the consequences. But what was the worst? Shaking with fear, teeth chattering, I lay motionless on the wet ground until the onset of darkness.

Toward the evening, screams from women mixed with the bawling of drunken Russians began to fill the air. They would not stop all night, nor in the weeks to come. "*Frau komm*" became the most feared two words in those days. The mass rapes were followed by mass suicides, brutal killings of husbands trying in vain to protect their wives, fathers in futile attempts to spare their young daughters. It was like an unending hell had broken loose. What I did not anticipate at this point was that the Red Army did not just pass through, but had come to a forced halt at the river behind which the American troops had installed themselves. Unable to proceed any further, thousands of Soviet soldiers kept pouring into the small village. Their resourcefulness in finding liquor as well as women would be unlimited, their permanent state of drunkenness leading to continuing disaster.

As darkness fell over the scene, I decided it was safe enough to creep along the western bank of the river in search of a human being other than a Red soldier. Where in God's name had the 82nd Airborne gone? Finally, I spotted one of my original liberators down by the water. The sudden appearance of an archangel in all his glory could not possibly have caused me to feel more relief. Giving me a lopsided grin, the young man greeted me with obvious relief. He proceeded to explain that, after depositing me at the *Ortsbauernführer's* house together with my horse, what happened next went so fast that no one had the opportunity to warn me.

The Americans had received the order to withdraw from the east bank of the river; within minutes, the village itself was cleared for the Soviet troops to move in, the innocent little stream now marking the border between East and West, or as far as I was concerned, between heaven and hell. It was only now that I understood the speed with which my former unit had been driven west; the Red Army had literally been around the corner.

My horse, I began lamenting, they have my horse. The twenty-one-year-old second lieutenant, who had identified himself as Charles Battaglia from Pennsylvania, his black eyes, dark curly hair, and olive complexion betraying his Italian descent, wrinkled his brow. After a few minutes of heavy thinking, he informed me that we would in fact have to get the white mare back. I learned quickly that once this young man made up his mind to do something, he would usually go through with it, no matter what; if the army had laws of its own, so had Charles. Two hours later, under the protection of night, we succeeded in sneaking across a bridge into the Red territory without being spotted by the drunken Soviet guards. Charles produced a French-style beret, under which he tucked my long, reddish curls. In case we were stopped, I was now a former French prisoner of war.

The decision to celebrate together as true Allies that first night after the victory turned into a gigantic flop; the boys from Texas, Kansas, Minnesota, and Idaho, not used to gallons of unrefined booze, got roaring drunk, and consequently, deathly ill, so that a repeat performance was never even considered. As the American "victims" realized, there seemed to be more than just a slight difference in mentality, habits, and manners.

In full realization of the fact that everybody was by now well on their way to getting drunk, Charles and I reached the other side of the bridge to the Soviet territory, and ultimately the house where I had spent the previous night. There, right in the yard, was the bush under which I had buried my treasures; Charles decided we should not waste precious time but first find the horse. The stable was empty; across from it was a fenced-in field with literally hundreds of Soviet nags. If Arabella had been of a darker color, we would never have stood a remote chance of detecting her, but being white as snow, she almost gleamed in the darkness against the black sky, a royal princess among peasants. As soon as she noticed me, she gave me a peeved look and began to scratch the ground with her dainty little hooves. Across her back lay a filthy blanket, an insult to her exquisite beauty. The scraggly creature next to her wore an elegant English saddle, which we removed at once to put on Arabella. At that moment, a drunk Russian zigzagged toward us, shining a flashlight into our eyes before aiming his Kalashnikov at us. What did we want with the horse, he demanded. At least that is what we assumed from his gestures. Charles signaled me to keep out of it and turned to the intoxicated hero. From the inside jacket of his uniform, he pulled the one magic weapon no Russian was able to resist: a bottle of booze, in this case a fifth of whisky. The soldier went for it like a hawk for a mouse—grabbed it, sniffed it first, put it to his mouth, and did not let go until the last drop had disappeared. The bottle was now empty, which was sad enough, but this sad reality was even sadder because the spot next to him was empty where, he could have sworn, two men and a white horse had just been standing! By the time he realized his loss, Arabella and I were charging across the bridge to the safety of American domain.

That same night I felt the strong urge to express my gratitude to God for Arabella's miraculous salvation, so I decided to finally part with my faithful little friend Ortgies. Not wanting him ever to be used by anyone again, I picked the bottom of the river for his permanent resting place. Seeing him sink into the water almost caused me to break into tears. "*Hitler, das Schwein, ist tot!*" "Hitler, the swine, is dead," I said in a whisper. And then I repeated it over and over again in a louder and louder voice, deciding it was an appropriate eulogy for the gun that served me so faithfully.

Charles had taken us to a small empty house with a barn next to it, where I could stay for a while. That night, however, I had no desire to lie down on one of the two beds, but remained in the barn, at the side of my horse. After Arabella had dropped onto the bed of straw, totally exhausted, I lay down next to her, covering both of us with a horse blanket. She graciously decided to tolerate my arms around her warm neck all night.

During the weeks following this adventure, all we heard were horror stories from the Soviet-occupied territory. A favorite pastime of the Red soldiers was fishing in the river by throwing hand grenades into the water, the surface of which soon filled with myriad dead fish displaying their white bellies. What also eventually came to the surface were the bodies of women who had chosen death over the never-ending molestations.

Not all the tales that made the rounds in the weeks to come were gruesome; some were very funny, for example, the one about the Russian who had admired a German skillfully riding his bicycle without touching the handlebars. *Karasho*! Snatching the bike from his owner in the belief that the magical German contraption could run without being steered, he promptly fell flat on his face.

Bike *nix karasho*! He gave it a kick. They stole anything and everything, so their term for stealing, "making *tsapptserapp*" became very popular. They did not necessarily keep their loot, meaning that what they stole from one house, they presented in the next one as gifts, with gestures of grandeur.

Most of the Mongols, Tatars, and Kirgiz from the steppes of Asia had never seen running water in houses. "Water from wall," they called this magical invention, with childlike awe. Under the erroneous impression that bathrooms were refrigerators, one of them put food into the toilet bowl on an upstairs floor, which promptly and irretrievably disappeared when he pulled the chain, causing him to run down to the lower floor, waiting for it to arrive in the downstairs facility. The results were devastating. In no time, the plumbing systems in almost every house were clogged.

Priceless antique furniture was dragged from houses into the park and tastefully remodeled to serve as open air latrines or chicken pens. Another story told of extremely intricate machines from the local furniture plant, confiscated as reparations to be shipped to the USSR. Just before the arrival of an inspecting team, little parts of the intricate machines sticking out of the boxes were swiftly sawed off. While the boxes now looked neat, the precious machines were rendered useless, ruined forever.

Chapter Fifty-Four
With the Americans

The platoon under the command of young Charles Battaglia settled in the village, while the rest of the regiment spread over the neighboring county. Signs were posted outside the commander's office, indicating in English and German that fraternization with the "Huns" was strictly outlawed at every level, with the possible exception of the horizontal one, which would remain a "gray" area. Superior officers, some of whom were themselves involved in such totally illicit activities, had no choice but to look the other way. With mass rapes a standard practice east of the river, taking women by force was unnecessary in the American-occupied area. In spite of the absence of professional prostitutes, the delighted GIs found enough volunteers among the female village population to happily meet their most urgent needs. American cigarettes, a cake of soap, or a bar of Hershey's chocolate sent a sufficient number of local girls into a state of ecstasy. Not only were these wonderful customers from the United States generous with gifts, but their gifts were accompanied with solemn promises of fabulous weddings, after which the lucky brides would be swept across the ocean into the land of plenty. Given the choice of either becoming a movie queen or the mistress of a luxurious castle, they would be showered with mink coats and Cadillacs, all standard possessions of each and every American GI.

The fact that the soldiers from this particular unit had, on their long and hard road to victory, not been exposed to the grim sight of a concentration camp, accounted for their general innocent friendliness, in sharp contrast to all those warriors who had been confronted with the mountains of emaciated corpses in the horror camps with their pitifully few survivors. After such an experience, American soldiers found it extremely difficult to detect anything but a monster in every German they met.

Also strictly forbidden was any kind of contact with the Red Allies across the river, where Russian soldiers did not offer presents to women in exchange for sex, nor did they promise castles or movie careers. In spite of the explicit order not to cross into the Soviet-occupied territory, Charles, for one last time, decided to sneak across the river so he could try to retrieve my jewels. Armed with a little shovel and a flashlight, he managed to make it there and back within ten minutes. From afar I saw him sadly shake his head, indicating that his search had been unsuccessful, but he was a poor liar, because in one tightly clenched fist I found my ring and the pin and in the other was the golden chain and medallion.

On the morning following my first night in the American zone, I was taken to headquarters for a thorough screening by the commander, a full colonel. The officer was familiar with the name of Pastor Niemoeller and his heroic resistance against Hitler, expressing the hope that he had survived. The name of Louis P. Lochner, American correspondent of the Associated Press in Berlin and my father's close friend, brought the unexpected surprise of the colonel's close acquaintance with him. Expressing my concern about the welfare of my parents, he told me that he would probably soon be in a position to find out.

But hadn't Berlin been taken by the Red Army? He only smiled; I would see, he said, and maybe sooner than I expected. That same afternoon, a GI pinned an imposing sign on the door of the little house where I was staying: "Off Limits—Official Interpreter."

In the middle of my second night of freedom, a jeep came to collect me for my first job. Survivors of a nearby concentration camp had gotten hold of two of their tormentors, who had donned striped garb in the hope of passing as liberated inmates. Without the interference of American soldiers, the imposters would certainly have been killed. In the course of the first week, we found a number of victims in the woods, obviously beaten to death, who were easily identified as members of the SS by the numbers tattooed under their arms. To say that I felt pity at the sight of the battered bodies would definitely have been an overstatement. Sometimes the interrogations, in most cases dealing with picked-up Nazis, took all night. We were also kept busy settling less spectacular incidents like quarrels among the village population, now robbed of their accustomed Nazi authorities, to whom they could denounce their neighbors. Since the mayor had fled—for obvious reasons—the Americans now represented the authority everyone craved. The populace quickly got into the habit of running to the commander's office with family squabbles, to report thefts and alleged robberies, insults or anti-American remarks, outdoing one another in slanderous accusations. The countless refugees from the advancing Red Army, almost all of whom had arrived without possessions, were now welcome scapegoats, blamed for all sorts of misdeeds.

More than once, when returning to my quarters, I found someone waiting for me behind the bushes with a covered basket of fresh eggs, the first harvest of white asparagus, home-churned butter, or meat from illegally slaughtered animals. All this was meant to serve as a bribe, tempting me to speak out in someone's favor. While I kept the food in order to survive, word spread fast that no bribe in the world could get me to do favors for Nazis.

One night, returning to the house after midnight, I could tell by a strange bundle on the kitchen table and some wet clothes draped over chairs that I was not alone. Automatically my hand reached into the inside pocket of my jacket where, until recently, the Ortgies had resided, when I heard a female voice from the bedroom, "Please don't be alarmed! It is only I, Emmy Bonhoeffer."

Emmy Bonhoeffer? I could not believe my ears, but there she was, sitting up in one of the two beds. After falling into one another's arms, she told me her story. On the road for weeks, she had escaped from the battle of Berlin with Hamburg as her ultimate goal. The last hurdle to overcome had been the little river separating the Soviet-occupied zone from the American territory. With her few possessions tied into a bundle on her head, she had managed to swim through the icy water without being detected. Someone in the village told her about me and my whereabouts. Finding the door of the house open, she simply walked in, took off her sopping clothes, and climbed into one of the beds, frantically trying to get warm.

Among the members of her family who fell victim to Hitler's bloodlust had been her husband Klaus, Pastor Dietrich Bonhoeffer's brother, and Hans von Dohnanyi, whose wife was a sister to the Bonhoeffer brothers. The shattering news that Emmy's own brother, Justus Delbrück, an active anti-Nazi who survived imprisonment by the Nazis only to be kidnapped by the Soviets for reasons unknown, had starved in a KGB camp, would only reach her many months later.

Hesitatingly, she asked if I had news from my parents. A rumor had reached her just before she left Berlin that my father also had been taken by the Soviets, which I dismissed as hearsay because it could not be true. He, too, had escaped death in a Nazi prison. We sat up in bed together until the break of dawn, devouring my provisions and, realizing our grotesque situation, alternated between streams of tears and outbreaks of hysterical laughter.

After a few days of rest, Emmy took off for the second part of her journey, traveling north to Hamburg on a bicycle that I had been able to "organize" for her. Over the following years, whenever we met in Berlin for the annual ceremony commemorating the victims of the July 20 assassination attempt, we never tired of reminiscing about our bizarre encounter in May 1945.

On the morning after Emmy's departure, I found the stable empty; Arabella was gone. There could not be any doubt that she had been stolen because horses, unlike dogs, do not run away to roam. Before fully grasping the new situation and allowing myself to break down over this terrible loss, I heard the clonkety-clonk of hooves on the cobblestones and, before I realized it, Arabella raced into the stable as if chased by the devil himself. The saddle hung under her belly, and there was a gaping wound on her right flank. Since her injury was too severe for me to take care of, I ran to the building where the American headquarters had been established. In the absence of a veterinarian, a military physician offered his help. Without him and his knowhow, I am not sure whether Arabella would have recuperated as fast as she did.

Neighbors told me that they had observed Polish ex-POWs outside the stable at dawn, one of them galloping away with Arabella. The rest of the story would forever remain speculation. What seemed the most likely explanation was that Arabella realized that this was the perfect occasion to throw a temper tantrum, one that her thief would not forget, if he survived the mare's unexpected onslaught. Usually, she was not satisfied with just throwing off uninvited riders, but loved to use her small hooves to give the victim a special treatment.

During the rare hours of leisure, Charles and I resorted to an exciting but mischievous, if not to say downright criminal, pastime. He had been able to secure a horse for himself, a huge bony nag, good-natured enough to tolerate a novice on his back. The first time he successfully managed to get on top, Charles had inquired where the brakes might be and what he was supposed to do to make the animal stand still. This was no problem, because standing still was the old gelding's most favored occupation; otherwise, he seemed agreeable enough to get himself in first gear and follow Arabella at a respectful distance.

With oats and hay in short supply, feeding Arabella became a problem. So, thanks to Charles' resourcefulness, we resorted to a practice for which, in the old American West, we would have been strung by a rope on the nearest tree: stealing horses.

Under the protection of night, making good use of the curfew rendering the area deserted after six o'clock, we caught horses in the fields, dragged them to a distant village, and sold them, not for money, but in exchange for hay and oats. The overjoyed peasants must have chuckled behind our backs, shaking their heads about such monstrous stupidity; a sturdy horse for a few bags of grain? The lawful horse owners, however, after first discovering the loss of their animals and ultimately their new whereabouts, would eventually retrieve their property in some stranger's stable, accusing the baffled farmers of horse-theft and worse. Nobody suspected us as the initiators of such gross mischief.

Chapter Fifty-Five

Joining the British

On June 1, the American 82nd Airborne unit moved out of the area. Charles, my liberator, and I bid each other a tearful farewell, after which he disappeared in his jeep, leaving a cloud of dust behind him. This twenty-two-year-old boy with the guts of a Rhett Butler had left my life. On the slim chance that we might meet again some day, we exchanged addresses. I gave him mine in Berlin, just in case.[31]

A unit of the British REME (Royal Electrical and Mechanical Engineers) moved into the village. The commander, Major John J. McGraw, a stout Scotsman, inquired politely if I was American. Why did I speak English with the funny Yankee accent? The officer, with iron-gray hair to match his iron determination and a remarkable ability to hold liquor, accepted me as an interpreter, so my life did not change all that much, except that I fell in love with my new boss. He told me that he was married and had two children, but the marriage existed only on paper since his wife had left him, not for another man, which would have been bad enough, but for a woman.

Although I was treated with the same courtesy I had enjoyed before, the new rulers turned out to be very different from their predecessors. After all, from the very beginning of the war in 1939, their country had been battered by the German Air Force—brutal attacks explicitly directed against the civilian population right up to the end of the war. So their attitude, although proper, was restrained, if not downright frosty. Nonfraternization laws stiffened considerably, and they were enforced as much as possible. Again, however, there remained the horizontal gray area, which proved very difficult to prevent. But even the ladies noticed that their new customers, not overly eager to share their sparse rations, were certainly in no mood to promise matrimony.

One morning, I had to accompany the major on a lengthy trip by jeep up north near the Danish border, for some negotiations in a German POW camp run by the British Army. Presenting me to the camp commandant as his interpreter, he was informed that my services were not needed because they had their own camp interpreter. The man in question, a German POW, displaying ostensibly submissive behavior, walked through the door. Taking one good look at me, he suddenly seemed to freeze and, like Lot's wife, almost turned into the proverbial pillar of salt. The monstrous ring with the SS insignia was missing from his big hand, the hand I had felt so painfully on my face less than a year before, in the Berlin Gestapo headquarters. He stared at me like a rabbit at a rattlesnake. But while once I had been the rabbit and he the snake, our roles were now definitely reversed. He was correct in his assumption that this totally unexpected and not very cordial reunion would at once terminate his lucrative job. His trial would take place in Lübeck at a later date, and I found out that I had not been the brute's only victim.

John, after learning all the gruesome details connecting me to the former SS officer, promised to personally check on my parents' fate. At this point, he let me in on the secret that within a few days, before July 1, the British and the American Armed Forces would withdraw from the area they had conquered and occupied since the first days in May. As far as our area in Mecklenburg was concerned, the Russians were already waiting in the wings to move into what had been determined at the Yalta Conference to be their assigned territory. The REME unit was assigned new headquarters somewhere north of Hamburg. John decided that not only would he take me with him, but Arabella, too. We should travel separately, but in style. He simply declared the horse property of the British, even though his only attempt to mount her had ended in disaster, netting him a badly bruised leg. The snow-white mare had just stood there in her favorite but treacherous pose of an angelic camel, ogling him with what seemed an ingratiating expression in her deep blue eyes. She had tolerated him on her back for no longer than a split second, and before the rider could even get his right foot into the stirrup, she simply leaped into the air with all fours at once. After applying a few hoof kicks in the direction of the man in the dust below her, she reassumed her previous pose.

For her transport, an Army truck was lined with a number of feather beds, so the proverbial "princess on a pea" would not injure her precious self or the truck, which the officers called a "lorry." The only problem was that Arabella could not be made to understand why in the devil's name she should exchange the comfort of her stable for the confinement of an army vehicle. It took all morning before four sturdy warriors with a lot of strength and even more perseverance managed to pull and push her up the ramp into her temporary domicile. Several times she went into one of her famous fits of rage, kicking and biting anything that moved. Finally, she gave up from sheer exhaustion and within seconds changed from Ms. Hyde back to Ms. Jekyll.

I spent the hours of the trip to Holstein in the major's jeep. Whenever British Military Police appeared at various checkpoints, in order to avoid unnecessary difficulties, John threw his army coat over me. On the evening of June 30, we reached our destination, which to my great surprise and even greater delight was the stately castle of Haseldorf northwest of Hamburg. Embedded in a beautiful park, the estate belonging to the Prince and Princess of Schoenaich-Carolath-Schilden, had been spared destruction. Untouched by the war, it was now bustling with refugees, including countless family members who had escaped from their own estates in the east. With the castle itself to be occupied by British officers, the whole family had moved to adjacent buildings.

All during my childhood, even during the war years, dozens of pheasants, partridges, hares, and venison had arrived at our home in Dahlem from Haseldorf for our consumption. Our connection with the princely family had been a romantic one, insofar as Prince Georg's sister-in-law, Princess Edelgard, had once been my father's fiancée. For various reasons, their romance had not come to a happy end. The princess, on her father's side an illegitimate Hohenzollern offspring, later married Prince Georg's younger brother Gustav von Schoenaich-Carolath-Schilden. While my heartbroken father had gone to war, fully intending to die a soldier's death, the princess immigrated with her husband to Portuguese Angola; the ties between the two families, however, were never broken.

My elation over having arrived in paradise was wholeheartedly shared by Arabella, who found the elegant surroundings and her new box in the noble stables more to her liking than her quarters of the recent past, not to mention the horrors of being stolen by those boorish Bolshevik vandals with their proletarian nags and unspeakably vulgar saddles. This sober realization most likely had prompted her to decide that, from now on, there was to be one other human being beside me to whom she was willing to extend the grace of tolerating on her back: Prince Georg. Never would she try a single one of her dirty tricks on him, instead conveying the feeling he was being carried on angel's wings.

During the first week in Haseldorf, Princess Agnes came into the little room to which I had been assigned very early in the morning. "There is someone to see you," she whispered. Barely awake, I noticed the shadow behind her. It turned out to be my brother, my beloved little brother. The nineteen-year-old was alive; he had survived the war. After telling his family's story to the British commander of a POW camp at the Danish border, the private was released on the spot and, without a clue where to turn, he had chosen Haseldorf because it was the only place he knew of, hoping that the prince could help him make a decision of what to do and where to go. He found more than he expected—me. Now, at least for a while, we had one another.

At the Yalta Conference in February 1945, it had been determined by Churchill, Roosevelt, and Stalin that some territories in Eastern Germany, originally conquered by either the Americans or the British, were to be turned over to the Soviets. In exchange, the Western Allies, including France, would each receive a slice of the capital, Berlin. Dahlem was to be part of the American zone. On July 1, to the infinite relief of the Berlin population, the Red Army retreated to the Eastern part of the city assigned to them, dead-set on leaving the three sectors reserved for their Western Allies an empty shell; they "tsaptserapped" everything that could be moved.

Chapter Fifty-Six
British Intelligence

My brother had begun to work as a farm laborer on the prince's estate, which meant ample food and a place to sleep. In the fall, he planned to return to Berlin. In August, REME relocated to Hamburg, where my services as an interpreter were not needed; I saw myself faced with the necessity to earn my living somewhere else. At this point, the *reichsmark* was not worth the paper on which it was printed. I applied for a job at the North German Radio Station in Hamburg, now operated by the British Forces, was immediately accepted, and really enjoyed my new position as an announcer.

Hamburg was close to Haseldorf, so I was able to commute between two worlds—the almost totally demolished city of Hamburg and an untouched Garden of Eden. Toward the end of the year, something happened that caused the British chief of the radio station to fire me. Unlike the other British officers at the network, he had struck me as somewhat shady. Tall and spindly, with a strong German accent and a protruding Adam's apple, this man combined a total lack of charm with absolute power over anybody working in "his" establishment. Having fled Nazi Germany to Moscow as a Communist, he had ultimately ended up in London. After refusing his unveiled invitations to try out the wonderful quality of the couch in his office, needless to say in a horizontal position, he fired me from my job. With memories of my fat old suitor in Danzig still fresh in my mind, I found this experience demoralizing but not very original. While losing my prestigious position as an announcer was sad enough, there was another job that kept me in Hamburg.

British Intelligence had put me in contact with an organization whose task it was to hunt Nazis. I was the only German among the group of agents who had to undergo rigorous training before being assigned their work. There were Greeks, Yugoslavs, French, Dutch, Belgians, and other nationalities, all eventually assigned to sniff out and observe certain suspicious domiciles in and around Hamburg, usually occupied by the spouses of Nazi criminals on the run. United by fierce determination, we had to use cunning, caution, patience, and restraint, certain that eventually, once the fugitives felt secure enough, they would seek contact with their wives and ultimately dare to come home. Most of the men were former members of the staff administering the concentration camps of Ravensbrück and Neuengamme, SS officers, noncommissioned SS, and civilians. Once they had decided it was safe to return home, it was up to the British to arrest those who emphatically denied their identities as well as the alleged crimes. Searches of their homes uncovered vast amounts of valuables:

money, jewels, platinum, silver, and gold. Some of the gold was in odd shapes, obviously from dental crowns and bridges. Sick to my stomach, I realized that this was my first physical encounter with what later would enter the vocabulary of the world as the Holocaust.

As the eventful year of 1945 came to an end, I decided it was time for me to attempt a journey to Berlin. Since there was no regulated interzonal traffic for civilians yet, I had no alternative but to try and reach Berlin by sneaking across the "black border." News from home had reached me with the help of John McGraw, who had been able to make contact with Charles, now stationed in Berlin. I made up my mind to take any risk, no matter what the consequences. The news, once dismissed by me as a rumor, was true; my father seemed to have disappeared.

Chapter Fifty-Seven
Return to Berlin

Only after my ultimate return to Berlin, in January 1946, would I learn the details about what had happened one day in July the year before. With the electricity out, my mother had answered a knock on the door to find an American officer outside; he wanted to speak to her. In mortal fear, she let him in, believing that he had come to tell her that her house was being confiscated as a residence for Americans. She just could not grasp that this handsome young man by the name of Charles had a wonderful message. Not only did he bring her the first authentic news about her children's fate, but he inquired what he, now temporarily stationed in Berlin, could do for her.

After overcoming her reservations, she confided in him that what she urgently needed was medication, complaining that the local pharmacist, a raving Nazi who hoarded his supplies like the treasure of the Nibelungen, would not give her anything without receiving something in return. Charles eyes lit up; he would pay the pharmacist a surprise visit. At the sight of an American jeep coming to a screeching halt just inches from his store window, the old scoundrel began to shake in his boots and came flying out to inquire what was going on. The sight of Charles, playing with his revolver, almost gave him a heart attack. The intruder stomped into the pharmacy and slammed my mother's list on the counter with the unmistakable order to fill it fast. With a bored look on his face, he added that, in case one single pill was missing, he would blast the store to smithereens. As a little foretaste, he aimed at a bottle on the shelf and fired. He would give him ten minutes and not a second more to gather all the medication without a peep if he intended to live. The pharmacist, now minus his SA uniform under the white coat, his teeth chattering, saw himself in no position to refuse such a heartwarming invitation. After stuffing the loot into his pockets, the militant intruder shot another jar, for educational purposes, and left, letting the engine of his jeep roar to a thundering volume.[32]

After receiving the heartbreaking news about my father's disappearance, I knew it was time to go home. John would still be there when I returned. He was, however, in no position to help in my illegal as well as dangerous attempt to make it all the way to Berlin. Having made contact with a dozen people willing to cross the "black border," from the British into the Soviet zone and ultimately into West Berlin, we set the date of departure for the first night of 1946. A so-called *"schlepper,"* for a fee of ten cigarettes each, would lead us through the woods to a certain point, from which we could cross over into the Soviet-occupied zone and eventually be able to catch a train in the direction of Berlin.

I filled a knapsack with a few necessities, packed a bottle of gin, upon which John had insisted, and on the afternoon of January 1, 1946, I boarded the slow train from Hamburg to Buechen, the last stop before the border. There I met my travel companions and the guide, who assured us that we had absolutely nothing to fear. After marching through dense woods for several hours in the bitter cold, snow began to fall. Our guide pointed at dimly visible lights in the distance, a village allegedly located in the Russian zone. The border was right ahead; there was no fence, no barbed wire, just a trench. All we had to do was sneak around the little booth with the barrier in front, where the Russian border guard would be asleep or drunk, most likely both. Tonight being the first evening in the New Year, we probably could not have picked a better date. We tiptoed around the closed barrier making as little noise as possible, while the Russian soldier inside snored like a bear hibernating in his cave. After safely making it to the other side, all we had to do was find the train station. Walking for almost thirty minutes on a paved road, we suddenly found ourselves surrounded by a Russian border patrol who screamed, "*Stoi!*"

Stoi was the most feared command aside from "*Frau komm!*" *Stoi* meant stop, or else! Before realizing what was happening, we found ourselves staring at the muzzles of four submachine guns, pointed right at our faces. What we finally understood was that we had to accompany our captors to the *Kommandantur*. *Dawai, dawai, schnell, schnell*, this instant! When I asked what we should do there, one of them said, "Sit in cellar little while." A little while in Russian thinking could mean anything from ten minutes to ten years. What a wonderful way to begin the year, I thought! Our pleas for release fell on deaf ears, until I produced the bottle of gin from the knapsack. Well, they grinned, *karasho*, which probably meant that we would have a wonderful party right there in the icy woods before being raped and then taken to the promised cellar. After opening the bottle Russian style by simply chopping the top off with a rifle butt, I was ordered to take the first swallow; if it was poison, I would be the first to drop dead. While I tried to drink without cutting my mouth, the situation changed again.

Out of the darkness came a figure on a bicycle, the sight of which caused the soldiers to freeze at attention. The moon had just appeared from the clouds, and I noticed that the man on the bike, rudely interrupting our cozy little New Year's celebration, was not only wearing a Russian officer's uniform, but a green hat, trademark of the NKVD, the secret police, later known as the KGB. Not familiar with Soviet insignia, I became instantly aware of something else; this man was, by all known standards, the most gorgeous-looking secret police officer who had ever sworn allegiance to Joseph Stalin.

After bellowing harsh commands at the flabbergasted Russians, he sent them flying. While the people in my group ran in the opposite direction, he signaled me to stay behind. Frozen with horror while speculating over my fate, the combination of Clark Gable and Robert Taylor grabbed me by the sleeve and said, "*Du stoi!*" What now? I had made it all the way through the Nazi era, the war, the bombs, I had shot a man, I had smartly avoided liberation by the Red Army, and now, on this first day of the new year, was I finally in for it? Almighty God, will you really do this to me? In a remote corner of my brain, I remembered the idiotic advice of the spinster teachers in the elite boarding school; if I ever found myself in a precarious situation, I should simply imagine what Frederick the Great or Martin Luther would do, and I could not possibly do wrong. The thought of the Great Frederick or the boorish Martin Luther being threatened with rape by a Soviet NKVD officer was nothing short of hilarious.

Taking another good look at the Russian Adonis, I still could not believe my eyes. The noble features of his finely chiseled face, the face of a true aristocrat, with its aquiline nose and deep-set eyes, would have caused any of Hollywood's movie heroes to hide in the nearest cave. In halting German he asked my name and what I was doing in the woods on such a cold night. Having regained control of myself, I told him that all I wanted was to go home. Home, to father and mother in faraway Berlin. Surely that was no crime, was it?

"Me colonel, me Nikolai," he said, introducing himself with the grace of a grand duke and lifting the knapsack off my back. He swung the sack across the handle of his bicycle, took me by the arm with his free hand, and proceeded to lead me down the road, obviously knowing where he was going. Suddenly overcome by a feeling of total trust, I did not mind being led wherever he wanted to take me. After a while, to my greatest surprise, we reached a railway station. There stood a rickety train, a regular war veteran with busted windows, groaning with old age. The engine emitted clouds of black smoke, the stationmaster having just lifted his staff, indicating imminent departure.

My savior tore the staff from the hands of the terrified official, telling him that "train not go when you say, train go when I say!" That was pretty clear, the stationmaster decided to agree.

Under the eyes of the terrified passengers, my designated guardian angel heaved my knapsack on board. And then, down on the platform, for everyone to see, he did what he had omitted doing in the privacy that the woods had offered. He took me into his arms and kissed me with gentle ardor, as if we had the entire night ahead of us. After which he returned the staff to its rightful owner.

"Now I say go! *Dawai, dawai!*"

As the train began to move, slowly gaining momentum, I watched the man who, by some cruel fate, was not going to be my lover after all, still leaning against his bicycle, waving his hand, and throwing kisses until he disappeared from my sight. God help me, but all I felt at that moment was the urge to jump off the train, to hell with Berlin. The oddly suspicious glances of the other passengers accompanied me all the way to the last stop. Nobody dared talk to me. I was either a terribly abused victim or, most likely, a Soviet spy or worse. Within the hour we reached the town from whence the train to Berlin was going to leave the next morning. Before drifting off into the twilight zone between being awake and asleep on the dirty floor of the station house, my head on the rucksack, it came to me like a revelation. Three guardian angels had protected me throughout the unbelievable adventures of the past year: an American lieutenant, a British major and a Soviet NKVD colonel. And it all seemed very natural.

The next morning was icy, with more snow coming down in thick flakes. Unable to make it inside the mobbed train, I was finally successful in climbing on one of the buffers between two cars. Straddling the cars, I tied myself to the buffer with a belt and arrived in Berlin ten hours later resembling an oddly formed icicle. Frozen to the buffer, a few helpful men managed to tear me loose. It took almost half an hour until I was able to move my legs and dive into the adventure of finding transportation to Dahlem. To my delight, there was a subway train. The city had already been bombed to a pulp when I departed the previous April, but I realized that the final blow had been dealt to it when the battle literally flattened the capital, which now resembled a moon landscape. Here and there were a few buildings, their outer walls barely standing, which resembled gigantic, hollow teeth. "Give me ten years," the self-styled architect from Braunau had screamed, "and you will not recognize Germany anymore!" It seemed that we all had underestimated Hitler's most outstanding gift: prophecy! As an island in the Red Sea of Soviet-occupied territory, the city of Berlin was now divided into four sectors. Only the outskirts were still inhabitable; the heart of the once bustling capital lay in ruins, a fate shared by almost every other German town. According to predictions, rebuilding would take at least half a century, clearing away the debris being by far the most formidable task. But even in the rubble, with no recognizable streets, there were people everywhere. Existing in cave-like cellars, they were out hunting for food, firewood, and other bare necessities, many in frantic search of surviving family members and friends.

On the badly rattling subway with its broken windows I spotted the first American soldiers in uniform. The pearly gates of heaven could not have offered a more welcome sight. It took me a while to come to the realization that it was not the ruins of the city where I had grown up, nor the pitiful sight of the gray faces of Berliners in their rags, many men with missing limbs, but, strangely enough, the GIs from the United States that gave me a warm feeling of having come home at last.

The desert that had once been a place brimming with life was still crawling with people who, after all, had to have a roof over their heads somewhere, but where? Survivors, victims, and murderers alike, I thought, and the murderers, I sensed with horrifying clarity, were still among us. In Dahlem, walking by St. Anne's Church, there were no more German soldiers hanging from lanterns, no more swastikas, no Nazi emblems anywhere. The price for their disappearance had been high.

Turning the corner onto our street, Am Hirschsprung, my heart pounding, I saw the house. From a distance it looked like a fortress. The house will survive, my mother had said when nobody believed it anymore. Surely my father would be standing at the garden gate where we had parted some nine months before. Charles, my only source of information so far, must simply have misunderstood and my father was at home, safe and sound and waiting for me. I was sure of it because I just could not face my life without him. Yes, the house, his house, although shaken to its foundations, was still there, with roof tiles missing and a few windows with cardboard or plywood nailed to the frames.

My mother, overjoyed by my unexpected appearance, looked considerably thinner but had obviously not lost her indefatigable stamina. Our house was now partially occupied by people who, after losing their own homes, had sought refuge with someone who not only offered them shelter, but reassurance. Residing in some of the upstairs rooms were two Russian aristocratic families who had escaped from their own country after the Bolsheviks had taken over in 1917.

My hopes about my father were soon shattered; he was gone, missing, lost. It was like he had never even existed. After talking about the initial facts surrounding his fate, we silently agreed to avoid mentioning his name. We relied upon the illusion that as long as we did not speak about what happened, maybe it really had not happened. Soon we would wake up from this horrendous nightmare, he would step into the house, and life would begin again.[33]

Chapter Fifty-Eight
The Confessing Accuser

Martin Niemoeller, the führer's only personal prisoner, was free, as free as anyone could be in the vast wasteland of post-war Germany, a defeated nation cut into four zones, like slices of cake. The former inmate of Sachsenhausen and Dachau now lived with his wife, the faithful housekeeper Dora, and two of his younger children in the idyllic village of Leoni on picturesque Lake Starnberg. His sons Herrmann and Jan, both members of the *Wehrmacht* in spite of their father's status, were still somewhere in the East. He had a hard time adjusting to an existence without barbed wire, windows without bars, no Sword of Damocles constantly threatening his life or drunken SS guards stringing up their victims before his eyes on the gallows that reminded him every second of the day or night that he might well be the next one to hang there.

Aside from the hardships of daily life, the pastor now carried an additional burden, the painful realization that he was separated from the overwhelming majority of his fellow Germans foaming with indignation that the Western Allies, instead of joining Hitler in his attempt to fight Bolshevik barbarism, subjected them to insults, hunger, and humiliation. Liberators, they call themselves? But the Allies had not come with the intention of liberating the Germans. The victors saw no reason to free a people who had permitted their elected government to throw the world into a disaster of hitherto unknown dimensions. The occupying powers pursued one purpose only, to prevent this nation from ever again doing what they had done twice in the same century—invade and attack their unsuspecting neighbors. Having learned a lesson from the grave mistakes of the Treaty of Versailles, the priority was now to "reeducate" a whole nation. But can the form of government, this precious institution called democracy, for which civilized nations had to fight, be taught by words, or simply by instituting it overnight? Would it ever work for a people who, for centuries, were used to giving and carrying out orders? Of the utmost importance, in the pastor's opinion, was the admission of guilt by the Germans, his own church not excluded.

Guilt? On top of being defeated, they are now supposed to feel guilty? Isn't it enough to be shamed and starved after being bombed to smithereens? The vast majority of the populace, who maintained that the Nazis had forced themselves onto an innocent people, falling from the sky like a swarm of locusts, denied participation or even knowledge of alleged atrocities. What deeply shocked the pastor was that not only had the unknown masses refused to beg forgiveness, but among them was an upright man, the Social Democrat Kurt

Schumacher, who himself had suffered hell in Hitler's camps, which he barely survived. Publicly he stated that "U-boat commanders in priests' frocks were to limit their confession of guilt to their own small caste, instead of extending it to an entire German people."

Martin's grave concern was the attitude of the official Protestant Church. He found himself confronted with an institution ready to resume "business as usual," without comment, taking up where they had left off twelve years before. Bishops and pastors of the old "neutral" clergy belonging to the old *Reichskirche*, the Evangelical State Church, after having successfully maneuvered their vessels between the German Christians and the Confessing Church through the Nazi period without risking anything, were still in their pulpits. They were in the same positions they held while the founder of the Confessing Church, which had not only suggested, but practiced resistance, languished in captivity. Neutrality and indifference, in Martin's view, were at the very root of evil in the world. The attitude of the established church met with the wishes of the rest of the Germans. Few realized that the initial step into a new future had to be preceded by the admission of wrongdoing, followed by sincere remorse, true repentance, and the humble request to be forgiven, before attempting to rectify in some way the horrible events that cost fifty-five million lives, among them six million Jewish children, women, and men who had been exterminated for who they were, not for anything they had done. Hitler's former prisoner knew that no precious time must be wasted; the church either had to come out with some kind of a declaration of guilt, or else forever forfeit the chance of being accepted in the civilized world as a halfway credible institution.

The church balked. As a visible sign of their disapproval, Martin was denied the pulpit in Dahlem, which legally and morally still belonged to him. Heartbroken over the decision, he realized that even among his fellow pastors there existed embarrassment over someone showing up as living proof that resistance had indeed been possible, a fact vehemently denied by 99 percent of the Germans.

If only he had died a martyr's death in Dachau, it would have been so easy and gratifying to build a beautiful chapel in his memory, where pilgrims could tearfully worship his memory.

Very much alive, however, he announced his intention not to let the church sweep the past under the rug. In Greek mythology, Hercules, confronted with the task of cleaning the stable of Augeas, flushed out the dirt with a powerful stream of water. Renewal through water was a cleansing procedure practiced by Christians in the act of baptism, by Jews by immersion in the Mikvah, but no one in post-war Germany wanted a Hercules.

The determined pastor decided, nevertheless, that the time had come for the Evangelical Church to publicly confess guilt, express remorse, and prepare for true repentance. After conferences in Frankfurt, Treysa, and Stuttgart, under the leadership of his ally, the Swiss theologian Karl Barth, the "Stuttgart Declaration of Guilt" was finally formulated. It ended with the following statement: "We, the church, accuse ourselves of not having borne witness more courageously, not having prayed more faithfully, believed more joyously, and having loved more arduously."

This declaration, accepted in foreign countries with a certain amount of satisfaction, was followed by an outcry of indignation in Germany. Not only did the general public protest, but hundreds of students voiced their dismay, branding Martin Niemoeller as a traitor, a *nestbeschmutzer*, one who soils his own nest. Addressing students in Heidelberg, the pastor said:

And the church and Christendom? In its eagerness to involve themselves in nationalistic expectations, it became part of the anti-Jewish campaigns begun hundreds of years ago. The church proved unwilling to fight anti-Semitism as it should have done. Those six million, therefore, are a heavy burden on Christendom and on the church and not on the Nazi party and SS and the one mass murderer Adolf Hitler. Yes, the church bears the heaviest burden of guilt because it knew what it was doing when it did nothing. Anti-Semitism is the one acute threat to the church—an anti-Semitic church being a contradiction in itself!

His last words were drowned in the loud protest of the audience.

Bearing all attacks with calmness, the pastor dismissed the formulation of the Stuttgart Declaration of Guilt as totally inadequate. He wanted to add a much stronger statement:

We are in no position to accuse Hitler and the Nazis because we, who call ourselves Christians, knew that the road would lead to disaster. It is not that we did too little of this and too little of that. We did NOTHING!"[34]

Denied the resumption of his Dahlem pulpit, he accepted the presidency of the Church of Hessen and Nassau. Refusing the title of "bishop," as well as the bishop's cross, as his own personal expression of remorse, he had his title changed to "church president." The man, now called "The (nagging) conscience of the Nation," had been through his own catharsis while visiting Dachau with his wife in the fall of 1945, for the first time as a free man. Led by an American officer, they found themselves in front of the crematorium. Nailed to a tree, Niemoeller noticed a crude, white painted board; on it, in black letters, the sign read, "Between the years 1933 and 1945, 238,756 human beings were incinerated here."

It was not the number of victims that shocked him; he was familiar with that. It was the other two numbers that made him shudder: "1933 to 1945." In his own words,

I felt a cold chill creep down my spine and knew instantly that this was God's warrant against Pastor Niemoeller. I knew my alibi was good between 1937 and 1945, but here God was asking me what I had done between 1933 and 1937 to stop Adolf Hitler? Adam—Man, where wast thou in those years between 1933 and 1937?

Cain, where is thy brother Abel?

From that day on, a modern Jeremiah, he traveled through the world, confessing his own guilt, and everywhere he was praised, admired, and respected for it, except in his own fatherland.

Chapter Fifty-Nine
Surviving in Berlin

As time went by, little by little I learned what had happened one day in early May of 1945. Among the first Red Army soldiers invading our house after the fall of Berlin, there had been an officer who could speak and read German. After examining my father's release documents from Nazi prison, he posted a notice in Cyrillic letters on the front door, declaring the house off-limits for Soviet soldiers. This did not mean that looting would stop altogether, because some of the roaming warriors in search of treasures were illiterate. Yet in spite of the monumental destruction, there seemed to be a silver lining, promising a new future. My parents were optimistic—no more Gestapo ransacking the house, dragging them to jail. No more fear of atrocities, a twelve-year nightmare had ended. Nothing that lay ahead could possibly equal the terror they had experienced.

This elation at having survived was cut short when, a few days later, a Russian soldier went door to door, announcing that all able-bodied men were to clean up the debris in front of their houses. My father, almost enthusiastically, took the broom and went to work. To him, this cleansing procedure was a symbolic act of finally sweeping away the evil spirits of the past. While he was still busy, a Soviet military vehicle came to a halt in front of the house, from which two officers with green hats, a trademark of the NKVD, emerged. With them was a man from our neighborhood in a state of hysteria, explaining to my father that he had been picked up in the street in front of his own house. Having lost all his papers, and thus unable to identify himself, he was arrested. He had persuaded his captors to take him to our house, where my father would certainly confirm he was not a Nazi on the run. The officers politely suggested that my father accompany them to the *Kommandantur*. and sign a written statement. Of course they would bring him back before nightfall, in a few hours. Since it was a cool spring day, my mother ran into the house and came back with a coat, so her husband, who was still recuperating from nine months of extreme hardship, would not catch cold. In the open car, he turned around, smiling and waving at her; that would be the last gesture she remembered, because he vanished without a trace.

The problems of basic survival confronting us each new day left little time to dwell on my father's fate. We were both relieved and grateful that Friwi was safe in Haseldorf and did not have to endure the hardships that life in the leveled city of Berlin imposed on all those who had defied death and now refused to leave. Our thoughts circled around the next slice of bread, a piece of coal or wood to feed the little stove in Anna's former room, which, over the next winter, kept my mother and me from freezing to death. Being hungry was bad enough, but being cold was something else.

For months to come, long lines of very young girls and very old women formed in front of a house on our street where the only neighborhood gynecologist, a raving Nazi, performed abortions assembly-line style, and tried to cure hitherto unknown venereal diseases, unwanted souvenirs of the victorious Red Army, without the benefit of penicillin.

Of all the damages inflicted on the battered house, the missing roof tiles created the worst problem, allowing cascades of rain and snow to penetrate the ceilings from the second to the first floor, ultimately seeping through to the cellar. Central heating was a luxury of the past, not only for lack of coal, but because the pipes were frozen solid, eventually bursting when spring came. My mother's pride, the once beautiful garden, now covered with debris, presented a deplorable sight. The disadvantage of growing our own vegetables, like potatoes, was that any possible crop had to be watched day and night or it just disappeared, so we soon gave up all efforts. Besides, we had no potatoes to spare for planting.

The last days of the war claimed a lot of lives in our neighborhood. A number of people were felled by shells in their own gardens. Entire families had preferred suicide over falling into the hands of Red soldiers; some were cut from ropes in the attics and endless numbers of women were fished out of nearby lakes. What they all had in common was that they were buried where they were found. On the hottest day of the summer, the Western Allies came up with a brainstorm, the decision to have all the corpses on private properties unearthed, so that they could be interred in cemeteries. Those bodies that could not be identified were to be buried in mass graves, a laudable idea had it not been the wrong season for such an undertaking. With the thermometer overshooting the one hundred degree mark, the Berlin air became a stinking mess. Too late the Americans, British, and French realized that they themselves were now trapped in the beastly stench of decayed bodies that hovered over the city for weeks.

According to my mother, the first Russians, hunting for valuables, had not even bothered to ransack the houses for liquor, the news having spread like brush fire that Germans favored their coal supply in the cellar as a safe hiding place for wine and jewels, so all they needed were long sticks to secure the loot. Whatever was not hidden under the coal was sure to be found in the compost pile of every garden, where my mother's bracelet of massive gold, a gift from the kaiser, produced a triumphant grin on the face of the lucky finder, sliding it into his pocket. Other favorite hiding places were family plots in the cemeteries, where the search for treasures, reminding everyone of Easter egg hunts for children, netted most pleasing results. There was almost nothing that a Red soldier was not able to sniff out in record time. The term "*tsaptserap*" became a household word wherever members of the Soviet Army showed their eager faces.

The Russians, proverbially generous by heart, enjoyed tsaptserapping stuff from one house, only to present a stunned neighbor with unexpected gifts. My mother became the proud owner of a more than slightly worn lady's corselette with real whalebone stays, offered to her like the crown jewels by a beaming little Kirgiz. One morning she found herself the lucky recipient of yet another thoughtful "present"; a black and white cow with a calf was dragged into the garden by two soldiers, who immediately proceeded to slaughter the calf on our dining room table. Soon after, she received a horse's head, complete with mane, ears, and eyes. Heroically suppressing the urge to vomit, she asked the kind donor's advice for just how she was to fit this monstrosity into a cooking receptacle. When he appeared with an axe to hack the head into manageable portions, she excused herself to step into the bushes.

The week following this rather unique incident, she heard some alarming noises coming from the terrace and detected a soldier busily shoveling a mountain of thick, sweet farina gruel from a wheel barrow onto the terrace floor, topping it with a gallon of melted butter from a pail. "Now Frau, eat!" he demanded, and personally saw to it that "Frau" ate, flushing the stuff down with the vodka he had been kind enough to bring along. When she finally declared that she was incapable of consuming another teaspoonful, he gave her a piece of advice she would never forget in the lean years to come: "You, Frau, not eat when hungry, you eat when have." She figured he knew from his own experience what he was talking about.

The one topic that remained taboo among family and friends was rape. I never dared to ask my mother how she had fared. With her kind of upbringing, I knew that she, unlike so many other women, topping each other with gruesome details of their own experiences, would never reveal what happened to her. However, one day she volunteered the information that indeed she had been approached with very indecent proposals by filthy individuals, obviously from the other side of the Ural Mountains. Just fifty years old and still extremely attractive, her appearance in spite of a carefully blackened face and purposely knotted hair under a dirty scarf—trademark of every female in an effort to avoid abuse—had not gone unnoticed by some of the less discriminating intruders, attempting to first seduce and then intimidate her with "balalaikas." They were in for a surprise. No tears, no pleading for mercy; instead, outraged by their audacity, my mother decided to yell at the assailants, following the old Prussian strategy that attack was still the best defense. Unlike a woman shrieking in utter despair, she sounded more like a Prussian general, causing the totally bewildered would-be sex offenders to shake in their boots. Even though they did not understand one word of her temper outburst, they got the message; before them stood the Baroness von Sell, née von Brauchitsch, a general's daughter with fourteen aristocratic ancestors, and "*Frau komm!*" was not applicable to her. They would leave her alone, or else!

If this friendly invitation did not net instant results, she quickly learned to resort to a trick that, once and for all, saved her from intended molestations; she proceeded to fake an epileptic seizure to absolute perfection by letting herself drop to the floor like a bag of potatoes, writhing in evidently uncontrollable convulsions, even managing to foam at the mouth. Remembering her ancestors from Russia, she intuitively knew that there were two things Russian soldiers detested; one was to be screamed at, and the other to be confronted with illness of any kind. A sick woman? Yuck, revolting, enough to make any man puke! The would-be assailant fled in total disgust. She gave me a demonstration, and we both ended up laughing until we cried. Her reputation as a heroine soon made the rounds, which had the great disadvantage that her house, declared a safe haven, was mobbed by far more women than she could accommodate. Not all females had been so bold or so lucky. Horror stories made the rounds, and they were all true. A strange fact remained; while obsessed with searching cellars the Russians were, for some unknown reason, reluctant to go up to attics, so hiding there became a good strategy.

We counted our blessings as well as our losses. Day after day, I set out on foot to find out who among our friends had made it through the inferno and who had not. To my great joy, I found Walter Franck and his wife, Dagmar, in their almost totally intact house. The star actor had a rather special story to tell. On the third day after the battle of Berlin had come to an end, a horde of Russians, some with the insignia of the NKVD, invaded his home and told him to come with them. He was sure he would be stood against a wall and executed, but to his immense surprise, they schlepped him to the *Rathaus*, the city hall and, once there, heaved him on their shoulders to carry him in triumph upstairs to the former district mayor's office. There they placed him in the chair, formerly occupied by a Nazi, and informed him that, from now on, he would fill the vacant position; "Now you burgomaster!"

It turned out that the Soviets knew everything about him, including his involvement in the resistance and his dedication and courage in saving Jews. Franck remained burgomaster for as long as it took for the theaters of the former capital to open again. Until then he experienced much the same proud sensation he had felt when seated on a throne in a Shakespearian drama.

Leni Riefenstahl's bombastic villa had been heavily damaged, and there was no trace of Paul and Inge. It would take several years until I found Paul, who had so masterfully fooled his Nazi mistress and the Gestapo. He assured me that not only did our unwitting hostess not have the faintest idea of all our illegal activities taking place in her house, he refrained from informing her afterward for fear that she, now furiously rejecting reports about her devotion to Hitler, might pretend she had known all the time; the fact remained that she was the one we had feared the most.

Frau Thiele had survived in Ditte's house, a living witness to the humanitarian actions of five brave Dahlem families, all of whom had remained undetected. Ditte's house was more or less intact, the daughters all alive, and even little Hermann, inducted into the Flak at age fifteen, had come home. Anita and Reinhard Frank were missing; only after decades would the truth of their deportation to Theresienstadt, Auschwitz, and Bergen-Belsen leak through. Anita Frank had succumbed to typhoid only days before liberation by British troops. She would never know that her little brother, for whose sake she had refused to go underground, was among the Auschwitz survivors. Fifty years after his disappearance I would be reunited with him in New York. It would take almost sixty years until Hanns Lange, who, with his Jewish mother Irma, had been granted immigration to England by Goering, stepped back into my life. Irma, however, died the year before our reunion.

Thanks to my parents' old friend Louis P. Lochner, the Associated Press correspondent in Berlin, who had returned to the city in US uniform, we learned that Uncle Otto and Aunt Edith Stargardt had been freed from Theresienstadt by the Red Army one day before their scheduled deportation to Auschwitz. Sent to Aunt Edith's son in Detroit, they would eventually return to the house that had been stolen from them by the Gestapo. My classmate Ursel Reuber, bravely fighting the Nazis from her various hideouts in Berlin, had been killed by a British air mine. Her Jewish mother returned from Theresienstadt.

It was only after my homecoming that I realized I had spent the past nine months in riding breeches and boots. Like any mercenary, I had led a warrior's life, acted like a warrior, and defended myself by using my gun like a soldier. Now, to my utter delight, I found some of my old clothes, which still fit me. After undergoing a regular metamorphosis, I found that walking in high-heeled shoes presented a real problem for a while. Much to my surprise I began to resemble what I had forgotten to be, a girl, and, in spite of everything, not a bad-looking one!

Chapter Sixty
Help from Many Sources

Soon after the occupation of Berlin's western sectors by the Western Allies, and with the help of Louis P. Lochner, my mother had been able to obtain what in those days could only be compared to a passport to heaven, the "red" identification card reserved for "Victims of Fascism," issued to surviving Jews and those Germans who could prove beyond the shadow of a doubt that by resisting, they or their families had suffered under the Nazis. Upon presenting my father's discharge papers from Nazi prison, she was duly registered by the American authorities, her house was declared exempt from American occupation, and she received special ration cards, exceeding the meager calories allotted to the greater part of the population. The fact that old Nazis were crawling out of the woodwork like vermin, grumbling about my mother's privileges, which included going to the head of the line wherever lines formed, did not bother her in the least. If necessary, she just yelled back at them, a twelve-year period of forced silence having accumulated a rather astounding vocabulary for a lady of her upbringing and social standing.

We soon found ourselves in the bizarre situation of being victims of Bolshevism as well as Nazism. A succession of Russian refugees, in exile since 1917, came to occupy some of our upstairs rooms. A Duchess, who resided with her husband of lower nobility, was very likeable, except that she stole like a magpie. Hiding the loot in the sanctity of one of her rooms left me with only one solution. Whenever they left the house, in order to retrieve the *"tsapptserapped"* items, I simply opened their locked door with the help of an old skeleton key, and stealing back what she had taken became a daily routine. At that point it dawned on me that *tsaptserapping* had not been invented by nor was it limited to the Bolsheviks.

My mother and I lived huddled together in Anna's former room next to the kitchen, the only one fitted with a makeshift stove, which served both for heating and cooking, despite serious difficulties in obtaining anything burnable. Once we let the fire die out, it was almost impossible to relight it for lack of matches, newspapers, or any other paper. With a pipe leading outside through a crudely cut hole in the plywood that replaced the glass pane, wind blowing from the west filled the room with black clouds of biting smoke. Feeding the stove needed all our wits, so we gathered wood from felled or fallen fir trees in the forest, painfully chopping it from the stumps, carting it home in our rickety little wagon, once the pride and joy of two happy children. These activities did not exactly serve to improve the look of the Grunewald nor that of our hands, which began to show painful and unsightly frostbite. For the first time, Germans had a taste of what it was like to be starving or freezing to death in the bitter cold of winter. Throughout the war, that fate had been reserved for the "subhumans," the population of the Nazi-occupied territories, bled dry over a period of six years. Even with our extra food rations and kind donations, we were almost always hungry.

Before my return to Berlin, there had been days when my mother realized that she had no choice but to offer some of her belongings, which had not fallen prey to "*tsaptserap*," on the black market on Potsdamer Platz. These items included Meissen porcelain, silver, and my prized possession, the portable phonograph encased in beige leather. Reaching the market by public transportation took hours, until she found herself amidst a bustling, bickering crowd. Prepared to be snatched in a surprise police raid and hauled off to the nearest precinct, she, the offspring of fourteen noble ancestors, sat on a pile of bricks, playing "Goody-Goody," one of my favorite records, to Russians and their buxom *matkas* flashing their silver teeth. After endless bargaining, my treasure was exchanged for a thick slice of bacon and a few loaves of black Russian bread.

It was shortly after my arrival in Berlin, through one of her mysterious connections, that my mother discovered what seemed like the key to the proverbial land of milk and honey. Somehow, she had gotten wind of the fact that whatever food the American Army did not consume was burned in a well-guarded area in the woods nearby, allegedly for sanitary reasons. A portion of these precious provisions was set aside to feed those smart pigs on the Dahlem estate that had managed the impossible, namely to survive the general carnage. A big farm wagon from the estate, pulled by two horses, with an old employee on the coachman's seat, was permitted into the inner sanctum, the dump of the US Army, where several dozen pails were filled each afternoon with leftovers destined to be devoured by animals.

The fact that the coachman's past as a member of the SA and the Nazi party had so far remained undetected caused my mother to make him an offer he found impossible to refuse. Every day, after dark, we went to a barn at the estate to collect from him our share of what rightfully belonged to the pigs. Since Americans were in the habit of neatly separating their various scraps before depositing them in different containers, we usually came home carrying several receptacles filled with manna from heaven. There was coffee with milk and sugar already added, baked beans with real bacon, and, to top it all, pancake batter with maple syrup on the side. At first, we had to swallow very hard, realizing our choice of either throwing up or simply ignoring items like cigarette butts, matches, toothpicks, pink pieces of well-chewed gum, and other unmentionable items. The food would keep us alive over a lengthy period.

On one of the coldest days, loud knocks at the front door almost scared us out of our wits. What now? More homeless people? Worse? Kidnappings of West Berliners by the NKVD, who sneaked into the Western sectors, had become a frightening practice. But it was not the NKVD. Outside stood a figure resembling a mixture of the Russian fairy-tale witch Baba Yaga and Santa Claus, so bundled up that it took us a while to identify her. After we had peeled the figure, like an onion, out of several layers of clothes and shawls, out came Anna! She had come back to us, frozen into an icicle; we had to thaw her by the little stove in her old room before she could give us a detailed report about the trip she had undertaken to see if "her family" was still alive. The journey, a lengthy and dangerous venture, had taken her a whole day. I do not remember how long we cried, laughed, danced, and shouted with joy. After completing our entire repertoire of Vendish songs and ditties, she dug into her bundles, from which emerged a freshly slaughtered chicken, wrinkled apples, canned red cabbage and ham, as well as fresh bread, butter, and a dozen eggs—treasures from another planet.

Anna, beside herself with happiness over finding us alive, proceeded to report, in a combination of equally loud German and Vendish, that at Friedrichstrasse train station, the official border between East and West Berlin, a miserable little creature in a "People's Police" uniform had insisted on confiscating some of her goods, declaring their import into capitalistic West Berlin as illegal. Would we believe it? "Why don't you compfercate all?" she had roared at the flabbergasted Communist official, who probably wished he had never been born. Then she proceeded to hurl a whole carton of eggs at his feet, which splattered all over the platform. In an acute state of shock he had fled, escaping possibly lethal attacks inflicted on him by a lunatic.

The vanguard of the victorious Red Army, evidently in a suicidal mood, had entered her little house, intending to invade her well-stocked pantry, when they found themselves face to face with the kind of babushka that they had not expected. Babushkas in Russia were gentle, loving, and kind, but this one, aiming a pitchfork at them, was even yelling in a language they understood, at least in the essential parts. What they grasped sounded like a very rude invitation to leave her grounds and not dare to return, ending with the Vendish version of the request to kiss her backside, "*rish me oblish!*"

Nix *tovarishch*, nix *karasho*, a bunch of dirty thieves they were!

From that infamous day on, having learned an essential lesson, Red soldiers made it their business to walk on tiptoes when passing her property, avoiding even touching her garden gate in mortal fear that this harmless gesture might cause a repeat performance.

Anna's happiness at being reunited with the two of us and learning that my brother was alive was only surpassed by her sadness about the disappearance of her revered *Herr Baron*. She installed herself in the same basement room where she had once endured the air raids. Scanning the neighborhood for former friends, she came home with new horror stories every day. Anna loved horror stories! After working like a farm horse for a week, chopping wood for the stove, washing laundry in cold water, and steadfastly declining to partake in our tasty, life-sustaining meals from American garbage cans, she left with the promise to return soon.

Chapter Sixty-One
A New Job

The first days of spring, so eagerly awaited, produced not only sweet-smelling flowers and green leaves on the trees, but also a revolting stench of sewage flooding the houses and even the streets, from broken pipes in baths, toilets, and gutters, until then mercifully frozen. But not even this calamity could diminish the overwhelming joy of having gotten through the first crucial post-war winter. John McGraw, still stationed in Hamburg and with whom I had managed to keep in touch thanks to the help of the British military stationed in West Berlin, suggested that I now return; he missed me, and his outfit was able to offer me a paid position. In view of the fact that there were still no regular passenger trains and no traveling passes for German civilians, this was easier said than done. Much as I relished the idea of being swept across the border by another angel in Soviet uniform, the chances that this were to happen a second time were pretty slim.

Someone gave me the tip that, in order to get across to the British zone, all I had to do was enter one of the refugee camps in the city, pretend that I was a displaced person from the East, and let myself be shipped by train to the West. After one day in a mobbed camp, I was carted with hundreds of others to the Grunewald train station in the British sector to board a freight train. The date was April 2, 1946.

The Grunewald station had been the main deportation point for thousands of Berlin Jews on their way to the camps. I wondered if the German *Reichsbahn* received the same compensation for our transportation, having charged Jews four pfennigs per kilometer in a freight car without windows, heat, water, food, or sanitary installations. The extermination of the Jews was, aside from being a monstrous crime, a well-organized, lucrative business from which quite a few individuals and organizations profited very nicely. No Jew was killed without being robbed before as well as after death. Stripped during his or her lifetime of businesses, homes, and all personal belongings, in death they still provided clothes, eyeglasses, gold fillings, bridges, and hair to be used by German industry. Finally, the ashes of their bones served to fertilize the fields, to the benefit of the "master race."

In sharp contrast to the Jews, we all boarded this freight train of our own free will, we were not deported, and none of us would starve. As far as comfort in the cattle cars was concerned, aside from some straw scattered on the floor and a few pails in a corner where the passengers could relieve themselves in full view, there was none. During the process of being screened by the British Military Police, I was stopped and politely asked to step aside. What now? My false papers were in order, weren't they? Of course, I was told, but with my command of English, I was considered a godsend. Would I act as the official train interpreter?

Rejoicing about this unexpected stroke of luck, I let myself be taken to a regular train car, centered between ten cattle cars. Sergeant Major Tom Atkinson, in charge of the train, informed me that they expected about two thousand refugees going west, accompanied by a troop of armed British soldiers, protecting the passengers from marauding Russians and Poles while en route to the city of Hannover. Although the distance between Berlin and Hannover was a mere two hundred miles, it would take the freight train at least twenty hours. My bundles were stashed in the British-occupied car, equipped with a number of cots and benches as well as a regular wood-burning stove with the pipe through the roof.

There was one snag, however, and I was told to prepare myself for it; at the frontier, in the middle of the night, the train would stop for the Russians to board in order to examine the passengers' papers, and it was not a good idea for a German citizen to be found traveling with the British military. So, just before the border, the train would come to a halt, giving me a chance to jump out, climb into the next freight car, and stay there until the procedure was over. Once the train stopped a second time, the signal that we had reached the British zone, I could come back. Very, very simple. Or so it seemed.

The crowded train began to move at two o'clock in the afternoon, and I had a wonderful time with the soldiers, who spoiled me with noodles and meat, prepared on the little stove, washed down with plenty of German lager beer. We then began to play poker, and just when I was about to experience what to most people only happens once in their lifetime, an honest to goodness royal flush, the signal came that, after nine hours, the border was about to be reached. In total dismay over forfeiting my fantastic stroke of poker luck, I jumped down from the military car, on to the next cattle car, and mingled with the other passengers.

Soon a Soviet soldier, the obligatory Kalashnikov on his back and obviously from the other side of the Ural Mountains, climbed aboard; from the way he held the passes upside down, I deduced that he could not read. As soon as all the cars had been checked, the train slowly resumed its journey and, after ten more minutes, came to the predetermined halt. Noticing what I believed to be the rotating flashlight signal from the British car, I took the plunge and jumped down on what in the total darkness looked like solid ground between the tracks. Only when something hit my forehead very hard and I began spiraling into black nothingness, did it occur to me that a mistake had occurred. In Hannover, it flashed through my mind, John would learn that I had disappeared from the face of the Earth. Within a few seconds, I felt icy water engulfing me; it went over my head, and I hit bottom, ultimately shooting up to the surface like the cork of a champagne bottle.

Before I was able to realize that my sheepskin coat, once it filled with water, would pull me down again, I heard voices and saw a flashlight that had followed me all the way down; before I knew it, half a dozen British soldiers came running down the bank of the river, and the sergeant major managed to pull me out. He carried me into the British car and immediately proceeded to strip me of all my clothes. After being wrapped in army blankets, Tom Atkinson, himself sopping wet from being in the water up to his hips, gently put me down on one of the cots, the others standing about, naked horror written all over their faces. Was

I hurt? Maybe even dead? No, as a matter of fact, I seemed alright; at least no bones were broken and there was no blood.

My clothes were immediately draped on a rope to dry near the stove. It would take the fur coat two whole weeks to dry out. I was then filled up with sweet hot tea and actually began to talk and laugh over this outlandish mishap, evidently caused by the fact that the sergeant major and I had gotten our signals crossed. While he had meant to warn me with the light, I had been under the impression that it was now safe to jump. We all laughed and then, without warning, I must have gone into shock, losing consciousness, becoming cold as ice, and hyperventilating before I stopped breathing. Somehow I was brought back to life and at once began to cry without being able to control myself. They were my first tears since the end of the war.

For the remainder of the night, Tom Atkinson sat by my cot holding my hand, stroking my hair, in an effort to comfort me. With a soft voice, he kept talking about his life as a car mechanic in Leeds, his wife and the two children who were waiting for him, and after a while, I must have drifted off. After being awakened an hour before we were scheduled to arrive at our destination, I demanded a mirror in which I did not recognize myself. My right eye was closed, a gigantic hematoma, which would display all the colors of the rainbow within the next few weeks, had formed above it. I must have hit some crossbar leading over what turned out to be the defective bridge from which I then plunged through a gaping hole into the river. The British physician in the military hospital in Hannover attested that I had survived practically intact and diagnosed a concussion. Years after the incident, undergoing corrective surgery, a hairline skull fracture was still clearly visible on the X-rays. Given the details by the sergeant major, John took one look at me and tactfully proceeded to sing "Black Eyed Susan," which at that point did not amuse me. A few days later, he drove me up to Haseldorf where Princess Agnes nursed me until I recuperated from the shock and injury.

Chapter Sixty-Two
The News of My Father

Tom Atkinson went back to Berlin a few weeks later and told my horrified mother about my adventure. When he returned to Hamburg in the fall of 1946, he contacted John and insisted on talking to me personally, because the nature of the message that he brought from my mother could not be conveyed over the telephone. He decided to drive up to Haseldorf; there the visitor, overwhelmed by the abundance of "royalty"—princes, princesses, dukes, duchesses, counts, barons, the white-gloved old butler, and the gorgeous castle—probably thought he was dreaming.

Noticing his awkwardness, I suggested we go out to the park, where we sat down on a bench. He did not know how to begin, so he just took my hand as he had done that fateful night on the train. But now, in full realization of my social status, my mother having turned out to be a "real baroness," he insisted on addressing me with my title, intermittently using "madam." On the train it had been a casual "girlie" or "ducky," and that was somehow not fitting anymore.

"I am sorry, baroness," the car mechanic from Leeds said in a soft, halting voice, "but your father is dead." Three times he had to repeat the words that somehow did not reach me. My head seemed to spin, as it had after my fall into the icy river; there was something unreal about this whole situation. "Are you alright, madam?" he inquired shyly, deep concern in his voice. Then he proceeded to tell me why he had come all the way to see me.

After my father's disappearance, attempts by my mother, by Louis P. Lochner, and by members of the Danish military mission to discover his fate had netted no results whatsoever. The Soviet authorities steadfastly maintained that they had never even heard his name. The police gave my mother the comforting advice to simply have her husband reported missing; after the mandatory seven years, he would be declared legally dead. If it had not been for a strange coincidence, his fate would forever have remained an unsolved mystery.

After I had gone back to West Germany, my brother managed to return to Berlin. His application to be accepted as a law student at Humboldt University in East Berlin, now under Soviet control, was rejected. The reason for refusal was that he was not the son of a laborer or a farmer. This rejection infuriated him enough to become one of the initiators responsible for the creation of the Free University of West Berlin a few years later. A rumor had come to his attention, according to which a famous actor, after his release from a top-secret camp in the Soviet zone, had mentioned my father's name. After his return to the West, the man kept his mouth shut for quite a while, remembering the stern instructions never to tell a living soul about his experience. "They" would find him wherever he went, and then he would be sent to Siberia for the rest of his life. Once he moved to West Germany, he realized that, for the sake of humanity, it was his duty to lift the veil of silence imposed on him. My brother decided to visit the man who, nine months before, had been among the few who left the death camp in Jamlitz alive.

Gustaf Gründgens, one of Germany's most prominent actors and a friend of Walter Franck, had held the position of general manager of Berlin's State Theater for almost ten years, during which time he had succeeded in saving a number of actors and their Jewish spouses from a terrible fate. This could never have been achieved, had not Hermann Goering, patron of the State Theater, at some point decided to really show his archrival Goebbels, in charge of the movie industry, who was more powerful. Just to annoy him, and by no means for love of the Jews, the non-Aryan spouses of his star actors remained unmolested. What more superbly elating sensation could exist for the obese, morphine addict Goering, the self-styled God, to be master over life and death?[35]

During the course of their conversation, Gründgens revealed that he and my father had already been through half a dozen makeshift places of detention including cellars, pigsties, and dirt holes, before arriving at the notorious camp in Jamlitz. Gründgens soon discovered that they were kindred spirits. After six months of indescribable suffering, he witnessed my father's death during the night of November 12-13, 1945.

Jamlitz, a particularly unattractive little village southeast of Berlin, not far from the Polish border, had been the site of a Nazi concentration camp. In the fall of 1944, over four thousand inmates from Hungary, the Soviet Union, Czechoslovakia, France, Greece, Holland, Italy, Norway, and Germany were held there, crammed into sixteen barracks. As the Soviet troops pushed westward, some nineteen hundred of those, who had managed to survive disease, hunger, and torture, were herded for a march all the way to Sachsenhausen, north of Berlin, the sick ones being shot by the wayside. Later in 1945, the NKVD found a bed already made, into which they now packed "enemies of the Soviet people" between twelve and eighty years of age, among them old and young Nazis, women, and children accused of having been werewolves, former Socialists, Communists, doctors, carpenters, lawyers, pharmacists, farmers, and laborers. Among them were a number of active anti-Nazis who had already suffered in Hitler's prisons, as well as Jews who had barely escaped the gas chambers. While some inmates had been actually tried and sentenced by Soviet military courts, most had been taken from their homes or simply plucked off the streets. In cases where the number of captives on a given transport did not correspond with the official number on the list, people were snatched at random from the fields to fill in for those who had either died or escaped.

Unlike in the Nazi camps, there were no beatings or executions in Jamlitz; they were considered unnecessary. Hunger, disease, and the cold completed the work. The captives, most of whom did not have the slightest idea what crimes they were accused of, ate grass, acorns, and bark from the trees until they died like flies. Of the twelve thousand to fourteen thousand people interned in the Jamlitz camp during its thirty-two months of existence, some four thousand to six thousand succumbed to exposure. The victims, at the beginning buried in single graves, were later thrown into ditches, hastily dug somewhere in the woods, the burial procedure usually taking place at night, so no one would notice. Forests and fields would soon cover all traces. In April of 1947, the camp was abandoned by the Soviets after efforts had been made to erase all signs of its existence. According to official statements, none of those who met their death there had even existed. Only after the unification of Germany did mass exhumations disclose that practically none of the skeletons showed outward signs of a violent death. Even the teeth with gold inlays and bridges were still found intact. The conclusion could safely be reached that the cause of death had to be a "natural" one: exposure and starvation.

On an icy November morning in the unheated barrack, Gründgens discovered that Ulrich von Sell, suffering from pneumonia, had fallen from his cot to the ground during the night and frozen to death on the bare earth. Together with a few others, he managed to bury him, so his friend would not end up in a mass grave. Just what prompted the Soviets to keep Hitler's emaciated ex-prisoner in their custody instead of sending him home after the promised few hours on May 8 will forever remain speculation. One version would have it that the neighbor, who asked my father to identify him, was a Communist spy, eager to deliver an aristocrat into the hands of the Soviets. This story, however, had to be dismissed as false because that man was also delivered to Jamlitz and died there. Still another suspicion was that when my father revealed his role in the plot against Hitler, probably mentioning the name of Admiral Canaris, once the chief of German counterespionage and a declared enemy of National Socialism and Bolshevism, he was at once classified as a dangerous "enemy of the Soviet people," probably a spy, a "Junker," a member of the hated aristocracy. We will never know.

⁓ Chapter Sixty-Three ⁓
GRANDMOTHER

In the Soviet-occupied zone, the facilities of former Nazi concentration camps, like Sachsenhausen and Buchenwald, continued to be used after 1945 by the Soviet administration, which, after 1949, turned them over to the East German Communist regime. Falsely declared as places of "detention and reeducation" for Nazis, they also served as prisons for all those under the suspicion of resisting Stalinism. The truth was that, behind the concrete walls with barbed wire on top, in the run-down, vermin-infested barracks, long-term prisoners were kept, among them women, children, and even Jews. On the iron gates at Sachsenhausen, the cynical Nazi message "*Arbeit macht frei*" ("Work will make you free") greeted the newcomers; in Buchenwald "*Jedem das seine*" ("To each his own").

The number, nature, and location of the NKVD camps, on the other hand, was kept top secret. Their mere existence within East Germany was vehemently denied, first by the Soviets and later by the East German authorities, dismissed as fantasies of the "Fascists." The first official and authentic information came out only after the reunification of Germany in the fall of 1989. Some of the camps with their mass graves had simply been ploughed over, planted with grass or corn; in the case of Jamlitz, housing developments were swiftly erected to cover all traces.

After my father's disappearance, my mother decided to seek out the whereabouts of my grandmother. Had she survived the inferno? Walking the twenty kilometers from Berlin, she found the house where the general's widow had resided, intact but occupied by Soviet officers and their families. Somehow, she was able to locate her mother-in-law at the other end of Potsdam in a shabbily furnished little room that the eighty-five-year-old woman now shared with Martha, her servant. After being thrown out of their home, with no place to go, Martha had propped up her mistress in a little wooden cart and pulled her through Potsdam in her long search for a roof over their heads.

Although my mother succeeded in withholding the devastating news of her last son's fate from his starving, bedridden old mother, she was not able to prevent a "well-meaning" friend from sending a note of condolence. Soon after, my grandmother succumbed not only to malnutrition and the cold, but the shock of the news. She was buried in the family plot among the "caste" she had been part of, in the ancient cemetery in Potsdam-Bornstedt, at her husband's side and next to Adolf, the third son, whose remains had been returned to his parents from France after World War I. My mother used cigarettes to bribe a carpenter in

Dahlem into carving a wooden cross for the grave, which she carried across her back from Berlin to Potsdam, later maintaining that now she was able to identify with Jesus Christ on his way to Golgotha. Not even a month later, the cross was stolen, most likely to be used for firewood. This theft so enraged her that she marched straight into the lion's den, my grandmother's old apartment, now occupied by a Russian major. After ringing the bell she was, to her amazement, courteously ushered in by the stocky master of the house, his buxom wife flashing her silver front teeth in a friendly grin, and an extremely well-behaved little girl with a pink taffeta bow in her hair.

Sitting on my grandmother's sofa, my mother spent a most enjoyable hour with Russian tea, cake, and more vodka than was good for her, in the company of three jolly Muscovites. Encouraged by the vodka and hospitality, she decided not only to spill the story of the stolen cross, but to go all the way. Noticing that practically all of my grandmother's belongings were still there, she boldly asked the officer, who had mastered sufficient German, why he, obviously a man of taste, bothered to surround himself with all these dreadful old pieces of junk? She, in fact, would be happy to take the stuff off his hands, relieving him for instance of the monstrous Steinway piano, the two-hundred and fifty-year-old desk clock, (a personal gift of Maria Theresa to one of my forefathers), the mahogany desk (pure Biedermeier style), and other outmoded Rococo items. She could see that he was obviously a modern man, a high-ranking officer of the victorious Soviet Army, who deserved better than living among totally outmoded paraphernalia. The nice major, unable to resist the determined look in her Hohenzollern-blue eyes, joyfully agreed to her selfless proposal. After several more vodkas, he told her that, since he was to return to Moscow in the not too distant future, she could pick whatever she liked; he would even send it to her.

"To West Berlin?" she inquired.

"Of course! Why not? No problem!," he replied. "*Karasho? Karasho!*"

A few weeks later, my mother had dismissed the officer's promise as a dream too good to be true, when an open Soviet military truck came to a halt in front of her house. Under the eyes of the perplexed neighbors, four sturdy Russian soldiers in battle fatigues began to unload their cargo: a black Steinway grand piano, a desk, the two-hundred and fifty-year-old clock with the Austrian Double Eagle on the pendulum, family portraits, and countless other equally valuable items. Taking great care not to chip anything, they carried the items into the house, after which my mother felt obliged to dig deep into her black market liquor and cigarette supply.

Chapter Sixty-Four
INTERLUDE: JOURNEY INTO THE UNKNOWN—JULY 1986

"Don't ever go *there*," my brother had warned me. He knew what he was talking about; he had been *there*. "You will regret it. There is no place to reminisce, to pay homage, or even to rest." In spite of the well-meant advice, I knew I could not stay away forever; I had to go *there*.

Erich Honecker, head of state of the Soviet zone, since 1949 known as the "German Democratic Republic" (GDR), in a fit of generosity had decided to issue me a permanent visa, which entitled me to enter his precious little island, walled in since August 13, 1961, a prerogative I took ample advantage of for as long as Germany was divided. Blacklisted since 1950 for my various anti-Communist activities, not even daring to travel between West Germany and West Berlin other than by air, this status had not been changed by my American citizenship, but by my marriage to Pastor Martin Niemoeller, whose name served as a protective shield no one in the "German Democratic Republic" dared touch. Over the years, I was able to smuggle tons of forbidden cargo in and out, including household items of those GDR residents hoping to eventually make it to the West, aware that they would have to leave all their property behind. But never had I dared to smuggle people, even though the Communist "People's Police" were not allowed to search my car. While feeling safe myself, the risk for a fugitive being caught was too high.

After attending the annual official ceremonies on and around July 20, 1986, in West Berlin, commemorating the 1944 assassination attempt, I decided to cross into the GDR via Checkpoint Charlie and drive the eighty miles southeast to the little Spreewald village where Anna was buried and where her relatives were eagerly awaiting me. After a heartwarming visit, I left my friends the next morning, and, fully intending to go straight back to West Berlin, I headed for the autobahn. At the intersection, against my will, I did not follow the signs pointing to Berlin, but turned right instead. It was as if the car did not want to go where I wanted to go. Soon, driving northeast instead of northwest, in the direction of the Polish border, I found myself passing through villages that I had never seen before, sleepy little places with neatly kept houses and an abundance of summer flowers in the front yards. After a good half hour, I noticed a sign by the road. I had reached the village of Lieberose, and immediately felt a chill, realizing it was too late to turn back.

Here the NKVD had taken over a Nazi concentration camp, filling it with their own prisoners, among them Justus Delbrück, brother of Emmy Bonhoeffer, Dietrich Bonhoeffer's brother-in-law and, for his involvement in the July 20 plot, a prisoner of the Gestapo.[36]

The sun suddenly hid behind clouds, and I drove through wild, dark woods. Huge trees, resembling black wings on a theater stage, lined the country road paved with cobblestones. For a few minutes, I was all alone, but then, from out of nowhere, I found myself surrounded by Soviet military vehicles, appearing from all directions. Somehow, I had managed to get myself wedged into what was evidently a Russian convoy, probably on its way to or from a military maneuver. Forced to proceed at a snail's pace as the only civilian car between a huge truck and a monstrous gray-green tank, I realized that attempting to pass or turn back was now impossible. The open vehicle in front of me was filled with young Soviet soldiers, some of whom risked a cautious grin. Jabbing one another with their elbows, I soon faced a whole truckload of red-faced boys with shaven heads, vastly amused at the sight of the *matka* trapped in her fire-engine-red Mercedes, the stars and stripes displayed on her front window shield, the unmistakable emblem of the United States of America. With the deafening noise of the tanks rattling over cobblestones, the idea suddenly hit me that, if I should happen to disappear here and now, not a living soul would ever find me, not in a hundred years.

Grinning back at the soldiers seemed advisable but became rather exhausting after a while. One of the boys in front of me reminded me of Pawlee, my little snot-nosed, bristle-headed POW at the riding academy. After what seemed a small eternity, the convoy suddenly turned onto a dirt road to the left, following the hand signal of a poker-faced Kirghiz. The maneuver, I figured, was probably a mock battle against capitalists like me. The man signaled me to proceed straight ahead; I was out, I was free, back among the living. The woods cleared, and after the darkness of the dense forest, the bright sunshine almost blinded me. What I had left behind, I realized, was a sinister foreboding of what was about to happen.

The next sign by the roadside read "Jamlitz"; I slowed down to get a good look at the place where I knew my journey would end. The dismal state of the unsightly, run-down village, so unlike Anna's pretty hometown of Werben, shocked me. From the walls of the buildings, Soviet and East German flags were interspersed with ghastly, huge signs reassuring the reader that, hand in hand with the Soviet Union, "Socialism would win"; in view of the dreary reality a rather brazen promise. Certainly it had not won during the past forty years.

Turning onto a dirt road to my left, I stopped the car and got out to ask directions. In the front yard of a desolate house, I spotted a bent old woman tottering about, wearing a babushka-style scarf and an apron, busily hanging laundry on a line between scratching chickens and a mutt on a chain going berserk at the sight of a stranger. Evidently half-blind, she approached the fence and even answered my question whether she had lived here in 1945. Yes, she had come that year as a refugee from Silesia. I inquired about the camp. Where had it been, what had become of it? To my surprise, she nodded, her arm pointing in the direction of what seemed to be a settlement of single, shack-like, shabby new houses. That is where the camp was, with all those poor people, so, so many, she muttered, she could see them behind the barbed wire. But, whenever she came too close, the guards had threatened her with machine guns; how could she forget? And then, she added, repeating over and over, "*Alle tot, alle weg, alle tot, alle weg*" ("All dead, all gone, all dead, all gone"), after which she disappeared in the house, closing the door behind her. The dog kept snarling and yelping, clearly conveying his message that I was not wanted there. It was then that I saw the street sign: *Strasse der Freiheit* (Freedom Street). What a horrible mockery! All dead! After 1947, the plough had erased all traces of the horror that had prevailed.

Deciding I had to find a place to rest for a few minutes, I drove up the narrow road until I could go no further. Parking the conspicuous Mercedes behind some bushes by the roadside, I climbed up a small hill. At least I would be able to overlook the territory where the camp had once existed. In total dismay I sat down on a lonely tree stump. Without having actually planned it, I had reached my destination; I was now as close as I could ever get to what once had been my father, with probably not even one hundred yards separating me from him. For a short while at least I had to rest after the long journey that had taken almost half a century. Goethe's words from "Faust" flashed through my mind: "Sorrow revives, her wail of anguish sending / Back o'er life's devious labyrinthine way, / The dear ones naming who, in life's fair morn. / By Fate beguiled, from my embrace were torn."

I found myself unable to cry; this was no place for tears. I was painfully aware of God's absence. Yet in spite of it, I opened my little prayer book and, having become a Jew by choice, did what I must have come for; I read *kaddish* for my father and all those nameless victims of Bolshevist terror buried with him somewhere under the fields, the roads, the houses: "Yit-gad-dal v'yit-kad-dash sh'mei raba" ("Let the glory of God be extolled, let his great name be hallowed, in the world whose creation he willed").

There was so much I had to tell him. Of foremost importance was the fact that his beautiful grandson, who uncannily resembled his namesake, the grandfather he had never seen, was, like his mother, an American citizen. I wanted him to know that I had not forgotten my promise, namely to go and find another star. In fact, I had found forty-eight, later to be fifty. Additionally, his only daughter, Kaiser Wilhelm's "little monkey," had married her fairy-tale hero, Martin Niemoeller. As a tangible reminder of my visit, I broke a small branch from an oak tree that, most likely, had witnessed my father's suffering and death.

One year later, on Yom HaShoah, at Jerusalem's Western Wall, called the "Wailing Wall" by Christians, I was finally able to get rid of all the tears that I had not been able to shed for four decades. "*At muchracha livkot*" ("you have to cry"), the woman next to me, who had been kind enough to lend me a scarf for my head, whispered in my ear, as if to encourage me. The Hebrew words sounded so familiar, the language that I had studied on my long way to embracing the Jewish faith. Here I felt at home, leaning my head against the stones left over from the destroyed Temple that, over thousands of years, had become used to tears.

A memorial has been erected in Jamlitz in an attempt to return to the victims of atrocity their identity and their dignity, denied them for so long. It reminds loved ones as well as casual visitors of what one barbarous regime following another barbarous regime can do to humanity.

Chapter Sixty-Five
New Sorrows, New Jobs

Sergeant Major Atkinson, the bearer of devastating tidings, disappeared from my life after that fateful day in Haseldorf. I never saw him again, even though hardly a day goes by when, if nothing else, the bump above my right eye reminds me of what happened during a night in April 1946. Seeing no purpose in staying on in what was now the British zone of Germany, I decided to return to Berlin to be with my mother.

There was still no legal way for me to cross the border; John decided to smuggle me into West Berlin in a British Army vehicle. Since he and I had decided to get married as soon as his divorce was final, he wanted to meet my mother. The only authority he had to be aware of was the British Military Police at the checkpoint in Helmstedt; the Soviets were not allowed to stop a British officer in uniform. Seated next to John during the first part of the journey, just before the border, he drove off the autobahn into the woods and made me climb into the trunk of his car, a procedure that would not have presented the slightest problem in the spacious Buick he usually drove; unfortunately, it had broken down the previous day, and he had been issued a German VW, a Beetle, for his trip to Berlin. In order to fit in the so-called trunk, located at the front of the car, I had to fold myself to the size of a newspaper, after which John succeeded in closing the hood by sitting on it. Locked inside, I found to my dismay that I shared my cramped quarters with another blind passenger, a wasp of considerable size, equipped with a very unpleasant disposition, determined to defend the confined space with his life. After a brief struggle, he ended up squashed to a pulp before he could sting me.

At the Helmstedt border, British guards, followed a few minutes later by the Soviets, lifted the barriers for the car to pass. After reaching a safe distance, John drove off once more into a small forest to extract me from my tight prison, unfolding my limbs one by one like the blades of a rusty jackknife. Unfortunately, the unpleasant maneuver had to be repeated before entering the island of West Berlin.

My mother could not believe her eyes and, after demonstrating to her how I had traveled, decided to fall instantly in love with John. When I told her that he and I were going to be married as soon as possible, she expressed some doubts. "I just don't believe you'll marry him," she said with the same firmness with which she had maintained that—against all odds—her house would not be destroyed. As expected, her prophecy would come true. In 1946, in Rhodesia, where he had gone to visit his son, John's car collided with a speeding train during a torrential thunderstorm at night. Whatever was left of him had to be excised with shears from the wreckage.

Unable and unwilling to deal with reality, I fell into what seemed a bottomless hole, even declining to resume my interrupted acting career. Not even my dear friend and former teacher Walter Franck could persuade me to return to my learned profession. He was starring in Samuel Beckett's *Waiting for Godot*, and I realized that I, too, was waiting for someone like Godot, whoever he was, only I did not really care if he ever came. But since I had to make a living, I accepted a position offered to me by a friend, who himself had narrowly escaped execution by the Nazis.

Dr. Rainer Hildebrandt, a dynamic young man and a well-known figure in the resistance, had been close to the circle around Albrecht Haushofer, murdered by the Gestapo on April 23, 1945. He asked me to join the "League against Inhumanity," an organization closely affiliated with the League of Human Rights. Officially limiting itself to the investigation and care of ex-prisoners and refugees from the Soviet zone, it was in reality an anti-Communist agency, operated and financed by the United States. After my rigorous training by British Intelligence, the position seemed perfect.

I was assigned to a job that required interrogating hundreds of escapees from the eastern zone, among them prisoners from Soviet concentration camps well as former political prisoners, before they were officially registered as political refugees by the Western Allies, after which they would be issued ration cards and taken to the West by military planes. I soon found myself handling the more intricate cases because, through my training and by nature, I was able to judge whether or not a person was telling the truth, and soon the word spread that I was hard, if not impossible, to fool.

Mingling with honest-to-goodness victims, there were small-scale as well as potential Nazi criminals posing as political refugees, whom I turned over to the authorities without compassion. Since our organization was on the Soviet hit list, almost all of us worked under assumed names, in acute danger of being kidnapped. Our office in an old villa in Berlin-Schlachtensee was infested with planted Communist spies, usually spotted by us before they could do any harm; we gleefully fed them false information. Naturally, we had our own agents in their respective organizations in East Berlin and the eastern zone. During that time, it still happened that people who felt safe in West Berlin were brutally dragged from their homes, even off the streets, by Soviet agents in broad daylight, seemingly to dissolve into thin air. The most spectacular case was that of Dr. Walter Linse, a lawyer, plucked from a West Berlin street, who disappeared without a trace. After Hildebrandt was almost snatched by the NKVD in front of his residence (had it not been for the watchfulness of his two huge dogs), all of us were placed under special American-supervised police protection.

It was in this capacity as an interrogator that, one day, a big bird landed in my net. Across from my desk sat a man who applied for status as a "recognized" refugee from Communist East Germany. I was sure that I had never seen his face before, yet something caused me to feel very uneasy. After examining the man's identity card, it hit me like lightning out of the clear blue sky; I was dealing with Dr. Paul Reckzeh, a physician and mass murderer, the infamous Nazi informer who had reported some seventy people to the Gestapo, of whom at least five paid with their lives. To my utter surprise he had not even bothered with a false identity.

With a shudder, I remembered the sordid case of the so-called "Thadden Tea Party," which had taken place on September 10, 1943, at the home of Anna Solf, widow of Kaiser Wilhelm's last German ambassador to Japan. Elisabeth von Thadden, headmistress of a renowned school for girls, had invited a guest, a physician, whom she introduced as having been recommended as politically absolutely reliable, who would gladly smuggle letters to and from Switzerland. After the get-together, the honorable physician wasted no time reporting everyone present at the party to the Gestapo. Among the first five executed by guillotine was Elisabeth von Thadden, an elderly lady of noble descent. Two of the invited guests had declined the invitation, later explaining their absence with a strange intuition warning them not to attend. One of them was the Countess Maria von Maltzan; the other one was my mother.

After the end of the war, the search for Reckzeh had begun, but he had disappeared like the proverbial needle in a haystack. According to rumors, the Soviets had allegedly caught, tried, and sentenced him, only to release him after a short time. He had resumed his medical practice while also spying for the Communists. What eventually caused his decision to leave East Germany would remain an enigma.

Something in my facial expression or my body language must have warned him. I left my office with the excuse of having to get a form for him to fill, in reality to alert the police, and, upon my return after not more than two minutes, I found an empty room; an intense search for him netted nothing.[37]

Chapter Sixty-Six
The Airlift

In the spring of 1948, Stalin had come to the conclusion that he was not satisfied with just a slice of the Berlin cake. He wanted to integrate the three Western-occupied sectors into his laborers' paradise, by force, if necessary. Yalta or no Yalta, where the agreement to divide the German capital between the occupying forces had been signed by Roosevelt, Churchill, and himself, this malignant growth, a capitalist island in the Red Sea, was not going to remain a thorn in his flesh forever.

A justification for taking swift action presented itself on June 21, 1948, when the Western powers, in a surprise move, devalued the old *reichsmark* and introduced a new currency, the *deutschmark*, in their zones, including West Berlin. For one fleeting moment in history, all Germans were equal; every citizen was handed the amount of forty *deutschmarks*, an amount which at that time was the approximate equivalent of ten American dollars. This step was immediately met by a currency reform in the Soviet-occupied zone; however, since no new money had been printed there, the old banknotes were adorned with stamp-like stickers, an emergency measure that prompted a friend of mine, still in possession of counterfeiting equipment from his days in Leni Riefenstahl's cellar, to print enough stickers to totally upset the financial situation in the Soviet zone, at least until new Eastern bills and coins could be produced.

The difference between the two monetary reforms became painfully evident; in sharp contrast to the new "Westmark," the "Eastmark" was not worth the paper on which it was printed. While stores in the Western parts of Germany overnight filled with goods not even imaginable a few weeks before, in the Soviet zone food, clothes, as well as all other "luxury items" remained not only rationed, but extremely scarce or simply nonexistent for years to come. The economic division of Germany, politically split since 1945, now caused insurmountable problems that, within days, led to serious complications on the highest level.

Stalin presumed that under no circumstances would the Western Allies risk a war over Berlin, so he imposed a total blockade on the Western parts of the city. The date when all access to and from the free sectors was barred to Western Allied traffic by land or water was June 28, 1948. But as Stalin, the man of "steel," soon found out, Berlin was not just another city, the Berliners not just another people, and neither were the Western Allies simply fortune-seeking mercenaries. His threat to starve the Berliners would not motivate the Americans, British, and French to relinquish their rightful claims on the city. Under the superb leadership of the US Military Governor General Lucius D. Clay, the mutual decision was reached to engage in a very unique joint venture, the Berlin Airlift. Until May 12 the following year, every item needed for the survival of the Western Powers as well as the Berlin population, from the size of a dried pea to that of Army trucks, would be delivered by air.

For the first time since the end of the war, life in Berlin became pleasantly exciting. Once we had gotten used to the noise of the prop planes, lovingly called "raisin bombers," roaring above our house at sixty second intervals twenty-four hours a day, we realized that this inhuman action by the Bolsheviks served a wonderful purpose. By finding themselves in the same boat, the Western Allies and Berliners joined together in a way never possible under normal circumstances. For eleven months, unlike in the previous three years, nobody came close to starvation. Realizing that our freedom was at stake, with death-defying determination we swallowed the rather disgusting contents of the bags containing the various dried foods issued to us. We even managed to joke over the twenty-five pounds of pressed coal allotted each household for the entire winter, easily carried home in one hand.

The one really annoying side effect was the electric current, now dished out in homoeopathic doses. We only received the benefit of electricity for two hours a day, frantically trying to make the best of it while it lasted. This meant jumping out of bed at two or four o'clock in the morning to do the ironing, vacuum cleaning, and cooking at lightning speed. No need to put on clothes because, at least during the winter months, we all went to bed fully dressed in order to keep from freezing to death. Fast meals were prepared from revolting but nourishing mixes, the containers wrapped in blankets for lack of newspapers and stashed in a place where they would remain hot. The warmest place was under the featherbed, which was a risky undertaking because forgetting about the pot of soup in the bed had very messy consequences. Electricity was strictly rationed for each household, and transgressors were punished. A term arose in those days, a name whispered behind cupped hands, "*Der kleine Gustav*" ("Little Gustav"), a small and ingenious device that enabled a halfway smart person to set back the meter. Since overdrawing one's allotment was punishable by prison, this devious procedure was practiced with glee by my equally devious mother, who had also developed into an expert when it came to bribery, which was an important skill in those days. Her Prussian blue eyes, beaming from an aristocratic face, betrayed nothing but highest integrity and sincerity; she became an absolute master in the art of melting an official's hard heart by "inadvertently" leaving a couple of cigarettes, a bar of soap, or half a loaf of bread, all black market goods, on or preferably under the obliging functionary's desk.

The Western Allies received only a little more of everything than the Berliners, like electric current, so Americans and their British counterparts graciously shared their fortune with German neighbors; the French were a little more reserved. On May 12, 1949, the combined perseverance of the Western Allies and the population of Berlin paid off; the blockade was lifted.

Chapter Sixty-Seven
Cold War

At this precise point in history, with life well on its way to normalcy, efforts could and should have begun on the part of the Germans to deal with the past, their own guilt, possibly even with a hint of remorse, preconditions for a new beginning. But just then, a true miracle happened; overnight, a powerful ally came to the rescue of the German morale, a new common enemy raising its ugly head: Communism. With the Iron Curtain now separating the two opposing ideologies, West Germany, physically wedged between them, was badly needed as a crucial buffer zone. The image of the despicable Huns had to be changed to that of a most desirable and vitally needed partner. With the outbreak of the Cold War, practically overnight, the Nazi era was dismissed as an unfortunate but probably not unforgivable period of a mere twelve years, now to be legitimately written off as past history. German rearmament, unthinkable just a few months before, was not only permitted, it was ordered. Convicted Nazi criminals were secretly let out of prison long before their sentences were completed, confiscated possessions returned to them, and soon, like cockroaches, old party members came crawling out of the woodwork to fill the highest positions not only in the new government, but in all walks of German life.

With the traditional submissiveness and servility displayed to Adolf Hitler, the Germans now eagerly served their new respective masters in East and West, throwing themselves into the reconstruction of their demolished cities. Democracy, the form of government that other nations had achieved by working, fighting, suffering, and even dying for, had been presented to them by the Western Allies on a silver platter. All they had to do was learn how to handle it by patterning themselves after their conquerors. The sad truth that far more lay in ashes than the devastated cities was now conveniently swept under the rug; the sense of a national shame gone, the nation of poets and thinkers once more prided itself as the "cradle of humanity." Only a handful of Germans took the time and trouble to ponder the true value of something that could be so totally destroyed in a mere dozen years. How much was tradition and civilization worth, if human beings had not been educated to concentrate on the most vital issues—to defend and, if necessary, stand up and fight for the rights of human beings?

The fact was that 55 million had lost their lives during the Third Reich, among them 20 million Russians, 259,000 Americans, 300,000 British, and 500,000 French. Four and a half million Germans had been killed in connection with the war that was supposed to provide unlimited new "*lebensraum*" for the Aryan "master race." And then there was that other number, one that had been hushed up and whispered behind cupped hands at first, growing in size like an avalanche from a few thousand to hundreds of thousands and finally to millions. Six million Jewish men, women, and children had fallen victim to Hitler's raging madness, exterminated like vermin, with the support and silent indifference of 60 million helpers. Germany, in ruins, at least was now "*Judenrein*"! That goal, having been achieved, or almost achieved, went unnoticed by the vast majority of the people concentrating on rebuilding their country. Even in the following decades, those leading to wealth and prosperity, nobody missed the Jews; no one seemed to be aware of the devastating consequences that this physical, mental, and spiritual self-mutilation entailed. But with the Jews gone, nothing would ever be the same in post-war Germany; a frightening degree of spiritual poverty in connection with an embarrassing degree of mediocrity would prevail after the loss of those who had contributed so richly to every aspect of German life. Like no other group, the German Jews had, over the centuries, excelled in every imaginable field, particularly in the arts and the sciences.[38]

The anti-Semitism of the past was now replaced by a new and sickening form of tearful philo-Semitism, expressed in actions like the so-called "Annual Brotherhood Week," where a handful of survivors on one side and German officials on the other professed understanding and tolerance. Totally bewildered by the general denial of dealing with the horrors of the Nazi era, voices among the new generation grew louder and more persistent. Young people turned to their fathers, grandparents, teachers, doctors, and pastors, demanding answers to their urgent questions; how could it have happened? But they all met with a wall of impenetrable silence. Silence about the past had become not only a habit, but a virtue.

One action, instigated by the Western Allies, was a political cleansing process called "denazification," a procedure to determine who had been a Nazi and, if so, in what capacity. This naive attempt at identifying Nazis and bringing them to justice turned out to be a disaster, producing shameless mass lies that resulted in the rehabilitation of all those who had "only been following orders" imposed on innocent people against their will. Of the 577 judges from the "People's Court" responsible for signing 32,000 death verdicts outside of the concentration camps, not one was ever indicted, let alone sentenced. It was established that, "under prevailing law, the judges had not been aware of any wrongdoing." All of them went back to their former jobs, and from there into well-rewarded retirement. *Nulle crimen sine legge, nulle poena sine crimen;* no crime without law and no punishment without crime.

Chapter Sixty-Eight
Discomfort and New Life

The realization that I would be doomed to live among people who had lost all moral orientation was more devastating than the duration of the Nazi regime. The once so close circle of friends, this small, death-defying community of human beings dedicated to resist and fight evil, had begun to drift apart. With the shared enemy gone, the group simply ceased to exist, irrevocably and forever. Everyone had gone in different directions. A common past, I came to accept with profound sadness, did not necessarily mean a common future. While united during times when religious convictions, political affiliations, and social standing had been of no importance, it now seemed that we were separated by light years.

When the staunch right-wing-oriented Konrad Adenauer was elected as the first Chancellor of the newly established Federal German Republic, it soon became evident that his regime was crawling with erstwhile Nazis. Seventy-five percent of the former Nazi-infested Foreign Ministry joined the new one. As ambassadors, they were sent to the far corners of the globe, particularly to South America, where they were welcomed (or rather, welcomed back) with open arms. Only eleven years after committing his heinous crimes against humanity in Auschwitz, Dr. Josef Mengele, having fled to South America, received a brand new passport, handed to him in Buenos Aires by the West German ambassador to Argentina, who must have been well aware of the recipient's identity. Criticized by a few constituents who were outraged about his choice of ex-Nazis in key government positions, the pious Catholic Adenauer dryly remarked that "since there was no clean water to cook with, he had to use dirty water." It was as simple as that. Hitler's effort to strip Germany of those few among the intelligentsia who had refused to turn rotten had been a thorough one, ending with the massacres after the July 20 assassination attempt; there just were not enough decent people left to take over. The Nazis' bloody harvest had claimed most of the lives of those morally qualified for responsible positions in the new government.

My mother was the recipient of three different pensions, the bulk of which came from the House of Hohenzollern; two smaller amounts consisted of restitution money by the state, to which she—a "victim of Fascism" and, grotesquely enough, at the same time a "victim of Bolshevism"—was entitled.

With not even a remote chance in sight to leave the country, I reluctantly accepted a job offer with *Heute* magazine in Munich, published and edited by the US Military Government. This position as a budding journalist would eventually enable me to immigrate to the United States. However, something unexpected happened; I fell in love with the editor, held in high professional esteem. The only son of a well-known German painter and art professor and a Jewish mother, he also enjoyed the legendary reputation of being absolutely immune to a woman's charms. Immune? This term had the same effect on me that music has on a circus horse. I decided to ignore warnings that he had been divorced at least three times and dove headfirst into a new adventure. A few months later, I found myself married to this high-strung, fascinating man, who was seventeen years my senior. One year later, we had a son, and shortly thereafter, his father and I split up—his fourth divorce, my first. Too late I had realized that neither fascination nor common interests in vitally important matters could keep two completely different and equally difficult people together.

I named my son Ulrich Marcus—Ulrich after my father. My son's beautifully shaped head uncannily resembled the grandfather he was never to know. To me, more than just a name had returned. The exquisite joy over his appearance surpassed anything I had ever experienced before. He was born in Berlin, the city where my own difficult childhood had taken place, darkened by Hitler's gigantic shadow, which would continue to haunt the world for generations to come. I was determined not to let it darken my child's future. He was not going to grow up among a people who had brought so much heartache to the entire world and certainly to my own immediate family. Waiting for my personal Godot was over, and the idea of taking my boy to the United States began to take shape in my head; the only crucial problem that remained was that we needed a sponsor.

The decisive factor favoring America over another English-speaking country was the realization that the prevailing laws would enable us to apply for citizenship after a mere five years. Furthermore, I knew that in the US, any position—with the exception of the presidency—would be open for my son. In England, Australia, and even Canada, it took at least two generations for any offspring of immigrants to be totally integrated. The United States, by tradition a nation of immigrants, accepted even a brand-new citizen as a full-fledged member of the "American family." The idea of going to New York took root in my thinking, until I was almost obsessed with the desire to live there and nowhere else.

A miracle I had not even dared to hope for happened when Uncle Otto and Aunt Edith Stargardt returned from Detroit to their house in Berlin. After their miraculous rescue in Theresienstadt by the Soviet Army, they had gone to the United States. After several years in Detroit with their son, they realized that the place where they really wanted to spend their old age was Berlin. Their home, confiscated by the Nazis, had been spared by the bombs and was now returned to the rightful owners. Among the sparse furniture were all the items that my mother had stolen from the Gestapo-sealed house in 1942. It was Aunt Edith who found the solution to my problem. Her son, Chief of Staff of the Children's Hospital in Detroit, became my sponsor. Within six weeks, I received an immigration visa for myself and my son; however, he would stay with my mother until I was able to establish something like a home for the three of us. Why should I not achieve what millions of immigrants had been able to accomplish over the centuries?

"Promise me you will go and live under a different star!" my father had begged. How could I possibly forget? How could I not keep this last solemn promise I had given my father? America! Yes, I would go to America! To New York—the ultimate city—*Urbs Ultima*.

Part Two Notes

1. Canaris himself was not so lucky. With Dietrich Bonhoeffer and Colonel Achim Oster, he was hanged in Flossenbürg Concentration Camp just days before the Allies liberated the camp.
2. A celebrity without a diva's whims, she would pay her native Berlin a brief visit after the war, but she would find herself the target of hate, denounced as a traitor for betraying her fatherland in time of need and siding with the enemy by joining the US forces. During that brief stay in her hometown, Marlene wanted to see just two of her old friends; one of them was Walter Franck.
3. It was also Thomas Mann who publicly appealed to the conscience of the world, using strong language: "Martin Niemoeller was delivered to the hands of a mass murderer, an act tolerated by an allegedly civilized world, accompanied by the silent approval of the Western nations that chose to look the other way for fear of jeopardizing their business dealings with Hitler's Germany."
4. The pastor would not see his father again. Hitler, alarmed and afraid of his star prisoner's growing popularity, refused permission for him to attend the funeral.
5. After his miraculous survival, the pastor was asked the same tactless question over and over again: "Was it really so bad?" His answer would always be the same: "No, it was a thousand times worse!" Not even with his wife or his closest friends would he discuss the gruesome details of life and death in the camps. However, his reluctance was not due to the usual block that prevented a victim from dealing with the past; it was due to the simple fact that he had accepted his past, mentally and spiritually working through it before putting it behind him.
6. The two officers were kept apart and would only meet again in the spring of 1945.
7. From Stevens, Martin learned details of the November 9 pogrom, seventeen months after his own arrest.
8. Anita came to see us a few times, always leaving the house with a food package. One day, she did not return. I went to the Jewish Hospital on Iraner Strasse to inquire regarding her whereabouts, and I learned that she and Reinhard had been deported to a labor camp in the East.
9. Until the date that Joseph Goebbels proudly declared Berlin as "*Judenrein*" ("clean of Jews"), a state that in reality was never reached, some fifty thousand Jews from the *Reichshauptstadt* were deported from that station in the Grunewald section of Berlin in broad daylight, actions that allegedly went completely unnoticed by the Berliners. After the war, no one seemed to remember the endless lines of people with stars on their clothes, winding their way to the waiting trains that consisted largely of cattle cars.
10. After a recuperation period in Switzerland, they went to the United States. To their dismay, they were told by their daughter-in-law that the real reason why they had been sent to a concentration camp, namely because they were Jews, should not be mentioned. In the circles into which their son had married, being Jewish was neither acceptable nor desirable. In view of this and other discrepancies, the two survivors eventually decided to accept the invitation by the city government of West Berlin to resume their rightful

residence in the house, which had been stolen by the Nazis. The only furniture with which to begin their new existence were the items saved by the two bold ladies, Edith and my mother, during one long, dark night.

11. What remains most remarkable is that her entire noble family turned, without exception, to the Nazis. Her unbelievable courage motivated the British movie industry, long after the war, to make a film about her life. She was portrayed by Jacqueline Bisset. Leo Gross wrote her story in the book "The Last Jews in Berlin."

12. This move probably saved my life. Sixteen months later, in April 1945, just before my original contract would have expired, almost the entire Danzig ensemble, in a desperate attempt to escape from the advancing Soviet Army, boarded a ship. With its pitiful cargo, the totally overloaded former Nazi party pleasure liner *Wilhelm Gustloff* sank in the icy waters of the Baltic Sea after being torpedoed by the Soviets; only a handful of survivors were rescued.

13. He usually appeared at our house in the company of his two male dachshunds, much to Schatzi's undivided delight. The admiral, a notorious amateur cook, lived around the corner from us with his old housekeeper, who had often voiced her complaints about her master's culinary orgies to Anna, during which her duties were reduced to those of a garbage carrier.

14. Of all the conspirators who met in our house, only Count Kraft von Henckel Donnersmarck, a famous patron of the performing arts, would survive the events following the ill-fated plot on July 20 that same year. The last to be executed were Dietrich Bonhoeffer, Wilhelm Canaris, and Achim Oster. The three of them were hanged on the gallows of Flossenbürg on April 9, 1945, just days before the Americans entered the camp.

15. The executioners aimed first at Stauffenberg, but my beloved cousin, Werner von Haeften, threw himself in front of his friend and was hit instead.

16. The check in the amount of one million reichsmarks was indeed presented to her by none other than the grateful führer himself at the Wolf's Lair. Helene, however, would never get the opportunity to spend even a fraction of this blood money. After the war she was among the handful of Nazi informers who were apprehended, arrested, tried, and sentenced to prison for life. But, like most of those punished for crimes against humanity, she was paroled after only ten years. From her prison cell, she wrote a letter of apology to Goerdeler's widow.

17. Only later did we learn that he was being held in Lehrterstrasse Prison.

18. Fortunately, our fears that he might be sent into battle in the East would prove unfounded.

19. Copies of the films would never be found after the war.

20. After the ordeal was finally over, all of the kidnapped children were eventually recovered by their mothers, none of whom would ever remarry.

21. One of the people who allegedly had inside information about an impending coup was Heinrich Himmler. After the failure, perhaps hoping to benefit personally from a change in government, he turned against the plotters.

22. The bloodhound Roland Freisler could never be brought to justice as an Allied bombing of the court building ended his life during a Berlin air raid. The scandalous leniency toward Nazi criminals, which became standard procedure in post-war Germany, encouraged Freisler's widow to demand higher survivor benefits for herself, with the explanation that her husband, through his untimely death, had been deprived of a "brilliant future career as a judge."

23. Her mammoth production *Triumph of the Will*, about the Nazi party convention in Nuremberg, had once delighted the Nazis. Even now, she was out somewhere making films to please her beloved führer. In spite of her audacious denials after the war, her unrestrained admiration for Hitler and her intimate relationship with him was common knowledge. The sad truth was that, with her outstanding talent, she could have made it to the top anywhere in the world without prostituting herself to a bunch of criminals over the entire length of their existence.

24. Not long after the officer's departure, I began to carry my father's gun, the little Ortgies I had been able to secure just before the Gestapo had come into the house on July 23, 1944.

25. The nice thing about him was that he did not hold this outrageous performance against us, although he was rather reluctant to go near our building from then on.

26. Frau Thiele did survive, not with us, but in Ditte's house. She ultimately went to England.

27. The van-like vehicle used by police to transport prisoners.

28. Hitler's death sentence came too late. All those he had planned to use as pawns would survive the führer, including Martin Niemoeller by almost forty years.

29. A slow ring movement in dressage, in which the horse balances on its hind legs.

30. At this point in history, I had no way of knowing that Soviet soldiers, captured by the German Army, after their liberation were treated as cowards and traitors by Stalin. The number of POWs who never made it home to their families—but instead were shot or sent to gulags—can only be guessed. The Western powers, allegedly in full knowledge of what was in store for them, as a friendly gesture to their war allies, refused to grant asylum to Soviet citizens in the West, forcing them to return to a possibly fatal destiny in their homeland.

31. That "just in case" did eventually happen, but it took forty years until, through a weird coincidence, I found my savior, then the respected and respectable head of a large California law firm.

32. Before leaving for duty in Nuremberg, where the first Nazi war criminal trials were being prepared, Charles presented my mother with a priceless—as well as illegal—farewell gift: ten cartons of Camel cigarettes, each one worth a fortune. She was now in a position to barter for the most urgently needed provisions to keep her alive. This was vital, because she had no one to take care of her; she was alone.

33. Little did I know then that it was to take four decades until I was finally able to speak about my father, his suffering, and his death. Even then, this was not by my own decision, but because one man, Elie Wiesel, tore down the wall of silence about the past,

which I had built around myself. Only after it had been broken did I become aware of having shared this behavior pattern with almost all survivors living with the treacherous fantasy that, as long as the unspeakable was not mentioned, there was a chance it had not occurred.

34. The so-called "Final Solution," the extermination of the Jews, was not even mentioned in the Stuttgart Declaration or in any of the following convocations and synods. At age ninety, Pastor Niemoeller would still regretfully state: "For decades I have tried to get the Germans to confess to their guilt. Unfortunately without any success, and I fear that this lies like a curse on my people."

35. The forty-five-year-old Gründgens attributed the miracle of his own survival to his relatively young age and stable health. Unlike my father, some twenty years his senior, he had not been exposed to hell in a Nazi prison for nine months.

36. After his miraculous liberation and before being snatched by the Soviets from his Berlin house, he had found time to enter the words *endlich frei*—"free at last"—into his diary at the sight of the first Russian soldiers. He, too, would eventually perish in Jamlitz.

37. According to the information passed through the grapevine over the years, Reckzeh had managed to escape his arrest by a split second. From West Berlin, he somehow made it back to the Soviet zone and practiced medicine in his own hospital until his retirement. In 1971, a West German magazine published an article about the doctor, who had allegedly delivered his own daughter to the Soviet authorities when he learned that she was ready to go West. As of 1990, the date of the German unification, this known murderer still resided in the splendor of his villa behind high walls in Zeuthen near Berlin. All efforts to bring him to justice had, as late as 1994, failed.

38. The question why those German Jews who had been lucky enough to survive in exile never came back is easily answered. For over forty years, not a single German president would see fit to officially invite them to return to the fatherland from which they had been driven.

Part Three
The Promised Land

Now the Lord had said unto Abram,

Get thee out of thy country, and

from thy kindred, and from thy

father's house, unto the land that

I will show thee.

—Genesis 12:1

Chapter Sixty-Nine
A Test Case

Through his gold-rimmed glasses, the white-haired judge focused on me with great intensity. His resemblance to Spencer Tracy was hard to overlook. "Madam," he said, "as I understand the situation, the Attorney General of the State of New York has denied you the right to vote in the elections because, during your recent naturalization procedure, you refused the mandatory literacy test. This court is asking you for an explanation." His clear blue eyes pierced me. Those eyes, I felt keenly, would not tolerate a lie.

Six months before, I had joyfully and wholeheartedly taken the oath of allegiance to the constitution of my new country, the United States of America, vowing "to forsake all other potentates." With this oath, I had honored the promise once given to my father that I would leave Germany and seek my fortune and that of my children under another star. Like his mother, my little son and all those coming after him would be members of the American family, not "German Americans" but "Americans of German descent."

Shortly after receiving my first American passport, I registered to participate in the upcoming communal elections. For the first time in my life, I would be entitled to cast my vote as a Democrat and an equal citizen of my chosen country. On Election Day, excited beyond description, I found myself among the first voters to arrive at the polls in the old Congregational Church in Brooklyn Heights, where Abraham Lincoln had worshipped almost a century before and where, a few months earlier, my American-born husband, Ross, and I had been in the crowd attending a service, at which the African American minister from the South had left an unforgettable impression on me. Never would I to forget the way Dr. Martin Luther King, Jr. firmly held my hand on the way out.

The date of the elections fell on one of those balmy late spring days, so rare in the city of New York, when the winter ice has just melted and stifling summer heat has not yet set in. I had left the house on Willow Street, enjoying the clear, refreshing air blowing from the East River; even the birds seemed to be singing just for me. In the distance across the river, the Wall Street skyline and the silhouette of the Brooklyn Bridge gleamed in the early morning sun. Later, after performing my duty as a citizen, I would drive across the one-hundred-year-old structure, down to the Fulton Fish Market to handpick a couple of live lobsters from a tank for that night's dinner. I was sure it was one of those days when absolutely nothing could go wrong.

In front of the church, two stocky, red-faced policemen, unmistakably of Irish descent, twirled their sticks with the elegance of professional jugglers. Already in light blue summer shirtsleeves, they greeted me with broad grins, "Good morning, ma'am." With nametags not yet mandatory, I could only guess that their names might be O'Reilly or O'Malley, here to uphold law and order, protecting the rights of the voters, including mine. In those days, most of the city's policemen still seemed to be Irish. They came from dynasties of policemen, the profession of New York cop handed down from father to son.

In the church vestibule I approached a long table behind which several women, representing the Board of Elections, were busy comparing the names of the voters to those in their registers. "Here you are," the woman said cheerfully, after locating my name. But then she suddenly hesitated, took a good look at me, again at the book, and slowly added, "Sorry, Mrs. Donaldson, but you cannot vote!" Twice she had to repeat the words, and still I was at a loss to grasp their meaning.

It was as if the floor had opened up to swallow me; I could not believe my ears. Tearing the register away from her, I turned it around and found something scribbled next to my name. My blood seemed to freeze because what I saw was "barred from voting by the State Attorney General." Barred from voting? But why? This, I decided, had to be a terrible mistake. As far as I could remember, I had not stolen silver spoons, threatened the president's life, or prostituted myself. The woman shrugged her shoulders, but seeing me dumbfounded, proposed that, if I really wanted to find out the reason, I should go at once to the Board of Elections in the nearby Supreme Court Building, the same edifice where, with my little son not too long before, I had pledged allegiance to the United States of America. However, she warned me, this would probably turn out to be a time-consuming undertaking and I had better prepare myself.

"Lady," I said, "you will not believe this, but I have done a lot of waiting in my life, and you cannot imagine just how much time I have got right now." She gave me an encouraging nod and, lowering her voice, added, "Good for you! Unfortunately, far too few citizens take the time to get what is rightfully theirs." Her remarks were directed at a black woman in a corner, who had just received equally disheartening news and was about to leave. I suggested to her that she and I should go together, an offer she declined. Her English was pitiful; she obviously came from one of the Caribbean Islands where English was not spoken. I would go alone!

Seized with red-hot rage, I sent a prayer of thanks to God, who had endowed me with the blessed disposition of an English bull terrier, determined to risk the loss of his teeth rather than let go of his prey. Remembering my martial ancestors and my own militant past, I assumed the air of a Prussian field marshal ready for battle and marched into the imposing structure of the Supreme Court of the State of New York at nearby Brooklyn Borough Hall. Upstairs, at the Board of Elections office, a young man seemed to have expected me. To my surprise, he did not even ask any questions, but motioned me to follow him through endless halls until we arrived in a large, dimly lit room with tables and chairs. He simply pushed me in and told me to wait.

Within the next half hour, the empty room began to fill with people, mostly men, none of whom paid the slightest attention to me. They carried attaché cases, pulling out documents that they heatedly discussed among themselves. With all these important cases, I pondered in dismay, where the hell did I fit in?

Maybe it was better to leave? But curiosity kept me in my seat.

Finally, the heavy double doors to a large courtroom were opened by a bailiff of rather impressive size, signaling everyone to proceed inside. With nothing else for me to do, I decided to tag along and watch whatever was happening—an interesting trial or maybe a juicy murder case? But before I was able to take a seat in the back, two well-dressed gentlemen, addressing me by my name, motioned me to a table right in front of the judge's bench. Seating me between them, the two strangers introduced themselves as counsel for my defense.

Defense? I should be defended? Against whom? Maybe they could prevent the worst, like being thrown into the clink or death on the electric chair. While I mused whether New York State still had the death penalty, the bailiff raised his voice and said, "Hear ye, hear ye. This court is now in session, the case of the State of New York against Sibylle Donaldson, Chief Justice Brenner presiding. All rise!"

I could hardly believe my ears! This whole pandemonium was for my sake? After the judge had taken his seat, we were motioned to sit also.

What in God's name could the State of New York have against me? I had nothing against the State of New York, except that its attorney general would not let me vote. Then I heard the sharp-sounding voice of a man seated by himself at a table next to ours: "Will the defendant please rise!" No sooner had he spoken, when he found himself interrupted by an angry judge. "Mr. District Attorney," he said, "Mrs. Donaldson is *not* here as a defendant; she is a witness. Please apologize to her!"

"Sorry, Your Honor; I am sorry, Mrs. Donaldson."

Aha—"Your Honor"—that was how one was supposed to address the extremely distinguished looking twin brother of Spencer Tracy in his most becoming black robe. I rose, and the bailiff led me to the witness box, where I was asked for my name and other basic information. I promised, my left hand on the Bible, to tell the truth, nothing but the truth, and was then motioned to be seated. In a corner, I noticed the flag, my flag with its stars and stripes, and I felt instantly reassured.

"Mrs. Donaldson," Chief Justice Brenner began, "you are here because you object to the charge brought against you by the Attorney General of the State of New York, accusing you of declining to take the literacy test, mandatory in the naturalization procedure as proof of being able to speak, read, and write English. Your refusal had as a consequence that you are now being barred from participating in today's elections."

A literacy test? What was he talking about? Feverishly, I began to search my memory. To the best of my knowledge, nothing faintly resembling such a test had been offered to me during my naturalization. The district attorney proceeded to elaborate that an error on the part of the State was out of the question, his files proving without a shadow of a doubt that, by my refusal to submit to the test, I had not only forfeited the right to vote, but that the legality of my citizenship was to be questioned. The judge turned to me and said, "Take your time, Mrs. Donaldson. I now want to hear from you, in your own words, exactly what happened in connection with these accusations."

Greatly encouraged by the kind undertone in his voice, I responded, "Your Honor, I do not need any extra time to think, because how could I have rejected a test that was not offered to me?"

"Not offered to you?" Chief Justice Brenner asked. Turning first to the district attorney, then to the audience in the courtroom, he repeated for the sake of all those present, "The test was not even offered to the witness?"

"Madam," he continued, once more addressing me, "I am now going to put a very important question to you. A lot depends on your reply, not only for yourself, but for countless others. Let us presume for a moment that you had been required to take the test in question at the time of your naturalization; would you have taken it?"

My reliable intuition told me that my answer meant a great deal to the man in the black robe across the bench from me. But what was the "right" answer? What kind of a game was this? What did he expect from me? I decided to jump headfirst into the water.

"No, Your Honor," I spoke in a firm voice, "I would definitely not have taken a literacy test!"

The judge's clenched fist hit the table in front of him: "Mr. District Attorney, counsel for the defense, ladies and gentlemen of the press, you have heard it. The witness would have declined to take the test had it been required of her."

I let out an audible sigh of relief; my answer had evidently been the one that the judge was hoping for, as he now continued: "You have all heard it! Mrs. Donaldson, a new citizen of the United States of America, obviously capable of reading and writing English, her spoken English putting some of my fellow Americans to shame, would have found a literacy test below her dignity, if not downright humiliating." Turning to me, he continued, "Am I correct in this assumption, madam?"

I nodded.

The judge said, "Let me, therefore, close the case in the hope that this discriminating procedure of a literacy test, offered exclusively in the English language, must be stricken from the naturalization procedures. It is my goal to achieve this before I retire. The request of the witness is granted. She will be able to vote in today's elections."

Case dismissed!

With everybody now leaving the courtroom, it dawned on me that the entire procedure of the past hour had been staged exclusively for me and my case. I could not believe it and felt a strong need to be enlightened. Before Chief Justice Brenner retired to his chambers, he motioned me to follow him. Seated in a comfortable chair in his office, I noticed the expression on his face, resembling that of a cat who had just swallowed a canary. A secretary poured coffee, after which he began to speak, this time in private.

"Madam," he said, "I believe I owe you an explanation. What you have witnessed during the past hour was democracy at its best. You demanded your rights, and you were granted your rights, because you stood firm and insisted on them. Attempts were made to bar you from performing your privilege and your duty as a citizen because you had not passed an exam that, in fact, you were intentionally not even informed about. For years I have done my best to have this unfortunate and unfair procedure stricken altogether. However, there are elements in our administration who, for a number of reasons, are eager to have certain minorities barred from becoming citizens. These despicable efforts are mainly directed against uneducated, mostly Spanish-speaking candidates, for whom the test in the English language presents an insurmountable hurdle. I call this attitude undemocratic and discriminating. Unfortunately, most of those rejected are too much in awe of the authorities to fight for their rights, a fateful omission that can lead to their deportation as undesirable aliens."

"Mrs. Donaldson," he concluded, "I do not know whom to congratulate first; you, for having chosen this country as your own, or the country, for the good fortune of gaining you as a citizen!"

I could barely suppress a strong urge to jump up and kiss him! Ovid, I was sure, would have approved wholeheartedly.

My case, I knew now, had been selected to establish a precedent. It could have been someone else, but by being in the right place at the right time, not in a mood to take no for an answer, I—a tiny cogwheel in the machine of democracy—had been instrumental in setting something in motion that would, in all probability, change the fate of countless others.

I skipped out of Chief Justice Brenner's office with a document stating that I, a literate citizen of the United States, was indeed entitled to cast my vote. Flying back to the poll site, the three women received me with applause. At last, someone had the guts to "let 'em have it!" Even "O'Reilly" and "O'Malley" pumped my hand in wholehearted approval. Not without an overwhelming feeling of triumph did I enter the booth to give my vote to the party and the candidate of my choice. A few months later, there was a short notice in the *New York Times* to the effect that the literacy test, given exclusively in the English language, was now a thing of the past.

↢ Chapter Seventy ↣
Living in America

Over five years had passed since the steamship *Italia*, sailing under the flag of Panama and groaning with old age, dropped its rusty anchor on Manhattan's West Side. A mere six weeks after applying for my immigration visa, it was handed to me by the American Consul in Berlin. Due to the speedy economic recovery, fewer and fewer Germans were willing to emigrate into the unknown, so the majority of those seeking a new beginning in the United States were "Displaced Persons" from the Eastern countries devastated by war. Most of these people were survivors of Nazi camps, robbed of their existence, and, in many cases, their families; they were accepted in the United States outside any quota.

My goal was New York City, where a friend had offered me temporary shelter. With the vast sum of twenty-two dollars in my purse, I had boarded the *Italia* in Hamburg harbor, filled with hope for a better future in the land of unlimited possibilities for myself and my son—the son I had to leave behind.

The inside cabin on the *Italia's* C-deck, an oversized broom closet, offered no unnecessary comfort for me and my fellow captives, three war brides. The "air conditioning" consisted of a few slits in the door, which meant that, in case you wanted to breathe, it was advisable to wait until you could go on deck. A little salad bowl in one corner, disguised as a wash basin, served as a cleaning device for two grown and two overgrown women, showers and toilets being located at the far end of a dark, endless corridor. We had to take turns dressing; there was room for only one to move about at a time.

On the second day of the voyage, which found me cursing my fate in all the languages at my disposal, including Vendish, a miracle happened. One of the kaiser's last birthday gifts to his "little monkey" had been an elegant notebook bound in red leather, engraved with the imposing initial "W" and the imperial crown in gold. After barely surviving the first night onboard the *Italia*, I noticed my little treasure was missing. Almost in tears over the loss, I went to the ship's chief purser in the faint hope that it might have been turned in by someone. To my surprise, the elderly official with his neatly parted hair, rimless glasses, and impeccable manners, obviously a gentleman of the old school, seemed to have expected me. The book had indeed been recovered by a steward in the library, he informed me, and after clearing his throat, he asked if the imperial crown was of any special significance? Was I, if he might be so bold to ask, a relative of "His Majesty"? Blessing the fact that, after my divorce, I had resumed my maiden name, I decided that it would probably be more advantageous for me to leave a veil of mystery over my relationship to the House of Hohenzollern and nodded my head ever so slightly. Excited beyond description, he inquired if the "gracious baroness" was satisfied with her accommodation on the ship.

Accommodation?

I was barely able to stifle the hoarse scream trying to escape from my throat. Noticing my reluctance to answer his well-meant inquiry, he hastened to inform me that, due to some good fortune, he was in a position to offer me a rather nice stateroom on the A-deck all to myself, at no extra charge. He would be honored if I would be gracious enough to accept his proposition.

A stateroom? The decision to honor him with my graciousness was not a hard one for me; within minutes, a steward removed my unsightly pieces of luggage from the rat hole in the ship's belly and, under the incredulous eyes of my former cellmates, carried it to my new domicile. Never before had I fully realized the true meaning of the term "splendid isolation," and I was now determined to enjoy the glory of my private domicile with bath to the fullest extent.

Unfortunately, the one factor I had failed to take into consideration was the elements. Due to the fact that the boat's stabilizers were either inadequate or totally missing, I spent the better part of the next twelve days in a horizontal position. The handsome young ship's doctor was unable to offer lasting relief; this trip being his maiden voyage, he was victim to the same seasickness that had befallen me. As a deplorable consequence, the only activities taking place in my lovely cabin, much to the chagrin of both of us, consisted of sharing a pail over prolonged periods, during which we prayed for our misery to end, if necessary, even by death. Never, he swore, would he set foot on a ship again! I wholeheartedly agreed.

On the evening before we reached our final destination, a boat from the nearby shore pulled up close to the *Italia*, and a dozen US immigration officials boarded for a last screening of the passengers. Having sufficiently recovered, I answered all questions, solemnly pledging to refrain from certain ugly activities like prostituting myself, becoming a financial burden to the United States, or attempting to assassinate the president. At that point of the voyage, I would have promised them the moon in exchange for solid ground under my feet.

Like most immigrants traveling with light luggage, I brought only a coat, three dresses, a couple of pairs of shoes, and one pair of nylons without noticeable runs. My true, intangible capital, setting me apart from my fellow immigrants, was a profound knowledge of the English language. The full significance of this advantage would dawn on me soon after my arrival.

Early the next morning, I joined the other passengers on the main deck. In the far distance, through the April morning mist, I was able to identify the first skyscrapers and the famous silhouette of downtown Manhattan. Then someone next to me whispered: "There she is!"

Yes, there *she* was—the tall lady with the torch, announcing, "Give me your tired, your poor..."

I, too, was tired, I was poor, I yearned to be free, I was alone, and I was crying. At the sight of her, an overwhelming yet strangely familiar feeling took hold of me; I had come home. At that moment, I would have given anything to share this overpowering emotion with my father who had, after his brave fight to stem the tide of evil, not been allowed to see the dawn of freedom.

Chapter Seventy-One
The New Yorker

I had been informed it would take me seven years to feel at home in New York. That might well have been true for anyone else; for me, however, it took barely two hours to know that this was my country, and New York was my city. Had I really lived somewhere else before? On the day following my arrival, I did two things. First, I went to the steamship company in Lower Manhattan to give back my return ticket. Not even wild horses would be able to tear me away from here. Then I registered with the Immigration and Naturalization Service, receiving my alien registration card, which entitled me to work for my living.

After a brief stay with friends in Yorkville, on Manhattan's Upper East Side, I was able to land a position with the National Broadcasting Company (NBC). My new boss asked if I was a "Brit." A slight foreign accent, very much en vogue in those days, was considered exotic and desirable. He could not believe that I mastered several languages, and I soon learned that multilingualism, while admired, was also a little suspicious, indicating that the person might be a Communist spy. The evil spirit of Joe McCarthy still hung heavily in the air. A true American, I discovered soon enough, after "taking" a foreign language in high school, was usually in no position to speak it.[1]

At NBC, already in the 1950s a pioneer in hiring minorities, I found myself in the company of colleagues representing many nationalities, races, and colors. What really floored me, at first, was the degree of helpfulness with which I, a total stranger, was treated. Even though my skills were less than ideal, I found that I had one advantage over my fellow workers who, without exception, needed Webster's help for spelling. Whenever in doubt, they turned to me, the new spelling expert.

The hiring formalities had mainly consisted of one question; had I worked in the field of research before? Of course, I answered, secretly praising my training by British Intelligence in Hamburg and the fact that I had learned to use a typewriter at an early age. Fortunately, the filing was done by special underlings, called filing clerks, so I was pretty sure I could handle the job, for which I received seventy-five dollars each Friday, an enormous amount, it seemed to me. Twenty dollars a week went into a savings account, a practice that my teller at the Chase Manhattan Bank on 34th Street praised each time I made a deposit.

One of the first things I did was to buy a few dresses at Lord & Taylor on 5th Avenue for outrageous prices, like fifteen or twenty dollars. All the girls I worked with were dressed to kill, and the only difference between their outfits and those of rich women was that one class wore the originals while the other was satisfied with the copies.

I had rented a small place in an old brownstone between Central Park and Columbus Avenue, on Manhattan's Upper West Side at 95th Street, a top-floor apartment; the adjacent one was inhabited by Leah, an exchange student from Tel Aviv. Shopping and picking up laundry for one another, we hit it off right away. Leah turned out to be more than just a neighbor; she was responsible for my initiation into the Jewish faith. When she lit the Shabbat candles for the first time, I found myself seized by the same inexplicable, intense feeling that had taken hold of me at the sight of the Statue of Liberty; everything was so familiar, I had seen it all before, maybe in a former life, but whatever the reason, I felt at home.

In the autumn, my mother and son were finally able to join me. My mother had volunteered to remain with us until I was totally settled. Now in a position to offer them a nice place to live, I had moved from Manhattan to a spacious apartment in Riverdale, near the Hudson River, with a park and playgrounds and a nursery school inside the building. All my belongings had safely arrived from Germany, so things began to look rosy. My move out of the city, however, meant three hours of commuting by bus and subway five days a week. I quickly learned the fine art of pushing myself into a subway car already packed like a sardine can. Wedged between fellow New Yorkers of all colors and races on the train speeding through Harlem, there were whole periods when my feet did not even seem to touch the floor. With air conditioning still a foreign term, traveling by subway in the intense summer heat was a living hell. Even in most of the executive offices in the RCA Building, the cooling devices consisted of huge, noisy fans on the ceiling busily whirling about dirty, hot air.

After a few weeks of getting used to life in the United States, my intrepid mother, displaying her usual death-defying vigor, threw herself into the exciting adventure of exploring the man-devouring Moloch, Manhattan. Crisscrossing the world's most famous island from the Hudson to the East River, from the Bronx to Wall Street, almost exclusively on foot, she usually came home filled with stories, making it evident that she must have missed very little.

One Sunday she returned with a particularly spicy story. Having seated herself on a bench in Central Park in order to feed the squirrels, an old black man pushing a baby carriage filled with bags had asked her politely if she minded him sitting next to her. Without delay, he proceeded to tell her the story of his life, of which she did not understand half because of his missing teeth. Her command of English was acceptable but would never advance to the level of her command of French. What she understood was that he was practically on his way down to Florida to visit his daughter, were it not for the fact that fifty cents were still needed to buy the bus ticket. Could she, such a great lady, possibly lend him this sum?

At that precise moment, bursting out of the bushes, a huge horse with an equally huge New York cop on top, came to a screeching halt just a few feet from her. With a meaningful glance in the direction of her neighbor, the policeman inquired if she was all right. All right? What did he mean? Of course she was all right, engaged in a very, very interesting conversation with this very, very nice gentleman. After convincing himself that there was no foul play, the mounted representative of the law, shaking his head about the naïveté of tourists, turned his horse around.

One Saturday evening, she had not returned from her outing at the usual time, and just when I was ready to report her missing, she showed up in suspiciously high spirits. Why was I worried? New York, a dangerous place? Not for her! The building's superintendent, such a dear man, had met her in the hall and invited her into a bar. A bar! She had never seen the inside of such a dubious establishment nor had she ever touched whisky. The janitor, an Irishman, enjoyed the reputation of being a lazy, notorious drunk and a ladies' man.

With the intense summer heat setting in, we had decided she needed a light summer dress, so one Saturday we went downtown to Bloomingdales. After trying on a dozen outfits, she found her own dress missing from the fitting room. Even a thorough search netted no results; it had simply disappeared! To the horror of the sales staff, this mysterious loss caused us to literally fall to the floor in one of our fits of hysterical laughter at the thought of her having to travel on the subway in her slip. Just when the dumbfounded salesladies were about to summon the professional help of an efficient crew in white coats from Bellevue Hospital, the quickly summoned floor manager came to a truly Solomonic decision. She let my mother have one of the new dresses free of charge, under the condition that we, evidently more than just slightly deranged, promised to remove ourselves from the scene at once.

At this point, it will have to be mentioned that, after my father's death, a relative, concerned about my mother's state of mind, pushed the first book about palmistry and ultimately astrology under her nose, which she devoured like a hungry lion consumes a lamb. Throwing herself into study of the stars and their positions in connection with her respective victim, she was soon able to produce intricately detailed horoscopes for all those willing—or not willing—to become her guinea pigs. What she came out with was often quite fascinating and surprisingly precise. Nobody was really safe from her efforts at predicting an either glorious or devastating future. One day, when I was sharing my concerns about my life as a single mother with a little boy in New York, she dryly stated in the same ominously firm tone with which she had predicted the indestructibility of our house during the bomb raids, "Something that you least expect will solve all your problems. You will marry again!"

Chapter Seventy-Two
The Today Show

Whenever arriving early enough at my job at 30 Rockefeller Plaza, I loved to sneak up to the eighth-floor studio to watch the tail end of the *Today Show*, which was shot between seven and nine o'clock, five days a week. Like most television shows in those days, it was done live. The undisputed star of this production was not Dave Garroway, Jack Lescoulie, Frank Blair, or even Helen O'Donnell (later replaced by the beautiful and talented Florence Henderson), but J. Fred Muggs, a chimpanzee!

Seated next to Garroway on a couch, this totally unpredictable ape of considerable size managed to keep everyone on the set in constant tension over the possible and totally unscheduled tricks J. Fred had up his little sleeve. Not even his trainer, hidden from view behind the camera, was always able to prevent his ward from throwing coffee or Coca Cola in Garroway's face or going into one of his uncontrollable temper tantrums, during which he would screech, scream, and bite, lashing out at anything that moved. Most of America watched *Today* in eager anticipation of some mishap caused by the chimp. Sometimes when J. Fred, dressed in one of his impeccable little sailor suits, was ready to go into a fit of rage, it was advisable to seek shelter wherever possible. When his behavior became intolerable, he was replaced with an even-tempered, ladylike little chimpanzee by the name of Kokomo who never lost her temper, which promptly caused the ratings to fall.

The *Tonight Show*, broadcast by NBC five evenings a week, in those days without competition, was hosted by Jack Paar, who had succeeded Steve Allen as host. One day he found himself fired on the spot because he had done something absolutely unimaginable for the puritan ears of the censors; he had used the unspeakably indecent word "WC" (water closet) on the air, a faux pas punishable by immediate dismissal. Those were the glorious old days, when it was even taboo to show two married people in bed together. After Paar's demise and several unfortunate attempts by a handful of substitute hosts, a modest young man with an irresistible pixie smile made a guest appearance, Johnny Carson. In time, he became the undisputed king of nighttime television, holding his position for thirty years.

Whoever was anybody in the glittering world of television would, at one time or another, pass through my office to negotiate terms for upcoming shows with my boss. These stars included Loretta Young, who only removed the restraining braces on her front teeth when on camera, Kim Novak, Milton Berle, and Nat King Cole. A noisy, jewel-bedecked chatterbox by the name of Jolie Gábor, with her obnoxious but authentic Hungarian accent, showed up with her equally noisy daughters, Eva and Zsa Zsa, whose accents were just as thick but perhaps not quite so authentic. Then there was Pat Boone, who sang "Love Letters in the Sand." Perry Como, the singer with the velvet voice, a devout Catholic, insisted that during his show one of us speed across 5th Avenue to St. Patrick's Cathedral to light half a dozen candles to assure him of the Madonna's grace. If this was not done, NBC and all of America could forget about his appearance! Since I was not Catholic, I was never asked to perform this service. My coworker, however, of Italian descent like Perry, and in the habit of placing a rather hideous picture of Jesus with the crown of thorns next to that of her mother on the desk each morning, was soon able to display the grateful star's hand-signed photograph.[2]

My private life, although now restricted by my duties as a breadwinner, housewife, and mother, had begun to bloom. Through my friend Hans Schwerin, grandson of Paul Ehrlich, whose Jewish family had been able to reach safety from the Nazis by the skin of their teeth, I was introduced to what was known as the "Black Society" during an era when blacks were still called "negroes" or referred to simply by the colonial term "colored people." Those African Americans who, in spite of discrimination, had made it up the social ladder, as a rule barred white Americans from their circles, while extending gracious hospitality to Europeans. Hans, unmarried, but with a fallibility for African American girls, took me with him to Harlem's Cotton Club, and through him I met Langston Hughes, the renowned author. During a party in the West End Avenue home of jazz musician Sy Oliver, a strikingly handsome young man was introduced to me; with his rasping voice, Harry Belafonte was already on his way to world fame as a singer. His lovely bride was with him, visibly suffering from the rather unpleasant side effects of an early pregnancy.

Chapter Seventy-Three
In Love Again

It all began in an elevator of the RCA building, where a man, evidently one of the network's executives, would sometimes greet me with an absentminded hello, a nod of the head, or just a faint smile. Inquiring about him among my colleagues, I learned that the attractive stranger was in charge of the script department, from which he was promoted to "Director for Television Evening Entertainment." There was a hint of melancholy about him that I found hard to resist. His wife, according to my informants, had deserted him after fifteen years of marriage for another man, and I should not waste my time on him; he had the reputation of being totally indifferent to female approaches. This character trait—once more—caused me to instantly perk up my ears.

Late one evening, we met after both having worked overtime, and he casually invited me for a drink. Without waiting for Ovid to give me the green light, I permitted myself the luxury of falling in love. Six months later we were married, although the marriage did not begin well, with a drunken justice of the peace in Mount Kisco barely able to sign the wedding certificates at eleven o'clock in the morning.

Ross Donaldson, of paternal Scottish and German Jewish descent, had come to New York from Indiana. His mother, who had died in a mental institution, was part American Indian, a fact that, in view of her son's ebony black hair and high cheekbones, could hardly be denied. From her, the soft-spoken man, who never raised his voice, had also inherited olive skin and fine bone structure. I never got quite used to his way of sneaking through the house without making the slightest noise, and I suspected that his green cat's eyes could see in the dark.

After fighting in Normandy during World War II, he had covered de Gaulle's triumphant return to France as a reporter for "Stars and Stripes." Returning to the United States, he soon decided that his future was not in the Midwest, but in New York City. A personal discovery of "The General" Robert Sarnoff, founder and chairman of RCA, Ross had begun his career with NBC in the script department, where his ability to judge the quality of a script in record time soon became legendary. My son adored his new father, but too late I realized the full impact of two problems that I would not be able to handle in the long run—women and alcohol.

After my mother's return to Berlin, the three of us moved from Manhattan to a spacious triplex in a century-old brownstone on Willow Street in Brooklyn Heights, a residential area preferred by artists and physicians as well as Wall Street lawyers and brokers. With Manhattan just a few blocks away, many of the inhabitants walked to and from work across the Brooklyn Bridge. The street names were as alluring as the whole area: Orange Street, Pineapple Street, Cranberry Street. Having come dangerously close to being razed for the purpose of "urban renewal," the "Heights," thanks to the massive protest of the population, did not share the fate of the Bronx, where Robert Moses had run amok, tearing down a huge area consisting of thousands of homes, in order to build his Cross Bronx Expressway. The Heights was spared destruction and eventually received the status of an historic monument, prohibiting even the slightest alteration without permission of the authorities.

Our eighteen-foot-wide house, located near the famous Promenade, once designed as a one-family home with the kitchen and dining rooms located in the basement, had a beautiful patio and a narrow garden in the back with several fruit trees and a miniature lawn. Through the trees, we enjoyed an unobstructed view of the downtown Manhattan skyline in all its unique glory. At night, the never-ending noises from the busy harbor, including the hooting of the ships' sirens and the chugging noise of the tugboats, would lull us to sleep.

Living in Brooklyn Heights, an area only five by ten blocks in size and referred to as "the Southern tip of Manhattan" by those not wishing to be identified as mere "Brooklynites," we found ourselves in the company of movie stars like Cary Grant, Rod Steiger, and Claire Bloom, who owned magnificent townhouses not far from us. Among our immediate neighbors on Willow Street were Norman Mailer and Norman Rockwell. The pint-sized man with the high-pitched voice, dragging a disgruntled bulldog behind him on a leash, was Truman Capote. Introduced as neighbors by Victor Marcolini, the local liquor store owner, he confided to me that the reason why he had named his slobbering, obese companion "Blessing" was because he was indeed a blessing![3]

My son Marcus began a childhood unlike any other. The quiet, tree-lined streets were considered safe enough to play stoopball and ride a scooter or a bike. Brooklyn Heights was more than just a part of the greatest city in the world; it was a regular "neighborhood" where everyone knew everyone. Most of the children either attended the renowned Packer Collegiate Institute, where Winston Churchill's mother had been a student, or the venerable Brooklyn Friends School, with its ancient Meeting House on Schermerhorn Street. This Quaker institution, which required a student to be enrolled before birth, offered the finest education from kindergarten through high school. Marcus was lucky. Just as we arrived in the area, a little girl had left mid-term, and he simply took the open slot. Seventy-five percent of the pupils came from Jewish families. They were too liberal to send their children to Jewish schools, but not liberal enough to let them attend public schools. This meant that, with both Christian and Jewish holy days observed, there were more free days than most of the parents would have preferred.

Thanks to his new stepfather's position, Marcus soon found himself the most popular child; on his sixth birthday, the entire class was invited to NBC Studios to attend the live shooting of the *Howdy Doody Show*, in those days at the top of the list for American children nationwide.

Having fallen in love with New York at first sight and feeling totally at home, I was convinced that, by some biological error, I had been born on the wrong continent. This was my true home, this was my nation, my people, a world I would never ever be able to leave. For Marcus, growing up in New York was pure joy. His musical "career" began when he was chosen by Grace Church, where he became the smallest member of their famous boys' choir. Not a weekend went by in the winter that we did not attend a show, an exhibition, or a concert. The small boy became familiar with Leopold Stokowski, Isaac Stern, Igor and David Oistrakh, Pablo Casals, Andrés Segovia, the Vienna Boys' Choir, and the Bolshoi Ballet, performing for the first time in the old Madison Square Garden. Then there were Leonard Bernstein's unforgettable concerts for children in Philharmonic Hall.

On a rainy fall night in the early 1960s, we found the Brooklyn Academy of Music almost empty. Nobody wanted to hear an obscure Soviet cellist nor cared to remember his unpronounceable name, Mstislav Rostropovich. His appearance so impressed Marcus that he expressed the desire to play the cello. We found a teacher from Juilliard to initiate him on that wonderful instrument.

With my husband, as director of evening entertainment, now in charge of casting, Marcus almost made it into show business as a star. The producer of the highly successful series *Flipper*, with its child star Luke Halpin well on the way to adulthood, was looking for another boy. Since the dolphin had over the years become used to Luke, he could not simply be replaced or dropped from the show, so the decision was made to give him a little brother, an orphan the family would eventually adopt. The new boy, according to certain legal requirements, had to be a resident of New York, photogenic, at ease with animals, equally at home under as well as above water, and conditioned to take directions. Marcus tested so well that Metro-Goldwyn-Mayer offered him a six-year contract, provided he moved to their location in Florida at once.

Determined not to let my son be torn from his surroundings, his new father, his school, and all his friends, I had no choice but to decline the tempting offer. Instead of Marcus, red-haired Tommy Norden, his chubby Irish face covered with cheerful freckles, stepped into the part. His seasoned stage mother, with several of her children already in show business, did not share my qualms.

The long summers were spent swimming and fishing in Hampton Bays, or Marcus went off to Camp Kemah on Lake Blaisdell in New Hampshire. The rest of the year, we explored the endless wonders of New York's unique surroundings, its empty off-season shores, the Hudson Valley, and the Catskills. From the Promenade, we were able to watch yet another miracle happening right under our eyes. Over a period of several years, we witnessed the Verrazano-Narrows Bridge rise, inch by inch, the majestic structure of steel and concrete eventually connecting Brooklyn with Staten Island.

After my husband had been put in charge of negotiating contracts between NBC and Metro-Goldwyn-Mayer, he took me with him on some of his frequent trips to the coast—California, Hollywood, Tinseltown!

Chapter Seventy-Four
Hollywood

"Pay attention—look here, pass uff, watch me, dis is de way I want you to do it!"

The lively little Hungarian-born man with the director's hat spoke an amusing mixture of American English, Berlin slang, and Viennese. Jumping up from his chair, he proceeded to perform a regular dance in front of the young actress to show her exactly what he wanted her to do.

"OK? OK!" He returned to his chair and let himself fall back into it.

Even though everybody was laughing, there could not be any doubt that, from star to cameraman, they were all paying the close attention that Hollywood's uncrowned king, Billy Wilder, demanded. He seized the megaphone and shouted, "All quiet on the set! Roll 'em—silence—action—shoot!"

On the slate, I deciphered the chalk-scribbled title of the movie that was being shot in front of me, *The Apartment*, a story about a little employee, played by Jack Lemmon, who rents out his apartment to couples and, consequently, finds himself confronted with unforeseeable difficulties.

Wilder, notorious for not tolerating outsiders on the set when directing a movie, had nodded his head in silent approval when Ross whispered his request that I be permitted to watch.

"Wat, aus Berlin biste?" he addressed me in his best Berlin slang. So, you are from Berlin? "Just sit and behave yourself," he added, turning back to his work.

The headlights went on and, with cameras buzzing, I watched a scene between Shirley MacLaine and Jack Lemmon in a bedroom being shot over and over, constantly interrupted by Wilder. Between endless takes, make-up girls fell all over the actors, lights went on and off, and on again until, after the fifteenth take, the vivacious little man was finally satisfied. "Wrap it—cut—print." A sigh of relief reverberated through the set.

The morning having passed, it was time for lunch, and I was cordially invited to come along to the commissary for some soup, a salad, or a sandwich. Over the frugal meal, Wilder, who never stopped talking, developed fascinating theories about the superior quality of films shot in black and white over those in color. Color, he said, being the natural enemy of drama and dramatic photography, had no real future in movies or in television—very likely none at all! Not only most of the actors, but everybody else on the set, had lunch at the studio commissary. It offered the opportunity to talk about problems, and only a few stars preferred the splendor of their private trailers. Nobody had ever heard of Greta Garbo lowering herself to mingling with ordinary people.

Our home away from home in Hollywood was the sugar-pink Beverly Hills Hotel, the "Pink Barn," as I called it, situated in a park with bungalows. It had more than style; it had real class.

"Call for Pheeleep Morreees!" a little man screamed.

With profound shock, upon my arrival for the first time, I realized that the beautiful plants climbing all over the walls in the hotel were artificial. Plastic, make-believe plants in the land of plenty, with the sun shining in this glamorous world of fantasy?

Among the celebrities we met were some whom I would never forget. Stan Laurel, his face bloated from a severe heart ailment, received us in his modest apartment, where wife number six, the only one he had married twice, took care of him. On top of the television set stood the only Oscar statuette that he ever received. He had named the trophy "Mr. Clean." Before we left him, he handed me a priceless photograph of himself with Oliver Hardy, signed by his partner before his death, and with a pen he added the words, "With warmest regards to Ross and Mrs. Donaldson and every good wish, Stan."

One night, Ross introduced me to a short, elderly man with a big cigar, who informed him that Gracie, his wife, had taken ill. I could not believe that I was standing in front of George Burns, who was, to me, along with Stan Laurel and Jack Benny, the greatest of all comedians. Looking me over between puffs, he expressed his hope to Ross that, even though I was probably not Jewish, I was at least able to prepare Jewish dishes. Like, for instance, pastrami sandwiches? He could not remember me or my name but, from that day on, whenever he met Ross, he would inquire how the "pastrami woman" was doing.

During a banquet honoring the crew of the highly successful NBC series *Victory at Sea*, for which my friend Richard Hanser wrote the scripts, I found myself seated next to a slender man with aristocratic features and prematurely white hair. Being a newcomer to the movie world in general and Hollywood in particular, I had to be enlightened by Ross that my dinner escort was none other than Robert Wise, at the time the most successful of all Hollywood directors. *I'll Cry Tomorrow*, *West Side Story*, and *The Sound of Music* were among his movies that made their triumphant way around the globe.

Chapter Seventy-Five
TRAGEDIES AND OTHER EVENTS IN EUROPE

During the summer of 1960, part of which Marcus and I had spent exploring Greece and Italy with my mother, Anna had come from her village in the East to be with us in Berlin. Just as I had been "her" child long before, she experienced the exquisite joy of having another baby when Marcus was born. Only five months later, a telegram informed us that she was dead at age seventy-three. I would never stop mourning for her.

Beginning with this shattering event, the year 1961 developed into a succession of disasters. On August 13, which would have been Anna's seventy-fourth birthday, the Berlin Wall went up, dividing Germany forever, or so it seemed. The population of East Germany, as Communist Party Chief Erich Honecker exclaimed, had to be protected from evil capitalist spies sneaking into his wonderful democracy.

The next blow came when the news arrived that my mentor and close friend, Walter Franck, was dead of cancer. The devastating report reached me on the same day that a news item appeared on the front page of the *New York Times*, according to which Hitler's famous foe, Pastor Martin Niemoeller, had been the survivor of a car crash in Denmark that claimed the lives of his wife, Else, and their housekeeper, Dora.

The President of the Church of Hessen and Nassau, Martin had resided in Wiesbaden since 1947 with his wife, their housekeeper, and young Martin, Jr., who was still attending high school. He spent the major part of his busy life traveling to the four corners of the globe; wherever he went, he not only preached the Gospel of Jesus Christ, but he talked about the guilt of the German people, not ever omitting his own part in it.

On August 11, 1961, Martin, Else, Dora, and eight-year-old Martin (daughter Hertha's son) were ready to begin a long-planned vacation in Denmark. Against the wishes of his wife, who was well aware of her husband's state of exhaustion, Martin refused to make use of his chauffeur-driven limousine; he insisted on taking the wheel of the private family vehicle, in those days a modest VW beetle.

Else's health was fragile. Her illness—Parkinson's disease—had recently taken a turn for the worse; treatment in the United States had brought only temporary relief. Reluctantly, she took the seat next to her husband, while Dora and the boy climbed into the back of the overloaded vehicle. After passing the Danish border, the skies darkened, a heavy wind soon turned into a raging storm, and, in a curve, the light car swerved out of control, hitting a tree with full force. The two women did not stand a chance; seat belts had not yet been introduced by the automobile industry, and they were thrown from the car. Else died on the spot, Dora in the ambulance. The police found a horror scene, with luggage strewn all over the area, while some Coca Cola bottles lay unbroken. Miraculously, young Martin had suffered only a broken arm. From behind the wheel, rescuers pulled the heavily bleeding, unconscious driver, his head having hit the windshield. The ambulance sped to the hospital in Apenrade. Against all prognoses, he survived, but when he came out of his long coma, he learned from his sons that Else, his faithful companion of forty-two years, had been laid to rest side by side with Dora at the Wiesbaden Cemetery.

Not even during his most trying times had Martin come remotely close to the state of total despair that gripped him now. Strong feelings of guilt tormented him, in spite of the assurance that the accident had not been his fault. "I killed them," he kept repeating. "I killed them both!" The initial shock was followed by a deep depression. Once more, Martin, a human being eager to share each thought with a loved one, was sentenced to the hell of solitary confinement. For eight years, it had been Hitler who imposed this cruel sentence on him. Now, was it God?

How would he live without Else? Why indeed should he go on living at all? He was almost seventy years old and, suddenly, tired of living. Heart seizures plagued him, and he suffered at least one full-fledged heart attack.

What would Jesus say?

Lord, what will Thou have me do?

And he heard God's voice, loud and clear, "I want you to live!" So, as in the past, Martin submitted to God's will.

Three months after the accident, the sixty-nine-year-old pastor was elected to be one of the six presidents of the newly established World Council of Churches, for a period of seven years. With this position opening new doors for him, it would eventually enable him to help the Russian Orthodox Church of Soviet Russia out of its forced isolation. With even greater vehemence, he threw himself into his work, furthering his ecumenical goals. The former submarine commander, a fighter by nature, realized to his own amazement that he was well on the road to pacifism. The peace of the world was at stake.

In order to establish the first connections with the Russian Orthodox Church, the president of the World Council of Churches traveled to the Soviet Union. Upon his return, he found himself maligned as a "traitor," a "Communist lover," a "peacenik," and he was officially called to order by the political right-wing party ruling West Germany since 1949. The fact that, as a goodwill gesture to the pastor on the part of the Soviet government, a sizeable number of German POWs were released was tactfully passed over by the media.[4]

In 1963, Martin decided to accept the personal invitation of Pope Paul VI to visit him in Rome. Back home after the trip, he found his house picketed again, outraged newspaper headlines once more condemning the Evangelical pastor. The headlines blared, "Protestant Leader Kisses Pope's Ring!"

Had he really kissed the Holy Father's ring?

Dutch Cardinal Willebrands had led the distinguished visitor to the private chamber where he was to be received by the pope. Seconds before the actual meeting, Martin suddenly wondered just what he would do in case the pope extended his hand to him, the hand with the ring? Before he could come to a decision, the Holy Father entered and, stretching out his arms in a spontaneous gesture, seized both his visitor's hands. "At long last I am meeting the man I have so long been praying for," he exclaimed. In a relaxed atmosphere, an hour-long intense exchange followed, begun in Latin and continued in German.

On that memorable day, the Vatican issued a special postcard with a photograph depicting the two dignitaries side by side, adorned with a special stamp, "Città del Vaticano, October 11, 1963." In three languages the stamp read, "Visit of Pastor Martin Niemoeller, President of the Church of Hessen-Nassau in Germany, with H. H. Paul VI."[5]

After the deaths of Else and Dora, the pastor's life in the empty Wiesbaden mansion became almost unbearable. Martin, Jr., having graduated from law school, was well on his way to the post he would ultimately hold, a federal judge on West Germany's highest court. A housekeeper, once a maid in the old Dahlem household, now took care of the lonely man, whose only companions were Racker and Rascal, two black dachshunds. He traveled even more frequently than ever before because, in his own words, "at home nobody is waiting for me anymore!"

Chapter Seventy-Six
Events in America

My husband's position as director of evening entertainment for NBC required extensive travel. Being in charge of casting for the shows he supervised, he soon found himself an irresistible target for all those starlets on their way to fame and glory, who would not leave a mattress unturned to get to the top. His time at home was reduced to occasional guest appearances, and our marriage began to crumble. Projects like pilot films for new network undertakings took him not only to Hollywood on a more frequent basis, but also to England, Brazil, and India. He was responsible for a revival of *Tarzan* as a television series, as well as other projects like *Maya*. While *Tarzan* became a great success, *Maya* would turn into a flop. His ability to spot a good manuscript within minutes was matched by a talent to predict the success or demise of a show. He promoted the financial support of a musical by the name of *Best Foot Forward*, which literally catapulted Judy Garland's unknown daughter, Liza Minnelli, to stardom. He was also responsible for persuading the "king" of the *Tonight Show*, Johnny Carson, to invite an unknown singer to his program. She was a timid young girl, whose most outstanding facial feature was her rather prominent nose. However, when she opened her mouth and began to sing, it became clear that a star was about to be born. She was sensational, but the nose, everyone agreed, would have to be corrected by a skilled plastic surgeon. Barbra Streisand, who turned into the greatest star that NBC ever discovered, had the good sense not to change her nose.

On Thursday, November 21, Ross had to go to England, leaving me behind in a particularly dark mood. Something, I felt, was going to happen. The events that occurred on Friday, November 22, 1963, threw not only America into a state of shock—for one brief moment, it seemed as if the heartbeat of the entire world had stopped. Around the noon hour in Dallas, Texas, John F. Kennedy was assassinated. In total despair, Marcus and I spent the next few days in front of television, becoming live eyewitnesses to the murder of the alleged assassin, Lee Harvey Oswald, by Jack Ruby.

On Monday, November 25, through a veil of tears, America bade farewell to her fallen hero. Unforgettable was the composed, black-veiled widow, little Caroline touching the casket, and John-John, still too young to fully comprehend the extent of the tragedy, saluting like a little soldier. Unforgettable was the riderless horse in the endless motorcade on its long route to Arlington National Cemetery, under blood-chilling, muffled drumrolls. What I felt was an indescribable pain, a physical hurt over the loss of the first president for whom

I had been able to vote. Nothing would ever be the same again; it was as if a gigantic black cloud had darkened our skies, leaving nobody's life untouched. The American nation realized that, with its president, she had lost her innocence.

"Don't let it be forgot that once there was a spot, for one brief shining moment that was known as Camelot."

The king was dead, and Camelot was no more. The joy over him, the pride, had given way to grief, sorrow, and fear.

Five years after JFK's meticulously planned execution, his brother, Bobby, would be shot to death in Los Angeles. Two months prior to this new tragedy, Martin Luther King, Jr. had been felled by a murderer's bullet.

Who would be next?

Chapter Seventy-Seven
Divorce, Despair, Deliverance

During my married years, I had begun to work for the American Friends Service Committee in downtown Manhattan. The Quaker organization, recipient of the 1947 Nobel Peace Prize, provided various interesting services, from establishing contacts between foreign students and American families to counseling conscientious objectors, particularly at a time when the war in Vietnam took on new dimensions. My work was stimulating and kept me from brooding over the sad realization that my marriage was doomed.

In 1966, Marcus and I had gone to Europe for the summer and, upon our return, I not only found that my husband's drinking had gotten out of hand, but sufficient evidence indicated that he had switched from fast-changing love affairs to a steady relationship with one particular woman, a movie scriptwriter in Hollywood. Since he did not seem inclined to leave me, I decided to hang on, in the vain hope that he might come to his senses. Over the next sixteen months, I went through the kind of hell that cannot be described in words; just when I began to believe that I might be spared the heartache of another divorce, the bomb was dropped on my head, turning my life to shambles. On January 27, 1968, my husband returned from Hollywood to pack his belongings, after which he left, without a single word of explanation. Since he had made no provisions for me, I found myself destitute within weeks.

For me, this meant the end of the world. What was I going to do, where was I going to turn, a single mother with a young son, who needed the security of a family? The only family I could offer him was in Europe. I shuddered at the prospect of moving back, even temporarily, until he was old enough to go to college. Just when I was about to give in to the total hopelessness of our situation and let myself fall into a black, bottomless pit, it seemed as if the heavens suddenly opened up, ready to send down another one of the inexplicable miracles my life had been blessed with in the past.

One morning, totally engulfed in grief over the fragments of my shattered life, I noticed a one-page article in our weekly newspaper, *The Brooklyn Heights Press*, announcing the visit of Pastor Martin Niemoeller at a nearby church in Brooklyn. His photograph brought back memories of another life, one that had taken place on some distant planet so very long ago. The seventy-six-year-old widowed pastor had accepted an invitation from his friend, the Reverend Turnipseed, to preach the sermon in his church on Brooklyn's Hanson Place. The date, April 20, Hitler's birthday, was a fateful day indeed for Niemoeller, who was filled with bittersweet memories because it also marked his forty-ninth wedding anniversary with Else.

There was no way for him to anticipate that, due to sad circumstances surrounding a woman he had known as a child, his own life was going to take a new and totally unexpected turn.

Should I dare to contact him? I wondered. Would the man who had risen to world fame remember the freckled child who had once roamed the rectory in Dahlem with his own children over thirty years before? For the first time in months, I was able to make a decision that would ultimately change my life. I picked up the telephone, and, within minutes, I heard his warm, familiar voice; of course he remembered me, and he wanted to see me. Would I be free to join him for lunch? At the Gramercy Park Hotel on April 20?

I could not believe it!

Twenty-four hours later, after feverish efforts to cover up the desolate state of my appearance, I entered the lobby of the Gramercy Park Hotel in lower Manhattan. Standing in front of the elevator, it hit me; my God, can this be true? Will I really see the man who, next to my father, had been the undisputed idol of my childhood? What will I say? What will he say? How should I address him? Before fainting from sheer excitement, the elevator doors slid open and there he stood, dressed in a conventional gray suit complete with a crimson vest and an elegant tie. How well I remembered the dark complexion of his ascetic face, the beautiful black eyes, undiluted inheritance from his southern French great-grandmother. His hair had turned from ebony black to a handsome iron-gray, and the smile that, according to his biographer, could charm the birds off a tree, was overwhelming. Stepping forward with the agility of a forty-year-old, he took me in his arms and said, "You have not changed one bit. I would have recognized you anywhere!"

Breaking into tears of relief, for a fleeting moment there was a flash, an illusion that the man who was holding me was my father. But then there was Ovid's voice, loud and clear. At last, he seemed to say, go ahead, plunge right in; I promise you that this time you have nothing to fear, nothing to lose, but a lot to gain!

Martin, who still remembered the audacious, scraggly child, addressed me by my first name and the familiar "*du*." But what in the world was I supposed to call him? Noticing my uneasiness, he cheerfully suggested that I simply call him "Martin." Martin, just Martin? Impossible! So I ended up carefully avoiding calling him anything.

He had to leave for Toronto the next morning, and when he gently kissed me good-bye, all I felt was infinite relief over the fact that he was *not* my father! It was the man, Martin Niemoeller, who had cast a spell over me, irrevocably and forever.

The following morning found me refreshed and filled with new energy; I contacted the Manhattan office of Vincent J. Malone, a renowned lawyer specializing in divorces who, within a week, was able to secure sufficient alimony from the man who had left me without a word. The law was clearly on my side.

It seemed as if the fog in which I had been engulfed for months was slowly lifting, and in spite of all the hardships, there seemed to be hope. I was now able to pick up the pieces of my life and decided to move to Berlin until my son was ready for college. My mother was there, my brother, cousins, and, most important, the indestructible house Am Hirschsprung, which would offer us shelter. With the John F. Kennedy School in Berlin, my son would not have to change the system of education nor his accustomed American lifestyle too drastically. So with a bleeding heart, I resigned myself to the fact that I would simply have to endure the next few years away from the city I loved, New York. Berlin would provide us both with familiar surroundings and a chance for me to work within the large American community. And then, of course, there was someone in Wiesbaden waiting for my visit. The die, a premonition told me, was about to be cast.

Not wanting to expose Marcus to the pain of witnessing his world breaking up, I sent him ahead to Berlin. As far as my own feelings were concerned, there were none left; the discomfort connected with the move kept me from falling apart. After all, I was not going to leave New York forever, I kept telling myself over and over again; someday I would return. With all of my belongings on their way to Europe, from the deck of the *Statendam* and through my tears, I watched the city I loved slowly disappear in the distance, bidding one last farewell to the tall lady who had welcomed me once.

"Give me your tired, your poor," she still repeated. This time, however, she seemed to add, "and let me comfort those among you who are heartbroken."

Chapter Seventy-Eight
Back to Berlin

Six months later, the disarray of the move behind me, I had rented a little townhouse in Zehlendorf, and with Marcus now attending the John F. Kennedy School, I felt the time had come to make good the promise I had given to Martin—to visit him in Wiesbaden. Arriving at Frankfurt Airport, I was met by the pastor's chauffeur at the gate, who led me to the waiting limousine. There he was, a little embarrassed, with a shy smile, the man I had not been able to get out of my mind. Seated next to him in the back of the car, he kept explaining the landscape around us; there was the Main River, a piece of information after which he almost accidentally put his hand on mine, and did not remove it until we reached Wiesbaden. His hands were perfectly formed, warm, strong, and sensuous, with long fingers and well-shaped fingernails, the most attractive and comforting hands I had ever seen or felt.

A true "mighty fortress," I thought, at the sight of the stately mansion on Brentanostrasse, with the four Evangelists' names carved in stone over the heavy entrance door. Later that same evening, seated across from him at the dinner table in Wiesbaden's exclusive "Schwarzer Bock," I asked the one question that had not let me rest.

During the previous months in Germany, I had made it my business to find out all I possibly could about the private life of the widowed pastor. I learned that while there were females practically standing in line, eager to get close to him, there was no mention of one particular woman. Fortified by the exquisite wine, I boldly inquired why he, at seventy-six still a most attractive man, obviously not meant to spend the rest of his life alone, had never remarried? Instead of an answer, he gave me an enigmatic smile, and I realized with horror that I had probably gone one step too far. The man I still found impossible to call by his first name might not forgive such indiscretion.

It was close to midnight when, stepping out onto Wiesbaden's elegant street, the Wilhelmstrasse, we found that steadily falling snowflakes had turned the town into a winter wonderland. With no cab in sight, we decided to walk all the way back to the house. After a few minutes of silence, the man by my side stood still and put his arm around my shoulder. His face close to mine, he said, "I am going to answer your question now. You might not believe this, but I am a very timid man. With me, a woman will definitely have to take the first step!"

The first step? I was thunderstruck! This was more than a hint or a suggestion; it was clearly an invitation, one that I had the good sense to accept. So I did the only sensible thing and kissed him. By the time we reached the house, we were almost fighting over the question who had been the first one to fall in love. The problem, although never quite solved, soon became irrelevant. Would I marry him? Of course I would marry him! Just as soon as my divorce from the man who had deserted me was final.

Well aware of my reluctance to stay in Germany, Martin, a true citizen of the world, cheerfully agreed to move to the United States with me, an offer that, after some thorough soul-searching, I felt I could not accept. Although retired from office as President of the Church of Hessen and Nassau, his position as a president of the World Council of Churches still required a great deal of travel. In other words, he had his roots in Germany, where four of his five remaining children as well as his brother and three sisters resided. After all he had suffered, how could I even consider tearing him away from his family?

Unfamiliar and rather skeptical about life in Wiesbaden, I found to my utter delight that it was inhabited by over thirty thousand Americans, mostly members of the US Air Force, which meant for me that living in this beautiful capital of the State of Hessen, the ancient Roman spa, would be endurable. I would not even be required to change my American lifestyle. Aside from the US Air Force Hospital, the largest such facility outside of the United States, there were the Erbenheim Air Base, Lindsey Air Station, housing and shopping areas, clubs, a chapel with Protestant, Catholic, and Jewish clergy, movie theaters, and the H. H. Arnold High School, where Marcus could finish his senior year. The one institution from which Martin would derive sublime pleasure was the Air Base Library with its fifty thousand volumes, well stacked with the works of all his favorite authors in their original language.

To his surprise, my husband-to-be found that the glad tidings of his impending marriage did not exactly cause undivided exultation among the members of his immediate family, but instead a havoc of unforeseen proportions. While the revered "older brother's" decision was accepted with respect and tolerance by his siblings, at least two of the five Niemoeller children reacted with totally inappropriate outbreaks of hysteria. Had their aging father taken leave of his senses? Had he, not long ago, informed them of his intentions to move to a home for senior citizens in Darmstadt, a project that had met with everyone's wholehearted relief? The institution in question offered the widower the kind of care that none of the children were willing or able to provide for him. But instead of surrounding himself with decrepit old people, he was plunging into a new, exciting adventure; the grandfather and great-grandfather decided to once more jump into the role of father to a young son. Most importantly, once more he would become a husband and live as a man! In the minds of many, the crowning insult of this endeavor was that the future Frau Niemoeller not only held an American passport, but was twice divorced, facts that in the eyes of some definitely indicated an undesirable degree of notoriety. The sullen housekeeper, her old-maid dreams of seeing herself in the role of lady of the house now shattered, fled in disgust.

My future husband took all brazen attempts geared to invade his privacy with amazing equanimity but, when reports reached his ears that certain members of his own clan seriously challenged his mental capacity, the pot boiled over. He summoned the family to the house for a showdown and threw a tantrum of hitherto unprecedented dimensions. In a stentorian voice, he told everyone that nobody, least of all his offspring, had the right to interfere with his life. To make himself perfectly clear, he added that, given the choice between them and me, he would chose me! After an extended period of moping, those among the children, having not only inherited their father's temper, but his sense of fairness and justice as well as his warmth, came to the happy realization that their old man could have done worse in his choice of a new life companion—a lot worse!

After my divorce by proxy in Chihuahua, Mexico, became final, we found out the hard way that it was not an easy endeavor for a German national to marry a foreigner. I was back in a country where, according to a pre-World War I law, the definition of a German was that he or she must be "of German blood." Of German blood, like Hitler, Goering, Goebbels, and Himmler? And this precious Teutonic blood must not be contaminated by unions with inferior foreigners. Mountains of ridiculously antediluvian legal obstacles, with which Germany was still amply endowed, had to be overcome; just when we, in total dismay, had decided to legalize our relationship in Denmark, England, or the United States, the last document arrived, signed by Hessen's Minister of Justice.

The simple civil ceremony in the old Wiesbaden City Hall was not followed by a religious service, which caused more tongue wagging. Martin's dry comment, that a marriage was an affair concerning only the two partners and God, was hard to swallow. The scandalous fact that I was not a member of the church remained a deep, dark secret between my husband and myself. I had left the institutional church long before I turned my back on my native country. Now I shared my husband's confidence that, in due time and with him by my side, I would come around and resume the faith in which I had been raised. Attending church on a regular basis and sharing every aspect of life with a man whose entire life revolved around Jesus Christ, how could I not embrace the man from Nazareth as the Messiah of mankind?

Chapter Seventy-Nine
Life with Martin

What really came as a surprise was the realization that the man I had married actually relished the fact that his new wife was more than just a little different from the traditional image of a German pastor's spouse. With a foreign passport, a decidedly different taste in clothes, favoring nail polish and make-up, driving an American street cruiser still adorned with New York license plates, my husband actually seemed to derive a sublime pleasure from showing me off in public like an exotic bird, a glittering butterfly he had been fortunate enough to catch. When a waiter in a restaurant referred to me as "*Frau tochter*" ("Madam daughter"), Martin would beam with pleasure and kick me under the table.

As far as the reactions of my own family were concerned, my mother, although shocked at first over my decision to marry a man the age of my father, welcomed her new son-in-law, a mere five months her junior, with her own special grace; however, she could not suppress the slightly reproachful-sounding remark that it had not been I, but she herself, who had once been designated by her friend Else as her successor in case she did not outlive her husband. She came to the conclusion, though, that at least the man in question stayed in the family.

Among those hesitant about coming to grips with the new situation was my own son. With his biological father never having shown much interest in him and barely over the heartache of losing a stepfather he had truly loved, Marcus balked at accepting stepfather number two. However, it was not long until he found out that Martin did not have any intentions of treating him as a stepson. The teenager came to realize that, for the first time in his life, he was going to have a *real* father. Giving up his resistance, he moved in with us and changed from the John F. Kennedy School in Berlin to the American military high school in Wiesbaden, planning to return to the United States for his college education. The relationship between father and son would deepen during the years to come, eventually motivating Marcus, while a college student in Greensboro, North Carolina, to change his name from Donaldson to Niemoeller by a simple court procedure, circumventing archaic German adoption laws. He broke the unexpected tidings to his father during a Christmas vacation, exhibiting a passport with the new name, which caused both to shed tears of unadulterated joy wholeheartedly shared by the entire Niemoeller family, including all his step siblings. Rarely would the two of them be seen sitting side by side without their arms around each other's shoulders, an expression of the bond of love that could not be broken by death.

Like no one else I had ever met, Martin craved affection and physical closeness. Only now did I comprehend the full impact of Hitler's cruelty; the demon knew exactly what he was doing when he sentenced this man, so desperately in need of sharing every feeling, every single thought with a human being, to total isolation. Alone in a cell over many years, surrounded by unspeakable horror, unable to touch anyone dear to him, never knowing what the next minute had in store for him, he had gone through the kind of hell that he could never truly describe to anyone.

Life and happiness had once more returned to the spacious house on Brentanostrasse, for the past years a place of dismal solitary confinement for the widower. With a competent new housekeeper, a typist, and a driver at my disposal, I enthusiastically threw myself into my various duties. Aside from numerous high-level social functions, I was expected to be an executive secretary, a confidante, an administrator, a cook, and a gardener.

In a surprise move, assisted by the Salvation Army, I had gotten rid of my husband's dreary wardrobe in his absence, substituting it with nice, conventional clothes like English tweed jackets, flannel trousers, ties of good taste, and handsome cotton shirts. The Salvation Army came back once more to collect a truckload of horrible makeshift furniture, including taste-defying fixtures like lamps, chairs, tables, and other household pieces, which I replaced with beautiful items, mostly family heirlooms, that I had once shipped to New York and now to Wiesbaden.

Obsessed with an almost physical aversion to handling money, my husband left financial transactions to me. All he claimed for himself were modest sums so he could periodically replenish his cherished supply of exquisite cigars, the only luxury he allowed himself. Purchasing them in a local store over a prolonged period of time was a regular ceremony, a pleasure shared wholeheartedly by the ecstatic shop owner.

My duties included those of private chauffeur for other than official functions. After the accident that had claimed Else and Dora's lives, Martin had not taken the wheel of a car again, so I soon found myself the victim of a seasoned backseat driver, whose main objection remained my nasty habit of driving, like Americans do, in a defensive style, refusing to join the Germans going berserk on their death trap called the autobahn, a free-for-all without any speed limits. Sometimes, in his eagerness to get ahead, he would pound the floor of the car with his right foot, pressing an imaginary gas pedal. One day in Berlin, when he had been especially insufferable, I brought the heavy Chevrolet to a screeching halt on the curb of a busy street, opened the door, pointed to a nearby taxi stand, and politely invited him to step out of my car and stay out.

Since that day, banned to the car's backseat, he tried to limit himself to entertaining me by singing songs at the top of his voice, from "Oh what a Beautiful Morning," "They've Got an Awful Lot of Coffee in Brazil," and "Get Me to the Church on Time" to "Why Can't a Woman be Like a Man?" Extremely fond of American musicals, he enjoyed the reputation of dashing into the nearest musical immediately upon landing in New York. He had seen them all, loved them all, and owned all the records, which he played on the prehistoric phonograph in his study until they were literally in shreds. His favorite singer was Bing Crosby, whom he had met on a movie set in Hollywood some years before, and nobody could say who of the two had more fun, the prince of the church or the prince of song.

Tucked into the backseat of the car, a safe enough distance away from me, he kept singing until merciful silence announced that he had drifted into dreamland. Since his days as a naval officer he was able to sleep anytime, anywhere, taking little catnaps that had a refreshing effect, particularly for me.

Although having just retired as the President of the Church of Hessen and Nassau, Martin remained a president of the World Council of Churches, was active in more peace organizations than I cared to count, and was still a pastor, who regarded it as his duty not only to attend, but also to hold services and officiate at christenings, weddings, and funerals, when and wherever he was invited. His day began early and ended late, working until the wee hours of the morning, sustained by black coffee, a sufficient supply of chocolate, and sour English lemon drops, generously provided by our American military friends. His frequent heart seizures had disappeared almost completely, so he continued to travel to the four corners of the globe and, whenever possible, I accompanied him. However, my husband had to accept my decision not to participate in demonstrations or other activities of a political nature, or discussions on the politics of my country outside the United States other than with fellow Americans.

Since the beginning of the war in Vietnam, a new kind of furious anti-Americanism had surfaced all over, in which I, regardless of my own opinion, was not going to join in a foreign country. Contrary to a widespread opinion, I had not "returned" to Germany; I had come to live in Germany as a guest, and a guest I would remain until my return home, to the United States. Often I was asked if and why I "still" had an American passport? After all, being married to Marin, did I not owe it to him to become a German national again?

I did not! And my husband would have been the last one to demand it. Politely, I kept rejecting offers by the authorities to issue me a German passport, the condition being that I renounce my American citizenship. I had sworn allegiance to the United States of America, an obligation my husband respected.

Chapter Eighty
Under the Rug

With the realization that Hitler's gigantic shadow still loomed over the world and particularly in Germany, where he and his minions had so badly disrupted my childhood, adolescence, and family, it did not take me long to realize the full impact of the devastating damage Germans had suffered in the successful but self-crippling act of sweeping their pernicious past under the rug. Wherever I looked, there were ostensible displays of obscene wealth, bordering on megalomania. This stark materialism, hard to match anywhere else, was totally unsuitable in a nation that had thrown the world into misery. Underneath the thin layer of shining glitter yawned an abyss of blatant spiritual poverty and provincial mediocrity. In all walks of post-war life, old and new Nazis gloated over the fact that the civilized world had, as a consequence of the Iron Curtain separating the free world from Bolshevism and in dire need for West Germany as an ally, hastily sanctioned the past by conveniently "letting bygones be bygones." Not long after the war, Bavarian Minister-President Franz Josef Strauss was heard to remark that "it was time for the Germans to stop walking about with backs bent by shame over Auschwitz." Wherever I looked, though, bent backs were extremely hard to find.

Hitler's existence, as well as the war he started, was now well on its way to being written off as a phase, an historic accident, bloodstained maybe, but no better or worse than other historical disasters. The advocates of this eagerly embraced philosophy diligently ignored the fact that no crime becomes any better by comparing it to another crime. A new kind of nationalism and anti-Semitism, hushed up and still a little subdued despite the almost total absence of Jews, was beginning to raise its ugly head. Deeply concerned over this situation, Martin had once more raised a lonely warning voice. He would not let the sins of the past be forgotten, including the part the Church had played in them. In Göttingen, addressing students on the subjects of nationalism and anti-Semitism, he had spoken the following words:

> The stronger nationalism becomes, the stronger becomes anti-Semitism. Hatred of the Jews is a deep, dark secret, totally different from the hate between nations, which is usually not directed against a suffering individual. And it is also totally different from the hate against foreigners. The Jew is not hated as a foreigner, he is hated as a Jew, and this hate cannot be explained. Because for too long the church went along with practicing or tolerating anti-Semitism instead of fighting it. Those six million are a heavy burden on Christendom and the church, and not just on the Nazi party and the SS and the one mass murderer. The church bears the heaviest burden of guilt because it was aware of what it was doing when it did nothing.

Anti-Semitism is anti-Christendom, so an anti-Semitic church is an anti-Christian church and as such the most acute threat to the church as a church. It is not the problem for the Jews, but for the Christians, who for centuries did their utmost to propagate xenophobia: hatred of anything and anybody foreign, a term under which falls anti-Semitism.

In spite of vile insults and open threats, he never tired of pounding into the minds of those Germans maintaining that they themselves had not participated in crimes, that the worst sin was that of omission, of indifference. Whoever had witnessed wrongdoing without protest was just as guilty as the henchman stringing up innocent victims. The fact that "restitution money" for six million lives had been paid by the Federal Republic of Germany to the State of Israel could never diminish the German guilt by one iota.

Almost totally missing from my husband's life in Wiesbaden was the usual circle of friends. It took a while until I understood that, for a man in his position, a patriarch standing high above the crowd, there seemed room only for admirers in total awe of him, or foes who would stop at nothing when it came to tearing him down. Quick-witted, gregarious, and open by nature, incapable of prejudice, hate, or hostility, Martin felt awkward in the presence of "worshippers"; what he needed were "buddies," good for exhilarating conversation and juicy debates over a fine cigar or a glass of vodka.

Soon after getting established in my new surroundings, I decided that I needed one niche of my life that belonged exclusively to me so, with my husband's full approval, I joined the volunteer staff of the American Red Cross in the Wiesbaden US Air Force Hospital, just a block from our house. I would be able to keep my position, which offered new and exciting challenges every day, until the end of Desert Storm some twenty years later. Looking back on this part of my life, I can truly say that there were few situations with which I was not confronted, in my capacity as a special caseworker.

During the 1970s, the hospital was blessed with almost one hundred and fifty volunteers, mostly spouses of servicemen, each donating a few hours a week in the various departments. This unique medical facility, housed in outmoded Luftwaffe buildings, even had its own chapters of Alcoholics Anonymous and Al-anon. The majority of Red Cross volunteers were totally inexperienced young women; being more mature, I soon found myself entrusted with particularly difficult cases. Having the entire medical staff, including the commander and the chaplains supporting the Red Cross in its extensive work, was very reassuring. Patients, military and others, such as the staff of the various US embassies, consulates, and the media were flown in by air evac from as far as the Azores in the west, Iceland in the north, South Africa in the south, Russia, India, and Red China. My typical day began by thoroughly scanning the hospital from top to bottom, in search of anyone in need of counseling. By far the hardest emotional task for me was dealing with families of the numerous accident victims, summoned from the United States to a critically ill, mutilated, or dying patient.

Being part of American life in Wiesbaden allowed me to make new friends, mainly among the hospital medical staff, so it was a new, young generation that filled our house from then on. They not only came in the role of friends, but as helpful physicians, if needed, not excluding the commander. To an amazing number of people it seemed to be a big issue whether I had not, in reality, "married my father." Indeed I had, I cheerfully retorted, but while daughters were never fortunate enough to see their dreams fulfilled, mine had come true. The father I worshipped had been taken from me in a most cruel way, so I felt that by sending Martin into my life, God had attempted to compensate me for my loss. It was that simple. Accustomed to meeting with disbelief, disapproval, or both, I usually relished volunteering the information that the man I married was certainly more than a "substitute father"; he was my husband, my lover, which usually put a stop to out of place curiosity. My lover? Had I just said "my lover"? Precisely.

Another audacious inquiry, clumsily veiled by elderly females who would have given their right arm to be in my role, was if I really and fully appreciated the supreme honor bestowed on me by being married to a true giant of the century, superior to me in every respect? The unspoken suggestion was that, overcome by Christian mercy, my husband, from high upon his pedestal, had stooped low enough to lift me, an undeserving little nobody, from the gutter. Furiously remembering my long line of distinguished noble Prussian ancestors, I had a fitting answer in store, one that shut up intruders into our privacy at once. Oh yes, I replied, deliberately misunderstanding the tactless inquiry, I was fully aware that there had to be something very, very special about me, something my husband had not been able to find in any other woman, otherwise he would have settled for one of his countless boring church mice, wouldn't he?

Chapter Eighty-One
Married Life

What was it like to be married to Martin Niemoeller? What was he really like in everyday life?

Not long after our wedding, in reply to my stepson Martin, Jr.'s tongue-in-cheek inquiry about how I was coping with his temperamental father, I was ready to admit to him that keeping a bag of fleas under control was probably a lot easier. Whereupon he comforted me with the reassuring statement, "that is precisely what we have you for now." Indeed, my high-spirited husband bore more than a faint resemblance to a rocket that had just been ignited, leaving everyone guessing when and in what direction it would go off. But off it would go!

From the first day, I realized that the man I had married was a bundle of inexhaustible energy, who applied to himself two famous sayings attributed to Ulrich von Hutten, the legendary knight and humanist of the fifteenth century: "The die is cast—I dared!" and "I'm not an intricately written book, I am a man with all his contradictions." There could be no better definitions of the former intrepid submarine commander and valiant Christian who had indeed "dared" to reject all the temptations of Nazi evil.

On the long road through life, undergoing his own, painful catharsis, he had emerged as a true pacifist, having reached the conclusion that the message of Jesus Christ, abused for centuries, must not be desecrated by serving as an excuse for an arms race that would end in the extinction of the human race. He summed up his convictions before the World Council of Churches, by saying, "I personally cannot imagine any situation in which God would answer my question, 'Lord, what willst Thou have me do?' with the command 'Drop an atom bomb!'"

His urgent plea for peace did not meet with the general approval of his fellow ecclesiastics whose fear of Communism, which they shared with the politicians, surpassed not only the dread of an atomic war, but led them to overlook the dangers from the right, dark powers that began to emerge and were allowed to develop unnoticed for many years. The new danger had a name—terrorism.

Martin expressed the hope that, in order to achieve lasting peace in the world, a new form of humane socialism might offer an acceptable alternative to capitalism. This expectation, however, dwindled when he came to recognize the pitfalls of socialism, the shrill discrepancy between the teachings and actual practice, and he predicted its eventual worldwide collapse long before anyone else was able to discern the inevitable. His anticipation that a Socialist society might be less susceptible to greed, to "mammon," as the most detrimental scourge haunting mankind, proved a fallacy.

Raising a warning voice against the growing exploitation of the underdeveloped countries, the "Third World," he even expressed skepticism over a lasting future for democracy as the one desirable and effective form of government best suited to serve the needs of a people. He did not live long enough to witness the disaster caused by an all too sudden change from dictatorial socialism to a free market society in those countries that, over decades, had been morally and economically weakened by corrupt regimes.

In sharp contrast to Hitler, who publicly boasted that "already as a young man in Vienna, he knew everything," Martin, ready to throw outdated convictions overboard, if and when necessary, was now called fickle and unstable. The French newspaper *Le Figaro* would, after his death, write about him, "He was never afraid to jump down from the pedestal he had been put on against his own wishes—and we loved him for it!" But this love was not shared by his fellow Germans, who branded him as a turncoat without principles for stressing the importance of continued dialogue over blatant threats between the political powers in a world now split by opposing ideologies. For him, the verbal exchange of diverse opinions, with the goal of eventually approaching some state of proximity, was more beneficial than rash and violent efforts to gain fast victories over "the enemies" at all costs.

In his own mind, changing his convictions whenever necessary did not result from a weakness of character, but was proof of inner strength and mental growth. This was a truly daring statement in view of the fact that flexibility of the mind was considered dangerously dubious in a country where sticking to one's principles was considered mandatory, an irrevocable virtue; a person had to have principles, or he was not to be trusted. However, the man so harshly admonished was in the best of company; none other than Johann Wolfgang von Goethe had maintained that a person of character did not need principles.

Being married to a living legend, a paragon of honesty, tolerance, and common decency, a man always ready to repent, I realized that his most outstanding characteristic was a unique singleness and purity of heart. In view of such outstanding qualities, I was almost relieved when I noticed one truly human weakness in him; in spite of his advanced years, he was still unable to control his temper outbursts, an undiluted legacy from his hot-blooded southern French ancestors, which enjoyed a legendary reputation. But even the most outrageous tempest was over as fast as it had begun, after which the terrifying Mr. Hyde returned to wonderful Dr. Jekyll who, with profound expressions of remorse, proceeded to seek forgiveness. While it had never occurred to Else, being of the old generation, to react other than with helpless tears to her husband's eruptions, he now faced a wife from the new generation; nobody, and especially not my beloved spouse, was allowed to scream at me and get away with it.

Not long after our wedding, up in his study, my husband gave a gala performance. A minor disagreement between the two of us had led to unduly rash remarks, and without the slightest warning, holding onto his desk, he began to stamp his feet, screaming at the top of his voice. Refusing to give him the satisfaction of seeing me seek a fast escape, I was determined to stay put and see this through, once and for all. Attracted by this noisy spectacle, Marcus came racing down the stairs and burst into the study, ready to defend whoever needed defending. Never had he experienced anything faintly resembling the scene unfolding before his eyes. Aghast and speechless, he and I exchanged glances at the sight of the raging volcano and soon began to giggle until, convulsed with uncontrollable laughter, we literally sank to the floor. It was only then that Martin, suddenly struck by strange sounds not exactly resembling sobs, must have sensed that something was definitely wrong and stopped his eruption. Letting go of the desk, he turned around very slowly and saw his wife and teenage stepson seized by a fit of hysteria. After not more than a second of stunned silence, he did what we least expected; grasping the absurdity of the situation, he decided the only thing to do was to join in, and the three of us ended up laughing until we cried.

After every tantrum, the remorseful culprit hastened to ask forgiveness of those he had insulted. Apologizing for a mistake, on any level, was easy for him. In turn, he readily granted forgiveness to those who had hurt him. Simon Wiesenthal, in his novel *The Sunflower*, which deals with the problem of forgiving and being forgiven, had invited the pastor's opinion on this complex subject, which he printed in the book: "Injustice or pain inflicted on us personally, we can forgive. But evil done to others we cannot forgive in their name. Only those who suffered can do that and no one else in their stead."

The question of collective forgiveness for Nazi crimes would again become a public issue, discussed worldwide one year following Martin's death. Forty years after the war, President Reagan had taken it upon himself to announce a general forgiveness for crimes that he himself had not endured. This monstrous act of appeasement, the public redemption of mass murderers, found open ears in Germany.

The mere fact that the President of the United States was planning to visit a place where SS men were buried was a slap in the face of survivors. A few days before Reagan was to depart for Germany, Elie Wiesel called me from Washington, asking my permission to suggest that the president, instead of going to the German military cemetery at Bitburg, pay his respects at the gravesite of Pastor Niemoeller. His plea was rejected. Ronald Reagan had already allowed a German chancellor to commit himself. Paul Celan, a Jewish survivor and poet from Czernowitz, who, in total despair later sought his death in the Seine, had expressed his feelings in his "Death Fugue," written in German, his mother tongue, and the language of the murderers: "Der Tod ist ein Meister aus Deutschland—sein Auge ist blau" ("Death is a master from Germany—his eye is blue").[6]

Chapter Eighty-Two
MARTIN AND THE WORLD

Being received by such distinguished personalities as the Queen of England, the monarchs of Sweden, Norway, and Denmark, Queen Juliana of the Netherlands, Dwight D. Eisenhower, Pandit Nehru, and Indira Gandhi, deeply honored but did not change Martin's way of dealing with regular people.

In the summer before our wedding, Yehudi Menuhin had invited him to spend a day on his estate in Gstaad, Switzerland, in the company of painter Oskar Kokoschka and actor Peter Ustinov. This casual and unrehearsed get-together of four rather unusual men, with the beautiful Swiss Alps as a backdrop, was made into an hour-long film for television.

With two exceptions, the countless honorary degrees bestowed upon my husband left him basically unaffected. The first, the "doctor theologiae honoris causa," from the ancient University of Prague while he was Hitler's prisoner, moved him to tears. The last degree, from the University of Puerto Rico, honored him together with the man whose violent death he would never stop mourning, Martin Luther King, Jr.

With equanimity, Martin accepted medals and decorations from right and left alike, provided that they were bestowed upon him for his peace efforts and for no other reason. Those honors included the Soviet Union's Lenin Peace Prize Medal and the International Lenin Peace Prize as well as both the German Federal Republic's highest and most distinguished order, the Cross of Merit, and its counterpart from the German Democratic Republic. The medals usually disappeared into a drawer.

Among his close personal friends he counted Albert Schweitzer, Robert M. Kempner, who had been assistant chief prosecutor at the Nuremberg Trials, and the American writer Dorothy Parker. In his campaign for peace, he was joined by Linus Pauling and the Bishop of Chichester George Bell, who, during the Hitler years, never ceased to protest the pastor's incarceration.

The first West German Chancellor, Konrad Adenauer, decidedly not one of Martin's admirers, was not amused by remarks that the churchman had dropped in a 1949 interview with the noted American reporter Margaret Higgins, in which he made the statement that, as far as he was concerned, "The Republic of West Germany was begotten in Rome and born in Washington."

In the fall of 1971, Pimen, the Patriarch of the Russian Orthodox Church, invited both of us for a rather spectacular stay in Moscow and Zagorsk. During the formal banquet in my husband's honor, I noticed something that almost caused me to choke. Before the meal, with the obligatory huge portion of black caviar as a starter, one of the nuns, noiselessly tending our table of twelve, approached Pimen to remove his headgear and to fasten a huge, snow-white, starched napkin the size of a table cloth to our esteemed host's front with a hideous black safety pin, after first lifting the long white beard that covered his chest.

At home, not all of our visitors who sought Martin's advice about personal problems, political issues, or church matters came with amicable intentions. Some of those barely able to disguise their animosity were quite baffled when they found that he, whom they had come to challenge and insult, never attempted to force his own convictions on them. It happened more than once that ideological adversaries, who stamped into Martin's study with the sole purpose of giving this political renegade a piece of their own minds, left visibly mellowed and in inexplicable awe over so much unexpected tolerance and kindness on the part of the pastor, who seldom failed to cast a spell on friend and foe. As one of his biographers expressed it, "He could charm the birds out of the trees."

Billy Graham, before holding a mass rally in Frankfurt, came to pay his respects to the man he so admired. "*Herr* pastor," he asked at the end of a long conversation, "can you tell me what might be wrong about my approach?" Martin answered, "Instead of telling the people that they *must* embrace Jesus Christ, ask instead the question if they *will* embrace Him!" Billy Graham never forgot.

A lasting concern for my husband remained the young generation in Germany, intentionally cheated out of the truth, willfully kept in the dark about their nation's sinister past. He maintained that it was not only the geographical and ideological border that split Germany; the infinitely more disastrous crack was the one separating the generations. "What can young people learn from us?" he kept asking. "Love of truth, of freedom? Sincerity? Tolerance? Courage? Responsibility? The fact is that they have to be protected from adults claiming to know the meaning of freedom. About liberty? Liberty is worthless without responsibility." Next to the Statue of Liberty in New York, he said, there should be a Statue of Responsibility!

Having reached the conclusion that the gravest of all sins was that of omission, the future of the church that had so miserably failed in its mission filled him with deep pessimism. If it had been up to him, he would have done away with the hierarchy that, in his mind, had grown out of proportion. "If we are to continue as a church, we will have to start from scratch, as a humble little group of beggars carrying the message of Jesus," he said. The attitude of the church, not different from any other business enterprise, caused him "more mental pain than he had suffered during all the years in the concentration camps." This confession, made repeatedly in public, even before television cameras, did not meet with the general approval of the institution that had only reluctantly, and under his pressure, admitted to a mere fraction of its guilt in a lukewarm statement.

In addition to holding services, he lectured in universities and churches all over the world. While able to jot down an address by pencil in one night, in German as well as in his faultless English, the preparation of a sermon was a different matter. As he grew older, this chore would take him at least a week. The word of God, the gospel of his Lord Jesus did not allow for improvisation; every word had to be carefully weighed before being put on paper.

We, who lived with him, soon spotted the first symptoms of the mysterious disease that I came to call "acute sermonitis." For at least two days, groaning and moaning, not unlike a woman about to give birth, he would labor over clearing his desk, moving stacks of papers in huge piles from one side to the other. The next step was to heave the rickety old typewriter, model 1923, on which he had written all his sermons during the Nazi era, onto the desk in front of him. After gathering the Bible and other necessary and helpful literature, it would take a while until he put the first sheet of paper in the machine. And then, like the sun breaking through dark clouds, came the first sentence. By that time, we knew that the patient would eventually recover.

During the week following these painstaking preliminary procedures, he would summon me to his study at regular intervals, needing to share his thoughts with me, asking for my approval or disapproval. He wrestled with every sentence before putting it on paper; after all, it was God's own word that he had the duty and privilege to convey to a congregation. During this week, he usually worked until the wee hours of the morning, enveloped in a thick blue cloud of cigar smoke, which made me gasp for breath each time I entered the study. It was my job to keep him supplied with thermos bottles of strong, black coffee, boxes of chocolate, and his cherished sour lemon drops; eating normal meals as well as getting a good night's rest seemed almost annoying to him.

The final stage of a week's labor was reached when he asked me to fold the finished manuscript, typed on half sheets, and secure it with thread, so he could easily turn the pages. Never using a sermon twice, at the end of his life there was an abundance of sermons and lectures, now preserved in the archives of the Church of Hessen and Nassau in the city of Darmstadt, available for generations to come.

With the same enthusiasm that prompted him to work hard, he threw himself into a state of utter laziness when vacationing on the islands of Madeira and Mallorca. Armed with an ample supply of books, stretched out on a deck chair, he would read through mountains of volumes written by his favorite authors like Agatha Christie and Georges Simenon. At regular intervals, he put binoculars to his eyes to follow a ship in the far distance, reminiscing about his years in the Imperial German Navy. Basking in the sun, his olive skin totally immune to sunburn, he soon turned the color of a coconut. The only activity interrupting this relaxed state was an occasional header into the water. Marcus and I, armed with fins and snorkels, waited at the bottom of the sea, ready to rescue him in case of an unexpected emergency. Filled with new energy and refreshed by the sun, the sea air, and the various regional wines, he would return to his desk at home.

Chapter Eighty-Three
Life in Germany

Getting used to daily life in Germany after years in New York turned into an exasperating experience. Everything was alien and most of it outright unpleasant, like the nightmare of shopping in markets that lacked most of the goods I was used to, from A to Z, meaning from avocados to zucchini. Only when Marcus, holding a part-time job with the US Armed Forces, gained PX and commissary privileges, was I able to obtain items like Kleenex, peanut butter, Jell-O, and meat cuts not mutilated by being butchered into little fragments. With checks not accepted and credit cards not yet invented, I found myself carrying bundles of cash all the time. Worse than anything else was the complete absence of what is called customer service, without which no business in America would survive.

Required to deposit purchases on a conveyor belt, they were then registered, after which it was up to the customer to bag them, if she had been clever enough to bring her own receptacle. Since no store would ever dream of delivering anything, be it food, liquor, drugs, or clothes from the cleaners, I wondered if anybody really cared about business or not. This state of non-service to customers would survive my entire stay in West Germany. Returning or exchanging items for whatever reasons was preceded by a Gestapo-like interrogation. In rigid compliance with yet another ridiculous law, all shops, whether their owners liked it or not, had to open and close at specific hours, minutes to be exact, a procedure that turned cities nationwide into ghost towns at early evening and for the duration of the weekend.

What I found particularly chilling was not so much the way the Germans treated foreigners—in those days a mere minority—but the manner in which they dealt with each other. The general lack of common courtesy, terms like "excuse me," "sorry," "please," and "thank you" were literally unknown, while the constant pushing and shoving without ever apologizing shocked me. Coming from New York, I was used to thanking the driver when leaving a bus. The same practice here got me stupefied looks of complete indifference, so I gave up the habit. Children were shouted at, at best treated in a patronizing style and without the respect they deserved, nobody minding their mental and physical abuse in public.

Another fact that never ceased to amaze and amuse me was the people's almost enthusiastic eagerness to comply with "the law." Pedestrians would rather hover at curbs for hours than dare to cross a street against the light, even with no car in sight. Those daring to cross against the light had to be prepared to find themselves verbally and sometimes even physically accosted by "law-abiding" citizens. Simple rules based on common sense were replaced with written directives, orders, and threats regulating every step of daily life, in view of which the general behavior behind the wheel of a car was hard to bear.

In Germany, as the only European country without a speed limit, the autobahn seemed the favorite place where all rules of simple civility could be disregarded. Aside from the nightmarish tempo, the liberal use of horns, murderous headlight blinking, and tailgating were commonplace. American soldiers had to undergo mandatory instruction before being permitted to take the wheel, a situation that led an American general to voice his own private opinion; "Impose a speed limit on the Germans," he maintained, "and they will start another war." If nothing else, the battlefield autobahn served as an equalizer; not the most expensive car, but the fastest one was the winner in this free-for-all that claimed record-breaking numbers of victims.

What few of the unsuspecting newcomers to the inhumane conditions existing on German highways realized was the fact that these hazardous driving habits were by no means restricted to uncouth rowdies; the refined, meticulously dressed gentleman with impeccable manners, with whom you had shared an interesting conversation at a cocktail party, minutes later could turn into a lethal enemy behind the wheel of his Mercedes or BMW. .

With practically nothing left to an individual's own initiative, I came to the conclusion that the population still enjoyed being told what to do and what not to do. After all, they were used to it. While I could appreciate a necessity for foreigners having to register with the local police, I discovered that German nationals also had to report every single change in their address, including a move within the same building. To me, while these laws interfering with personal freedom were detrimental enough, much worse was the general opinion that these measures were not only justified, but served everyone's safety. The carrying of an identification card, unthinkable in the free society of America, was mandatory for every German citizen. It had to be produced upon demand for a policeman without prior provocation. This law had been extremely helpful during the Nazi era in rounding up unwanted citizens. Even some twenty-five years after the end of the Third Reich, Germany bore the earmarks of a police state. While in other democracies, the job of the police department was the maintenance of law and order, preventing and fighting crime, in Germany, the police were involved in every private aspect of life. They issued passports, driver's licenses, and something called a *fuehrungszeugnis*, an official document confirming a citizen's "good behavior," issued to future employers.

To my dismay, I found the standards of theater and movie productions at a deplorably low level. Tear-jerking trash and shallow slapstick junk replaced the outstanding performances immediately following the war when, freed from the Nazi-imposed "culture," in spite of the destruction, hunger, and cold, the arts seemed to derive almost uncanny strength from the devastation. Plays and movies dealing with the gruesome past were now considered a bore and certainly no longer desirable. Already in 1968, Franz Josef Strauss, the Bavarian minister-president, had advised his overjoyed fellow citizens to "step out of the shadow of Auschwitz." He saw no discrepancy between admonishing the Jews for holding a grudge over something that happened a quarter of a century before, and the innate Christian right to continue blaming the Jews for the death of Jesus Christ two thousand years ago. But that was, of course, a very different matter.

In the 1970s, American television productions of a rather questionable quality by far outnumbered those made in Germany. In order to make the shows palatable for a German audience, instead of presenting them with subtitles, they were subjected to the brutal procedure of dubbing. Not one movie or television show was spared, mutilated literally beyond recognition by sometimes hilariously distorted translations of the script, not to mention the obvious difference in lip movements. A gigantic industry had mushroomed after the war, which over the years developed into an independent subculture. It provided an army of lesser talented actors with the unique opportunity to substitute the unmistakable voices of Clark Gable, John Wayne, Marlene Dietrich, and Marilyn Monroe with their own, most of the time grotesquely incongruous to the originals they aimed to imitate. It remained a rather dubious pleasure to hear J. R. Ewing's alluring Texas drawl substituted by the nasal twang of a Prussian officer, Ben Cartwright's deep, sonorous voice replaced by a drill sergeant's bark, while both Marlene Dietrich and Marilyn Monroe came across with equally high-pitched squeaks.

My busy life at my husband's side and in the US Air Force Hospital left few opportunities for me to explore the city and its people, but I could not help noticing a certain species, mostly white-haired males between the ages of fifty and eighty, who still made me shudder. I kept wondering where they had been between 1933 and 1945. Just how many among them had been Hitler's eager helpers—ranging from pitiless spectators to savage henchmen—was anybody's guess. There was little doubt in my mind that the murderers were still among us. The myth of the *Wehrmacht* having been like any other army was stubbornly retained for decades. Only little by little did the rotten truth leak out, revealing that the legend of the "good German soldier" had been a fallacy. While atrocities, particularly those directed against Jews, had been blamed on the SS *Einsatzgruppen* and the police battalions, it was becoming known that wherever horrendous crimes were committed, the German Army had not been distant. Officers and simple soldiers had, in most cases without pressure, actively and not without pleasure participated in acts of mass slaughter.

Chapter Eighty-Four

REBELLION

In 1968, student uprisings in West Germany shook the Federal Republic. Young people, thoroughly disgusted with the fact that universities still operated under archaic rules, first suggested and then demanded the removal of old Nazis from leading positions. Twenty years after the war, the faculty of most teaching institutions still harbored a considerable number of those professors who, after the dismissal of their Jewish colleagues, had eagerly stepped into the gaps. The students' voices were brutally stifled by the police with truncheons, the scornful rebels branded as outcasts and potential enemies of the establishment, accused of willfully jeopardizing the young democracy. Only after their demands for peaceful reforms had continued to fall on deaf ears, did they proceed to violence, at first limited to the damage of public property. In their dismay over atrocities attributed to the Americans in Vietnam, they began to concentrate on damaging American military installations.

The core of the alliance that had begun as a mere student protest, now calling itself the Red Army Faction (RAF) under the leadership of Andreas Baader, Ulrike Meinhof, Jan-Carl Raspe, and Gudrun Ensslin, turned to militancy and naked terror. Having spurned the opportunity of discussing the problems with the rebels, the authorities went on a rampage. In a state of total hysteria, they mercilessly hunted everyone suspected of ideologically supporting the "enemies of the state." A new term was created: "sympathizers." The major culprits were eventually apprehended, tried, and sentenced to life in Stuttgart-Stammheim's high-security penitentiary where, despite all watchfulness, they still directed all RAF actions.

On September 9, 1977, those members of the RAF not yet apprehended dropped a bomb that shook the German Federal Republic to its foundations. In a meticulously prepared action, Hanns-Martin Schleyer, president of the West German Employers' Association, was snatched from his private car in broad daylight, an action in which his driver and four others were killed by bullets. The frantic search for Schleyer's whereabouts netted no results.

The abductors made the prompt discharge of eight jailed fellow terrorists a condition for Schleyer's safe release. They further demanded an aircraft, ready to transport them and their freed comrades to a country of their choice. Making sure that no foul play on the part of the government was involved, they decided that two hostages were to accompany them on the flight to their final destination, most likely located in the Near East—one of the hostages was to be a Swiss lawyer, the other was Martin Niemoeller. Without batting an eye, the eighty-five-year-old pastor agreed to offer his life in exchange for that of Schleyer, a former high-ranking member of the Nazi party and the SS, of whom he had never even heard.

Before the plan could be carried out, however, the German Lufthansa jet "Landshut," packed with tourists, was hijacked on the island of Mallorca with the support of Palestinian terrorists. After a five-day odyssey, refused landing permission at various airports, the craft finally managed to set down near the Somali capital of Mogadishu. There it was taken in a surprise attack, not without considerable bloodshed, by the G-9, the special German anti-terrorist task force, on October 18.

Their hopes now shattered, three of the incarcerated terrorists, Andreas Baader, Jan-Carl Raspe, and Gudrun Ensslin, ended their lives in their cells. Ulrike Meinhof had already committed suicide. On the day following the triple suicide, Hanns-Martin Schleyer was found murdered in the trunk of a car outside the French Alsatian town of Mulhouse, close to the German border. Not one member of the Schleyer family ever saw fit to thank the eighty-five-year-old pastor for his readiness to lay down his life for someone he had never met. This spectacular case, as well as those that followed, handled with brutality, insensitivity, and inefficiency on the part of the German authorities, would haunt the country for years to come. It had become an established and generally accepted fact that the dangers threatening the democracy came from the left, and from the left alone. Once singled out as a "leftist sympathizer," the victim of an almost medieval witch hunt was practically barred from all walks of professional and social life, his or her existence wiped out in a wave of mass hysteria, matching that of the McCarthy era in America.

Martin raised a warning voice that this kind of stubborn myopia, giving the far right a unique chance to develop, grow, and spread like a poisonous fungus, would eventually present a lethal danger to a republic that vehemently continued to deny the very existence of right-wing, nationalist tendencies. Not long after his death, this prophecy came true; Nazi-oriented skinheads, dead-set on ousting undesirable foreigners from their Aryan fatherland, met with little, if any, resistance from the authorities, while they roamed the streets, marched in well-organized torchlight parades, bawled Nazi songs, and swung their flags with swastika-like emblems right under the noses of the police. Houses occupied by asylum seekers were set afire, and innocent blood was shed.

Chapter Eighty-Five
Film and Farewell

In the summer of 1981, our house on Brentanostrasse was converted into a film studio. Twice a week over a period of two years, the "Doc-Film," noted for several award-winning documentaries, came for a few hours at a time to shoot what was to become a feature-length movie depicting the life of Pastor Martin Niemoeller, from his days in the Imperial German Navy, to his courageous resistance against Hitler, to pacifism as the final goal in his long life. Under the title "What Would Jesus Say?" the finished product was, after Martin's death, presented to audiences in West German movie theaters as well as in the GDR before being exported to other countries.

With the final scenes in the process of being wrapped up, Martin suffered a decline in his health so severe that I knew what was coming. Our last trip abroad had taken us to Greensboro, North Carolina, for Marcus' graduation with honors from Greensboro College. Martin was one of the two dignitaries invited to speak at the commencement exercises, the other being Senator Sam Ervin, the tough old man who had been instrumental in bringing about the downfall of Richard Nixon.

With his father's health failing, instead of entering Duke University School of Medicine, Marcus decided to enroll as a foreign student at the venerable Johannes Gutenberg University Medical School in Mainz, founded some five hundred years prior. With Mainz just seventeen kilometers from Wiesbaden, he was able to live with us, a fact that filled me with confidence and my husband with sheer joy. While Marcus completed an "externship" at the US Air Force Hospital, something occurred that turned the focus of the world on the city of Wiesbaden.

On January 17, 1981, the hospital had been notified that the fifty-two American hostages, held by Iran for a total of four hundred and forty-four days, would be released; their first destination would be the Wiesbaden US Air Force Hospital. As soon as news of the hostages' possibly imminent arrival leaked out, the international media invaded the area. They settled bumper-to-bumper for a possible long wait in their vans, outside the barbed wire fence that had been installed earlier to keep out terrorists. In spite of top security, there was no trick the reporters did not try to smuggle themselves into the hermetically sealed facility, including posing as cleaning personnel or hiding in laundry trucks. Inside, hasty preparations had been made to convert an entire second floor wing of the main building, later named "Freedom Hall," from ordinary wards to comfortable living quarters for the victims of Ayatollah Khomeini's rage.

In order to avoid having my car searched twice a day from top to bottom, and equipped with a special pass, I walked the short distance from the house to my office. After days of almost unbearable tension, the arrival at Rhein-Main Airport in Frankfurt finally took place in the early morning hours of January 21. In Wiesbaden, now in a regular "hostage fever," church bells throughout the town had begun to ring when the buses with their precious cargo reached the city limits, a beautiful gesture expressing the citizens' gratitude over the salvation of fifty-two human beings. While the media lay in ambush at the front gate, we managed to sneak the buses inside the compound through the back. Once all of the ex-hostages were safely tucked away in their quarters, we regarded it as our foremost concern to protect them from the media before being debriefed. Their worn-out bodies and minds deserved a chance to recuperate. On the evening of their arrival, a beaming Jimmy Carter disembarked from a helicopter on the hospital landing pad. Both Marcus and I had the opportunity to shake the president's hand.

Four days after this joyful event, on January 25, Martin collapsed in the sacristy of the Luther Church after preaching a sermon. Apparently suffering cardiac arrest, he stopped breathing. Warned by a dark foreboding, I had carried an adrenaline shot in my purse that, administered by Marcus, brought him back to consciousness before his brain was affected. After being taken home, friends from the US Air Force Hospital, among them its commander, sped to his bedside. With rest and medication, the patient slowly recuperated, but somehow it was as if his life now seemed to take place on a different level. He had been too close to death, in his own description almost reaching the shore on "the other side" before being forced to return to us.

"Why?" he asked. "Why did you not let me go?"

A six-week stay in a sanatorium in the Bavarian Mountains, near the village of Kreuth, where I had spent my childhood summers, brought temporary relief but only delayed an irreversible process. Over the following months, the patient began losing weight, and the diagnosis, which Marcus and I shared only with his doctor, confirmed our worst suspicions: cancer. How long? Would he suffer pain? Should we tell him? We did not, for the simple reason that he would have come to loathe his decaying body, the body that had served him so well for almost a century. Though he never asked, we were certain he knew.

One of his last visitors was his revered friend Linus Pauling, the recipient of two Nobel Prizes who, like Albert Schweitzer, was a close ally in the fight for world peace. On an enchanted Indian summer afternoon, Marcus carried his father, now light as a feather, into the garden, and we were touched to see the two seasoned old peace veterans holding hands, laughing, and crying with joy over their unexpected reunion.

A few months later, on Christmas Eve, we lit the candles on a little tree in his bedroom for one last time. On January 14, 1984, Martin's ninety-second birthday, I arranged a big party in his honor, welcoming not only the entire family, but all those who wanted a chance to say their good-byes. Among the guests was the Metropolitan of Moscow, the patriarch's emissary. From his shabby suitcase, he brought forth a heavy gift, wrapped in brown paper—a kilo of caviar meant to speed up the revered patient's recovery. At the end of the day, I found the old priest hiding in a dark corner of the dining room, sobbing into his beard.

Before sending the visitors upstairs in groups of two or three, I warned everyone that tears were definitely out of order in the patient's presence. Overcome by emotion, some of them sat on the stairs outside the bedroom, seeking comfort by holding on to each other, while a trombone trio played all of Martin's favorite music. Propped up in bed by pillows, his emaciated face shone with joy. My hope that God might take him after that blissful day was not fulfilled, however.

With a nurse who came in once a day for one hour to lend a helpful hand, I was able to keep my promise never to send him to a hospital. In the comfort of familiar surroundings and far removed from the life-preserving, death-detaining devices routinely used in hospitals, he patiently awaited the end. Our family doctor had entrusted full medical care to Marcus, in spite of the fact that he was not yet a certified physician, limiting herself to the supervision and prescription of the necessary medication.

"Lord, what willst Thou have me do?" I kept asking.

"Let him go," said the Lord.

Chapter Eighty-Six
The Work Is Finished

During the final phase of his life on Earth, a cherished companion other than Marcus, his lovely fiancée Claudia, and myself, was Lassie, a little long-haired dachshund who belonged to my English friend Bertha. Each morning the little animal was delivered to the house, and she promptly ran up the stairs to the bedroom, jumped onto the bed, and placed herself across the patient's midsection. Martin stroked her silky-soft fur, enjoying the warmth of the small creature so aware of the comfort she was giving him.

Waiting for his Lord to call him home, my husband rarely spoke anymore; when he did speak, it was of the sea, the Mediterranean he loved so well, his thoughts drifting back to the days of his service in the Imperial German Navy. When he felt strong enough to read, it was not the Bible, worn out by the eight years of use in the cells of one prison and two concentration camps, but the hymnal of the Evangelical Church, a uniquely beautiful collection of all the anthems he knew by heart, particularly his favorite, "*Die Güldene Sonne*" ("The Golden Sun"). Soon he would see it in all its glory. Up to the end, he chuckled about the fact that he had survived Hitler for almost forty years, maintaining that, by keeping him safely locked away until the end of the Third Reich, the führer had most certainly saved his life. As a free man, sooner or later, he would have joined the resistance and ended on the gallows. And he smiled, in anticipation. We waited with him, each in his own way.

The family came, the children and the grandchildren from near and far, one after the other tiptoeing into the bedroom for one last word, one final embrace. On the Sunday before his death, a motion of his hand signaled that I should come close. With a faint gesture, too weak now to open his eyes, my husband put the golden wedding band that he had taken off his finger into my hand. Two days later, on Tuesday, March 6, at the peak of the carnival season, with a city having turned into a madhouse of drinking and dancing, Marcus, Claudia, and I realized that the end was imminent. Marcus, concerned over my state of exhaustion, had spent the previous night next to his dying father.

With the first blackbirds singing their jubilant evening song in the birch tree outside the window during the last minutes before the dusk turned to darkness, at seventeen minutes after five o'clock, Martin Niemoeller took a final deep breath under a simple crucifix, the one that Jack Bowling, the American admiral and a close friend, had made for him as a token of his love. Marcus placed the stethoscope on his father's chest. Turning around to us he said softly, "He has gone out to sea." Surrounded by those he loved best, Martin, after ninety-two years and fifty-two days, joined his ancestors, the peaceful expression on his still face conveying the reassuring message that he had reached the other shore.

No stranger was to touch him, so the three of us prepared him for his last journey. Only when they came to put him in his coffin did Marcus and Claudia send me out of the room. In his black pastor's robe, well-worn in the service of his Lord, a small bouquet of snowdrops from the garden in his folded hands, he lay in state in a downstairs room, so all his friends could bid their final respects. We kept him in the house for two days, days that were filled with utter peace.

As Luke 2:29 reads, "Lord, now lettest Thou thy servant depart in peace, according to Thy word, for mine eyes have seen Thy salvation."

Filled with deep gratitude, we returned the unopened package containing morphine to the pharmacy. God had been merciful; Martin died without suffering the agonizing pains usually accompanying the deadly disease that had ravaged his body.

In accordance with his wishes, he was laid to rest in the red Westfalian soil of the little rural cemetery in the village of Wersen near the city of Osnabrück, from which his four grandparents had come. One year later, the gravesite that I had designed would bear a cross of black African granite with the words "Lord, what willst Thou have me do?" Next to it, a granite plate bore the necessary data:

D. Martin Niemöller
Pastor in Berlin-Dahlem 1931-1945
Hitler's prisoner 1937-1945
President of the Church of
Hessen and Nassau 1947-1964
President of the World Council
of Churches 1961-1968
Confessor of the faith
Defender of peace

So gentle was the manner in which the Church of Hessen and Nassau supported me through the hardships following their former president's death, that I felt carried on angels' wings.

The neighborhood church, the Lutherkirche in Wiesbaden, where Martin had collapsed, was the scene of a memorial service, attended by dignitaries from all over the world, who paid their respects to Hitler's most outstanding foe. The three-hour ceremony was broadcast live in its entirety on German National Television. William Shores, the African American baritone who was a close family friend, sang Martin's favorite hymn: "Rock of ages, cleft for me," which had also been the one Christian hymn cherished by the man who had never stopped praying for Adolf Hitler's personal prisoner, Mahatma Gandhi. Traffic in Wiesbaden stood still while, in a peaceful demonstration, thousands of mourners marched silently through the streets of the city. Holding the first daffodils of the season, which they ultimately placed at our front gate, they paid homage to the man they had loved.

With profound feelings of gratitude for the many blessed years far outweighing the grief over the loss of my husband, I now had to accept the fact that a door had irrevocably closed on the most wondrous chapter of my life.

Chapter Eighty-Seven
EAST GERMANY

Among those who wished to express their condolences during the reception following the memorial service was a delegation from East Germany, the so-called German Democratic Republic. A long-winded letter from Erich Honecker, praising my late husband, was handed to me by the country's chargé d'affaires. My casual remark that the GDR, the "other" Germany, was practically unknown to me, had consequences that I could not possibly foresee. One week later, I found myself in the possession of another Honecker communication, an official invitation to visit the German Democratic Republic, not just for a day, but for two weeks, and in the style usually reserved for heads of state, as I was soon to find out. The invitation, placed in a red folder with the GDR's emblem of hammer and circle, was hand-delivered to me by a messenger. Vastly amused by the thought of having been on the Communist hit list until the day I married Martin Niemoeller, I accepted.

On June 29, 1984, I boarded a train to Erfurt, an undertaking that in itself was nothing short of a miracle. Since the erection of the Berlin Wall, with the exception of a handful of foreign tourists as well as political functionaries, the right of Germans to travel back and forth was strictly reserved for aged pensioners in both directions.

Having flatly rejected the GDR's request to mail my US passport to their Diplomatic Mission in Bonn to have it stamped with the entry visa, I was informed that the required permit would be issued to me on the train. Sharing the first-class compartment with several elderly pensioners, I noticed that, as we approached the "Iron Curtain," some of them were frantically trying to hide forbidden items like Western magazines from sight, for fear that the "People's Police" would confiscate them, or worse. Following a hunch, I told them that, at least today, they had nothing to fear, being certain that the police would know better than to search the compartment in the presence of their president's guest of honor. As it turned out, I was correct in my assumption; at the border, displaying almost embarrassing servility, two policemen entered the compartment, saluted, and, leaving my co-travelers gasping, restricted themselves to stamping my passport, after which they saluted again and left.

On the platform of the Erfurt station, the same one on which West German Chancellor Willy Brandt recently had been received by Erich Honecker on his first and only official state visit, I was met by two friendly but nervous females, one of them carrying a bouquet of red carnations, the only flowers abundantly available in East Germany, I would soon surmise. The women introduced themselves as my "escorts" for the weeks ahead. In truth, those "ladies-in-waiting" were obviously not solely delegated to please me, but to make sure I was never out of their sight, so I would only notice the sunny side of socialism and not the ever-present shabbiness and poverty lurking just around each corner, inches away from the ostensibly displayed Communist party splendor in every city and village we visited. It did not escape me that my two companions took turns each evening sending detailed telephone accounts to East Berlin, most likely reporting every remark to the "*Stasi*" (*Staatssicherheitsdienst*), the feared Secret Police. Wondering how much they really knew about me and my anti-Communist past—including the spy activities that I had been involved in some thirty-five years before while working for the anti-Communist, American-supported League Against Inhumanity—our way of communicating with one another turned into a rather amusing game. We reached what would be a silent understanding; not only did they probably know exactly who I was, but they also knew that I knew that they knew. Once that seemed an established fact, we had a wonderful time together.

Included in the red-carpet treatment was an official, government-owned, black Volga limousine, complete with Uwe, the baby-faced chauffeur, probably also a *Stasi* snitch. The wonderful German "Democratic" Republic, a worker's paradise, was presented to me on a golden platter. Undoubtedly, I would come to understand just why Honecker's precious jewel deserved to be protected by a wall, one that was constructed of concrete and tastefully adorned with control towers and ample supplies of barbed wire. I received the information that, contrary to the capitalists' false belief, it was not meant to prevent citizens from leaving the GDR, but solely to keep out vicious spies, common criminals, and the rest of the capitalist world, all green with envy and eager to destroy the unique achievements of Communism. At the time of my visit, some three dozen GDR citizens attempting an escape had been shot dead at the Berlin Wall, while those caught in the act faced long-term prison sentences.

With all sightseeing tours meticulously scheduled ahead of time, wherever we turned up, be it at a church, Luther's Wartburg, or a museum, as soon as we approached, other visitors were chased aside like chickens with the gruff explanation that we were a "delegation," the one magic word in the alleged "classless society" that, like "sesame," opened all doors for those who were a little more equal than others. I became used to the fact that, wherever I appeared, some eager official, party emblem displayed proudly in his or her lapel, would surely be laying in ambush to greet me with the obligatory, oversized bouquet of red carnations. I do not remember just how many hotel chambermaids happily profited from this generosity.

Dining in posh restaurants, restricted to the party elite and out of bounds for those underlings not in the possession of hard Western currency, I tasted delicious food, not excluding Russian caviar, served Russian style in soup plates with thick slices of black bread, accompanied by streams of vodka, champagne from the Crimea, and excellent local wines. Residing exclusively in plush VIP hotel suites, all probably bugged, a vastly amusing incident in Leipzig's top hotel caused my two ladies-in-waiting to almost sink through the floor with sheer embarrassment. A dumpy-looking, high-ranking officer in the uniform of the rich and mighty Soviet Union had hammered at the door of my suite. Profusely sweating and swaying from more than a slight overdose of vodka, he urged me to buy his prize collection of cheap plastic spoons, in the ardent but futile hope of receiving US dollars in exchange.

It was in Leipzig's Thomas Church, while placing flowers on Johann Sebastian Bach's grave, that I came to the conclusion that this deeply moving moment had made the entire trip worthwhile. After visiting Anna's village and her grave in the Spreewald region, our two-week tour ended in Potsdam, where a true and unexpected surprise was waiting for me. I was received by a city delegation, red carnations and all, in the modest house, actually the shabby room, where I was born. With an abundance of garbage trucks in the yard, the deteriorated building was now fittingly occupied by the city's sanitation department.

A few hours later, in the full realization that, in spite of all efforts, respective ideological differences had definitely not been overcome, we bade a tearful good-bye at Checkpoint Charlie.

Displaying my best manners, I sent a thank-you note to Erich Honecker and was surprised by the announcement that yet another representative of the GDR was on his way to me. With the conspicuous black limousine tactfully parked around the corner, the Communist Party chairman's messenger, between sips of the tea I offered him in one of the kaiser's own dainty porcelain teacups, informed me of his lord and master's special message to me that, being of a rather delicate nature, was best not put into writing.

The chairman was extending an invitation to take up permanent residence in the German Democratic Republic, where Pastor Niemoeller's widow would enjoy all the privileges of a highly honored guest, including a villa in the town of my choice, a chauffeur-driven limousine, and, last but not least, an "open"—meaning unlimited—bank account. Furthermore, I would be allowed to keep my US citizenship and slip through the "protective wall" in my own American car whenever I wished. My visitor made it quite clear that I was going to be not just a little, but a lot more equal than the vast majority of happy workers in the classless society.

In a written note, I politely rejected the generous proposition.

One year before the unification that caused Honecker's fall, I sent him one last letter, asking that a family of six, a physician, his dentist wife, their three children, and the grandmother, be let out of his gilded cage. The Bishop of Berlin had turned to me as a last resort to help this particular family who, for years, had been harassed beyond description by the *Stasi*. The party chief must have been too dumbfounded to turn down my audacious request for the simple reason that I had never before asked him for a favor. After the family indeed received immediate permission to leave, the chairman saw fit to express his dismay over my demand in a letter, one that was not delivered by hand, but came by ordinary mail. From the message's admonishing tone, I gathered that he had not been overly amused by my demand, but decided that I could live very well with his scorn.

To my surprise, the permanent visa entitling me to enter the GDR was not withdrawn, so I kept on driving through Checkpoint Charlie whenever I pleased. Until the day in November 1989 when the Berlin Wall crumbled, I visited friends in their wretched isolation, smuggling tons of forbidden goods back and forth. The only "merchandise" I never dared take across the border was fugitives; if caught, while I had little to fear, the illegals faced possible life sentences.

Chapter Eighty-Eight
New Beginnings

During the weeks following my husband's death, thousands of condolence messages poured in from all over the world; it would take me eighteen months to answer them all. The Church of Hessen and Nassau offered to stick my notes into envelopes, address, and mail them to save me time and costs. Without their help and generosity, I do not know how I would have coped with the situation. The first telegram from the United States reached me on March 7. It came from Washington and read as follows:

> When he finally realized the onslaught of Nazi ideology on human values, Martin Niemoeller, the Pastor of the Protestant congregation of Dahlem, spoke out in an unmistakable voice. In a speech delivered before students at Göttingen on June 17, 1946, he confessed to his silence. Quote: I am guilty, I kept silent. I only began to speak up when the church was affected. And yet, he of all people surely was not guilty. Quite to the contrary, he did speak out and he did suffer. He spent eight years in the concentration camps of Sachsenhausen and Dachau, for he had the courage that so many were lacking. On behalf of the United States Holocaust Memorial Council, I extend my deepest condolences to you and all mankind on the loss of a man who defied the forces of evil. Elie Wiesel, Chairman U.S. Holocaust Memorial Council.

Auschwitz survivor Elie Wiesel, no stranger to me as author of the book *Night*, had entered my life. With one window forever closed, it soon became evident that another was about to open.

In September 1984, I traveled to Washington to attend a four-day Holocaust conference held in honor of "Righteous Gentiles," those death-defying individuals who, during the Nazi era, had risked persecution and death by saving Jewish lives. Upon my arrival in the State Department's huge Dean Acheson Auditorium for the opening ceremony, someone in the large crowd pointed out the host who had asked me to participate at this great gathering as an honored guest. When I introduced myself to him, without a word, the slender man with the melancholy dark eyes took me into his arms. There was no need for words.

A few hours later, I found myself included in the small circle of handpicked guests, asked to attend a luncheon hosted by the sponsor of the conference, Secretary of State George Shultz. After four magnificent days, the Chairman of the United States Holocaust Memorial Council Elie Wiesel closed the conference with a few remarks about Pastor Martin Niemoeller's outstanding courage during the days of inhumanity. Six months later, in Elie's wood-paneled library on New York's Central Park West, something of an earthshaking nature occurred, causing my life to take a totally unexpected turn.

Following a decision never to speak about his own fate, the death of his parents, and his little sister, the survivor of Auschwitz and Buchenwald had reluctantly broken his vow of silence only after François Mauriac, the noted French writer, humanist, and Nobel Prize laureate for literature, had convinced him of the necessity not only to speak, but to put his painful experiences into writing. When I declined to answer his detailed questions about my own past, he must have sensed that I, too, was a victim of the widespread illusion among survivors that, as long as I did not talk about the tragedy that had struck my family, there was still a remote chance it had not happened. He was absolutely correct in this assumption because, in my mind, the loss of my father, my cousins, Werner and Hans-Bernd von Haeften, as well as the constant persecution by the Nazis, would become an irrevocable reality only if I spoke about it. Ignoring my frantic objections that I could not and would not under any circumstances elaborate upon this dark chapter, he said, "*You must!*" Elie made it quite clear that he was not going to take no for an answer.

Standing by the window, my eyes focusing on the park below me in its fresh spring beauty, for the first time in forty years, I found myself grasping for words that described my father's suffering, his lonely death, not leaving out a single painful detail. When I had finished, the man who had freed me from the heavy burden of silence took me gently by the shoulders. Looking me straight in the eyes, he simply said, "And now you have to begin speaking about it in public!" When I protested that I could never do that, he said four words that would determine my future, "Of course you can."

In the same soft tone, he would later tell me to write a book about my life. Write a book? I could never do that either!

"Of course you can."

On October 12, 1984, a few days after my return from Washington, my mother died. Like my husband, she was allowed to take her last breath surrounded by loved ones in her own home, in the house she had courageously defended against destruction. With her own stamina, she had fought the aftereffects of a massive stroke that she had suffered twelve years before. Against all medical predictions, motivated solely by her iron will, she managed to recover for the simple reason that she would not permit a handicap to change her accustomed lifestyle more than absolutely necessary. Her attending physician had taken me aside and said, "Have no illusion, this clock has run out," to which I retorted, "dear doctor, you do not know my mother!"

Toward the end, which came gently a few weeks after her ninety-third birthday, she began making an honest effort to overcome her antipathy to God, whom she somehow imagined to be an awesome and cantankerous old man, in all likelihood bearing a distinct resemblance to her own unloved father. She just could not forgive him, the allegedly Almighty One, for permitting his only begotten son to be sacrificed on the cross and still expect to be loved by her or anybody else. Furthermore, she kept maintaining that if God had only been married, the world He created would not be in such a deplorable mess.

On a golden October day, the trees afire with bright autumn colors, we laid her to rest in Dahlem's ancient cemetery of St. Anne's, in the shadow of Martin's church. Having lost both my husband and my mother within seven months, I knew the time had come for me to go home, but where was home?

After all these years, I still felt like a total alien in Germany. Home was New York, but my plan for an immediate return to the United States was ruled out by Marcus' decision to accept a position as a physician at the University Hospital in Zurich, Switzerland, the world-famous Canton Spital. He and Claudia, now also a certified physician, had married and were planning their future together.

How could I possibly put the Atlantic Ocean between myself and my only son, my daughter-in-law, and eventual grandchildren? After having made the decision to stay on in Wiesbaden until they both were ready to go to the United States, I decided to put closure to my years with Martin and left the spacious "fortress" on Brentanostrasse, even though the church was ready to remodel it in order to fit my requirements. I moved to a smaller residence and picked up my life by returning to my job as a caseworker at the US Air Force Hospital. I had no reason to regret my resolution to remain in the Hessian capital for the time being, as one of over thirty thousand US citizens, most of them affiliated with the military. Headed by its young and energetic Lord Mayor Achim Exner, Wiesbaden's city government generously extended to me all the privileges of an "honorary citizen," the same status my husband had enjoyed.

In the fall of 1985, following what at first seemed like a whim but grew into an inexplicable urge, I enrolled in a special Hebrew course for beginners at a local language academy, my initial goal being the ability to read the Bible in its original language. To my surprise, I found the Hebrew letters, beginning with aleph, beth, and gimmel, so uncannily familiar that I could not rid myself of the feeling that long ago, in a previous existence, maybe a totally different dimension, these characters had actually been part of my life, the circumstances of which I could not remember.

Chapter Eighty-Nine
A New Life

Through my friends Elsie and Fred Meininger, Jewish refugees from Wiesbaden who now resided in New York, I received my first invitation to give a lecture at their Upper Manhattan synagogue, Hebrew Tabernacle. After receiving the rabbi's invitation to be the speaker on the forty-eighth anniversary of the November pogrom, "Kristallnacht," I learned that Dr. Ruth Westheimer, better known simply as "Dr. Ruth," with her family active members of the Temple, was sponsoring my appearance. On November 9, 1986, my host Dr. Robert Lehman, rabbi of this large Reform edifice on Fort Washington Avenue, graciously permitted me a glance into the sanctuary fifteen minutes before the service was to begin. I could not believe my eyes, and neither could my host; every seat was taken, causing him to remark dryly that a crowd that size was usually only expected during the High Holy Days.

Seated on the bimah between Dr. Ruth's husband, Manfred Westheimer, and the rabbi, I regretted the fact that I was still not able to follow the service in Hebrew, but had to use the English translation in the prayer book. Following Dr. Lehman's introduction, I stepped forward and did what I had believed to be impossible; for almost forty minutes, I was able to hold the congregation's undivided attention. When I was finished, I received a standing ovation that brought tears to my eyes. Light years seemed to have passed since I had heard Elie Wiesel's fateful words, "Of course you can!"

During the reception that followed the service, a long line of worshippers formed to greet me, to shake my hand, and to share some of their stories with me. Most of them were elderly people, almost all of German origin, now residing in Washington Heights, jokingly called "Frankfurt on the Hudson." Some just wanted to touch the widow of the man they all admired who, in spite of all his suffering, found it necessary to stand up and publicly confess to his own part of the guilt while still a free man. One old lady rolled up her sleeve, and there it was, *the number*. Totally overcome with emotion, I did what Martin would have done; I asked her to forgive me, for not having a number tattooed on *my* arm.

My appearance at Hebrew Tabernacle resulted in my receiving more invitations than I could handle. Apparently, it was through word of mouth that one rabbi handed me to the next. In addition, my dear friend Henry Marx, editor in chief of the *Aufbau*, America's only German Jewish biweekly publication, and Dr. Eric Stoerger, also connected with the newspaper, went out of their way to negotiate speaking engagements for me. So over the following years, I took my message to Reform and Conservative congregations, as well as universities and colleges mainly in New York City, New York State, Connecticut, New Jersey, and Pennsylvania. I was even asked to address the Board of Rabbis in Philadelphia. With each appearance, even though I was still not quite certain about the goal I wanted to achieve, I realized that I was now walking in the right direction, in the direction of home.

After speaking at Temple Habonim on Manhattan's West Side, I received an invitation from Dr. Gunter Hirschberg, rabbi of Rodeph Sholom on West 83rd Street, to address his congregation. Originally from Berlin, Gunter became a cherished friend until his untimely death only a few years later. The best, however, was yet to come! Franz and Marianne Winkler, originally from Munich and Berlin, respectively, patrons and members of Temple Emanu-El on New York's 5th Avenue and close friends of the Temple's Senior Rabbi Dr. Ronald B. Sobel, suggested to him that I address his congregation, the largest Reform Jewish synagogue in the world. The date was set for April 23, 1987, a fateful day for me because on that date, forty-two years earlier, I had left the raging battle of Berlin on horseback.

Having imagined the revered head of this famous institution, which had three more rabbis, as a white-bearded patriarch bent with old age, I was very much surprised to see before me an athletic and extremely handsome, slender, and, in spite of his prematurely gray hair, youthful and alert-looking man. His radiant smile, the warm expression in his beautiful, dark eyes, and his keen sense of humor swept away my fears almost instantly. Before the service was to begin, my host asked me to spend a few minutes with him in his study, where I asked him who was going to preach the sermon. Looking at me, he simply said, "You, my dear! You are the sermon!"

Seated on one of the high-backed chairs on the bimah of the gigantic sanctuary, to my right Dr. David Posner, one of the Temple's associate rabbis, and to my left the senior rabbi, I felt all my nervousness had disappeared. Throughout the liturgy preceding the sermon, Dr. Sobel reassuringly held my hand until it was time to step forward and begin addressing the crowd of over eight hundred worshippers. Throughout my forty-minute presentation, one could have heard a pin drop.

Looking back on this particular day, which marked a true highlight in my life, I can honestly say that, in spite of the vastness of the structure and the large congregation, I never felt safer or better protected than in the enormous, octagonal marble pulpit, its walls surrounding me like those of a mighty fortress. I knew that this was *my* Temple, this was *my* rabbi, and this was *my* congregation. This was the home where I belonged.

Chapter Ninety
QUESTIONS OF FAITH ... AND ANSWERS

Almost three years prior to my appearance at Temple Emanu-El, while attending July 20 memorial services in Berlin, I had met Albert Friedlander, keynote speaker for the somber occasion. I had no idea that this eminent liberal rabbi of Westminster Synagogue in London, Dean of the Leo Baeck College, was to become a key figure in my life as a future Jew. He would gently lead me, step by step, as my mentor and close friend on the road toward my goal. Prior to telling him of my decision to leave Christianity for the Jewish faith, I had shared my intentions only with Elie Wiesel. Without batting an eye, the man just remarked, "Of course—you want to go back to the roots."

Upon my return to Germany from yet another Holocaust gathering in Philadelphia on April 21, 1985, commemorating the end of the Third Reich, I traveled to Dachau to attend ceremonies observing the fortieth anniversary of the camp's liberation. Prompted by Elie Wiesel, the US Senate in Washington had approached me with the request that I accompany New Jersey's Jewish Senator Frank Lautenberg on his official visit to the camp at exactly the same hour when Ronald Reagan, having given in to the West German chancellor's pressure, visited SS graves at the Bitburg Cemetery. The senator arrived in Dachau with his entourage, including several survivors and officials, among them Dr. Franklin Littell, noted Methodist clergyman and scholar, and the only non-Jewish member of the US Holocaust Memorial Council. Lautenberg remained at the campsite long after the departure of the US media, insisting on learning every detail of its gruesome history. Deeply moved, he stood by my side in the cell where my husband had spent the worst four years of his life.

With the public focus being on Bitburg, the German media chose to ignore the senator's visit to Dachau; the event was covered exclusively by the American networks CBS, NBC, and ABC. This had as a distinct advantage the fact that all my friends in the United States were able to watch me on their TV screens that day.

One month later, Elie Wiesel came to Germany and, accompanied by our mutual friend, the filmmaker Erwin Leiser, we went to Martin's grave in Westfalia. The year before, during a visit to Buchenwald, I had picked up a little stone at the site of the former children's block, from which the orphaned Elie was liberated. Handing it to him at the cemetery, he placed it on my husband's grave, and I was sure that it carried a very special message.

Although I had left the church as an organization some twenty-five years prior to my marriage to Martin, never to be officially reinstated, the fact remained that I was raised as a Protestant Christian in more than just the religious sense of the word "Protestant." Even as a small child, the example of my parents had taught me the importance of protesting against injustice. Martin Niemoeller, the century's most noted Protestant, and his futile appeals to a Christian Church to repent for its appalling failures during the Shoah made me see the church through his eyes.

On my journey to shores yet unknown to me, I began to assess Jesus anew—Jesus the human being, Jesus my Jewish brother and my "rebbe," who never pronounced himself a god, but was elevated to divine honors only long after his death. It was not hard to accept Jesus as God's son, insofar as we were all His children, carrying within us the divine spark God Himself had planted. Driven by an irresistible impulse to travel beyond the beginnings of Christendom, in the hope of finding answers to all the questions withheld from me until now, I felt like all through my life, much like a spectator in a theater, I had been confined to watching a drama that began with the second act instead of the first.

If I were to embrace the Jewish faith, with all the consequences, it had to be for the right reasons, particularly at a point in history when "turning Jewish" in Germany had become some kind of a fad, particularly among certain groups with which I, the daughter and wife of active members of the resistance against the Nazis, an American of German heritage, did not wish to be identified. Stories made the rounds, according to which sons and daughters of Nazi perpetrators were using the act of conversion, identifying with the "victims" by becoming one of them, as a welcome alibi, a means by which the past could be rectified and the guilt of their elders in the Holocaust miraculously erased. Living in Israel, some of these chameleons became notorious for dramatically demonstrating their newly acquired Jewishness by parading through the streets of Jerusalem in black caftans, wearing payes, tzitzit, yarmulkas, and even shtreimels in the summer heat. The fact that they were the offspring of dictatorial fathers seemed to make them particularly well-suited for teaming up with ultra-orthodox fundamentalists in often violent efforts to force their own rigid religious laws on less observant Israelis.

To me, having been born into the nation of murderers, it was clear that, no matter what, I would have to live with my share of the German guilt for the rest of my days. This burden was in fact a new version of the "original sin," one that every native German would have to bear for centuries to come. As an adopted white American, I carried, as an additional load, part of the responsibility for having contributed to the slaughter of the Native Americans as well as the fate of African slaves.

In the summer of 1989, only months before the downfall of Communism, I went to Hungary for two weeks as the honored guest of the country's strong Reformed Church, whose presiding bishop felt that he owed this generous gesture to the widow of the man who had stood up for them in never-ending efforts to ease the chicanery directed by the Communist regime against the church. During a week's stay in Budapest, obviously the Communist showcase, I was able, through Bishop Toth's intervention, to visit the renowned Rabbinical Seminary, where I was received with great reverence by its director Rabbi József Schweitzer. At the Budapest Reformed Theological Academy, I addressed the students and future pastors at the annual commencement exercises, a solemn event after which a young Reformed pastor took me across the country to Debrecen, the stronghold of Hungarian Calvinism and the place where Hungarian independence had once been proclaimed.

Having successfully translated a friend's biography, *Elie Wiesel: Witness for Life*, from English into German for its publication in Germany, I was familiar with this district town near the Rumanian border, where the son of Shlomo and Sarah Wiesel, after reaching high school age, had to travel from his native Sighet at regular intervals to take the annual state exams required by the government. More than forty years of Communist mismanagement had been sufficient to turn the stately city into a shabby place. Particularly annoying were thick clouds emerging from stacks emitting black industrial smoke that caused a poisonous stench to settle over the town, making breathing difficult.

The six-hundred-year-old Debrecen was nicknamed the "Reformed Rome" because of its numerous churches. During a sightseeing tour, some of the dilapidated town's synagogues were pointed out to me, not a single one of which served as a house of worship anymore, for one obvious reason: there were no Jews. Looking at all the church spires stretching toward heaven, where "God in the Highest" was allegedly dwelling, something happened to me; like scales falling from my eyes, I suddenly realized that God in his glory, "God in the Highest," was not to be sought up there, at some immeasurable distance in the far blue yonder, but right here on Earth. Wherever I turned, there was God; *He* was not only in every creature, but in every stone, every grain of dust, and in every breath of air.

Throughout the years of learning, I would be taught that it was not faith in God that was of foremost importance, but rather the observance of His commandments; faith, if not transformed into deeds, was dead. I learned that the Jewish interpretation of "Love your neighbor as yourself" was "Love your neighbor, he is like you!" A Jew's entire faith can be expressed in this one commandment from the Torah, which basically means "Do as you would be done by." Nothing made more sense to me than the Jewish concept that God would only forgive trespasses against Him, while forgiveness of sins committed against fellow humans would have to come from those we had injured after humbly begging their forgiveness. Yom Kippur!

In Debrecen, I was received by the presiding bishop of the Reformed Church in his magnificent residence within the gigantic Reformed Academy's compound and extended the honor of signing the Golden Book. Attending Sunday services in the packed cathedral, I found myself squeezed between two Reformed pastors, who took turns translating every word of the liturgy and the sermon for me. Toward the end of the service, with the entire congregation moving single file toward the altar in order to receive Holy Communion, I knew that, in spite of the curious glances of the worshippers, I would not be able to join them. I felt glued to my seat. A voice within me told me that I would never again partake in this holiest of the sacraments, accepting the body and blood of Christ in the form of bread and wine.

Looking back, I can pinpoint this particular instant in the cathedral of Debrecen as the fateful one during which I consciously closed the door of Christianity behind me. I still remember the tremendous relief—spiritual, mental, and physical—over having rid myself of an awesome burden. The answer to my question "Lord, what willst Thou have me do?" was now clearly audible: "I want you to be Jewish!"

The exquisite joy that I felt on my journey back to the beginning was only slightly dampened by the realization that even the overwhelming influence of Martin Niemoeller, whose entire life had revolved around Jesus of Nazareth, had not been strong enough to convince me that I should accept Christ as the Messiah who, according to the Evangelist John, had stated that he alone was "the Way, the Truth, and the Life," that "no man cometh unto the Father, but by Me." These alleged declarations cost the lives of untold masses of Jews and others all over the world.

Fully aware of the pain my momentous step would have caused the husband I had adored, I knew that the driving force behind my decision was more powerful. For centuries, the Jews had been chastised for their refusal to accept Jesus as a moderator between God and themselves. In total agreement with them, I now felt certain that, without a "middleman," God in his immediacy was beginning to become truly alive for me.

In the Christian interpretation, the incontestability of the "original sin" was as self-evident as the belief that faith counted considerably more than deeds. The aim of the church had always been to have the focus directed to life eternal rather than to life on this Earth. Faith and fear, the promise of paradise to the obedient on one side, the threat of eternal damnation hanging as a sword over renegades on the other, had been successful in keeping the intimidated, ignorant masses teetering on an eternal seesaw between the hope of reward in a life hereafter and the mortal fear of forever burning in purgatory. This practice had, over the centuries, been a proven means for the church to maintain its power by keeping the flock under its control in a perpetual state of bondage, their sole hope being the promise of a better life in another dimension. If Jesus had indeed been the Messiah promised to us by God, why had his life and death neither improved the lot of mankind nor brought any lasting positive changes to the world? I, for my part, was willing to join the ranks of those still waiting for the first coming of the Messiah.

Chapter Ninety-One
Conversion

There was little doubt in my mind that the God I sought was going to be different from the one I, as a child, had been taught not just to worship, but to fear. There would be little resemblance between the awesome, nameless, unimaginable God and the white-bearded, stern old patriarch on his golden throne who, surrounded by angels and archangels, sat in judgment over "the living and the dead"; this was a procedure by which He, assisted by Jesus and the Holy Spirit, separating the chaff from the wheat, divided humans into two categories, those who had believed in Him, His son, and the Holy Spirit, and those who had not. While the pearly gates to heaven opened for the believers, the faithless were doomed to purgatory and eternal hell; it was that simple!

So far, my search for God seemed to have consisted chiefly of questions to which, in all likelihood, there were no answers. A most crucial one was why He, in His omnipotence, had chosen to leave His only begotten son, the Messiah, sent by Him into the world, to die a miserable death on the cross? I had come to the conclusion that, if my redemption depended on regarding this act of bloody barbarism as one of heavenly mercy, I wanted no part of it anymore.

The Christian acceptance of blood as the ultimate cleansing factor had always seemed revolting to me. A popular children's prayer suggested "Thy grace and Jesus' blood will wash away all sins." The cross, a stark and frightening instrument of torture, synonymous with suffering and salvation alike, now appeared to me as a symbol of sacrilegious obscenity, whether displayed in a church, a museum, as a work of art, or particularly as an "ornament"—a piece of jewelry around someone's neck. If Jesus was truly divine, how could his followers violate God's explicit commandment, "Thou shalt not make unto thee any graven image, or any likeness of anything that is in heaven above"? This unequivocal order had never been revoked, altered, or supplemented, so the wretched figure of the crucified Jesus caused me to cringe with compassion for him and embarrassment for those who tolerated this outrageous blasphemy. The "dogma of the Holy Spirit" as part of a "Trinity," totally incomprehensible to me, was as easily dismissed as the myth of the Immaculate Conception, the virgin birth of Jesus and the cult built around his mother Mary, the "mother of God."

What I began to see clearly was the disastrous part Christendom had played in the history of mankind. In the name of the "Prince of Peace," violent crimes, instigated and sanctioned by the church, had been committed for almost two millennia: from the Crusades, the

Spanish Inquisition, Martin Luther's suggestion to burn the synagogues of those Jews who stubbornly refused to accept the divinity of Jesus, all the way to their nearly total eradication amidst an enlightened and civilized Christian society.

During the Holocaust, in the hour of its greatest challenge, when the need for simple, decent human behavior became a vital issue, the church of Jesus Christ, including the figure of the "Holy Father," declared infallible deputy of God, proved a disaster of hitherto unknown dimensions. Only fifty years following the Shoah would there be a pope who asked the Jews' forgiveness for the Catholic Church's fatal role during the Third Reich. It was not, as Martin had expressed it so appropriately in his Göttingen address to students in 1946, that the church had done little, if anything, over the centuries to stem anti-Semitism in all its unexplained and unsurpassed cruelty; it had done nothing! The institutional church had not just been a fellow traveler of evil, but, in fact, was the instigator of all the pain and suffering connected with the abuse of those who refused to accept Christ as the Savior. When the centuries-old legend of the Jews being responsible for the death of God's son proved to be insufficiently effective, a brand-new concept of them as a foreign, alien, and therefore evil "race" was not only not protested, but actually supported by the Christian church. The statement of the self-styled German philosopher Heinrich von Treitschke, "The Jews are our misfortune!" was taken up with blissful enthusiasm. This eagerly accepted ideology, allowed to grow and fester without restraint, spread like a poisonous fungus, ultimately leading to the almost total elimination of the Jews as an unwanted race. The straight road to Auschwitz, in clear contrast to Hitler's twisted cross, had been paved by hatred, indifference, and pitilessness.

How could God have tolerated the nearly total extinction of His chosen people? How could the slaughter of six million humans ever be explained as an act of His benevolence, His mercy? If God had created all humans in His image, could it be that with each slaughtered victim a piece of Himself had been murdered, leaving Him only a minute fraction of the entirety He had originally been? Was it conceivable that He might have simply chosen to look the other way for a fraction of a second of His eternity while it all happened? With one and a half million children dead, where indeed had His eye, supposedly watching even over the sparrow, been? Would it be easier, from now on, to believe in a God who was not quite so perfect, not quite so omnipotent and merciful? A God who was possibly not infallible after all?

What about the perpetrators? Had not they, too, been created by Him in His image? I remembered Martin Niemoeller, who never ceased to blame himself for not having done enough to teach the Nazi butchers he had met the Gospel of Jesus Christ and the meaning of the Ten Commandments. By omitting to do so, had he not missed a God-given chance? After all, in prison and in the concentration camps, he had come into close contact with an abundance of SS henchmen, and before that, even with Hitler himself.

My journey back to the roots took six years. It was as toilsome as I had hoped it would be, yet I was determined to let no obstacle block my path. My mentor, Albert Friedlander, shared his knowledge and wisdom with me, providing advice, gentle guidance, and all the reading material I needed to study before he declared me ready for my formal conversion before a "Beth Din" at the Leo Baeck College in London. All during those years of learning, I could never rid myself of the feeling that the curtain to the first act, the one I had been prohibited from seeing, was about to open. By the spring of 1990, when I had mastered Hebrew sufficiently, Rabbi Friedlander felt that I was ready for the ultimate step, but I was uncertain; there seemed so much more to learn. I postponed my trip to London from one month to the next, until the day when I realized that the process of learning would not end with my conversion; it would truly begin only after I had been accepted as a bona fide member of the Jewish family.

In April of that year, during a lecture tour in the United States, I had asked my friend Rabbi Ronald Sobel for assistance. While the American Reform Movement does not require immersion in a ritual bath for a newcomer to the faith, it remained mandatory for Liberal Jews in England. However, with no *mikveh* available to other than Orthodox Jews in the vicinity of London, converts had to travel as far as Cardiff, Wales, to undergo the ceremony. Rabbi Sobel knew the answer to my problem and delegated his Assistant Rabbi, Amy Ehrlich, a stunningly beautiful, scholarly, and warmhearted woman, to accompany me to a *mikveh* on Manhattan's Upper West Side, where I underwent the procedure of ritual cleansing and rebirth that prepared me for my new Jewish identity.

In England, on June 11, 1990, my heart pounding, I entered the Leo Baeck College in the northern section of London, where my examination before the rabbinical court was to take place. Accompanied by Albert Friedlander, I found myself facing the three rabbis who would decide my fate. What came across to me, when I stepped into the room that I would hopefully leave as a member of the Jewish faith, was a wave of friendliness and sympathy, causing my nervousness to dwindle. The questions put to me, mainly by the officiating rabbi seated between two others across the table from me, were not strictly confined to my religious convictions, my knowledge of Hebrew, of the laws, and of the Torah, but focused mainly on the personal attitude that had led the offspring of a Christian noble family and widow of the century's most outstanding Protestant Christian to take this solemn step. My case was unusual, insofar as most of those seeking conversion do so for the sake of a Jewish spouse rather than of their own accord. While my reading of a passage in Hebrew in the prayer book was a bit halting, I had no difficulties expressing my motives. It all seemed so natural, so logical, so clear.

I did not find it hard to promise to observe the laws of the Torah, to light the candles, to read the appropriate prayers every Friday night, to abstain from working on the Shabbat. Like all my fellow Jews, I was going to recite the *Sh'ma* three times a day, and as an outward sign of my commitment to Judaism, I would observe the laws of *kashrut* by avoiding pork and, during Passover, confine myself to consuming only unleavened bread.

Having chosen Sarah for my new Jewish name—the compulsory name for every Jewish female under the Nazi regime—I signed the document presented to me as "Sarah Bat Avraham Avinu"

Sarah, daughter of Abraham, the first "convert," father of us all. Abraham's wife, Sarah, had given birth to Isaac at a rather ripe old age, so it seemed quite in order for me to promise "future children would be reared in the Jewish faith." In a spontaneous gesture, the rabbis presented me with the Bet Din's own *siddur*, the prayer book, as a token of their respect. I was so touched that, when I opened it to read the inscriptions by the rabbis, including that of Albert Friedlander, my tears fell on the paper, leaving a trace forever reminding me of that glorious day.

All the way back to Knightsbridge by Rabbi Friedlander's side, in a state of euphoria, I felt like skipping and dancing, singing and shouting, eager to share the news with everybody, the good news that now I "belonged" and was indeed part of the greatest family on Earth.

On the following morning, in the Westminster Synagogue, his own sanctuary, Rabbi Friedlander accepted me into the community of Jews with Psalm 23: "Adonai roi; lo echsar" ("The Lord is my shepherd; I shall not want").

My long journey was over; I had safely reached my destination. I was home!

Even though I had decided not to publicize my decision to leave the Christian faith, I knew it would eventually leak out. How would the church, of which my husband had been president, react to the step his widow had taken? Unaware of the fact that I was now Jewish, one of Germany's most prestigious national television interviewers asked me to appear on her show *Wortwechsel* (*Debate*), a one-hour affair with only a single guest. My books had been so successful that Christa Schultze-Rohe expressed the opinion that I should go public with the story of my life. What a perfect occasion to reveal my "secret."

One of the first telephone calls I received was from my husband's successor in office, the President of the Church of Hessen and Nassau, Pastor Helmut Spengler. The sole purpose of his call was to assure me that the step I had taken would change nothing in our relationship, and he continued to assure me of his friendship. Similar messages reached me from other clergymen, all of them positive and understanding. I was deeply moved. Like my own son's positive reaction, the understanding, acceptance, and tolerance I experienced from the Niemoeller family surpassed all my expectations. In sharp contrast, my own biological relatives saw fit to appoint themselves as self-styled prosecutors and judges, unanimously reaching the verdict that this act of treason disqualified me once and for all from being welcome in their midst.

Epilogue: August 1996

Several months after my acceptance into the family of Jews on June 11, 1990, an official letter from Temple Emanu-El informed me that, following a recommendation by their Senior Rabbi Dr. Ronald B. Sobel, the decision had been made to name me an honorary member of their congregation. Now I had a spiritual home in the city to which I hoped to return in the not too distant future.

However, before being free to leave Europe behind me for a second time, there still remained tasks to be accomplished, loose ends to tie up, promises to keep. The Wiesbaden US Air Force Hospital closed its doors in 1993, concluding my twenty-two years of work as a member of the American Red Cross. One year later, my son returned to the United States as a practicing physician in Pennsylvania; his departure left little reason, if any, for me to stay behind.

In 1990, I had begun to write my first book, a German-language autobiography, which was soon followed by a second volume. Published in Berlin by Ullstein, it is the story of a child and adolescent growing up during the Nazi era, on the "other side of the tracks" amidst a family, their actions guided solely by their conscience, who decided to light a candle instead of cursing the darkness. The shining examples of my parents and Pastor Martin Niemoeller, who dared to practice simple common decency in the face of evil and inhumanity, instilled in me values that forever shaped my life.

Writing about what happened in the world, my world of confusion and turmoil, where traditional standards seemed to have been abandoned, served more than one purpose. By expressing in writing all that I had never been able to speak about, I rid myself of some of the shadows that had darkened my own life, while creating a lasting memorial for my parents, especially for my father, who did not live to see freedom. Furthermore, I felt a strong obligation to bear witness, in the hope that my humble contribution, albeit a pebble in a large mosaic, might help young people in their struggle for better understanding of the incomprehensible.

Whatever I was able to achieve on the long and arduous road toward the goal I set for myself after the death of my husband, I owe to the guidance and constant reassurance of magnificent teachers who, each in his own way, set lasting standards for me: Albert Friedlander, Ronald Sobel, Gunter Hirschberg, Raul Hilberg, Robert Kempner, Erwin Leiser,

Franklin Littell, Hubert Locke, and Henry Marx. My deep gratitude goes to Elie Wiesel, without whom this book would never have been written.

One question still remained: could I trust myself to dare take the drastic step of moving back to the United States so late in a life that has been one long succession of miracles? The answer was clear: of course I can!

After my son had settled in Bucks County, Pennsylvania, I returned to the United States on April 28, 1998. Another window was about to open.

Part Three Notes

1. I also found out that nobody really cared to see certificates about qualifications for a job in the network's research department. You either could do it or you could not, in which case you were fired as fast as you were hired, not only on my level, but on all levels. I once witnessed a high-level executive of NBC, upon returning from a week's vacation, find his office occupied by someone else, his belongings thrown into a cardboard box, and his coworkers not terribly eager to speak to him anymore.

2. The only celebrity I would, to my dismay, never meet or even see from afar, was Marlene Dietrich, with whom I felt a strong kinship for more than one reason. The superstar had come from much the same Prussian background as I had, her rigid upbringing having probably been vital in her ability to overcome trying situations with the discipline instilled in her. She had become an American citizen with much the same enthusiasm that motivated me.

3. Victor Marcolini, a delightful source of local gossip, made no secret of the sinful fact that among his best customers by far were the Jehovah's Witnesses, whose world headquarters—the Watchtower—was located at the northern tip of the Heights. The fact that liquor was among the strict taboos for the sect's followers did not seem to overly concern a sizeable number of them.

4. When, only a few months later, West German Chancellor Konrad Adenauer, among those calling the pastor a traitor and whose cabinet was filled to the brim with former Nazis, accepted an official invitation from Moscow, nobody seemed to find fault with his decision. Because that was different, of course!

5. Later, as his wife, I asked him what indeed he would have done, had the pope offered his right hand. Would he have kissed the ring? Of course he would have kissed the ring, he answered.

6. The Kolmeshöhe Cemetery, near Bitburg, included the graves of forty-nine members of the *Waffen-SS*, a fact not discovered by the American advance team before the trip was announced to the public.

Index

Adenauer, Konrad, 227, 273, 304
adoption laws, 264
African Americans, 82, 247
African slaves, 295
Agnes, Princess, 190, 211
Air Force Hospital, 278, 281
air mines, 140, 162
air raids, 132, 140, 152, 160, 162, 164, 169, 231
Albert, Carl Edward George, Duke of Saxe-Coburg and Gotha, 14
Alexander, Marshal, 173
Alexander, Tsarevich, 107
Alexanderplatz Prison, 70
Alexandra, Viktoria, Princess of House of Hessen and bei Rhein, 60, 61
allegiance oath, 235
Allen, Steve, 246
American Friends Service Committee, 258
American Red Cross, 268, 302
Andersen, Hans Christian, 30
Anschluss, 94
anti-Americanism, 266
anti-Bolshevism, 112
anti-Communism, 287
anti-Semitism
  and Catholic Church, 299
  Jewish concentration camps, 49
  Jewish student surveys, 63
  Judenstern, 128

kin liability ("*Sippenhaft*"), 148
Kristallnacht ("Night of Broken Glass"), 101–102
legal codification of, 51
liquidation orders, 172
and nationalism, 79, 267–268
and Nazi party, 82
and Niemoeller, Martin, 107
and philo-Semitism, 226
popularization of, 74
profiting from extermination, 209
propaganda, 74
race laws, 73, 128–129
Semi-Gotha, 9, 10
slave labor, 49
theories, 9
Arabella, 170, 171, 174, 178–182, 186, 187, 189
aristocracy, 145, 214
Aryan descent questionnaire, 63
"Aryan paragraph," 52
assassination, 112, 148, 256–257
astrology, 80, 245
Atkinson, Tom, 210, 211, 212, 220
Aufbau, 292
August Wilhelm, 53
Auguste Viktoria, Empress, 6, 11, 12, 43
Auschwitz-Birkenau Extermination Camp, 130, 135, 204, 227, 267, 289, 290
autobahn, 49, 217, 221, 277

Baader, Andreas, 280
Bach, Dr., 105
Bach, Johann Sebastian, 288
ballet school, 118
Baranowski, Officer, 96, 97
Barbara, 159
Barth, Karl, 199
Battaglia, Charles, 181, 182, 184, 186–187, 188, 192, 193, 231
battle of Berlin, 176, 204
battle of St. Quentin, 13
Bavarian Alps, 66
Bayern, Albrecht von, Prince, 68
Beckett, Samuel, 221
Behnke, Colonel, 156–157, 163, 170
Belafonte, Harry, 247
Bell, George, 92, 122, 273
Bellevue Hospital, 245
Benny, Jack, 252
Berchtesgaden, 66, 153
Bergen-Belsen, 129, 204
Bergner, Elisabeth, 118
Berlin Airlift, 224
Berlin blockade, 224
Berlin State Theater, 117
Berlin Wall, 253, 286, 287, 288
Berlin Zoo, 153
Bertha, 284
Best, S. Payne, 121, 167, 172
Best Foot Forward, 256
Bethmann-Hollweg, Theobald von, 22, 23, 31
Beverly Hills Hotel, 252
Bitburg Cemetery, 294
"black border," 193
Black Maria, 165
black market, 150, 153, 165, 207, 216, 224
"Black Society," 247
blacklisting, 94
Blair, Frank, 246
Blockwart, 80

Bloom, Claire, 249
Blum, Léon, 167
Bodelschwingh, Pastor von, 38
Bolshevism, 51, 143, 149, 206, 214, 227
Bonhoeffer, Dietrich, 229, 230
Bonhoeffer, Emmy, 185–186, 217
Bonhoeffer, Klaus, 186
book burning, 54, 117–118
Boone, Pat, 247
Bote & Bock, 58
Bowling, Jack, 284
Brauchitsch, Augusta Bertha Ottilie Helene von, née von Korn-Rudelsdorf. *see* Sell, Baroness Augusta von
Brauchitsch, Eberhard Hubertus Hellmut Konrad von, 7, 8, 9, 73
Brauchitsch, Hans-Conrad von, 73
Brauchitsch, Hellmut von, 7
Brauchitsch, Herta von, 7, 8
Brauchitsch, Hildegard von, 7, 8
Brauchitsch, Konrad Louis Eduard von, 6, 7, 8, 9, 106
Brauchitsch, Konrad von (grandson), 7
Brauchitsch, Siegfried von, 7
Brauchitsch, Walther von, 78, 112, 132
Brecht, Bertolt, 117, 138
Bremer, Else, 37, 38. *see also* Niemoeller, Else
Bremer, Herrmann, 37
Brenner, Justice, 235, 236–237, 238–239
bribery, 154, 185, 215–216, 224
British Broadcasting Corporation (BBC), 95, 121, 140
British Intelligence, 191, 221, 243
British Military Police, 209, 220
British Royal Air Force (RAF), 127, 132
Brocovice, Velislaus von, 6
Brooklyn Academy of Music, 250
Brooklyn Friends School, 249
Brooklyn Heights, 249
Buchenwald, 172, 215, 290

Budapest Reformed Theological Academy, 295, 296
Bund Deutscher Maedel, 64
Burns, George, 252
Bussche, Axel von dem, 140

Cäcilie, Crown Princess, 60
Calvinism, 296
Canaris, Wilhelm, 111, 142, 214, 229, 230
Canterbury, Archbishop of, 122
capitalism, 270
Capote, Truman, 249
Carson, Johnny, 246, 256
Carter, Jimmy, 282
Casals, Pablo, 250
Catholic Church, 51, 66, 79, 94, 121, 299
Celan, Paul, 272
censorship, 92, 96
Central Park West, 290
Chamberlain, Houston Stewart, 9
Chamberlain, Neville, 140
Chase Manhattan Bank, 243
Checkpoint Charlie, 217, 288
Chiang Kai-shek, 100, 101
"Chief One," 85, 87, 103–104
"Chief Three," 85
"Chief Two," 85
Children's Hospital of Detroit, 228
"Christmas tree" devices, 162
Church of Hessen and Nassau, 200, 253, 266, 275, 285, 301
Church of Jesus Christ, 52, 104
Churchill, Winston Spencer, 190, 223
Claudia, 284, 291
Clay, Lucius D., 224
Coburg and Gotha, Duke of, 10, 13
cognitive dissonance, 140, 162
Cold War, 225
collective forgiveness, 272
color film, 251

Communism, 48, 50, 67, 225, 243, 270, 286, 287, 295, 296
Como, Perry, 247
concentration camps, 69–71, 82, 97, 121–122, 135, 148, 152, 162, 167, 185, 217, 221, 240
Confessing Church, 52, 63, 74, 82, 87, 91, 92, 104, 107, 142
constitutional state, 73
Cotton Club, 247
"Council of Brethren," 52
cows and calving, 67
Crosby, Bing, 265
Cross of Merit, 273
currency, 25, 223, 287

Dachau Concentration Camp, 119, 120, 122, 141, 167, 168, 172, 294
Dahlem, 84, 92, 96, 100, 141, 196, 291
Danzig State Theater, 138, 139
Dean Acheson Auditorium, 289
"Death Fugue," 272
Debrecen, 296
Delbrück, Justus, 186, 217
democracy, 198, 225, 280
denazification, 226
deportation, 130, 137, 167, 204, 209
Der Stürmer, 74
Desert Storm, 268
deutchmark, 223
Deutschlandfunk, 95, 146
dictatorial socialism, 271
Dietrich, Marlene, 118, 304
displaced persons, 3, 240
Ditte, 63, 84–85, 99, 104, 128, 134
"Doc-Film," 281
Dohnanyi, Hans von, 186
Döhring, Pastor, 124
Dolchstosslegende, 22
Donaldson, Ross, 237, 248, 251, 256, 258

Donaldson, Ulrich Marcus
  adult life, 303
  birth, 228, 253
  childhood, 249–250, 256
  education, 259, 261–262, 264, 281
  employment, 276, 291
  family life, 271
  and Niemoeller, Martin, 283–284
  personal life, 284, 285
Dönitz, Karl, 36, 106
Dora, 38, 90, 141, 198, 253
Dosse River, 176
Duke University School of Medicine, 281
Dulles, Allen, 149

East Germany, 253
Edda, Aunt, 42
Edith, 230
Ehrlich, Amy, 300
Ehrlich, Paul, 247
elections, 236
electricity rationing, 224
Elie Wiesel: Witness for Life, 296
Elizabeth II, Queen of England, 10
Ellis Island, New York, 4
Elser, Georg, 121
Ensslin, Gudrun, 280
Ervin, Sam, 281
eugenics, 79
euthanasia, 79
Evangelical State Church, 199, 284
excommunication, 121
executions, 80, 134, 144, 148, 164
extermination camps, 135, 140–141, 164, 209

family coat, 20
Faust, 219
Federal Republic of Germany, 268
Ferdinand, Franz, 22
Field Police, 174

"Final Solution," 135, 232
Flak munitions factories, 153, 155, 204
Flipper, 250
Flossenbürg Concentration Camp, 229, 230
forced labor, 113, 117, 130
foreign registration, 277
Forell, Pastor, 93
Franck, Walter, 116–118, 127, 136, 137, 204, 221, 229, 253
François-Poncet, André, 58
Franco-Prussian War, 143
Frank, Anita, 128–129, 204, 229
Frank, Reinhard, 128, 204, 229
Franz Joseph, Kaiser, 22
Frederick the Great, 22, 86, 103, 120
free market society, 271
Free University of West Berlin, 212
Freisler, Roland, 148, 159, 166, 231
Frick, Wilhelm, 75
Friedlander, Albert, 294, 299, 300, 301, 302
Friedrich Wilhelm III, 12, 106
Friwi, 201
frugality, 56
fuehrungszeugnis (good behavior certificate), 277
Fulton Fish Market, 235
Fyodor, 157, 163, 171, 174–175

Gandhi, Mahatma, 119, 285
Garber, Zev, xi
Garibaldi, Sante, 167
Garroway, Dave, 246
Gaulle, Charles de, 248
Gavin, James, 177
German adoption laws, 264
German Air Force, 188
German Army, 94, 172, 278
German businesses, 276
"German Christians," 52, 75, 87
German currency collapse, 25

German Democratic Republic (GDR), 217, 286, 288
German Federal Republic, 279, 281
German marriage laws, 263
German military center, 272
German National Television, 285
German people
  aristocracy, 145
  cognitive dissonance, 140, 162, 226
  collective forgiveness, 272
  conscience of, 253
  denial, 199, 226
  guilt of, 253, 268, 278, 295
  legal observations, 276
  post-war observations, 276–277
Gertrud, Aunt, 30
Gestapo
  censorship, 92
  deportation, 130, 137
  domestic spying by, 70, 75
  executions performed by, 134
  fear of, 164
  informers, 221–222
  interrogations by, 70, 94, 147
  kidnappings by, 121
  methods, 154
  murders by, 221
  and Niemoeller, Martin, 76, 90, 91, 119
  post-war escape, 164
  theft, 204
  torture, 137, 151
  and Ulrich von Sell, 146
  and von Sell, 94–95
Gisevius, Hans Bernd, 93
Gobineau, Comte de, 9
Goebbels, Joseph
  Catholicism, 94
  entertainment industry involvement, 137
  vs. Goering, 117
  lies of, 229
  music industry involvement, 117
  and Niemoeller, Martin, 91, 122
Goebbels, Magda, 117
Goerdeler, Karl, 146
Goering, Hermann, 44, 50
  Catholicism, 94
  vs. Goebbels, 117
  personality, 72–73, 75, 103, 132, 213
  slanders Niemoeller, 75
  vindictiveness, 72
Goethe, Johann Wolfgang von, 219, 271
Goldschlag, Stella ("Blonde Ghost"), 137
Gollwitzer, Helmut, 104
good behavior certificate (*fuehrungszeugnis*), 277
Gotha Almanach, 9
Göttingen, 289
Graham, Billy, 274
Grant, Cary, 249
Grimm's fairy tales, 30
Gross, Leo, 230
Grossdeutscher Rundfunk, 135
Gründgens, Gustaf, 213, 214, 232
Grunewald, 130, 209, 229
Gsovsky, Tatjana, 118
Gürtner, Franz, 91, 96

Haeften, Agnes von, née von Brauchitsch, 148
Haeften, Hans-Bernd von, 142, 290
Haeften, Werner von, 142, 144, 147, 230, 290
Hahn, Freda, 7
Hahn, Kurt, 128
Hans, 153–154, 154
Hanser, Richard, 252
Harrach, Mathilde von, 12
Hassell, Ulrich von, 142
Haushofer, Albrecht, 221
Hebraicum, 37
Hebrew Tabernacle, 292

Heinrich (brother to Kaiser Wilhelm II), 61
hemophilia, 107
Henckel Donnersmarck, Count Kraft von, 230
Henderson, Florence, 246
Hermann, 204
Hermine, Princess of Schoenaich-Carolath, née Princess Reuss, 43, 45–47, 94, 124, 126
Hess, Rudolf, 92
Heute, 227
Heydrich, Reinhard, 135
Higgins, Margaret, 273
hijacking, 280
Hilberg, Raul, 302
Hilde, 29, 30
Hildebrandt, Rainer, 221
Himmler, Gudrun, 62
Himmler, Heinrich, 76, 135, 230
Hindenburg, Paul von, 40, 42, 48, 66, 73
Hirschberg, Gunter, 293, 302
Hirschel, Hans, 111, 137
historical plays and movies, 277
hit lists, 286
Hitler, Adolf
   anti-Bolshevism, 112
   arrogance, 271
   attempts on life, 112, 140, 143, 144, 148–149, 186, 217, 227
   and Catholic Church, 121
   death, 175
   declares war on Soviet Union, 118
   drug addiction, 140
   "Final Solution," 135
   gesticulations, 63
   and Holocaust, 200
   ideology, 74, 79, 144–145
   infamy, 228, 267
   interference in church affairs, 51
   legal family name, 54
   liquidation orders, 172
   Mein Kampf, 41, 50, 74, 92
   Munich putsch, 25
   and Mussolini, 115
   names successor, 106
   and Niemoeller, Martin, 52, 76, 82, 91–92, 94, 96–98, 120, 122, 229, 231, 284
   and Niemoeller, Sibylle Sarah, Baroness von Sell, 89, 105
   oaths of allegiance to, 159
   omnipresence of, 62–63
   personality, 107
   prophecy, 196
   resistance against, 185
   rise to power, 42
   strategy of, 153
   terrorism, 132
   vindictiveness, 146, 148
   and Wilhelm II, 123, 124
Hitler Youth, 42, 64, 78, 90, 95, 101, 114, 128, 160
Hitlerputsch, 79
Hoeck, Michael, 120
Hohenstein, Ernst von, 6, 13
Hohenstein, Hans von, 13
Hohenzollern, House of, 6, 123, 125, 190, 227
Holocaust, 192, 199, 200, 225–226, 268, 289, 294, 295
Honecker, Erich, 217, 253, 286, 288
horse theft, 186–187
Howdy Doody Show, 249
Hughes, Langston, 247
Humboldt University, 212
Hungarian Calvinism, 296
Hutten, Ulrich von, 270

Igor ("Goliath"), 178
Il Duce. see Mussolini, Benito
I'll Cry Tomorrow, 252
illicit alliances, 43

immigration, 3–4, 266, 288
Ina Maria, 61
Inge, 153–154, 204
"International Jewry," 51. *see also* anti-Semitism
International Lenin Peace Prize, 273
Iran hostage crisis, 281
Irene, Princess of House of Hessen and bei Rhein, 61
Irish policemen, 236
Israel, 137, 268, 295
Italia, 3, 5, 240, 241

Jakob, Major, 154
Jamlitz, 213–214, 218, 219
Japan, 135
Jerusalem, 219
"Jew-catchers," 137
Jewish concentration camps, 49
Jewish Hospital, 128
Jewish identity, 300
Jewish Old Testament, 52
Jewish race, 9, 63
Johannes Gutenberg School of Medicine, 281
John F. Kennedy School of Berlin, 259, 261, 264
Jonge, Alfred de, 173
Judenschweine, 74
Judenstämmlinge, 73
Judenstern, 128–129, 129
Juliana, Crown Princess of Netherlands, 103
Junkers Werke, 9, 73

Kadner, Dr., 78, 79
Kafka, Franz, 117
Kalláy, Miklós, 167
Kaltenbrunner, Ernst, 164
Karl, 57
Katharina, 9

Kempner, Robert M., 273, 302
Kennedy, Caroline, 256–257
Kennedy, John Fitzgerald, 256–257
Kennedy, John Fitzgerald, Jr., 256
Kennedy, Robert Francis, 257
KGB, 186, 194. *see also* NKVD
kin liability ("*Sippenhaft*"), 148
King, Martin Luther, Jr., 235, 257
Kirgiz, 182
Knuth, *Unterscharfüher*, 151, 160, 165, 166
Khomeini, Ayatollah, 281
Kokomo (chimpanzee), 246
Kolmeshöhe Cemetery, 304
Kortner, Fritz, 118
Krause ("Monsieur Jean"), 99
Kreuth, 114
Kristallnacht ("Night of Broken Glass"), 102, 292
Kroepel, Adolf, 80

Labor Service ("*Arbeitsdienst*"), 117
Lange, Hanns, 102–103, 107, 204
Lange, Irma, 102–103, 104, 204
Lange, Walter, 103
Langen, Margret, 118
Laurel, Stan, 252
Lautenberg, Frank, 294
Laws for the Protection of German Blood and Honor, 10
League Against Inhumanity, 287
League of Human Rights, 221
Leah, 244
lebensraum, 42, 49, 226
"leftist sympathizers," 280
Lehman, Robert, 292
Lehrterstrasse Prison, 160, 164, 230
Leiser, Erwin, 294, 302
Lemmon, Jack, 251
Lenin Peace Prize, 273
Leo Baeck College, 294, 299, 300
Leonore, 85

Lescoulie, Jack, 246
Libowitz, Richard, xi
Linse, Walter, 221
liquidation orders, 172
literacy testing, 235, 238–239
Littell, Franklin, 294, 303
Lochner, Louis P., 58, 204, 206, 212
Locke, Hubert, 303
Louise, 9
Lubbe, Marinus van der, 49–50
Luther, Martin, 86, 103, 194–195, 299
Luther Church, 282
Lutze, Inge, 62
Lutze, Viktor, 62

Mackensen, August von, 143
MacLaine, Shirley, 251
Madison Square Garden, 250
Maike, Aunt, 17, 18, 106
Mailer, Norman, 249
Majdanek extermination camp, 135
Malone, Vincent J., 259
Maltzan, Countess Maria von, 111, 137, 222
"Mamsel," 113
Mann, Heinrich, 138
Mann, Thomas, 119, 138, 229
Marcolini, Victor, 249, 304
Maria, 9, 73
Marie, 17
Marie Gabriele, Duchess, 68
marriage and social status, 12
marriage laws, 263
martyrdom, 199
Marx, Henry, 292, 303
mass arrests, 91
materialism, 267
Matthias, 73
Mauriac, François, 290
Max Emanuel, 68–69
Maya, 256

McCarthy, Joe, 243
McGraw, John J., 188, 189, 192, 193–194, 209, 212, 220–221
meals, manners, and table behavior, 56
Mecklenburg-Schwerin, Duke of, 20, 106
Mein Kampf, 41, 50, 74, 92
Meinhof, Ulrike, 279–280
Meininger, Elsie, 292
Meininger, Fred, 292
Mengele, Josef, 227
mental institutions, 79
Metro-Goldwyn-Mayer, 250
Minnelli, Liza, 256
Mirbach, Maimi, Baroness, 137
Mirko, Uncle, 70–71, 113, 114
Mischlinge ersten Grades, 73
Moabit Prison, 91, 93
Mongols, 163, 182
morganatic marriage, 61
Mount Kisco, 248
Muggs, J. Fred (chimpanzee), 246
Müller, Friedrich, 77
Müller, Ludwig ("Ludwig the Desperate"), 52, 75, 76
Munich putsch, 25
munitions factories, 153
Mussolini, Benito, 114–115

National Broadcasting Company (NBC), 243, 250, 252, 256, 294, 304
National German Woman's League, 107
national identification card, 277
National Socialist German Workers' Party
    anti-Semitism, 129
    astrology laws, 80
    book burning, 117–118
    brutality of, 82
    vs. Communism, 67
    defeat of, 148, 225
    "Final Solution," 135
    function and precision, 74

goals of, 41–42
hierarchy, 80
Holocaust, 200
ideology, 76, 79, 138, 289
Labor Service ("*Arbeitsdienst*"), 117
Nazi hunters, 191–192
propaganda, 95
race laws, 128–129
territorial expansion, 94, 103, 123, 141
nationalism, 267, 280
Native Americans, 295
Nattermann, Frau, 134
"Nazi hunters," 191–192
Nell, 65
Neuengamme Concentration Camp, 191
New York City, 243, 244
New York Times, 239, 253
Nicholas II, Tsar of Russia, 22, 61
Niemoeller, Else, 37, 38, 75, 77, 90, 92–93, 97, 141, 161, 167–168, 173, 198, 253–254, 258
Niemoeller, Emil Gustav Friedrich Martin
   accident and recovery, 253–254
   and anti-Semitism, 107
   appearance as child, 35
   arrest by Gestapo, 90, 91
   attempts on life, 76
   birth, 35
   in Brooklyn, 258
   cancer, 282
   career ambitions, 36, 76
   on Catholic Church, 120
   conscience of, 199–200, 299
   death of, 77, 272, 280, 284–285, 289
   death of children, 161
   death of wife, 253–254
   early childhood, 35–36
   family of, 37
   fatherhood, 77
   film about, 281
   friendship with Niemoeller, Sibylle Sarah, 34, 84–85, 104, 259, 261
   habits, 106
   health issues, 281, 282
   and Hitler, 49, 51, 75–76, 82, 91–92, 98, 120, 122, 173, 185, 229, 231
   hostage negotiations, 279–280
   imprisonment, 92, 94, 96–98, 119, 167–168
   isolation punishment, 97–98, 265
   leisure activity, 275
   liberation, 172, 173, 198–199
   marriages, 37, 217, 219, 262–265, 269–272, 278, 286
   mental anguish, 274
   naval career, 37, 76, 106, 266, 275, 281, 284
   on Nazi ideology, 51–52
   personality, 35, 76, 120, 199, 264–265, 265, 268, 271, 272, 274–275, 302
   as president of Church of Hessen and Nassau, 200, 266
   prophecy of, 280
   recognition and awards, 273, 289–290
   relationship with Niemoeller, Sibylle Sarah, 88
   religious education, 37, 121
   sermons of, 37, 91, 119, 274–275
   slandered by Goering, 75–76
   targeted by Hitler, 52
   temper, 271, 272
   transfer to Dachau, 118
   trial against, 93, 96
   and von Sell family, 38–39, 95
   "What would Jesus say?" 36, 281
   and World War I, 36–37
Niemoeller, Heinrich, 35, 37, 40, 119
Niemoeller, Herrmann, 198
Niemoeller, Herta, 161
Niemoeller, Jan, 198
Niemoeller, Jochen, 161

Niemoeller, Jutta, 161
Niemoeller, Martin Friedrich Eberhard, 77
Niemoeller, Martin, Jr., 92, 253, 255, 270
Niemoeller, Paula, 35, 119
Niemoeller, Sibylle Sarah, Baroness von Sell
  acting career, 104, 221
  agricultural school, 114
  American citizenship, 266, 288
  anti-Communism, 287
  attends Holocaust conference, 289
  birth, 24
  boarding school, 84–88, 90
  and British Intelligence, 191, 221, 243
  Brooklyn Heights, 249
  cavalry service, 155–156, 157–158
  character, 185
  death of father, 212, 231–232, 242
  death of mother, 290–291
  divorce, 228, 259, 263
  Dosse River incident, 174–175
  early life, 25-28, 29, 30, 32, 33, 99, 263
  encounters Hitler, 54, 89, 105
  escapes Red Army, 180–181
  family life, 27–28, 29, 63
  fear of Hitler, 71
  foreign registration, 277
  friendship with Niemoeller, Martin, 34, 84–85, 88, 104, 259, 260–261
  general education, 84–88, 136
  on German people, 276–277
  and Gestapo, 146, 147
  godparents, 25, 85, 104
  grandmother, 169, 170, 215
  health issues, 99, 163, 210–211
  and Hitler Youth, 78, 105
  horse riding, 65
  horse thievery, 187
  immigration to United States, 227–228, 240
  as interpreter, 178, 185, 188, 210
  as interrogator, 221
  and Judaism, 291, 291–293, 295, 296–299, 300, 301
  language skills, 86, 171, 241, 243, 300
  literacy testing, 235–239
  literary career, 302
  marriage to Donaldson, Ross, 235, 248, 258
  marriage to Niemoeller, Martin, 217, 219, 262–265, 269–272, 278, 282–283, 286, 289
  meals, manners, and table behavior, 56
  meets Jimmy Carter, 281
  morals, 227
  motherhood, 228
  move to Berlin, 27, 259–260, 276
  at NBC, 243
  near-death experience, 210–211
  in New York City, 243, 249
  Olympic Games, 82
  "Ortgies," 170, 178, 180, 182, 231
  post-war life, 224, 267, 276
  as prisoner of war, 177–178
  promise to father, 228, 235
  and Protestantism, 294–295
  relationship with Kaiser Wilhelm II, 44–45, 84, 85, 104, 107, 240
  religious experimentation, 33
  reputation of, 221
  rescues Arabella, 181–182
  resistance activity, 136–137, 150, 152, 154, 160, 174
  reunion with father, 164–165, 166
  reunion with mother, 196
  romances, 100–101, 128, 136, 248
  school days, 62–64
  sixth sense, 127
  smuggling, 220, 288
  and SS, 150
  summer vacations, 65–66
  survival in Berlin, 201–205

theater career, 116–117, 138, 139, 142, 153
travels to West Coast, 250
use of deadly force, 174–175
visits Doorn, 125
visits Jamlitz, 218–219
visits Orangerie, 125–126
voyage to United States, 241
"Night of Broken Glass," 102, 292
"Night of the Long Knives," 59, 72
Nixon, Richard, 281
NKVD (Soviet secret police), 194, 195, 201, 204, 207, 213, 215, 217
Nobel Prize, 119, 282, 290
nobility, 44, 58
"Noblesse oblige," 55
nonfraternization laws, 188
Norden, Tommy, 250
Normandy invasion, 140, 177
North German Radio Station, 191
Northern German Naval Academy, 36
Nuremberg Race Laws, 73
Nuremberg trials, 106, 231, 273

O'Donnell, Helen, 246
Olbricht, Friedrich, 144
Olga, 113
Oliver, Sy, 247
Olympic Games, 82, 92
Operation Valkyrie, 143–144, 148
Oskar, 61
Osnabrück, 285
Oster, Achim, 111, 142, 229, 230
Oswald, Lee Harvey, 256
Ovid, 138, 248
Owens, Jesse, 82

Paar, Jack, 246
Pacelli, Eugenio, 94
pacifism, 254, 270
Packer Collegiate Institute, 249

palm reading, 245
panhandling, 244
Panzerfaust weapon, 176
Papagos, Alexander, 167
Parker, Dorothy, 273
parliamentary democracy, 48
Pastor's Emergency League, 52, 76, 92
Paul, 153–154, 204
Paul VI, Pope, 254–255
Pauling, Linus, 282
Paulus, Field Marshal von, 142
Pavlik, 157, 158, 163, 171, 174, 176
Pearl Harbor, 135
People's Court, 148, 226
People's Police, 286
Philip, Prince of Hessen, 69
philo-Semitism, 226
Pimen (Patriarch of Russian Orthodox Church), 273–274
Pius XI, Pope, 51, 94
Pius XII, Pope, 94, 121
Plettenberg, Hans von, 166
Plettenberg, Kurt von, 154
Plinke, Minna, 8, 13
Plötzensee Prison, 80, 151
pogroms, 103, 292
police state, 277
political prisoners, 97, 167, 221
Porsche, Ferdinand, 49
"positive Christendom," 52
Posner, David, 293
Potsdam, 7, 16, 169, 215
prisoners of war
  conditions, 157
  German, 188, 254
  "grapevine," 163
  Niemoeller, Sibylle Sarah, 177–178
  Polish, 113, 186
  Russian, 177, 178, 231
  Soviet, 122, 157, 170, 171, 174
"prolet-Aryans," 62

propaganda, 95
prophecy, 80–81, 98, 196, 220
Protestant Church, 199
Prussian Garrison Church, 49
Prussian virtues, 36, 56, 86, 149
Prussian War Academy, 21
"pulpit clause," 93
purification, 8–9
Putzi, Uncle, 41, 42

Quirnheim, Mertz von, 144

rape, 163, 180–181, 184, 195, 202, 203
Raspe, Jan-Carl, 280
Ravensbrück Concentration Camp, 191
RCA, 248
Reagan, Ronald, 272, 294
Rebecca, 9
Reckzeh, Paul, 221–222
Red Army Faction (RAF), 279
Red Cross, 171, 268
reeducation camp, 153
refugees, 206, 221
regicide, 143
"Reich Bishop," 52, 75
Reichmuth, Pastor, 88
Reichsfrauenfuehrerin, 62
Reichsgericht, 50
reichsmark, 223
Reichsrundfunk, 73
Reichstag Building fire, 49–50, 51
Reichswehr, 53
religious assimilation, 17
religious suppression, 82
resistance center, 153–154, 164
resistance movement, 64, 130, 134, 136–138, 146, 152–154, 164, 174, 185, 204, 221
restrictions and shortages, 115, 132
Reuber, Ursel, 204
Ribbentrop, Bettina von, 62

Riefenstahl, Leni, 153, 164, 204, 223
Rockwell, Norman, 249
Rodeph Sholom, 293
Röhm, Ernst, 72
Röhricht, Eberhard, 77
Rominten, 72
Roosevelt, Franklin, 190, 223
Rosenstiel, Hedwig von, 20
Royal Electrical and Mechanical Engineers (REME), 188, 189, 191
Ruby, Jack, 256
Rupprecht, Knecht, 41
Russian Orthodox Church, 254, 273
Rust, Mechtild, 62

Sachsenhausen Concentration Camp, 49, 70–71, 96, 97, 119, 120, 215
Sahm, Heinrich, 58–59
Salem School, 128
Sarah, 9
Sarnoff, Robert, 248
Schacht, Hjalmar, 167
Schindler, Oskar, 154
Schleicher, Kurt von, 59, 72
Schleyer, Hanns-Martin, 279, 280
Schneider, Reinhold, 125
Schoenaich-Carolath-Schilden, Prince Gustav von, 189, 190
Schoenaich-Carolath-Schilden, Princess Edelgard von, 189
Scholl, Hans, 134
Scholl, Sophie, 134
Scholz-Klink, Gertrud, 62
Schroeder, Dr., 62
Schultz, George, 289
Schultze-Rohe, Christa, 301
Schumacher, Kurt, 198–199
Schuschnigg, Kurt von, 167
Schutzstaffel (SS), 53, 59, 121, 123, 150, 151, 168, 174, 278
Schwärzel, Helene, 146

Index

Schweitzer, Albert, 36, 273, 282
Schweitzer, Józef, 295
Schwerin, Hans, 247
Schwerin, Ilse von, 142–143
secret police, 287, 288
Segovia, Andres, 250
Sell, Baron Ulrich von
    business and financial acumen, 23
    change of nobility title, 44
    death of, 125, 212–214, 245
    disappearance with Soviets, 201
    education, 20, 21
    fate of, 196–197
    and Gestapo, 111, 147–148
    health issues, 22–23, 166
    and Hitler, 133
    imprisonment, 148, 150, 152, 159, 160, 165–166
    military academy education, 20–21
    nickname, 60
    and Niemoeller, Martin, 95
    and Niemoeller family, 38–39
    personality, 22, 125, 127
    physical appearance, 14, 29
    post-World War I employment, 23
    release from prison, 164–165
    romances, 189–190
    rumors of, 192
    Selecta, 21
    suicide plan, 111–112
    targeted by SA, 72
    torture, 165
    and Wilhelm II, 21–22, 94, 107, 123, 125–126
Sell, Baroness Augusta von
    and Anna Troppa, 133
    astrology, 80, 245
    attends Imperial Ball, 11
    bribery, 215–216, 224
    consumption, 14
    cunning, 130, 224, 230
    death of, 290–291
    early life, 6, 8
    education of children, 84
    encounters Hitler, 71
    first marriage, 13, 14
    health issues, 7, 164, 193
    mourning, 13–14
    in New York City, 244–245
    and Niemoeller family, 141
    pensions, 227
    personality, 80, 130, 152, 203, 206, 216, 245, 290
    resourcefulness of, 206–207, 216
    return to Berlin, 248
    sixth sense, 220, 222
    and Ulrich von Sell, 146, 160
Sell, Friedrich Wilhelm Adolf Konrad Ulrich von, 28, 31, 83, 128, 148, 152, 190, 191, 212–213, 217
Sell, Sophie-Charlotte von, 24, 25
Sell, Ulrich Adolf Wilhelm Günther von, 20
Sell, Wilhelm von, 14–15, 20
Semi-Gotha, 9–10
Senatra, Edoardo, 58
Seydlitz, Field Marshal von, 142
Seyss-Inquart, Arthur, 124
Shirer, William, 92–93, 144
Shores, William, 285
shortages and restrictions, 115, 132
Siemens forced labor factory, 130
sin of omission, 274
Sippenhaft (kin liability), 148
sixth sense, 127, 220, 222
skinheads, 280
slave labor, 49
Sobel, Ronald B., 293, 300, 302
Sobibor extermination camp, 135
socialism, 79, 270, 287
Solf, Anna, 222

Soviet Army, 130, 155, 162, 163, 167, 176, 177, 180–181, 202
Spandau Prison, 106
Spanish Inquisition, 299
Special Court, 93, 96
Spengler, Helmut, 301
St. Nicholas Day, 41
St. Patrick's Cathedral, 247
Staatssicherheitsdienst, 287, 288
Stalin, Joseph, 112, 176, 190, 223
Stalin, Joseph (son), 122
Stargardt, Edith, 58, 74, 82, 130–131, 204, 228
Stargardt, Otto, 58, 74, 82, 130–131, 204, 228
starvation, 121, 214
Stasi secret police, 287, 288
State of New York versus Sibylle Donaldson, 237
Statue of Liberty, 3, 4, 241, 244, 274
Stauffenberg, Claus Count Schenk Graf von, 142, 144
Steiger, Rod, 249
Stevens, Richard "Dick," 121–122, 167–168, 172, 229
Stöcker, Adolf, 9
Stoerger, Eric, 292
storm troopers, 48
Strauss, Franz Josef, 267, 277
Strehlow, Major von, 18
Streisand, Barbra, 256
Strindberg, August, 117
Stuttgart Declaration of Guilt, 199–200, 232
suicide, 181, 202, 280
Sunday school, 33

Tartars, 163, 182
Tarzan, 256
teaching, 62–63
television, 246, 250
Temple, William, 122
Terezin ghetto, 131
terrorism, 83, 92, 132, 140, 270, 280
Thadden, Elisabeth von, 222
The Apartment, 251
The Brooklyn Heights Press, 258
The Sound of Music, 252
The Sunflower, 272
Theresienstadt, 58, 204, 228
Thiele, Frau ("Wittenberg"), 137, 163–164, 204
Third Reich
    Anschluss, 94
    astrology laws, 80
    beginning state, 48–50
    and Catholic Church, 299
    concentration camps, 135
    death toll during, 225–226
    end stage, 294
    "Final Solution," 135
    gender roles in, 155
    and Hitler, 284
    Holocaust, 225–226, 294
    invasion of Soviet Union, 112
    life during, 55–59, 128, 152
    as police state, 277
    relationship with Catholic Church, 51
    and teachers, 62–63
    territorial expansion, 141
    war restrictions and shortages, 132
    war with America, 130
third world countries, 271
Time Magazine, 120
Today Show, 246
Tonight Show, 256
torture, 121, 137, 148, 151, 154, 162, 165
Toth, Bishop, 295
Trafalgar Square, 122
Trakostjan, Countess Draskovich von, 68
treason, 93
Treaty of Versailles, 42, 198

Treblinka extermination camp, 135
Treitschke, Heinrich von, 9, 299
Troppa, Anna, 16–19, 34, 84, 90
    death of, 253
    departure, 133
    employment activities, 18, 23
    on family vacation, 66
    on men, 57
    menu choices, 56, 65
    Munich putsch, 25
    opinions of, 59
    personality, 29, 30, 106
    pregnancy, 24
    return of, 207–208
"tsaptserap," 202, 206
Tucholsky, Kurt, 117, 138
Turnipseed, Reverend, 258

Ullstein, 302
underdeveloped world, 271
United German Protestant Church, 76
United States Armed Forces, 276, 278
    US 7th Army, 172
    US 82nd Airborne, 177, 181, 188
    US Air Force, 262, 302
United States Holocaust Memorial Council, 289, 294
University Hospital in Zurich, 291
University of Münster, 37
Uradel, 58
urban renewal, 249

V2 bomb, 154
Vatican, 94, 121, 254–255, 273, 299
Vendes, 17
Venlo Incident, 121
Victoria, Queen of England, 43
Victory at Sea, 252
Vietnam War, 266, 279
Volksgerichtshof, 50
Volkswagens, 49

voting rights, 236

Waiting for Godot, 221
Waldeck-Pyrmont, Duke Josias von, 10
Waldemar, Prince, 61
Warsaw ghetto uprising, 138
Wedekind, Frank, 117
Wehrmacht, 105, 111, 123, 162, 176, 278
Weill, Kurt, 117, 138
Wersen, 285
West Berlin, 220
West German Employers' Association, 279
West Side Story, 252
Western Wall of Jerusalem ("Wailing Wall"), 219
Westheimer, Manfred, 292
Westheimer, Ruth, 292
"What would Jesus say?" 37, 254, 281
White Rose resistance group, 134
Wiesbaden, 261, 262, 281, 292
Wiesbaden Cemetery, 254
Wiesel, Elie, 231–232, 272, 289, 292, 294, 303
Wiesel, Sarah, 296
Wiesel, Shlomo, 296
Wiesenthal, Simon, 272
Wilder, Billy, 251
Wilhelm, August, 41
Wilhelm, Crown Prince ("Willy"), 53, 57, 60, 103
Wilhelm Gustoff, 230
Wilhelm I, 43
Wilhelm II, Kaiser of Germany
    abdication, 60
    death, 123, 124
    flight from Germany, 30
    as godfather, 45
    military experience, 106
    obsessions, 44
    personality, 123, 124

Wilhelm II, Kaiser of Germany
(*continued*)
    relationship with Niemoeller, Sibylle Sarah, Baroness von Sell, 11, 44–45, 84, 104, 107, 240
    tree-cutting, 44
    and von Sell, 125–126
    wealth disposition, 31–32
    and World War I, 6, 13
Willebrands, Cardinal, 254
Winkler, Captain, 159
Winkler, Franz, 293
Winkler, Marianne, 293
Wipper, Kommissar, 147, 150, 152–153
Wise, Robert, 252
Wittelsbach, Crown Prince Rupprecht, 68–69
Wittelsbach, House of, 69
Wittelsbach, Mafalda, 69
Wittelsbach, Marie-Charlotte, 68–69
Wittelsbach, Marie-Gabrielle, 68–69
Woelle, Major, 156, 157, 159
Wolff, Louise, 58
World Council of Churches, 36, 254, 270
World War I
    blame for loss of, 22
    combatants, 22
    declaration, 13
    and Niemoeller, Martin, 36–37
Wortwechsel (Debate), 301

xenophobia, 268

Yalta Conference, 189, 190, 223
Young, Loretta, 246

Zehlendorf, 261
Zolorin, Burchardus de, 123

www.ingramcontent.com/pod-product-compliance
Lightning Source LLC
Chambersburg PA
CBHW060940230426
43665CB00015B/2016